D1266970

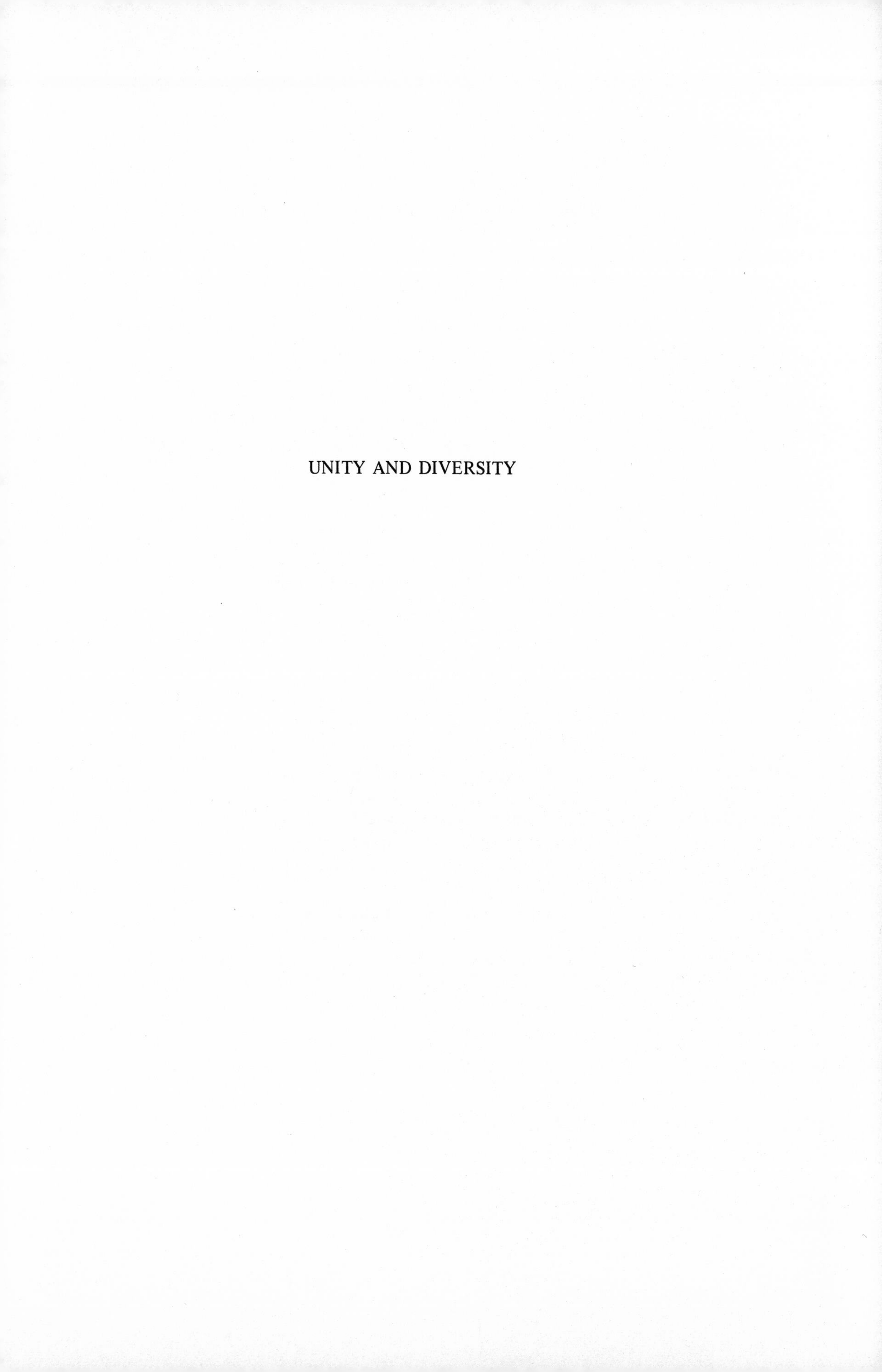

UNITY AND DIVERSITY

THE JOHNS HOPKINS NEAR EASTERN STUDIES

Hans Goedicke, General Editor

Hans Goedicke, *The Report about the Dispute of a Man with His* Ba

J. J. M. Roberts, *The Earliest Semitic Pantheon*

John D. Schmidt, *Ramesses II: A Chronological Structure for His Reign*

David Lorton, *The Juridical Terminology of International Relations in Egyptian Texts through Dyn. XVIII*

Bernard Frank Batto, *Studies on Women at Mari*

Hans Goedicke, *The Report of Wenamun*

Hans Goedicke and J. J. M. Roberts (eds.), *Unity and Diversity: Essays in the History, Literature, and Religion of the Ancient Near East*

UNITY AND DIVERSITY

Essays in the History, Literature, and Religion of the Ancient Near East

Edited by
Hans Goedicke and J. J. M. Roberts

THE JOHNS HOPKINS UNIVERSITY PRESS
Baltimore and London

Manufactured in the United States of America

The Johns Hopkins University Press, Baltimore, Md. 21218
The Johns Hopkins University Press Ltd., London

Library of Congress Catalog Card Number 74-24376
ISBN 0-8018-1638-6

Library of Congress Cataloging in Publication data will be found on the last printed page of this book.

CONTENTS

PREFACE

Near Eastern studies at The Johns Hopkins University are inextricably connected with the name of Dr. William Foxwell Albright, former W. W. Spence Professor of Semitic Languages. After studying at this University, he joined its faculty in 1927 and gave its Oriental Seminary a lasting imprint in his many years of affiliation until his retirement in 1958.

Very few scholars have ever demonstrated so profusely the unity of the ancient Near East and the interwoven texture it had. Others may have probed deeper in one particular area, but Albright's combination of thoroughness and breadth of scholarship remains unmatched. After thorough training in Hebrew, he grew up with the new disciplines of Hittitology and Ugaritology, participated in the rapid expansion of the still young field of Assyriology, and laid the groundwork for many of the modern advances in Palestinian archaeology. Such breadth has never been easy to achieve, but the rapid increase of knowledge and the subsequent specialization in the various areas of Near Eastern studies has made it even more difficult. Nevertheless, Albright's concern for an integrated view of the ancient Near East, rooted in sound philology and grounded in a historical method demanding objective controls--archaeology in that broad sense in which he used the term–continues as the basic orientation of the present Department of Near Eastern Studies.

When Professor Albright died on September 19, 1971, the Department lost its mentor, but it did not lose the direction he gave it. Thus, when plans were made to honor the late scholar with a symposium in his memory, it seemed only appropriate to organize it pursuing his vision of the interrelatedness of the ancient Near East. The American Council of Learned Societies most graciously supported the endeavor with a substantial grant, and from January 9 to 12, 1973, The Johns Hopkins University hosted a number of leading scholars, several of them former students of Albright, representing various disciplines of Near Eastern studies. For three and one-half days they presented formal papers and participated in sometimes heated discussions. It was an intellectually exciting event, very much reflecting the spirit of William Foxwell Albright.

It was the intention from the very beginning to collect and publish the papers offered at the symposium. We are pleased to make these important contributions available to those who could not participate personally in the symposium. They demonstrate the approach to the ancient Near East as an interdependent and closely textured period in the development of the human spirit.

We want to thank those who made the meeting and this publication possible. We are particularly grateful to the American Council of Learned Societies, which made it possible to conduct the symposium. Thanks are due to Mrs. Gail Wiest who typed the manuscripts during the symposium and conducted this demanding task under high pressure. Last, we want to thank all those who participated in one form or another in the meeting and the organization of the symposium.

LIST OF ABBREVIATIONS

AAR — American Academy of Religion

AASOR — *Annual of the American Schools of Oriental Research*

ABoT — *Ankara Arkeoloji Müzesinde . . . Boğasköy Tabletleri*

AfO — *Archiv für Orientforschung*

AHw — W. von Soden, *Akkadisches Handwörterbuch* (Wiesbaden, 1959-)

AJA — *American Journal of Archaeology*

AKA — E. A. W. Budge and L. W. King, *The Annals of the Kings of Assyria* (London, 1902)

Am — Amarna

ANES — *Journal of the Ancient Near Eastern Society of Columbia University*

ANET — James B. Pritchard (ed.), *Ancient Near Eastern Texts Relating to the Old Testament* (Princeton)

AOAT — *Alter Orient und Altes Testament*

ARAB — David D. Luckenbill, *Ancient Records of Assyria and Babylonia,* 2 vols. (Chicago, 1926)

ARM — *Archives royales de Mari* (= TCL 22-)

ArOr — *Archiv Orientální*

AS — Field numbers for the tablets from Tell Asmar

AS — *Assyriological Studies* (Chicago)

AS[2] — W. von Soden, *Das akkadische Syllabar* (Analecta Orientalia 42)

ASAE — *Annales du Service des Antiquités de l'Egypte,* Le Caire

ASKT — Paul Haupt, *Akkadische und sumerische Keilschrifttexte . . .* (Leipzig, 1881-82)

ASTI	*Annual of the Swedish Theological Institute*
AT	D. J. Wiseman, *The Alalakh Tablets,* Occasional Publications of the British Institute of Archaeology at Ankara, 2 (London, 1953)
AWAW	*Österreichische Akademie der Wissenschaften Abhandlungen,* Philosophisch-historische Klasse, Wien
BA	*Biblical Archaeologist*
BA	*Beiträge zur Assyriologie und vergleichenden semitischen Sprachwissenschaft*
BASOR	*Bulletin of the American Schools of Oriental Research*
BB	C. Bezold and E. A. Wallis Budge, *The Tell El-Amarna Tablets in the British Museum* (London, 1892)
BE	*Babylonian Expedition of the University of Pennsylvania,* Series A: Cuneiform Texts
*BH*³	*Biblia Hebraica,* ed. R. Kittel, 3rd ed. (Stuttgart, 1937)
BibOr	*Bibliotheca Orientalis*
BIFAO	*Bulletin de L'Institut français d'Archéologie orientale,* Le Caire
BM	Tablets in the collections of the British Museum
Bog.	Boghazkeui
Boson, *TC*	G. Boson, *Tavolette cuneiformi sumere degli archivi di Drehem e di Djoha dell' ultima dinastia di Ur* (Milan, 1936)
BoTU	*Die Boghazköi-Texte in Umschrift . . .* (= WVDOG 41-42)
BWL	W. G. Lambert, *Babylonian Wisdom Literature* (Oxford, 1960)
CAD	*The Assyrian Dictionary of the Oriental Institute of the University of Chicago* (Chicago, 1956-)
CBQ	*Catholic Biblical Quarterly*
CBS	Tablets in the collections of the University Museum of the University of Pennsylvania, Philadelphia
CMHE	F. M. Cross, *Canaanite Myth and Hebrew Epic* (Cambridge, Mass., 1973)

CT	*Cuneiform Texts from Babylonian Tablets in the British Museum*
CTH	Emmanuel Laroche, *Catalogue des textes hittites* (RHA fasc. 58 [1956] 33ff.; 59 [1956] 69ff.; 60 [1957] 30ff.; and 62 [1958] 18ff.)
DA	A. Boissier, *Documents assyriens relatifs aux présages,* 3 vols. (Paris, 1894-99)
EA	J. A. Knudtzon, *Die El-Amarna-Tafeln* (= VAB 2); EA 359-79: A. F. Rainey, *El Amarna Tablets* 359-79 (= *AOAT* 8)
Friedrich, *Staatsv*	J. Friedrich, *Staatsverträge des Ḫatti-Reiches in hethitischer Sprache* (= *MVAeG* 31, 1; and 34, 1), 2 vols. (Leipzig, 1926 and 1930)
GAG	Wolfram von Soden, *Grundriss der akkadischen Grammatik,* AnOr 33 (Rome, 1952)
Goetze, *AM*	A. Goetze, *Die Annalen des Muršiliš, MVAeG* 38 (Leipzig, 1933)
HAB	F. Sommer and A. Falkenstein, *Die hethitisch-akkadische Bilingue des Hattušili I (Labarna II),* Abh. der Bayer. Ak. der Wiss., Phil.-hist. Abt. NF 16 (Munich, 1938)
Ḫatt.	A. Goetze, *Ḫattušiliš, MVAeG* XXIX/3 (Leipzig, 1925)
W. Helck, *Die Beziehungen . . .*	W. Helck, *Die Beziehungen Ägyptens zu Vorderasien im 3. und 2. Jahrtausend v. Chr.* (Wiesbaden, 1971[2])
HiAV	*Hilprecht Anniversary Volume. Studies in Assyriology and Archaeology Dedicated to Hermann V. Hilprecht* (Leipzig, 1909)
HSS	*Harvard Semitic Studies*
HTR	*Harvard Theological Review*
HUCA	*Hebrew Union College Annual*
HWb	J. Friedrich, *Hethitisches Wörterbuch, Kurzgefasste kritische Sammlung der Deutungen hethitischer Wörter* (Heidelberg, 1952-)
ICC	*The International Critical Commentary on the Holy Scriptures of the Old and New Testaments* (New York), C. A. Briggs, S. R. Driver, A. Plummer (eds.)

IEJ	*Israel Exploration Journal*
ISET	M. Çiğ and H. Kizilyay, *Istanbul Arkeoloji Müzelerinde Bulanav Sumer Edebî Tablet ve Parçalari* (Ankara, 1969)
JAOS	*Journal of the American Oriental Society*
JBL	*Journal of Biblical Literature*
JCS	*Journal of Cuneiform Studies*
JEA	*Journal of Egyptian Archaeology*
Jean, *ŠA*	C-F Jean, *Šumer et Akkad, contribution à l'histoire de la civilization dans la Basse-Mésopotamie* (Paris, 1923)
JEN	*Joint Expedition with the Iraq Museum at Nuzi*
JNES	*Journal of Near Eastern Studies*
JRAS	*Journal of the Royal Asiatic Society*
JSS	*Journal of Semitic Studies*
KAR	Erich Ebeling, *Keilschrifttexte aus Assur religiösen Inhalts,* 2 vols., *WVDOG* 28 and 34 (Leipzig, 1915-19, 1920-23)
KAV	Otto Schroeder, *Keilschrifttexte aus Assur verschiedenen Inhalts, WVDOG* 35 (Leipzig, 1920)
KBo	*Keilschrifttexte aus Boghazköi,* Heft 1-6 (= *WVDOG* 30, 36) (Leipzig, 1916-23); Heft 7ff. (= *WVDOG* 68ff.) (Berlin, 1954-)
Keiser, *STD*	Clarence Elwood Keiser, *Selected Temple Documents of the Ur Dynasty, YOS* 4 (New Haven, 1919)
KUB	*Keilschrifturkunden aus Boghazköi* (Berlin, 1921-
LEDEHP	David A. Robertson, *Linguistic Evidence in Dating Early Hebrew Poetry,* SBL Dissertation Series 3 (Missoula, Montana, 1972)
LKA	Erich Ebeling, *Literarische Keilschrifttexte aus Assur* (Berlin, 1953)
LKU	A. Falkenstein, *Literarische Keilschrifttexte aus Uruk* (Berlin, 1931)
LSS	*Leipziger semitistische Studien*
MA	Middle Assyrian

MAD	*Materials for the Assyrian Dictionary*
MAW	S. N. Kramer, *Mythologies of the Ancient World* (Garden City, N. Y., 1961)
MB	Middle Babylonian
MDIK	*Mitteilungen des Deutschen Archäologischen Instituts,* Abteilung Kairo, Wiesbaden
MDOG	*Mitteilungen der deutschen Orient-Gesellschaft*
MIO	*Mitteilungen des Instituts für Orientforschung*
MSL	*Materialien zum sumerischen Lexicon*
MVAeG	*Mitteilungen der Vorderasiatisch-Aegyptischen Gesellschaft*
NA	Neo-Assyrian
Nik	M. V. Nikolskii, *Dokumenty chozjajastvennoj otčetnosti drevnej Chaldei iz sobranija N. P. Lichačeva, čast' II* (Moscow, 1915)
OA	*Oriens Antiquus*
OA	Old Assyrian
OAkk	Old Akkadian
OB	Old Babylonian
OECT	*Oxford Editions of Cuneiform Texts*
OLZ	*Orientalistische Literaturzeitung*
Or	*Orientalia*
OTS	*Oudtestamentische Studiën*
PAPS	*Proceedings of the American Philosophical Society,* Philadelphia
PN	Personal name
Poeble, *GSG*	Arno Poeble, *Grundzüge der sumerischen Grammatik* (Rostock, 1923)
PRAK	H. de Genouillac, *Premieres recherches archéologiques à Kich,* 2 vols. (Paris, 1924-25)
PRU	*Le palais royal d'Ugarit*
R	H. C. Rawlinson, et al., *The Cuneiform Inscriptions of Western Asia,* 5 vols. (London, 1861-1909)
RA	*Révue d'assyriologie et d'archéologie orientale*

RdE	*Révue d'Egyptologie publiée par la Société française d'égyptologie,* Paris
RHA	*Révue hittite et asianique*
RLA	*Reallexikon der Assyriologie*
RŠ	Field numbers of tablets excavated at Ras Shamra
RSO	*Rivista degli studi orientali*
SBH	G. A. Reisner, *Sumerisch-babylonische Hymnen nach Thontafeln griechischer Zeit* (Berlin, 1896)
von Schuler, *Dienstanw.*	Elinar von Schuler, *Hethitische Dienstanweisungen für höhere Hof- und Staatsbeamte; ein Betrag zum antiken Recht Kleinasiens, AfO* Beiheft 10 (Graz, 1957)
SITP	M. Weippert, *The Settlement of the Israelite Tribes in Palestine,* trans. J. D. Martin (Naperville, Ill., 1971)
SK	H. Zimmern, *Sumerische Kultlieder aus altbabylonischer Zeit,* VS II, X (Leipzig, 1912-13)
SKT	H. Winckler, *Sammlung von Keilschrifttexten,* 3 vols. (Leipzig, 1893-95)
ŠL	Anton Deimel, *Šumerisches Lexicon* (Rome, 1928-50)
SLB	*Studia ad tabulas cuneiformes collectas a F. M. Th. de Liagre Böhl pertinentia*
SLTN	Samuel N. Kramer, *Sumerian Literary Texts from Nippur in the Museum of the Ancient Orient at Istanbul, AASOR* 23 (New Haven, 1944)
SMEA	*Studi Micenei et Egeo-Anatolici*
Sommer, *AU*	F. Sommer, *Die Aḫḫijavā-Urkunden* (= Abh. der Bayer. Ak. der Wiss., Phil.-hist. Abt. NF 6) (Munich, 1932)
Sommer and Ehelolf, *Pap.*	F. Sommer and H. Ehelolf, *Das hethitische Ritual des Papnickri von Komana,* Boghazköy-Studien 10 (Leipzig, 1924)
SRT	Edward Chiera, *Sumerian Religious Texts* (Upland, Pa., 1924)
SSAW	*Sächsische Akademie der Wissenschaften, Sitzungsberichte,* philosophisch-historische Klasse, Leipzig
StBoT	*Studien zu den Boğazköy-Texten* (Wiesbaden, 1965-)

STT — O. R. Gurney, J. J. Finkelstein, and P. Hulin, *The Sultantepe Tablets,* 2 vols. (London, 1957, 1964)

Sturtevant and Bechtel, *Chrest.* — E. H. Sturtevant and G. Bechtel, *A Hittite Chrestomathy* (Philadelphia, 1935)

TAPS — *Transactions of the American Philosophical Society,* Philadelphia

TCL — *Textes cunéiformes du Louvre*

TIM — *Texts in the Iraq Museum*

TIT — Thorkild Jacobsen, *Toward the Image of Tammuz* (Cambridge, Mass., 1970)

TLB — *Tabulae Cuneiformes a F. M. Th. de Liagre Böhl collectae*

TTG — George E. Mendenhall, *The Tenth Generation: The Origins of the Biblical Tradition* (Baltimore and London, 1973)

UET — *Ur Excavations Texts*

Ugar. — *Ugaritica* (Mission de Ras Shamra; Paris)

VAB — *Vorderasiatische Bibliothek*

VAS — *Vorderasiatische Schriftdenkmäler der königlichen Museen zu Berlin* (Leipzig, 1907-)

VAT — Tablets in the collections of the Staatliche Museen, Berlin

VT — *Vetus Testamentum*

WA — Hugo Winckler and L. Abel, *Der Thontafelfund von El Amarna* (Berlin, 1889-90)

WVDOG — *Wissenschaftliche Veröffentlichung der Deutschen Orient-Gesellschaft*

YGC — W. F. Albright, *Yahweh and the Gods of Canaan* (New York, 1968)

YOS — *Yale Oriental Series,* Babylonian Texts

ZA — *Zeitschrift für Assyriologie*

ZAS — *Zeitschrift für Ägyptische Sprache und Altertumskunde,* Leipzig-Berlin

ZAW — *Zeitschrift für die alttestamentliche Wissenschaft*

ZDMG — *Zeitschrift der Deutschen Morgenländischen Gesellschaft*

PART I: HISTORY

- 1 -

EARLY ISRAELITE HISTORY IN THE LIGHT OF EARLY ISRAELITE POETRY

David Noel Freedman

In a previous paper I attempted to establish a sequence dating for the early poems of Israel.[1] A principal conclusion was that the oldest substantial poems of the Israelite confederacy which have survived are the Song of the Sea (Exod. 15) and the Song of Deborah (Judg. 5). In my opinion, both poems belong to the earliest phase of Israel's national existence, and their original composition may be dated with some confidence to the twelfth century B.C. Of the two, the Song of the Sea is older: it describes the episode in which corporate existence effectively began for this people, and may be assigned to the first half of the twelfth century, or about 1175. The Song of Deborah describes the major victory of the Israelites over the Canaanites near Taanach, as a result of which Canaanite political hegemony and military superiority were overthrown, and Israelite possession of the land was confirmed. This poem may be assigned to the third quarter of the twelfth century, or not later than about 1125.

The conclusions reached in the previous article, which form the premise of the present study, do not depend for their acceptance entirely on the validity of the criteria or the reliability of the procedures adopted. Other scholars, using different criteria and methods, have arrived at very similar results with respect to the two poems under consideration.[2] We may affirm a growing consensus about their early date. Regardless of the merit of my particular analysis of the material and the proposed identification and sequence dating of the corpus of early biblical poetry, there is a sound basis for the early dating of these poems, and hence for their use in the reconstruction of the initial phases of Israelite history.

The purpose, therefore, of the present paper is to examine the two songs and attempt to extract from them valid historical data for a reconstruction of Israel's earliest national experience. The assumption is that these are the oldest sources available for such a reconstruction, are roughly contemporary with the events, and should therefore provide an accurate description of the central and most important occurrences in the saga of early Israel. At the same time, it must be borne in mind that we are dealing with poetry with its characteristic literary features and emphases, not a journalistic report of battle actions. That means that we cannot expect a simple, sober, sequential account, but must deal with an impressionistic reflection and refraction of the events as they impinged on the creative, emotive mind of the poet. By balancing the various factors, it should be possible to recover significant historical information, not only about the events, but the impact they had on the people who participated in them, and how they perceived their importance and meaning.

Clearly the two poems do not provide anything like a complete or continuous account of Israel's early days, or even of the central events themselves. But they are the primary witnesses to those events, and their testimony must be weighed accordingly. They constitute the foundation upon which a more complete reconstruction may be attempted, and the standard by which the prose data of the Bible are to be measured and evaluated. It is of interest that in the case of both poems there is an accompanying prose narrative (Exod. 14 for the Song of the Sea; and Judg. 4 for the Song of Deborah). The priority of the Song of Deborah and its superiority as a historical source in relation to the prose account have been widely acknowledged.[3] The opposite has been the case with the Song of the Sea, though no adequate reasons have ever been adduced for this reversal in method and treatment of essentially equivalent phenomena.[4] It is my intention to rectify this distortion in scholarly tradition and custom, and treat the literary remains consistently, and in the same order of priority.

THE SONG OF THE SEA (EXOD. 15:1-18, 21)[5]

Both of the biblical poems belong to the genre of victory hymn, examples of which happily have survived from neighboring cultures. Thus we have the Egyptian poems which celebrate the victories of Rameses II over the Hittites at Kadesh on the Orontes, and of Marniptah over the Libyans and others,[6] as well as the Assyrian poem about Tukulti-Ninurta's triumphant campaign against the Kassites of Babylon.[7] All three of these date to the thirteenth century B.C. and are, therefore, somewhat older as well as being much longer than the biblical examples.

It is not my intention to compare these poems or their formal characteristics in detail, but rather to emphasize certain points in common about their structure and the mode of treatment of the central subject matter. While the poems tell a story which is generally consecutive, there are variations in detail from a strict chronological sequence. Attention is focused on the central event or series of actions which culminate in the utter defeat and rout of the enemy. The total time span is relatively short: the story line includes some background material, preliminary actions leading to the central event, the decisive engagement itself, and something of the immediate consequences for both victor and vanquished.

Typically, the poems establish the fact of victory as well as its importance. Then there are flash-backs, filling in details of the preparations and preliminaries leading to the decisive engagement. The victory is again celebrated, and the consequences described.[8]

The Song of the Sea opens with a vivid couplet summarizing the victory at sea (v. 1), which is repeated as a closing refrain (v. 21):

> I will sing to Yahweh for he has triumphed gloriously,
> Horse and its charioteer he hurled into the sea.[9]

The account of the sea victory is filled out in verses 3-5, and reaches a climax in the description of the mighty storm at the Reed Sea generated by Yahweh himself. It was not a battle in the usual sense, since only Yahweh was active against Pharaoh and his host, not the people of Yahweh. Under the circumstances it is difficult to reconstruct the episode with any precision, although the prose compilers made a valiant stab at it, aided presumably by other source materials.[10] There is enough evidence to make it clear that the decisive moment came with the destruction of the Egyptian chariot force by a violent storm at the Reed Sea. It is noteworthy that the song celebrates the defeat of an armored contingent (i.e., chariotry), as does the Song of Deborah. Possession of chariots was the sign of military superiority in the world of the second millennium B.C., and under normal circumstances a show of this force would have been sufficient to intimidate any rebellious band armed only with hand weapons. For a militia without sophisticated weapons or training, to challenge a chariot army would seem to be the height of folly, and victory could only come about through the miraculous intervention of God. Just that is precisely the theme of both poems. In Israel's infancy, when it was little better than a rabble in arms, crucial victories over heavily armed opponents were achieved by Yahweh, the God of Israel.

There is a break in the sequence after verse 8; verse 9 is a flash-back, depicting the boastful enemy equipped and ready to set forth in pursuit of Yahweh's people, to overtake, destroy, and despoil them. While the language is typical, and should not be pressed for historical details, nevertheless it provides background for the central event. With verse 10, the unit resumes the theme of victory at sea, and closes with the drowning of the Egyptians.

It is not until the next section that the aftermath or consequences of Yahweh's triumph are described. The main result is the liberation of the people from Egyptian domination and further military intimidation, and their subsequent march through the wilderness under divine guidance to his holy habitation (v. 13).[11] The same theme is continued in verse 17, with 16cd serving as a link. But at the same time, or rather, prior to the movement of the people from the sea to the mountain, another consequence or by-product of the victory is described. This lengthy digression (vv. 14-16ab) concerns the neighboring peoples who are involved in the aftermath for two reasons: (1) they occupy land still claimed by Egypt as part of its Asiatic empire, and hence must be considered vassals of the pharaoh. While Egyptian power was somewhat attenuated in this period (the first quarter of the twelfth century B.C. in my opinion), nevertheless the pharaoh (presumably Rameses III) was a powerful monarch, and after the repulsion of the sea peoples, exercised some control over the remaining Asiatic territories, including Philistia, Canaan, Edom, and probably Moab[12] and (2) the second consideration is that the line of march of the people of Yahweh took them near or into regions claimed by one or more of the nations mentioned. While no direct encroachment of their territories is affirmed or even hinted at, the movement of a sizable group in proximity to ill-defined border regions would be enough to generate concern. When such a movement is associated in popular report with a spectacular victory over one of the major powers, that concern would naturally escalate into consternation.

According to the poet, the magnitude of the victory is best seen in the reaction of the neighboring vassal domains. Terror and dread overwhelm them; they are paralyzed by sheer fright. This theme, which is common to campaign oratory of the ancient Near East and a cliché in the prose Assyrian annals, is used to heighten the political impact of the engagement at the Reed Sea. The poet links the primary victory over the Egyptians with the secondary effect on their vassals through a play on the word "stone," two properties of which are exploited in his imagery. Thus the chariot army of Pharaoh is said to sink into the depths "like a stone" (v. 5); and the four nations which occupy the Asiatic territory of Egypt are said to be struck dumb "like a stone" (v. 16).[13]

Instead of coming to the aid of the suzerain in his hour of need, or afterward, they remain silent and motionless behind their borders; they permit, and by their cowardly inaction, encourage the second aftermath–the march through the wilderness of the people of Yahweh. Thus the latter not only escape from Egypt and the armored pursuit force, but are able to turn their flight into a triumphal parade across potentially hostile regions to the sacred area surrounding Yahweh's holy mountain.

The passage of the people through this region is recorded in verse 16cd, which connects the terrified acquiescence of the peoples in this trespass with the advance of Yahweh's people through the wilderness and ultimate arrival at its destination. Thus verse 13 summarizes this aspect of the aftermath, with emphasis on Yahweh's faithful and powerful guidance, and the people's safe arrival at the sacred area. Verses 16 and 17 spell out the details of the movement across the wilderness (v. 16cd) and the entry and settlement in the holy territory of Yahweh (v. 17).

The identification and location of the sacred habitation of Yahweh (v. 13; see related expressions in v. 17) is the principal remaining problem of the poem.[14] With respect to this question, I propose the following: (1) that *n^ewē qodšekā* "your holy habitation" and *har nah^alāt^ekā* "your mountain possession" are parallel or complementary expressions for the same place; (2) that the action in the verses under consideration (vv. 13 and 17) is all in the past, in spite of the variation in the form of the verbs employed (two suffixed forms in v. 13, two prefixed forms in v. 17a), as already observed many years ago by S. R. Driver;[15] and (3) that the place in question is none other than the mountain of God at Sinai or Horeb. According to the tradition this area was the immediate goal of the people who left Egypt, and it fits well into the context of the victory at sea,[16] whereas a location elsewhere, e.g., in the land of Canaan, not only disrupts the unity and continuity of the poetic narrative, but represents the entry and settlement in the promised land as peaceful and without the resistance of the inhabitants, contrary to the practically unanimous testimony of all other sources.[17]

That the phrases *nwh (qdšk)* and *hr (nḥltk)* are in fact complementary is confirmed by a passage in Jeremiah where we find the same terms paired: *n^ewē (ṣedeq)* and *har (haqqōdeš).*[18] In the latter passage, the reference is certainly to the land of Canaan, very likely to the holy city Jerusalem and Mt. Zion. The terms would inevitably be applied to the central sanctuary of Yahweh wherever that happened to be. From the tenth century on, it was at Jerusalem, to be sure, but before that time it was elsewhere. In Jer. 31:23, we have a good example of transference, since the terms are more appropriate to a wilderness region (i.e., *nāweh* is a pastoral habitation) and an authentic mountain range. Such terms would not have been used to describe Jerusalem and Mt. Zion, if they had not been hallowed by tradition, a tradition originally associated with Sinai/Horeb and its great mountain.[19] They are especially appropriate to that place in the period to which the poem has been assigned by me and other scholars on independent grounds. The preservation of the terminology and its adaptation to other sanctuaries in other places is typical of the conservatism of all religious groups, and only serves to emphasize the antiquity and tenacity of these original traditions. Parallel to this phenomenon is the persistent assertion, found in several early poems (and restated in the archaizing Psalm of Habakkuk) that Yahweh came from Sinai, i.e., from the southland (his primordial dwelling among men) to acquire a new permanent abode in Canaan (Judg. 5:4-5, Deut. 33:2-3, Ps. 68:8-9; cf. Hab. 3:2-3).

Furthermore, the description of the divine throne (*mākōn l^ešibt^ekā* "dais of your throne," i.e., the platform on which the throne of Yahweh is set) and sanctuary (*miqdāš*) in Exod. 15:17 reflects the heavenly or mythic palace and throne-room of the deity, made by his own hands, and hence to be distinguished from man-made temples wherever they may have been erected. Yahweh's own palace was in the heavens at the top of the sacred mountain, generally hidden from view by the clouds. Such a picture of Yahweh's residence made by him fits the scene at Sinai and nowhere else.[20] The use of the critical phrase at the dedication of the temple in Jerusalem in the days of Solomon brings out the distinction between the heavenly and earthly sanctuaries; the Massoretic Text of 1 Kings 8:13 reads:

bānōh bānītī bēt zᵉbūl lāk	I have surely built a royal house for you
mākōn lᵉšibtᵉkā ʿōlāmīm	A dais for your eternal throne.

This is an adaptation of the original mythical reference to the current occasion.[21]

My conclusion is that verses 13 and 17 refer to the march through the wilderness from the sea to the mountain. The various nouns *nwh qdšk, hr nḥltk, mkwn lšbtk,* and *mqdš* all describe the holy abode of Yahweh in the southland. Similarly, the verbs *nḥyt, nhlt, tb'mw,* and *tṭʿmw* describe the march through the wilderness and the entry into and settlement at the holy site. That place was surely Sinai/Horeb (the exact location of which remains uncertain), though Kadesh-Barnea has some claim to be considered as an alternate site. In any case, the poet had in mind a settlement in the vicinity of the holy mountain, which was dedicated to the worship and service of Yahweh.

The phrase *hr nḥltk* "the mountain of your possession" (i.e., the mountain to which you have rightful claim, or your own mountain which belongs to you by right) establishes legal ownership, whether that possession is a matter of inheritance or conquest. As has been noted by scholars, an almost identical expression, *ğr nḥlty*, has turned up in Ugaritic as a description of the mountain sacred to Baal. The mountain itself, while draped in mythological terms and associations, not only bears a distinctive name, *ṣāpōn* "North" (i.e., the northern peak), but has been identified with classical Mt. Casius modern Jebel Aqraʿ, just north of Ras Shamrah.[22]

In addition, Cross has shown that a particular mountain was sacred to the god El, chief of the Canaanite pantheon, namely, Mt. Amanus, which is even higher than Mt. Casius.[23] In other words, the expression is to be understood as the designation of a real mountain which has a special role in relation to a particular deity, i.e., it is his own mountain. In the original instance, it will be a towering peak (at least in relation to its environment), on which the palace of the god is located, where he holds sway, and where his retinue of heavenly servants wait upon him. In this respect, Yahweh is like El and Baal, having his own sacred mountain. It is Sinai/Horeb, traditionally identified with Jebel Musa, an imposing peak in the Sinai peninsula. Questions have been raised about the location, and other sites (and other mountains) have been proposed, including the volcanic peaks in the northern Hejaz.[24]

Wherever it was in the southern region, that mountain was known to Israel and identified as Yahweh's own, just as he was identified as the God of this mountain: *zeh sînay* "the One of Sinai." In Cross's view, which I have adopted, Yahweh was the patron deity of a Midianite league (which included Kenites as a specialized group) in the general area around the Gulf of Akaba (the region variously called Seir, Edom, Paran).[25] The association of Yahweh with Sinai is therefore pre-Mosaic, and may be reflected in the place-name *yhw3* preserved in a thirteenth-century Egyptian list.[26] Presumably the full name would have been *bēt yahweh*; both name and location are appropriate for the Midianite sacral center including both settlement (at Qurayya) and mountain (Sinai).[27]

We may suppose that the Midianite settlement there was of relatively recent origin (Late Bronze Age), and that the phrase *hr nḥltk* reflects the establishment of the cult of Yahweh at Sinai. The language used to describe Yahweh's ascendancy there is typically mythical and belongs to the pre-Mosaic form of this religion. Other echoes of the older tradition may be found scattered through the poetry of the Hebrew Bible, though the mixture of presumed Midianite motifs with those of Canaanite religion cannot easily be untangled (e.g., Rahab, the mythical monster in Ps. 89:11, may be Midianite; Leviathan, on the other hand, has a cognate in Canaanite mythology). It is only after the transfer of Yahweh's earthly center from Sinai to Canaan that such language would be applied to one or more sites in Canaan. Not until the capture of Jerusalem and the erection of the sanctuary there, is the shift in language and terminology completed.

There is an interesting parallel passage in Ps. 78, a lengthy historical poem which deals primarily with the Exodus and Wanderings, though it carries the story as far as the accession of David and the establishment of his dynasty.[28] After an extended introduction (vv. 1-8), the narrative opens with the deliverance from Egypt and continues through the Wanderings in the wilderness and the miracles and murmurings which punctuated them (vv. 9-39). Then, beginning with verse 40, the poet returns to the Plagues in Egypt and the Exodus. With the slaying of the first-born (v. 51), the stage is set for the departure of the people, which is then described in language reminiscent of Exod. 15:13, 16-17. Thus we read:

52) Then he led forth his people like sheep,
and guided them in the wilderness like a flock;
53) He led them to a safe place so that they would have nothing to fear,
but the sea overwhelmed their enemies;
54) Then he brought them to his sacred region,[29]
to the mountain which his right hand had created;
55) He drove out the nations before them, and assigned their landed
property to them by lot,
he settled the tribes of Israel in their tents.

It is important to recognize that this is a summary statement covering the period from the departure from Egypt down to the occupation of the land of Canaan, including as principal and representative events the drowning of the Egyptians, the Wanderings in the wilderness, and the entry into the land. It is clear that verses 52-53 deal with the complex of incidents leading up to the destruction at the sea. On the other hand, verse 55 presumptively refers to the invasion of Canaan and the apportionment of the conquered land.

The question is: to what does verse 54 refer? Since it is placed between the departure from Egypt and the drowning of the Egyptians, on the one hand (vv. 52-53), and the forcible dispossession of the nations and the division of the land among the Israelite tribes, on the other (v. 55), it would be reasonable to see in verse 54 a description of the Wanderings in the wilderness and the sojourn at the holy mountain there. After all, the poet was fully aware of the wilderness tradition, having devoted the bulk of his composition to a detailed account of Israel's experience there. It would be strange if in the resumé all reference to the wilderness were omitted, or if that part of the tradition were simply submerged in the account of the Conquest.[30] Prevailing scholarly opinion to the contrary notwithstanding, any reference to the hill country of Judah here or Mt. Zion in particular would be out of order, and would disturb the dramatic build-up of the poem, which reaches its climax with the explicit designation of Judah and Mt. Zion as the real focus of God's interest in verses 68-69; David is mentioned in verse 70 as the one who attained this goal. Any such reference would be premature before the historical narrative in verses 56-67 (note, e.g., the mention of Shiloh, vv. 60f., which preceded Jerusalem as the site of the central sanctuary), and especially so before the invasion and occupation of the land, v. 55.[31]

In my opinion, Ps. 78:54, like Exod. 15:13 and 17, describes the wilderness mountain sanctuary as the initial goal of the march from Egypt. This is the natural reading and interpretation of the passages in both poems, and there is nothing in either of the latter to suggest otherwise. It is only the accumulated weight of scholarship that has obscured this point. Furthermore, we note that Ps. 78:55, with its clear statement of the dominant themes of the conquest of Canaan and the division of the territory, has no echo in Exod. 15. There is no hint in the latter of either of these matters, or of any other element in the Conquest tradition.

If the scope of the poem in Exod. 15 is limited to the victory at the Reed Sea and its immediate consequences–the march through the wilderness and the settlement at the holy mountain there–what can we say about the date of these events, on the basis of the internal data of the poem? The principal clue is to be found in the list of four peoples in verses 14-15. These are described as having heard the news of the Egyptian disaster at the sea, and as responding with shock and great fright, so much so that they were paralyzed with fear and unable to impede the triumphal march of Yahweh's people through the wilderness. The identity and collocation of these peoples are both interesting and important. The order of the names is geographical and stylistic: (1) The news of the Egyptian catastrophe reached the Philistines in southwest Palestine first, since they were nearest to the place where it occurred; from there the word was passed on to the Edomites in the southeast quadrant, and then to the Moabites in the northeast. Finally it came back across the Jordan to the Canaanites in the northwest.[32] (2) The phrases are organized in an envelope construction, in which the first and last terms form a linked pair, while the second and third terms form a balancing pair:

1) *yšby plšt*	//	4) *yšby kn'n*
2) *'lwpy 'dwm*	//	3) *'yly mw'b*

From a historical and chronological point of view, there is only one period during which these four peoples coexisted in the area from the border of Egypt to the northern perimeter of Palestine: the twelfth century B.C. The critical terms are the first (*plšt*) and the fourth (*kn'n*), though all are important. There is no explicit mention of the Philistines in Egyptian sources before the early twelfth century (during the reign of Rameses III, who repelled an invasion of the sea peoples, among whom they are listed).[33] Doubtless they were present in the area earlier (in the thirteenth century, certainly, perhaps even before that), but they were not settled as a national entity in Palestine before the first quarter of the twelfth century, so far as one can tell from the records.[34] The reference here, in which Philistia is grouped with other settled peoples cannot be earlier, but might be later. It is often claimed, moreover, that it must be much later, since other occurrences of the term *p^eলešet*

are in either late (e.g., Isa.14:29, 31; Joel 4:4) or undatable poetry (Pss. 60:10, 83:8, 87:4, 108:10).[35] Standard usage in prose (and other early poetry, e.g., 2 Sam. 1:20) is the masculine plural form, *p^elištîm*. While this argument may carry some weight, it is clear that the singular form, *plšt*, was in use in a neighboring culture (Egypt) as early as the twelfth century, and must therefore have been known by the Israelites. Its haphazard and sporadic use in Hebrew poetry can hardly be used to prove anything about its introduction into the language.

It may also be argued that the term *yšby*, which I have rendered "enthroned ones,"[36] is inappropriate for the Philistines, who did not have kings (*m^elākîm*) in this period, but were governed by a council of tyrants or lords (*s^erānîm*, which is etymologically related to Greek *tyrannos*). The word *yōšēb* is less specific than *melek*, and hence may have served as an equivalent for *seren*; at the same time, it could represent "kings" in the complementary phrase *yšby kn'n* "kings of Canaan." In the eyes of the Israelites, the formal distinction between Philistine and Canaanite political structures may have been obscured by the functional similarities, especially in the leadership. It is also possible that in Exod. 15:14, the phrase *yšby plšt* simply means "the inhabitants of Philistia,"[37] though in view of the expressions in verse 15 referring to the leaders of Edom and Moab (and presumably Canaan), it is not likely.

At the other end of the period, i.e., by the eleventh century, the situation on both sides of the Jordan had changed drastically: on the east bank the Ammonites had intruded upon the domestic tranquillity of the Moabites by seizing large chunks of their territory; and on the west bank the Israelites and Philistines had practically demolished the Canaanites. It is instructive that after the decisive defeat of the Canaanite kings recorded in the Song of Deborah there is no further mention of the Canaanites in any early poem of Israel, or in the prose accounts after the period of the Judges (except for an occasional stereotyped phrase: 1 Kings 9:16, 2 Sam. 24:7; cf. Neh. 9:8, 24). If the battle of Kishon, celebrated in the Song of Deborah, occurred around 1150 B.C., or slightly later, then we could fix the events described and the situation reflected in the Song of the Sea in the first half of the twelfth century, preferably in the first quarter. I do not see any sufficient basis for pushing the principal occurrence–the victory at the sea–back into the thirteenth century, though that is possible. The further back it is set, the greater the discrepancy in the picture of the four nations in verses 14-15. The earliest possible date for the Exodus would then be the last quarter of the thirteenth century, while a preferable date would be around 1200, or very early in the twelfth century.

An apparent conflict between this proposal and the evidence in the Marniptah "victory stele," in which "Israel" is mentioned in a series of peoples and cities located in Syria-Palestine may be resolved in the following manner. If the identification with biblical "Israel" is accepted, and there seems to be no significant argument against the equation, we would agree that there was a confederation of political units in the land of Canaan collectively called "Israel" during the thirteenth century B.C. or even earlier.[38] Already in the thirteenth century the league had gained sufficient autonomy to merit mention in Marniptah's list of enemies in the Asiatic provinces. But it had not yet attained statehood or adopted Yahwism, which was introduced into the country at a later date. It seems likely that many if not most of the tribal names were attached to districts in Palestine in pre-Mosaic times.[39] In other words, the framework or territorial structure of the twelve-tribe confederation was already present in Palestine at least a half-century before the movement initiated by Moses under the banner of a militant and triumphant Yahweh penetrated the west bank of the Jordan river.

Having attempted to determine the chronological horizon of the poem, and to fix the approximate date of the events and circumstances described in the poem, namely, the first quarter of the twelfth century, we may proceed to consider the date of the poem itself. A substantial mass of evidence and argumentation has been assembled by a number of scholars pointing to a very early date for the composition of the Song of the Sea; in fact it is held by several to be the oldest of all Yahwistic poems of any length in the Bible.[40] More specifically, a date in the twelfth century for its composition seems very reasonable.[41] On the basis of the present analysis and some of the inferences drawn from it, I now propose a date of composition in the second quarter of the twelfth century, and in any case before 1150. In my opinion, the poet was restricted in his vision of the historical experience of his people, the people of Yahweh, to the period ending with the settlement at the southern wilderness sanctuary. He was, therefore, acquainted with Mosaic Yahwism in its pristine form, before its first radical adaptation to a territorial state with a developed political structure. He lived within a generation of the events described in the poem, and may even have been a participant in or observer of them. The conclusions to which I have come, while not quite as traditional as those of the compilers of the Pentateuch, who attributed the poem to Moses himself and the refrain to Miriam and her companions, are nevertheless sufficiently drastic to pose questions for orthodox critical scholarship, as well as to offer suggestions for the reconstruction of biblical history.

The picture presented by the poem and supplemented by extrabiblical data may be described as follows:

1. Behind the poem is the flight from Egypt, here barely touched on by the enemy in his speech in which he boasts that he will overtake, put to the sword, and plunder the people.

2. The central content of the poem is the miraculous deliverance of the people at the Sea of Reeds. While numerous details are provided, including information about Pharaoh's chariotry and officers, about the violence of the storm which wrecked the armored force and drowned the fighting men, it is extremely difficult to reconstruct a rational sequence of events or the exact circumstances of the occurrence.[42] That there was a decisive shift in the fortunes of the fleeing group seems certain.

3. From that time on they were free of the threat of Egyptian reprisals or punitive action. According to the poet, the effect of the victory was not limited to Egypt, but extended to overwhelm the other neighboring and interested states: Philistia, Edom, Moab, and Canaan. Paralyzed by fear at the awesome display of Yahweh's power against the most powerful nation in that part of the world, these lesser peoples could offer no opposition as the people marched across the wilderness from the sea to the holy mountain of Yahweh. The poem closes with the vivid description of the people planted in the sacred precinct, the peculiar possession of Yahweh, where his sanctuary stands, the dais of his throne, all made by his own hands. The language is rich with mythic terminology, derived from the older religious traditions preserved in Canaanite literary texts. Such expressions, which were used of other gods and their sacred areas and temples,[43] were applied to Yahweh and his sacred mountain in this passage, and would be adapted to worship at the different central shrines of Israel and Judah in the centuries to come, finally being fixed on Jerusalem and Mt. Zion, Yahweh's permanent earthly abode in the biblical tratition.

The poem is also important for what it does not say: there is no mention or presumption of the Conquest, i.e., the entry into and settlement in Canaan. Furthermore, there is no reference to the patriarchs or awareness of the theme of the promised land. The objective of the people who fled from Egypt was the holy land of Yahweh, but that territory was in the sourthern wilderness, Yahweh's traditional home, not Canaan.

In short, there is no obvious link between Yahweh and the God of the Fathers.[44] In this poem we have a clear expression of a new religion, not simply the adaptation of an old one. The accommodation of the new faith introduced by Moses to the traditional El religion of Israel was the work of a later generation.[45] Furthermore, the group that was the object of divine intervention, who were rescued from the pursuing chariots is known only as the people of Yahweh. Although they have been redeemed by him, even created by him, they are not called Israel and claim no patriarchal descent: they are not necessarily children of Abraham, Isaac, and Jacob. The group is perhaps best described as a heterogeneous collection: an undefined mixture of the stateless people at the bottom of the Egyptian class and power structure, sharing little more than a common language (in biblical terms, *'ereb rāb* and *'ᵃsapsūp*).[46] But these slaves secured a unique leader, were delivered by a miracle; they were welded into a community through a common faith, hardened and toughened by a terrible ordeal in the wilderness, to emerge as the people of Yahweh. That is their only designation in the Song of the Sea. There is no confederation called Israel (or Judah) in the poem, no tribal divisions with the familiar names of Jacob's sons, no traditions of the past, no promise of posterity, no conquest of the land–only permanent dwelling with Yahweh and continued life under his protection.[47]

THE SONG OF DEBORAH (JUDG. 5)[48]

A drastically altered scene is reflected in the Song of Deborah, to which we now turn. The battle between Israel and Canaan at Taanach by the waters of Megiddo (Judg. 5:19) was the decisive episode in the struggle for control of the central and northern areas of Palestine. With the destruction of Sisera's chariot force, and the defeat of the Canaanite kings allied with him, the main phase of the warfare between Israelites and Canaanites was over.[49]

The central action is described briefly but vividly in verses 19-22, with the preceding sections of the poem being devoted to preliminary and preparatory actions and summary statements, while the particular fate of Sisera is narrated in the succeeding units of the poem (verses 24-27 and 28-30, which relate the concern of his mother). The time-span of the poem is relatively brief, a characteristic of victory odes.[50] The major battle and its immediate aftermath take place on a single day, while the specific preparations for the battle, including the muster of the Israelite militia are a matter of a few weeks or months, hardly more. The only extended flash-back is to be found in verses 4-5, which refer to Yahweh's march from the southland to Canaan. While it is sometimes argued that this passage reflects only the immediate situation in which Yahweh, the One of Sinai, comes from the region of Edom//Seir, i.e., the location of his terrestrial base, to the aid of his beleaguered people in their critical encounter with the Canaanites, that is a questionable inference.[51] The passage reflects rather the permanent displacement of Yahweh's earthly abode from the southern wilderness to the land of Canaan, and corresponds to the movement of his people from Sinai or Kadesh to the northern region. That this migration of God and people was not immediately related to the battle at Taanach described in the Song of Deborah, but had an independent status in the traditions of Israel, is to be seen in the fact that several versions of the divine march from the southern plains to Canaan occur in various early or archaizing poems: e.g., Deut. 33:2-3, Ps. 68:8-9, and Hab. 3:3.[52] None of these refers directly to the episode described in Judg. 5, but rather imply that Yahweh's march north was at the head of his people and took place in preparation for the entry into and settlement in the land of Canaan. While the southern mountain range, where Yahweh revealed himself to Moses and was worshipped by his people in their first permanent settlement, would always retain its sacred associations and have a central place in the traditions of the founding of the community, it is instructive that its importance was only in terms of reminiscence, and the ongoing cult could accept the transfer of holiness to the land of Canaan as permanent and complete. The tabernacle and ark symbolized the continuing presence of Yahweh whether in motion or at rest in one or another of the major shrines of early Israel. This practice continued until the final stabilization of worship in the temple at Jerusalem. There were deviations from this norm in later times, e.g., the persistent heresy of the northern kingdom with its sanctuaries at Dan and Bethel, but the official view was held firmly in the biblical writings. There is only one recorded instance of a pilgrimage to the ancient mountain of Yahweh: Elijah's flight to Horeb after the episode at Mt. Carmel.[53] There may have been others, but their absence from the record indicates that there was no regular practice of this sort. In short, the transfer of sanctity was complete and irreversible. The God of Sinai became in turn the God of the promised land (Canaan, including Trans-Jordan), and ultimately the resident deity of Jerusalem on Mt. Zion.[54]

Even though the march from the south is not directly related to the battle at the Kishon river, it forms a necessary part of the story of the Conquest, and serves also as the link between the Exodus and Wanderings on the one hand, and the Wanderings and the Conquest on the other. The sequence of events is closely knit, and while the poems emphasize only the most important occurrences, there are no significant gaps, from the beginning with the Exodus from Egypt until the final displacement of the Canaanites. According to the chronology proposed above, not more than one or two generations were involved, perhaps only forty to sixty years. If the Exodus and initial settlement in the south are to be dated around 1200 or shortly thereafter, then the march from the sacred mountain north should be placed in the second quarter of the same century, with the climactic battle at Taanach around 1150 or a little later. If the Song of the Sea was composed in the second quarter of the twelfth century or roughly around 1175, then we should date the composition of the Song of Deborah in the third quarter of the same century, hardly later than about 1125. In other words, both poems were occasional pieces composed to celebrate recent decisive victories.[55]

The next unit of the Song of Deborah, verses 6-7, which begins in the epic manner, "In the days of Shamgar ben-Anat / in the days of Jael . . . ," is usually taken to be retrospective, describing the desperate condition of the Israelites before the appearance of Deborah and the great victory at Taanach. The disappearance of the yeomanry or militia (*ḥdlw przwn*, v. 7)[56] was difficult to square with their victorious reappearance (v. 11), while the references to the "days of Shamgar," apparently a contemporary, and Jael, an active participant in the victory, were seen to be problems if not outright errors (Jael has often been emended right out of the text).[57] In the light of a new analysis of the content of the verses, however, it has become clear that they describe the consequences of Deborah's leadership and the victory in battle, not its antecedents. Hence the references to Shamgar and Jael are quite appropriate, and the retrospective tone reflects the standpoint of the poet who views the scene as a whole, including the background, the preparations, the battle, and the aftermath.

The unit may be read as follows:[58]

bīmē šamgar ben-^{a}*nāt*	(6) In the days of Shamgar ben-Anat,
bīmē yā'ēl ḥād^{e}*lū*	In the days of Jael, they enriched themselves,
'^{o}*rāḥōt w*^{e}*hōl*^{e}*kē n*^{e}*tībōt*	From caravans and highway travelers,
yēl^{e}*kū '*^{o}*rāḥōt '*^{a}*qalqallōt*	From caravans which travel the crooked roads,
ḥād^{e}*lū p*^{e}*rāzōn*	(7) The yeomanry enriched themselves.
b^{e}*yiśrā'ēl ḥādēllū 'ad*	In Israel, they enriched themselves on booty,
šaqqamtī d^{e}*bōrāh*	Because you rose up, Deborah,
šaqqamtī 'ēm b^{e}*yiśrā'el*	Because you rose up, a mother in Israel.

The new analysis and interpretation of this passage depend upon the identification of the root *ḥdl* II in the three-fold occurrence of the verb *ḥdlw*. In contrast with *ḥdl* I, which means "to cease, leave off," *ḥdl* II means "to become fat, rich, prosperous," and then also "gross, stupid"; but we are concerned with the basic meaning of this root. The decisive evidence for this interpretation is to be found in the Song of Hannah (1 Sam. 2:1-10), where the phrase *ḥādēllū 'ad* is found (1 Sam. 2:5), and where the meaning cannot be questioned: "(The hungry) have grown fat on booty." The identical expression in Judg. 5:7, including the peculiar Massoretic vocalization, requires the same translation, which dramatically alters the sense of the whole unit.

The success of the yeomen of Israel in amassing booty is thus a consequence of Deborah's leadership, and easily understood in the light of the smashing victory over the Canaanites. The two occurrences of *ḥdlw* in verse 7 must be understood in the same way, as describing the recent prosperity of the Israelite militia; the pattern of repetition is found throughout the unit: e.g., *bymy . . . bymy*, *'rḥwt . . . 'rḥwt* (v. 6); *šqmty . . . šqmty*, *byśr'l . . . byśr'l* (v. 7). The proper interpretation of *ḥdlw* in verse 6 is less certain. If the subject of the verb is *'rḥwt* "caravans," then the meaning should be "cease"; the thought would be that the rich caravan trade conducted by and in behalf of the merchant princes of the Canaanite cities, and protected by their chariot forces, had been forced to stop by the threat and actual depredations of the Israelite militia, who were essentially guerilla fighters. Alternatively, if the verb is to be identified as another instance of *ḥdl* II, then the meaning would be that the same militia was enriching itself by plundering the aforementioned caravans. It seems to me that the latter understanding is more in keeping with the data already adduced, and presents a consistent picture of Israel's position after the victory at Taanach.

If there is material reflecting the period before Deborah's activity, it may be found in verse 8. The first part remains difficult, and may be beyond recovery or restoration, but I believe that it should be analyzed and interpreted in the light of Deut. 32:17.[59] The explicit remark in the latter part of the verse about the lack of heavy-duty weapons for the infantry would seem to reflect the sad state of Israelite military strength before Deborah. The usual rendering of the number of men in the army of Israel as 40,000 is obviously questionable, but it is not just a case of poetic hyperbole. The term *'elep* is to be understood in its etymologic sense as a village or a population center, which was responsible for providing a unit of troops.[60] Apparently there was a potential army of forty such units in Israel. If the average number of men in an *'elep* was 10, that would make up a fighting force of 400 at full strength, a substantial army for the hill country of Palestine.[61] In the prose account of the battle in Judg. 4, reference is made to Barak's army of 10,000 men (vv. 6 and 14); we can interpret this figure as signifying ten units (perhaps 100 men) from two tribes, Naphtali and Zebulun (see Judg. 5:18). How many additional troops were provided by the remaining eight tribes is not clear, especially since several of them may not have sent any at all (e.g., Reuben, Dan, Gilead, and Asher; vv. 15-17), but if the total was around 400 (official strength), then the share of the four other participating tribes (Ephraim, Benjamin, Machir, and Issachar) would have been 300.

The first major unit of the poem closes with verse 9, which forms an envelope construction with verse 2: note the repetition of the expression *brkw yhwh* "Bless Yahweh," and the subtle interchange between *byśr'l . . . 'm* (v. 2) and *yśr'l . . . b'm* (v. 9). We may render as follows to show the interconnection:

biprōaʿ pᵉrāʿōt bᵉyiśrāʾēl	(2) When locks were long in Israel,
bᵉhitnaddēb ʿām	When the people volunteered,
bārᵃkū yhwh	Bless Yahweh!
libbī lᵉḥōqᵉqē yiśrāʾēl	My heart was with the commanders of Israel,
hammitnaddᵉbīm bāʿām	Who volunteered among the people,
bārᵃkū yhwh	Bless Yahweh!

The next unit, verses 10-13, initiates the celebration of the great victory: verse 10 is the announcement to the audience; verse 11 is the recitation of the mighty deeds of Yahweh; verse 12 recalls the beginning of the action, with the summons to the leaders, Deborah and Barak; and verse 13 is a reprise of some kind (see v. 11).

The central unit of the poem in its present form concerns the mustering of the tribal units for the battle (vv. 14-18). The material is in some disarray and not always intelligible. But it seems to be a roll call of the tribes or political units which were expected to supply troops for the engagement. It is clear that some tribes were more enthusiastic about the battle than others, and perhaps more to the point, some participated and others did not.[62] It is important to note that tribes which did not take an active part in the struggle are listed along with those which did. That means that the list does not derive from the circumstances of the battle, but rather reflects an already existing organization, i.e., a confederation of some kind. While the sequence is irregular and there is some unexplained overlapping and repetition, the list appears to be complete (at least in the mind of the poet). It is always possible that lines and names have dropped out of the poem, which may be only a torso;[63] and there is the glaring omission of three well-known tribes (Simeon, Levi, and Judah). But until and unless convincing evidence is forthcoming, it is methodologically more reliable to suppose that the list reflects the reality in the twelfth century B.C.[64]

The list gives the impression of originality and authenticity. It does not conform to the standard lists of the prose materials with respect to number, order, or designation, though there is sufficient correspondence and overlap to show that we are dealing with essentially the same groups.[65] At the same time, the divergences are so striking, that we must regard the list in Judg. 5 as independent of the others, and not influenced by the traditions reflected in Gen. 49, Deut. 33, or the prose accounts. As is well known, Judg. 5 includes the ten northern tribes, but not the southern tribes, Simeon and Judah, or the tribe of Levi. It is often supposed that the southern tribes were cut off from the north by a line of fortified Canaanite cities, and that they are not mentioned in the poem because there was no way for them to join in the affair.[66] But this is conjectural and depends upon the view that the traditional twelve- (or thirteen-) tribe structure was operational in the twelfth century.

I believe that the Song of Deborah reflects the actual state of affairs at that time: namely, that there was a ten-tribe league which bore the name Israel.[67] The existence of such a confederation can be traced back to or postulated for the thirteenth century on the basis of the Marniptah stele, while certain tribal (and territorial) designations in Palestine may be even older.[68] But of the geographic extent of such a confederation, or the number and names of its constituent elements, we must rely on biblical evidence which is not available before the twelfth century, although presumably more ancient data are embedded in some of the sources. For the twelfth century we have only the Song of Deborah, which is the subject of debate. The earliest biblical evidence for the twelve-tribe federation is to be found, in our opinion, in the Testaments of Jacob (Gen. 49) and Moses (Deut. 33), which are to be dated in their present form not earlier than the eleventh century B.C.[69] Other lists come from different literary strata and sources, reflecting a basic consensus about the number and distribution of the tribes, though with variations in detail.[70]

As pointed out in another place, I believe it is significant that the poems containing the twelve-tribe lists also regularly couple Israel with Jacob, whereas in the Song of Deborah, with its ten-tribe list, only Israel is named.[71] Whatever this datum may imply about the particular relationship between Judah (and perhaps Simeon and Levi) and Jacob, it seems clear that there was a distinctive correlation between the name Israel and the ten northern tribes. That correspondence is fully attested at the time of the divided kingdoms, when the northern group of ten tribes separated from the dynasty of David to establish its own realm.[72] That this move was a restoration rather than an innovation is confirmed by the fact that after Saul's death, Ishbaal, his son, was crowned king of Israel (2 Sam. 2:8-9), while David became king of Judah at Hebron (2 Sam. 2:1-4). Thus as early as 1,000 B.C. there were two nation-states, Israel and Judah, the former of which consisted of ten tribes, while the latter may have included other units besides Judah, as for example, Simeon, which were fully absorbed.

According to the tradition, David reigned for seven and one-half years at Hebron before becoming king of both Israel and Judah (2 Sam. 5:1-5). Ishbaal is said to have reigned for two years over Israel before his assassination. The discrepancy of five and one-half years is curious; if we assume that the figures are correct, then we may explain the circumstances in one of several ways:[73] (1) If David and Ishbaal began to rule over their respective kingdoms at the same time, then we must suppose that there was a five-year interregnum in Israel before David became king there. (2) If, on the other hand, there was little or no gap between the death of Ishbaal and the accession of David over Israel, then we must suppose that David became king of Judah five and one-half years before Ishbaal became king of Israel, i.e., while Saul was still alive. So far as the biblical narrative is concerned there is no support for either supposition: David's accession to the throne of Judah is placed immediately after the death of Saul, and his accession to the throne of Israel is similarly placed after the death of Ishbaal. Of the two alternatives proposed, the former seems less likely; it is difficult to imagine that there was any significant delay in making David king of Israel after the death of Ishbaal. In my opinion it is more likely that David became king of Judah during Saul's reign as king of Israel, and as a consequence of the rupture between them. Since David became a vassal chieftain under the authority of Achish, the Philistine ruler of Gath, after David's break with Saul, it is not difficult to imagine that he was installed as king of Judah with Philistine approval. Judah, after all, had been a protectorate of the Philistines since the time of the Samson stories (see Judg. 15:9-13, esp. v. 11). The question may legitimately be raised as to whether Saul was ever king of both Israel and Judah or, put another way, whether Judah was part of the kingdom of Israel over which Saul reigned as king. It is my judgment that if Saul ever exercised even nominal rule over Judah, it was through an arrangement separate from that which bound Saul to the northern kingdom; and that such an arrangement with Judah was terminated when David broke with Saul, and in effect became his successor as ruler of Judah. The effective establishment of a dual monarchy united in the person of a single king was the achievement of David and Solomon.

Briefly, we suggest that the original twelve-tribe league, located in Canaan and dating back to pre-Mosaic times, included Simeon and Levi, as well as the ten mentioned in the Song of Deborah (possibly with some name changes). The two "missing" tribes (Simeon and Levi) were banished from the league, as the result of some serious breach of confederation regulations, as indicated by the severe condemnation pronounced against both of them in Gen. 49:5-7. There may be a connection between this pronouncement and the scandalous events at Shechem involving the two brothers reported in Gen. 34, but it is difficult to say. If the same episode is in mind, then it would seem that the poet and the prose writer saw things somewhat differently (see Gen. 34:7 and vv. 30-31). The inference that the two tribes were banished from the league is based on a new interpretation of Gen. 49:7, which I render as follows:

'ārūr 'appām kī 'āz	(7) Cursed be their wrath–how fierce it was!
w^{e}'ebrātām kī qāšātāh	And their rage–how cruel it was!
'^{a}ḥall^{e}qēm b^{e}ya'^{a}qōb	I will divide them from Jacob,
wa'^{a}pīṣēm b^{e}yiśrā'ēl	and I will banish them from Israel.[74]

In accordance with this interpretation, I suggest that both groups moved off in a southerly direction, with Simeon finding refuge and settling in the territory of Judah. The account of this settlement in Josh. 19:1-9 implies that Simeon's move into territory assigned to Judah was secondary and unplanned. Levi seems to have relinquished its territorial claims, and left the country, ultimately finding its way to Egypt. There is no reason to doubt the tradition that Moses and his family belonged to this group, or that Levites were among those at the center of the Exodus movement.

To summarize: It is my contention that an original twelve-tribe league in Canaan bore the name Israel, and included Simeon, Levi, and the ten tribes mentioned in the Song of Deborah, but not Judah, which had a separate history. The two tribes, Simeon and Levi, were dropped from membership, and the remaining ten-tribe group, pictured in the Song of Deborah, constituted the Israelite federation in the twelfth and early part of the eleventh century B.C. It is possible that efforts were made to reconstitute a twelve-tribe league including Judah and Simeon during the eleventh century under the leadership of Samuel, but clear evidence is lacking.[75] Out of this league, the monarchy emerged, with Saul as the first king (*melek*) or dynastic ruler (*nāgīd*) of Israel. A similar development took place in the south with David becoming king of Judah, apparently before the death of Saul. After the death of Ishbaal, under David's forceful leadership the two kingdoms were united,[76] only to fall apart again after the death of his son Solomon.[77]

The remaining parts of the Song of Deborah deal with matters relating more directly to the battle and its outcome: i.e., verses 19-22, the destruction of the Canaanite forces by the torrential wady Kishon; verse 23, the cursing of Meroz; verses 24-27, the execution of Sisera by Jael; and verses 28-30, the mounting concern of Sisera's mother over the absence of news and the delay in the return of her son. There may be some reasonable doubt as to whether the poem is complete as we have it in the biblical text, but we must deal with it in its present form. Aside from a possible resolution of the tension created by the juxtaposition of the two dramatic scenes in the latter part of the poem–Jael and Sisera, on the one hand, and Sisera's mother and her chief lady-in-waiting, on the other–the essential story of the battle and the events leading up to and away from it is in the record.

A brief summary, in general chronological sequence, follows:

1. The earliest point of reference in the poem is the march of Yahweh, the God of Sinai, from the region of Seir//Edom (vv. 4-5). This event is subsequent, in my opinion, to anything recorded in the Song of the Sea, including the Exodus, the Wanderings through the wilderness, and the settlement at the Sinai sanctuary by the people of Yahweh. What

this mythopoeic statement signifies in historical terms is not entirely clear, but we may infer reasonably that a movement both of ideas and of people is involved. While Yahweh's march northward is linked to the subsequent battle at Taanach in the poem, there is no suggestion that Yahweh returned safely to his mountain abode once the victory was achieved. A permanent change of address was involved, though it seems clear that the southern mountain, Sinai, and the holy encampment there, remained identified with and sacred to Yahweh. It is not, however, a crude shift of residence and jurisdiction on the part of a local deity, but the transfer of a distinctive religious faith to a new community. Ideas, especially of this kind, do not travel by themselves, but are carried by people, so at least some segment of the population that worshipped and served Yahweh at Sinai must have accompanied him on his march to Canaan, or to reverse the image, he must have accompanied them on their march north. The new Mosaic faith attracted adherents along the way, and rapidly became the religion of important elements in the population of Canaan. This group included settlements scattered through the hill country especially, and constituted the Israel of pre-Mosaic times. The migrants from the far south merged into the larger entity with its geographic base in Palestine to form Israel, the people of Yahweh, to use the language of the Song of Deborah.[78]

2. There is an apparent reference to an earlier period in Israel's experience, though the precise chronological relationship to Yahweh's march from the south is not clear. The mention of *ᵓĕlōhīm ḥădāšīm* "new gods" (v. 8), is suggestive of a time of conflicts, especially if it is related historically to a similar passage in Deut. 32 (v. 17). The confederation seems to have been in a state of military disarray then, in contrast with the later situation described in verses 6-7 and summarized in verse 11.

3. This people, which had lived in an uneasy, generally subordinate relationship to various Canaanite city-states, now under the impetus of the new faith, and doubtless influenced by other socioeconomic and political factors (including the steady decline of Egyptian power and influence), challenged Canaanite hegemony. The next scene is the mustering of the militia: a roll call of the tribal units or politicomilitary districts is given, along with the responses of the tribes in terms of providing manpower and active participation. According to the text, five of the tribes responded favorably (vv. 13-15): Ephraim, Benjamin, Machir (for Manasseh), Zebulun, and Issachar; four others failed to show any enthusiasm for the enterprise (vv. 15-17): Reuben, Gilead, Dan, and Asher. In an appendix (v. 18), Zebulun and Naphtali are cited for conspicuous bravery on the field of battle. The two latter tribes are also mentioned in the prose account (Judg. 4) as the principal participants in the struggle against Sisera.

4. The battle itself is described briefly but dramatically. In ordinary terms, the odds against Israel were overwhelming, but with Yahweh on their side, the outcome could not be in doubt. Divine power was manifested in the sudden flooding of the Kishon; the Canaanite chariot force was wrecked by the river, and the battle ended. The summation in the Song of the Sea applies as well to Sisera and his army as it did to Pharaoh and his host (Exod. 15:1):

> I sing of Yahweh that he is greatly exalted,
> Horse and charioteer he hurled into the sea.

5. The story then focuses on Sisera and his unseemly fate. To fight and die in battle was tragic but honorable; a man could be a hero even in a lost cause. But to die at the hands of a woman was a disgrace, an irreparable blow to a warrior's name and reputation.

The poet has taken full advantage of Sisera's mischance to immortalize the enemy and oppressor, who fell by a woman's wile and mighty stroke. For he is not merely recording the circumstances and outcome of the battle, but expressing exultation at victory over a hated foe, and special satisfaction at the scandalous demise of their leader. The dramatic and emotional possibilities of this drastic judgment on any who dared to oppose the will of Yahweh for the well-being of his people are exploited, not only in the grim account of Sisera's death, but also in the story of Sisera's mother and her attendants vainly waiting for news of expected victory, and nervously reassuring themselves with unlikely reasons for the delay.

6. The aftermath of victory is described, according to a new interpretation, in verses 6-7.[79] Freed from the intimidation and menace of Canaanite forces, the Israelites were able to regulate commerce in their territories, or in other words, intercept and plunder the caravans as they crossed over the mountain passes. Thanks to the great victory engineered by Deborah and Barak, the Israelites achieved a considerable measure of security, stability, and prosperity, in stark contrast with the deplorable conditions which prevailed before the battle.

7. Finally, there is the summons to everyone in Israel to sing and celebrate, to rehearse and proclaim the great triumph of Yahweh and his militia; there is also a proud if not boastful warning to kings and princes to give heed and pay close attention to this new and dominant force in international affairs (vv. 2-3, 9-11). The liturgical close (v. 31) makes it clear that the ancient victory, which gave Israel its place in the sun, has continuing and repeated relevance in the life of the community of faith.

SUMMATION

The two poems under consideration, the Song of the Sea and the Song of Deborah, are the oldest substantial compositions preserved in the Hebrew Bible, in my opinion, and both may be dated in the twelfth century B.C. As such, they offer both historical data and immediate reactions to the circumstances of Israel in its formative years. Always remembering that lyric poetry is not prose narrative, still less journalistic reporting, we may nevertheless learn much from these ancient sources, both from what they include and omit, and how they treat central and peripheral matters.

Essentially, the poems taken together confirm the historicity of key events, and establish their chronological relationships. Thus the Song of the Sea links the flight from Egypt with the deliverance of the people from the Egyptian chariotry at the Reed Sea. The victory at the sea is also tied to the march through the wilderness, and the settlement at the holy mountain, Sinai. The basic sequence--Exodus, Deliverance, Wanderings, Settlement at the sacred mountain--is attested by the poem. The Song of Deborah, for its part, confirms the settlement in the southern plateau (in the region of Seir//Edom), and the subsequent march north by Yahweh. The occupation of Canaan is presumed, but what is proclaimed now is decisive victory and effective control of that land.

The story of the twelfth century for Israel the people of Yahweh, according to the poems, is as follows:

1. Exodus from Egypt and deliverance at the sea.
2. Wandering through the wilderness and settlement at Sinai/Horeb.
3. Yahweh's march north at the head of his people.
4. The conversion of Israel, or parts of it, already in being as a confederation of

tribes, to faith in Yahweh.

5. The struggle against Canaanite oppression, which comes to a climax in the battle at Taanach and results, not only in the defeat of Sisera and his chariot army, but in the effective elimination of the Canaanites as a political force in the country. Israel, as the successor of Canaan, enters a new phase of its national existence.

The summary just given is in general conformity with the dominant tradition in the various prose strands of the Pentateuch or Primary History, and it may be wondered whether such an apparently harmonious result is really justified.[80] Actually, the placid surface is deceptive, and there are a number of radical divergences from the traditional reconstruction. A critical point is the continuity posited in the prose narrative from the patriarchs through the sojourn in Egypt, and the subsequent events culminating in the return to Canaan and settlement there. The poems offer a significantly different picture, revealing the tell-tale seams by which originally independent and disparate traditions have been sewn together.

In the Song of the Sea there is no mention of the patriarchs or any traditions derived from them. According to our analysis there is no direct link to the land of Canaan, either of a patriarchal past there, or of a promised future. So far as the poem is concerned, Yahweh is not just a new name for the God of the Fathers, but a new God.[81] He has no primary connections with the Fathers or the land of Canaan. Similarly, the people of Yahweh are just that, and not Israel at all, or as yet. They were redeemed and acquired (or created) by him, and owe their freedom and status to him. Their origins, which are not traced beyond their presence in Egypt, may well be complex, and included in the Exodus group may be elements which traced their descent to the patriarchs, and claimed kinship with Israelites; but they are defined in the poem only as Yahweh's people.[82]

Whatever may be Yahweh's own background, geographically, linguistically, or mythologically,[83] by the time he is introduced in the poems of the twelfth century, he is a distinct deity, independent of the chief gods of the Canaanite or Amorite pantheons.[84] In the poems, the term Yahweh is used only as a name, and not as a verb, which it is formally.[85] Even if the original form of the name was *yahweh-'ēl*, as I believe, any ultimate connection with El, the principal deity of one or another of the northwest Semitic pantheons, has long since been severed.[86] In short, the Song of the Sea tells us of a new religion, and a new people, and a new experience.

We have argued for a date in the twelfth century, preferably in the first half of that century for the Song of the Sea. It is also our contention that the events which it reports occurred at the beginning of the same century. Taking the names and places, as well as the rest of the data at face value, there can hardly be any other conclusion. The mention of *p*^{e}*lešet* "Philistia" in precisely the same form in which it appears in the inscriptions of Rameses III (the earliest recorded references) strongly supports a twelfth-century date.[87] While Philistines were undoubtedly present in the area at an earlier date, there is no significant evidence for the systematic occupation of the southwestern coastland of Palestine until after the attacks on Egypt by the Sea Peoples had been repulsed. These date from the early years of Rameses III at the beginning of the twelfth century.[88]

The flight from Egypt was followed immediately by the deliverance at the Reed Sea, which liberated the people of Yahweh from further Egyptian oppression or intimidation. The march across the plain and settlement at the holy mountain followed soon after. Here the community of God was established and cultic and civil life was organized.

At this point we postulate that a series of critical episodes affected the life of the community and drastically altered the course of its history.[89] Successful wars of defense may have encouraged the group to expand in a northerly direction.[90] At the same time, divisions and controversies may have produced severe strains in the community, which are amply reflected in a variety of prose accounts.[91] Dissidents were thus forced out and obliged to make their way to other places. One way or another, reports of the new movement along with advocates and adherents reached civilized centers on both sides of the Jordan. Undoubtedly visitors came south to observe and left to proclaim the wonder of what they had seen.[92]

The response to the new faith would have been mixed, and this situation is reflected in the literary sources. Yahwism apparently took hold among the *b^{e}nē yiśrā'ēl* "the sons of Israel," a federation of ten tribes then occupying the hill country of central and northern Palestine. It was subject to various forms of political and economic pressure by the rulers of the Canaanite city-states which claimed possession of that territory. After a series of engagements which began in an earlier period (fourteenth-thirteenth centuries),[93] the Israelites under new leadership represented by Deborah and Barak, and as a result of Yahweh's personal intervention, were able finally to overthrow Canaanite authority and eliminate the oppressive system under which they had suffered.[94]

The stories in Joshua and especially Judg. 1 may well reflect efforts by the tribes individually and in various groupings to establish a footing on the west bank of the Jordan in the fourteenth-thirteenth centuries, before their conversion to Yahwism. Their God, El Shadday, probably of Amorite origin and associated with the patriarchs who migrated from Harran in the Middle Bronze Age, was identified with El, the chief god of the Canaanite pantheon, as seen in the adoption of certain epithets: El Elyon, El Olam.[95] He was typically the God of revelation, law, and justice, bound by covenant ties of promise and obligation to his people. The claim to possession of the land was based upon the patriarchal presence in various localities, certain shrines dedicated to El, and the tradition of a divine commitment to the Fathers. The tribal league was organized around a common religious commitment to the patriarchal God, who was worshipped in these places, e.g., Shechem and, above all, Bethel. We may suppose that patriarchal religion was reactivated by the new faith in Yahweh, and the community was infused with a new spirit of militancy which won the day and established the federation as master of the former Canaanite enclave.

A similar process may be posited for the southern group of tribes, including Judah and Simeon, where Yahwism must also have penetrated, as reflected in archaic traditions preserved in Judg. 1 and 3, and Josh. 15.[96] Many of the connecting pieces are missing, however, so a detailed reconstruction is not yet possible.

Cross has recently proposed a new view of the history of the priesthood in Israel on the basis of an ancient rivalry between a Mosaic or Mushite priestly group and one derived from Aaron.[97] The Mushite priesthood apparently had its point of origin and headquarters in the far south, in Yahweh's homeland; but it also established centers in Israel, in the northern part of Canaan, at Shiloh and Dan among other sites. The Aaronids, on the other hand, were in control in the sanctuaries in the area between, stretching from Hebron in the south to Bethel in the central part of the country, and including Jerusalem. Lines of demarcation could hardly be maintained rigidly, but in general the Mushite priests would have been responsible for the form of Yahwism adopted in the north, while the Aaronids would have determined the character of the faith in the south. The Song of Deborah in particular would have been a product of Mosaic Yahwism, reflecting a special interest in Jael, whose family was related to the Mushite priesthood.[98]

We can set up a series of correlations as a general guide to the division between Mushites and Aaronids:

	Mushite	*Aaronid*
Geographic distribution	North (and far south)	South (and central)
Collective designation	*bᵉnē yiśrā'ēl* Israel	*bᵉnē yaʿᵃqōb* (?) Judah
Chief deity	Yahweh	El (with Yahwistic component)
Iconography	Cherubim	Bull images
Origins	Exodus, Wanderings, Sinai	Patriarchs Promise of the land

By the time the formal twelve-tribe pattern emerged in the eleventh-century Testaments of Jacob (Gen. 49) and Moses (Deut. 33),[99] several significant changes from the Song of Deborah may be noted:

1. For "Israel, the people of Yahweh" in the Song of Deborah, there is now a fixed pair, "Jacob // Israel," which is used repeatedly in the two Testaments (and in the Oracles of Balaam, which we have also dated to the eleventh century).[100] In other words, the ten-tribe league called Israel has become a twelve- (or thirteen-) tribe federation called properly Jacob-Israel, though the term Israel could be used for the expanded group. In time the two major units would be identified as Israel and Judah, though the former would continue in use as the more generic term.

2. With respect to divine nomenclature, we find that the nearly exclusive use of the name Yahweh, characteristic of the twelfth-century poems, has yielded to an expanded list of names including in particular the patriarchal designation, El, along with the epithets for this deity recorded in the Book of Genesis: Shaddai, Elyon, Olam.[101] These poems reflect an accommodation or blending of Mosaic and patriarchal traditions: Yahweh and El have come together as a single God. Such a development must also reflect political adjustments of some kind. The most obvious is the union of northern and southern tribes to form a larger and more powerful confederation. The occasion for such unifying activities can only have been the emergence of a greater threat than the one posed by the now defeated Canaanites. By the end of the twelfth century, the Philistines had established themselves as the major power in Palestine, and with the collapse of other resistance, the Israelites had to face this enemy alone.

The process of consolidation must have been encouraged by the severe pressures exerted by the Philistines, and it may have come to a head after the fall of Shiloh around 1050 B.C. Under the leadership of Samuel, the Israelites were still unable to offer effective resistance, but he initiated the process which led to success. First, he established a permanent executive authority in the person of Saul, the *nāgīd* "chieftain." Second, David, a Judahite military genius, was recruited as Saul's lieutenant, thus combining the forces of north and south. If the anointing of David by Samuel has a basis in fact, we may regard it as the proleptic or actual coronation of David as king of Judah, just as Samuel anointed Saul to be king of Israel. We may also see in David's marriage to Michal, Saul's daughter, a diplomatic attempt to cement the ties between Israel and Judah, looking forward to a merger not only of families but of states. The latter was in fact achieved by David after the collapse of the house of Saul.[102]

NOTES

[1] The article, "Divine Names and Epithets in Early Israelite Poetry," will appear in the forthcoming *Festschrift* in honor of G. Ernest Wright, to be published by Doubleday and Co.

[2] On the early dating of the Song of the Sea, see *YGC,* 12-13; *LEDEHP,* 153-56, esp. 155; P.C. Craigie, "An Egyptian Expression in the Song of the Sea (Exodus XV 4)," *VT* 20 (1970) 83-84; and "Psalm XXIX in the Hebrew Poetic Tradition," *VT* 22 (1972) 144-45; and F. M. Cross, "The Song of the Sea and Canaanite Myth," chap. 6 in *CMHE,* 112-44, esp. 121-25.

The antiquity of the Song of Deborah is affirmed by most scholars, with slight variations as to the precise date; see, e.g., G. Fohrer, *Introduction to the Old Testament,* trans. D. Green (Nashville, 1965) 209; O. Eissfeldt, *The Old Testament: An Introduction,* trans. P. R. Ackroyd (New York, 1965), 100-101; P. C. Craigie, "The Song of Deborah and the Epic of Tukulti-Ninurta," *JBL* 88 (1969) 253-65, esp. 253-55; and "The Conquest and Early Hebrew Poetry," *Tyndale Bulletin* 20 (1969); D. Harvey, "Deborah," in *The Interpreter's Dictionary of the Bible,* ed. G. A. Buttrick (New York, 1962), vol. 1, 809.

[3] See J. M. Myers, "The Book of Judges," in *The Interpreter's Bible* (New York, 1953), vol. 2, 717-18.

[4] See the discussion of this point in F. M. Cross and D. N. Freedman, "The Song of Miriam," *JNES* 14 (1955) 237-50, esp. 237-39. See S. R. Driver, *The Book of Exodus,* in "The Cambridge Bible" (Cambridge, 1911) 113-40.

[5] For a basic bibliography, see the article "The Song of Miriam" mentioned in n. 4; for more recent literature, see n. 2.

[6] For a translation of the victory narrative of Rameses II, see J. H. Breasted, *Ancient Records of Egypt* (Chicago, 1906-7), vol. 3 §§ 298-351; pertinent sections are given by John A. Wilson, in *ANET,* 255-56. Wilson has also translated the Marniptah victory hymn, *ANET*, 376-78. See the discussion by Sir Alan Gardiner, *Egypt of the Pharaohs,* paperback ed. (New York, 1964) 259-64, 272-74.

[7] P.C. Craigie provides bibliographical data on the Epic of Tukulti-Ninurta in "The Song of Deborah and the Epic of Tukulti-Ninurta," 255, n. 13.

[8] The Song of Deborah is much longer than the Song of the Sea, and supplies more details of the engagement and its immediate aftermath: e.g., the death of Sisera at the hands of Jael. Nevertheless, it may not be complete, and seems to break off abruptly in the course of a vivid description of Sisera's mother, expectant yet anxious, not yet aware of the disaster that had befallen her son and his army. From a literary point of view, the poem seems to be a torso, lacking at least a concluding section (not to speak of other narrative parts relating to Deborah and Barak), which would balance the lengthy Introduction (vv. 2-9). The Song of the Sea is a more symmetrical composition, and seems to be complete as it has come down to us (see my forthcoming article, "Strophe and Meter in Exodus 15," in the Jacob M. Myers' *Festschrift*).

[9] The first person singular form of the verb is probably original, as the same form is found in the Song of Deborah (Judg. 5:3); but see Cross, *CMHE,* 127 and n. 47. The plural

imperative form (v. 21) is appropriate as a summons to the people, or the choir representing them.

[10]For the most recent and efficient treatment of the problem, see the discussion in Cross, *CMHE,* 121-44.

[11]For the identification of the "holy habitation" with the wilderness sanctuary, see *CMHE,* 125, and n. 41; see also Cross and Freedman, "The Song of Miriam," 248, n. 42. I think that a location in the wilderness is virtually certain, and that Sinai is a much more likely site than Shittim (against Cross, *CMHE,* 141). For additional details and discussion, see below.

[12]There is evidence to support these claims, though only for Palestine and the southern regions around the Dead Sea. Syria definitely had been lost, in spite of the survival of traditional and anachronistic phraseology in the wall inscriptions at Medinet Habu, and the remaining Asiatic territory would disappear in the course of the twelfth century; see Gardiner, *Egypt of the Pharaohs,* 283ff. and 288. See also A. Malamat, "The Egyptian Decline in Canaan and the Sea-Peoples," chap. 2 in *Judges,* ed. B. Mazar (Tel-Aviv, 1971), vol. 3 in "The World History of the Jewish People; First Series: Ancient Times," 34-35.

[13]Against the argument of M. J. Dahood, "*Nāda* 'To Hurl' in Ex 15, 16," *Biblica* 43 (1962) 248-49, I hold that v. 16 refers to the condition of the four nations mentioned in vv. 14-15, not to that of the Egyptians. Thus the standard analysis and interpretation of the passage are to be preferred; see *CMHE,* 130 and n. 66.

[14]The most recent discussion is that in *CMHE,* 141-43. In an unpublished manuscript on the "History of the Religion of Israel," Albright deals with the question of the location of the sanctuary in v. 17; he suggests two possible solutions: Sinai or Canaan, but is unable to decide between them.

[15]*The Book of Exodus,* 139-40. Cross comes to the same conclusion, *CMHE,* 125, as does Robertson, who has made a thorough study of verb forms in Hebrew poetry, *LEDEHP* 8-55.

[16]See Exod. 3:1-12, esp. v. 12: "And he said, 'Indeed I shall be with you, and this is the sign that I have sent you. When you bring the people out of Egypt, you shall serve God at this mountain.'" The association between Yahweh and Sinai is very ancient and must be pre-Mosaic. One of the oldest and most distinctive epithets of Yahweh is *zeh sīnay* "the One of Sinai" (Judg. 5:5; Ps. 68:9).

[17]The common view, that the land of Canaan is meant by the description in v. 17, is expressed by Driver and others; see, e.g., Cross and Freedman, "The Song of Miriam," 249-50, n. 59. Since there is no mention of an armed invasion or military conquest of the land in the poem, the difficulty with this identification of the sanctuary of Yahweh with the later shrines at Shiloh or Jerusalem becomes apparent. Cross (*CMHE,* 141ff.) plausibly suggests a location for this shrine at Gilgal, which served as the first cult center for the confederation in the land of Canaan; and this was before any military action in Canaan itself. In order to justify the proposal, Cross points out that the mountain terminology, which may have been associated with Sinai originally, might well have been transferred even to an unimpressive site like Gilgal, in much the same way that similar

terms were later applied to Mt. Zion, which is a rather modest hill.

Nevertheless, I find it hard to believe that a poet, recounting the decisive moments in the formation of the community, would omit entirely any reference to the original sacred mountain of Yahweh, i.e., Sinai, which figures so prominently in all surviving traditions, in favor of a secondary and temporary center of worship, without further specification. Unless the obvious, primary reference can be shown to be impossible or highly improbable, it is a better choice, especially in an early poem, than a secondary transferred reference.

18 Jer. 31:23 reads as follows: "Thus has said Yahweh of hosts, the God of Israel, 'Again they will say this word in the land of Judah and in its cities, when I restore their fortunes, "May Yahweh bless you, legitimate habitation, O holy mountain."'"

19 For discussion of this point, see *SITP,* 105-6, n. 14.

20 According to later tradition Sinai was the place, not only where the first tabernacle was erected, but indeed where Moses received detailed directions concerning its construction. The point is emphasized that Yahweh showed Moses "the pattern of the Tabernacle and the pattern of its furnishings" (Exod. 25:9). The key term is *tabnīt,* which is rendered "pattern" in the standard translations. It is derived from the root *bnh* "to build," and normally signifies something constructed. In other words, Moses was shown something constructed on top of the mountain (see Exod. 24:17), rather than a blueprint. The heavenly tabernacle itself, in my judgment, served as the model for the earthly replica; that is what Moses saw when he ascended the mountain to confer with God.

21 C. D. Ginsburg, in his *Biblia Hebraica, Massoretico-Critical Text of the Hebrew Bible . . .* (London, 1906), offers a slightly different reading: *bānītā* "you have build" for *BH*^{3} *bānītī* "I have built." The second person singular reading may be a legitimate variant, corresponding to the viewpoint expressed in Exod. 15:17, in which Yahweh's own action in erecting his temple is emphasized. The Solomonic edifice is only the earthly replica of the glorious heavenly original, which was made without hands (i.e., by God's rather than man's hands). The ambiguity reflected in the shift between the first and second person forms of the verb, is also present in the opening line of the couplet (v. 12; see LXX 1 Kings 8:53 which is the corresponding text, but has an additional colon, which may well be original): "Yahweh said that he would dwell in thick darkness." Here we have a reference to the cloud which surrounded the divine presence, and protected the privacy of his heavenly abode; at the same time it has an earthly counterpart in the incense cloud which rises in the temple and obscures the holy of holies and the sacred objects on solemn occasions (e.g., the Day of Atonement as described in Lev. 16:12-13).

22 See *YGC,* 117-18.

23 See *CMHE,* 37-38.

24 On the location of Sinai, see M. Noth, *The History of Israel,* trans. S. Godman, rev. ed. (New York, 1960) 127-33.

25 See *CMHE,* 71.

[26]See *CMHE,* 61-62 and n. 63; also *SITP,* 105-6, and n. 14.

[27]On the Late Bronze settlement at Qurayyah, see the preliminary reports by P. J. Parr, G. L. Harding, and J. E. Dayton, "Preliminary Survey in N. W. Arabia, 1968," *Bulletin of the Institute of Archaeology* 8/9 (1970) 219-41; and J. E. Dayton, "Midianite and Edomite Pottery," *Proceedings of the Fifth Seminar for Arabian Studies* (London, 1972) 25-33.

[28]See O. Eissfeldt, "Das Lied Moses Deuteronomium 32:1-43 und das Lehrgedicht Asaphs Psalm 78 samt einer Analyse der Umgebung des Mose-Liedes," *Verh. Sächs. Acad. Wiss. Leipzig, Phil.-hist. Kl.* 104, no. 5 (Berlin, 1958) 26-41; also *YGC,* 17, n. 41; 25, n. 58.

[29]Dahood renders Hebrew *gbwl* as "mount" on the basis of Ugaritic *gbl* "mountain" (*Psalms II* [New York, 1968] 237, 245; also Albright, *YGC,* 26, and n. 59). If the translation is correct, then it would serve to strengthen the case for connecting the various expressions in Exod. 15 (*nwh qdšk, hr nḥltk*) and Ps. 78 (*gbwl qdšw, hr zh qnth ymynw*).

[30]See H.-J. Kraus, *Psalmen,* vol. 15, pt. 7, in the *Biblischer Kommentar* (1960) 547; Dahood, *Psalms II,* 245.

[31]It is possible that the movement in v. 53a is to be understood as subsequent to the victory at sea in v. 53b, but even that would only signify that the people had escaped from Egyptian territory and power: the flight to a place of safety is the counterpoint to the destruction of the Egyptian force. The poet has already alluded to the safe departure of the Israelites (vv. 12ff.) and may well have that aspect of the episode in mind in v. 53.

[32]It is possible to see in this arrangement a reflection of the traditional line of march of Yahweh's people, who came near but did not enter the territories of the Philistines, Edomites, and Moabites in that order before finally reaching the land of the Canaanites. See Craigie, "The Conquest and Early Hebrew Poetry," 86. However, the passage in Exod. 15 makes no distinction between Canaan and the other three nations; it does not imply contact with any of them, much less conquest.

[33]See Gardiner, *Egypt of the Pharaohs,* 284-85; Albright, *YGC,* 157-64; Malamat, "The Egyptian Decline in Canaan," 32-35.

[34]See Malamat, "The Egyptian decline in Canaan," 23-25. For a contrary view, see *CMHE,* 124-25, where Cross places the settlement of the Philistines in the thirteenth century. The fact that the name does not occur in the records of either Rameses II or Marniptah is difficult to explain if the Philistines were organized as a political entity in Palestine in the thirteenth century.

[35]See *YGC,* 46-47; Cross and Freedman, "The Song of Miriam," 248, n. 44; also my discussion in "Divine Names and Epithets."

[36]See Albright's comment, quoted in "The Song of Miriam," 249, n. 49.

[37]For this translation, see "The Song of Miriam," 242; and *CMHE,* 130.

[38]The fact that the determinative preceding the name is that of a people rather than of a state indicates that in Egyptian eyes "Israel" was either a recent arrival in the country,

or as a political confederation a recent development. The name "Israel" is pre-Mosaic, non-Yahwistic; it is patriarchal in origin and was applied to a tribal league which was already in existence in Palestine for some time before the Exodus or the emergence of Mosaic Yahwism. See my discussion in "Divine Names and Epithets."

39 See *YGC,* 20, 265-66.

40 See my discussion in "Divine Names and Epithets"; Albright dates the poem in the thirteenth century (*YGC,* 12, 45-47); Robertson assigns it to the twelfth century (*LEDEHP,* 135, 153-156, esp. 155); Cross and I put it in the twelfth century in "The Song of Miriam," 240; Cross alone now dates it in the twelfth or eleventh century (*CMHE,* 124).

41 Albright's date in the thirteenth century seems too early to me; in order to maintain it, he must emend *plšt* out of the text (*YGC,* 46-47). The presence of that word in the text would not bother Cross, but his date for the poem is a bit low in my opinion. My present view is about the same as the one expressed in "The Song of Miriam," i.e., not later than the twelfth century in its original form, and not later than the tenth century in its final form (see my discussion in "Divine Names and Epithets").

42 For a persuasive and probable account of what happened, see Cross, *CMHE,* 126-32; cf. Albright, *YGC,* 45-46; "The Song of Miriam," 238-39.

43 Cross has shown that Canaanite El is associated specifically with Mt. Amanus (*CMHE,* 24-39); Baal's mountain, on the other hand, is Mt. Casius (*YGC,* 118, 125, 128).

44 Exod. 15:2, with its reference to "the God of my father," may represent an attempt to link Yahweh to patriarchal religion. Two observations are in order, however: (1) The verse as a whole seems to be secondary, a later interpolation designed to serve a liturgical purpose (see our comments in "The Song of Miriam," 243-44; and mine in "Strophe and Meter in Exodus 15" and "Divine Names and Epithets"). (2) A distinction is to be drawn between the singular form "father," used here, and the plural "fathers" which is the standard designation of the patriarchs. In other words, the term does not identify the deity as the "God of the Fathers," but only as the family God; see J. P. Hyatt, "Yahweh as the 'God of my Father,'" *VT* 5 (1955) 130-36; also "The Origin of Mosaic Yahwism," *The Teacher's Yoke: Studies in Memory of Henry Trantham* (Waco, Texas, 1964) 75-93. If the wording derives from an old tradition, and is to be considered as anything more than a poetic equivalent to *'ēlī* "my God," then we may see here an allusion to Moses' adopted family in Midian, whose God he (and Israel) came to worship (cf. *CMHE,* 71).

45 See my discussion in "Divine Names and Epithets"; but cf. *CMHE,* 71 for a somewhat different view. I would agree that the name Yahweh originates in a liturgical formula describing El. By the time of Moses there was a sharp disjuncture, so that in all the early poems, Yahweh appears only as a name, and never with its original verbal force. The link with El had been broken, and was not forged again until after the settlement in Canaan.

46 For the Hebrew words see Exod. 12:38 and Num. 11:4. While the biblical editors are careful to distinguish between the Israelite core and the accompanying rabble, the description probably fit the whole group. See G. E. Mendenhall, "Early Israel as the King-

dom of Yahweh," chap. 1 in *The Tenth Generation* (Baltimore, 1973), esp. 5, 19ff., 21-23.

[47] For a provocative analysis of the nature of early Israelite society under the impact of Mosaic Yahwism, see Mendenhall, "Tribe and State in the Ancient World," chap. 7 in *The Tenth Generation,* 177-87.

[48] For recent discussion of the Song of Deborah, see Craigie, "The Song of Deborah and the Epic of Tukulti-Ninurta," 253-65, esp. 254-55 with bibliographical references. See *YGC,* 13-14, 48-51; R. G. Boling deals with the Song in detail in his forthcoming volume on *Judges* in the Anchor Bible series.

[49] For the distribution of the term "Canaan," see the discussion above and my article, "Divine Names and Epithets." Except for an occasional allusion to the past or in a stereotyped expression, the word Canaan is no longer functional as a historical-political title. It is not found in any early poem later than the Song of Deborah, though it occurs in the prophetic oracles of the eighth century and following, and in a few Psalms as well. The title "Canaan" and the gentilic "Canaanite" occur repeatedly in the Pentateuch and Joshua, as expected. The usage continues in Judges through chap. 5 (and once more in Judg. 21:12). It appears twice more in the Deuteronomic History: 2 Sam. 24:7 and 1 Kings 9:16; and crops up occasionally in the Chronicler's Work (1 and 2 Chron. and Ezra-Neh.). Among the prophets, it occurs in Isaiah (19:18, 23:11), Hosea, Zephaniah, Obadiah, and Ezekiel. It appears in the historical Pss. 105 (v. 11), 106 (v. 38), and 135 (v. 11): these are all references to the past, when Canaan was an active political entity. The contrast in usage is dramatic, and clearly deliberate. In the eyes of the biblical writers, Canaan ceased to exist as a geopolitical entity after the great battle between Israel and Canaan described in Judg. 4 and 5.

[50] See Craigie, "The Song of Deborah and the Epic of Tukulti-Ninurta," 256-64. The same considerations are applicable to the narrative of Rameses II.

[51] See G. F. Moore, *A Critical and Exegetical Commentary on Judges,* ICC (New York, 1895) 139-40.

[52] See *CMHE,* 86, n. 17; 100-102, 157.

[53] 1 Kings 19. In spite of persistent efforts to reconstruct a ritual pilgrimage to Sinai// Horeb and a celebration there, the paucity of supporting data is noteworthy. Cf. *CMHE,* 308-9 and n. 56.

[54] The special association of Yahweh with different local sites in no way conflicts with his character as a cosmic deity. The tension between the local and particular manifestations of the deity, on the one hand, and his transcendent, universal aspects, on the other, is characteristic of biblical religion, and higher religion in the Near East generally. See Cross's perceptive remarks in "The Priestly Tabernacle," in *The Biblical Archaeologist Reader* 1 (Anchor Books; New York, 1961) 225-27.

[55] On the dating of these poems, see my discussion in "Divine Names and Epithets."

[56] On the translation of the key term, see *YGC,* 49, n. 101.

[57] Albright changes "Jael" to "Jabin"; see *YGC,* 49, n. 99.

58 The translation and analysis are based upon the work of Professor Marvin Chaney of San Francisco Theological Seminary, who graciously provided the relevant material from his unpublished doctoral dissertation, and through oral communication. The material can be divided into eight lines with the following syllable count: 7 + 7, 10 + 10, 6 + 8, 6 + 8. The second bicolon seems to overbalance the other lines, and perhaps a slightly different strophic arrangement is in order (see my translation): 7 + 7 + 10 = 24; 10 + 6 + 8 = 24; 6 + 8 = 14.

59 See D. R. Hillers, "A Note on Jdg. 5:8," *CBQ* 27 (1965) 124-26. For comments on the relationship between the two passages, see *CMHE,* 122-23, n. 34.

60 See G. E. Mendenhall, "The Census Lists of Numbers 1 and 26," *JBL* 77 (1958) 52-66.

61 For example, King Mesha of Moab reports that he led a fighting force of 200 men against Jahaz, a town in Israel (line 20 of the Mesha Inscription); see Albright's translation in *ANET,* 320.

62 The latter is emphasized by the curse hurled at Meroz, which must have been notably delinquent (v. 23). This verse, which is often challenged as secondary and intrusive, actually closes the unit dealing with the battle itself, vv. 19-23. The key word is *bā'ū,* which controls both the first line of the unit (v. 19) and, with the negative particle *lō',* the last line (v. 23). The enemy, the kings of Canaan, came to the battle, but the people of Meroz, who belonged to the federation, did not, though under covenant obligation to help in time of need. The verse is also a link to the next major unit, vv. 24-30. Note the contrast between *'ōrū* "curse" (v. 23), and *t^{e}borak* "let her be blessed" (v. 24).

63 It is difficult to imagine that the poem proper ended with v. 30 (v. 31 is commonly understood to be a liturgical signature, which is linked thematically and grammatically with vv. 4-5; note, e.g., the agreement in second person singular pronominal suffixes). At the same time, this impression of incompleteness cannot be demonstrated, and nothing more than educated guesses can be made about the supposedly missing parts.

64 In view of the persistent tradition of a twelve-tribe league, and the prevalence of twelve- and six-tribe groups in the surrounding regions (as reported in the Bible), it may be agreed that the original configuration included twelve units. That the number and names of the tribes may have varied from time to time, and that there were changes in the participating units is also clear from the biblical records.

65 Eight of the tribal names given in the Song of Deborah are identical with those in the standard lists: Ephraim (v. 14), Benjamin (14), Zebulun (14, 18), Issachar (15), Reuben (15, 16), Dan (17), Asher (17), Naphtali (18). The other two are related to known tribal names, and can be regarded as valid surrogates: Machir (14) for Manasseh (in the tradition he is identified as Manasseh's first-born son); Gilead (17) for Gad (although Gilead is represented as the son of Machir, Num. 26:29, 30; etc.).

66 See Y. Aharoni, "The Settlement of Canaan," chap. 6 in *Judges,* ed. Mazar, 109.

67 See J. Liver, "The Israelite Tribes," chap. 9 in *Judges,* ed. Mazar, 201-4, esp. 203, n. 34. See E. Meyer, *Die Israeliten und ihre Nachbarstämme* (Halle a. S., 1906) 232-35 on the subject of a ten-tribe league; also S. Mowinckel, *Zur Frage nach documentarischen Quellen in Josua 13-19* (Oslo, 1946) 21ff.; and A. Malamat, "The Period of the Judges," chap. 7 in *Judges,* ed. Mazar, 138-39.

68 See Aharoni, "The Settlement of Canaan," 115-16; and H. H. Rowley, *From Joseph to Joshua* (London, 1950) 3, 33-35.

69 In my opinion, both poems contain older materials; see Albright, *YGC,* 265-66, on the Blessing of Jacob. The presence of Judah in both lists reflects developments toward the end of the eleventh century.

70 The classic treatment of the tribal lists is that of M. Noth, *Das System der zwölf Stämme Israels* (Stuttgart, 1930). The order of the tribes in Gen. 49 is as follows: Reuben, Simeon, Levi, Judah, Zebulun, Issachar, Dan, Gad, Asher, Naphtali, Joseph, Benjamin. The Leah group (six tribes) comes first, followed by the children of the concubines (four tribes), with the Rachel group (two tribes) coming at the end. The basic pattern is indicated in Gen. 35:22-26 (after the narratives detailing the births of the successive children of Jacob, Gen. 29:31-30:24, and 35:16ff. for Benjamin). The following table indicates the range of variation among representative lists:

Judg. 5	*Gen. 49*	*Deut. 33*	*Gen. 29, 30, 35*	*Gen. 35:22-26*
Ephraim	Reuben	Reuben	Reuben	Reuben
Benjamin	Simeon	Judah	Simeon	Simeon
Machir	Levi	Levi	Levi	Levi
Zebulun	Judah	Benjamin	Judah	Judah
		Joseph		
Issachar	Zebulun	Ephraim	Dan	Issachar
Reuben	Issachar	Manasseh	Naphtali	Zebulun
Gilead	Dan	Zebulun	Gad	Joseph
Dan	Gad	Issachar	Asher	Benjamin
Asher	Asher	Gad	Issachar	Dan
Naphtali	Naphtali	Dan	Zebulun	Naphtali
	Joseph	Naphtali	Joseph	Gad
	Benjamin	Asher	Benjamin	Asher

Gen. 46	*Exod. 1*	*Num. 1:5-15*	*Num. 1:20-43*	*Num. 2*
Reuben	Reuben	Reuben	Reuben	Judah
Simeon	Simeon	Simeon	Simeon	Issachar
Levi	Levi	Judah	Gad	Zebulun
Judah	Judah	Issachar	Judah	Reuben
Issachar	Issachar	Zebulun	Issachar	Simeon
Zebulun	Zebulun	Ephraim	Zebulun	Gad
		Joseph		
Gad	(Joseph)	Manasseh	Ephraim	Ephraim
			Joseph	
Asher	Benjamin	Benjamin	Manasseh	Manasseh
Joseph	Dan	Dan	Benjamin	Benjamin
Benjamin	Naphtali	Asher	Dan	Dan
Dan	Gad	Gad	Asher	Asher
Naphtali	Asher	Naphtali	Naphtali	Naphtali

Num. 7	*Num. 13*	*Num. 26*	*Num. 34*	*Deut. 27:12-13*
Judah	Reuben	Reuben	Judah	Simeon
Issachar	Simeon	Simeon	Simeon	Levi
Zebulun	Judah	Gad	Benjamin	Judah
Reuben	Issachar	Judah	Dan	Issachar
Simeon	Ephraim	Issachar	Manasseh	Joseph
Gad	Benjamin	Zebulun	Ephraim	Benjamin
Ephraim	Zebulun	Manasseh	Zebulun	Reuben
		Joseph		
Manasseh	Manasseh	Ephraim	Issachar	Gad
Benjamin	Dan	Benjamin	Asher	Asher
Dan	Asher	Dan	Naphtali	Zebulun
Asher	Naphtali	Asher		Dan
Naphtali	Gad	Naphtali		Naphtali

Josh. 13-19	*Ezek. 48:1-29*	*Ezek. 48:30-35*	*Apoc. 7*
Reuben	Dan	Reuben	Judah
Gad	Asher	Judah	Reuben
½ Manasseh	Naphtali	Levi	Gad
Judah	Manasseh	Joseph	Asher
½ Manasseh	Ephraim	Benjamin	Naphtali
Ephraim	Reuben	Dan	Manasseh
Benjamin	Judah	Simeon	Simeon
Simeon	Benjamin	Issachar	Levi
Zebulun	Simeon	Zebulun	Issachar
Issachar	Issachar	Gad	Zebulun
Asher	Zebulun	Asher	Joseph
Naphtali	Gad	Naphtali	Benjamin
Dan			

Except for Num. 34 (in which the Trans-Jordanian tribes have been omitted) and Judg. 5, all the lists count twelve tribes, although the names and the order vary. In general, the lists from Genesis and Exodus give the twelve sons of Jacob, including Levi and Joseph. From Numbers on, Levi is generally omitted and Joseph is divided into two tribes, Ephraim and Manasseh. In Deut. 33, Simeon is dropped rather than Levi, while Ephraim and Manasseh are appended to the Joseph oracle, which otherwise is similar to the Joseph oracle in Gen. 49. Ezekiel has both kinds of lists: in the geographic distribution of the tribes, Levi is omitted (he is located in the sacred precinct) while Ephraim and Manasseh are included (Ezek. 48:1-29); in the list of the gates of Jerusalem, Levi is included, along with Joseph, which displaces Ephraim and Manasseh (Ezek. 48:30-35).

71 See discussion of this point in "Divine Names and Epithets."

72 See 1 Kings 11:26-39, esp. vv. 30-32, 35-36.

73 H. W. Hertzberg, *I and II Samuel: A Commentary,* trans. J. S. Bowden (Philadelphia, 1964) 249-51, questions the validity of the figure for Ishbaal.

74 In archaic poetry the preposition b^e often has the meaning "from" as in Ugaritic. The

force of the verb *pwṣ* in the Hiphil is illustrated by Gen. 11:8, "And Yahweh dispersed them from there. . . ." Similarly the basic meaning of *ḥlq* in the Piel is "to divide, separate"; see Ps. 60:8 = 108:8.

[75]In Deut. 33, Judah apparently has been substituted for an original Simeon in v. 7, where the verb *šᵉmaʿ* (the same root as in the name *šimʿōn* "Simeon") and the sentiment expressed would seem to suit Simeon better than Judah. Since the statement is vague, and the particular circumstances are not known to us, it is best not to press the point. Since Simeon was actually part of Judah by this time, the substitution is quite understandable (see Josh. 19:1).

[76]Note that in 2 Sam. 19:43 the status of Israel as a ten-tribe entity during the reign of David is emphasized in the controversy between Israel and Judah.

[77]See 1 Kings 11:31,35, in which Israel is described as consisting of ten tribes, while Judah is offered one tribe as a consolation prize. Traditionally, this extra tribe would have been Simeon, since Simeon apparently was transferred from Israel to Judah in earlier times; but in the immediate historical context, it was understood to be Benjamin (cf. 1 Kings 12:21 in the light of 1 Kings 11:32 and 36). The latter shift should have been reflected in a reduction in the number of tribes assigned to Israel (i.e., nine), but the tradition of ten was too strong to be altered at this late date.

[78]According to tradition, the route followed by the people of Yahweh took them past the territory of the Edomites and the Moabites, and into direct conflict with the Amorite kingdoms of Og and Sihon in Trans-Jordan. I wish neither to deny nor to diminish the importance of the tradition, but simply to note that the two poems with which I am dealing say little if anything about the experience of Israel in this region. One must look to poems like the Song of Heshbon (Num. 21:27-30) and the Oracles of Balaam (Num. 23-24) for possible information on this point.

[79]See discussion above.

[80]See the discussion by Craigie, "The Conquest and Early Hebrew Poetry," 76-93.

[81]See the discussion of Exod. 15:2, above. The issue is a subtle one, since in matters of religion and culture nothing is brand new: there are always antecedent models and influences. The origins of the term *yahweh* in a sacral context are to be found in the cultic traditions associated with the God El; on this point I agree fully with Albright and Cross; see Cross, *CMHE* 1-77, especially the section on Yahweh and El. Albright's formulation of the matter is found in a variety of his writings; a useful summation appears in an unpublished manuscript on the "History of the Religion of Israel." In the earliest poems of Israel, however, Yahweh is a fully autonomous deity, independent of El, and with his own history.

[82]A link through the family of Moses with the tribe of Levi, and hence with Israel, is at least plausible and may be probable. Given a cultural-linguistic continuum, other connections between the Exodus and patriarchal groups are also likely.

[83]Cross's analysis of the origins and setting of the worship of Yahweh is persuasive, see *CMHE,* 71ff. It may be observed that Yahweh emerged from a description of El as the creator; the classic expression *yahweh ṣᵉbāʾōt* "he creates the armies" must be

predicated of El, not Yahweh. Later editors misunderstood the construction, and saw in the word *yhwh* not a verb but the name of the deity; so they inserted the word *ʾᵉlōhē* before *ṣᵉbāʾōt*, to ease what they considered to be a grammatical anomaly. See Albright's review of B. N. Wambacq, *L'épithète divine Jahvé Ṣᵉbāʾōt: Étude philologique, historique et exégétique,* in *JBL* 67 (1948) 377-81. Yahweh, for his part, is an *ʾēl* "god," and from early times he is so designated: e.g., *ʾēl ḥannūn wᵉraḥūm*, *ʾēl qannāʾ*.

84 So far as I am aware, the term *yhwh*, as the name of a deity, has not turned up in any religious literature outside of Israel. All known nonbiblical occurrences are either explicit references to the God of Israel (e.g., *yhwh* in the Mesha Inscription), or are otherwise associated with the same God (e.g., the place-name in the region of Edom mentioned earlier).

85 See my discussion in "Divine Names and Epithets."

86 See my discussion of the original form of the name in "The Name of the God of Moses," *JBL* 79 (1960) 151-56. The revival of old formulas like *yahweh ṣᵉbāʾōt* and *yahweh šālōm* "he creates peace" (Judg. 6:24) in the period of the Judges reflects a rapprochement between the groups worshipping Yahweh and those worshipping El; see "Divine Names and Epithets," Appendix.

87 See A. Malamat, "The Philistines and their Wars with Israel," chap. 8 in *Judges,* ed. Mazar, 164-79.

88 See W. F. Albright's discussion, "The Sea Peoples in Palestine," chap. 33, pt. 1, in *Cambridge Ancient History* (Cambridge, 1973) vol. 2, 26-28, 33; Malamat, "The Philistines and their Wars with Israel," 170ff.

89 Other poems in the Pentateuch and the prose narratives undoubtedly preserve historical details of Israel's experience in the wilderness and subsequent march northward, but a precise chronology or exact determination of the events eludes us.

90 The reliability of the traditions concerning Og and Sihon has been questioned repeatedly, and most recently and vigorously by J. Van Seters, "The Conquest of Sihon's Kingdom: A Literary Examination," *JBL* 91 (1972) 182-97. In spite of Van Seters's direct challenge, I believe that the poem preserved in Num. 21:27-30 is very old and supports the tradition; see P. D. Hanson, "The Song of Hashbon and David's *NÎR,*" *HTR* 61 (1968) 297-320.

91 For example, the stories of the murmurings in the wilderness, of the golden calf, of the controversial report of the spies, of the rebellion of Dathan and Abiram, and of Korah, and of the episode at Baal-Peor.

92 The story of Balaam, who was brought in to curse and remained to bless and praise the unique people of God, is a prime example. While the Oracles of Balaam can hardly be dated in their present form before the eleventh century, they doubtless contain accurate historical information about the early period of Israel's existence; see my discussion in "Divine Names and Epithets." The isolated sayings at the end of Num. 24 may be somewhat older than the longer poems; in Albright's judgment, they reflect the movements of the Sea Peoples toward the end of the thirteenth century B.C. (see "The Oracles of Balaam," *JBL* 63 [1944] 207-33, esp. 227-31).

[93]The stories in Joshua, and especially Judg. 1, may reflect the struggles of pre-Yahwistic Israel to gain and maintain a foothold in Canaan, as well as later activity in those areas.

[94]See G. E. Mendenhall, "The Hebrew Conquest of Palestine," *BA* 25 (1962) 66-87; reprinted in *The Biblical Archaeologist Reader* 3 (New York, 1970) 100-120. For a recent discussion of the Conquest traditions, see Weippert, *SITP.*

[95]See Cross's discussion of these epithets, *CMHE,* 3-12; M. Haran, "The Religion of the Patriarchs, an Attempt at a Synthesis," *ASTI* 4 (1965) 30-55; also "Divine Names and Epithets."

[96]The Caleb traditions, including the story of Othniel (Judg. 1:11-21, and 3:7-11), must be very old; as Albright has shown, there is an archaic poem embedded in the text: Judg. 1:14-15 = Josh. 15:18-19 (*YGC,* 48).

[97]*CMHE,* 195-215.

[98]On this relationship, see B. Mazar, "The Sanctuary of Arad and the Family of Hobab the Kenite," *JNES* 24 (1965) 297-303; and *CMHE,* 201.

[99]On the dating of the Testaments of Jacob and Moses, see "Divine Names and Epithets." As Albright maintains, individual blessings may be considerably older (see *YGC,* 265-66). I would now hold that the incorporation of Judah in the lists reflects the attempts to amalgamate the northern and southern groups. These efforts were initiated in the eleventh century, perhaps by Samuel and Saul, but did not reach fruition until the time of David.

[100]See discussion in n. 92, above.

[101]See discussion in "Divine Names and Epithets."

[102]See discussion above.

- 2 -

ASSYRIA AND THE WEST: THE NINTH CENTURY AND ITS AFTERMATH

Hayim Tadmor

I

In the course of several decades of systematic and ruthless raids under the warring kings of the ninth century,* Assyria emerged as the victorious overlord of southern Anatolia and northern Syria, imposing her political-economic domination over the small but prosperous states west of the Euphrates.

The ferocious, yet irregular, sorties of Ashurnasirpal II were followed by the well-planned annual campaigns of his son Shalmaneser III, the subduer of northern and central Syria. The accounts of the military exploits of Ashurnasirpal II, composed in the "early Neo-Assyrian" dialect of Akkadian,[1] enumerate those massacred, impaled, burnt, and taken captive, and earned him the reputation of being the most fearsome of Assyrian emperors. This is the policy which Olmstead in his pioneer studies of the Assyrian expansion of the ninth century aptly described as "calculated frightfulness."[2] The historical records of Shalmaneser III refrain from describing atrocities. His annals, composed no doubt by a new royal scribe, are mainly concerned with economic and material gains: numbers of cities conquered, quantities of metals and other commodities received as booty and tribute. One wonders whether the absence of atrocities reflects an actual change of Assyrian policy toward the West, or whether it is a refinement in the character of historical writing. In these eloquently exaggerated records of royal self-praise,[3] the protagonist is naturally the ever-victorious king. Yet the role of the gods there is not a mere figure of speech. Wars were always sanctioned by gods.[4] It is mostly Ashur's "trust-inspiring oracle" (*takultu*), his glory, or his mighty weapons in the king's hands that bring about the victory. It was only later, in the eighth and seventh centuries, that kings usurped the divine epithets, attributing to themselves the terror-inspiring radiance (*puluḫtu*)[5] that overwhelms the enemy. This religious-literary style cannot allow for a setback. An actual defeat is not recorded; a draw or a setback, such as the battle of Qarqar, is related as a glorious victory. The gory descriptions of blood running like water, corpses piled up like a bridge, often cover up the inability to admit that Ashur's foe could in fact prevail over his armies.

It is no surprise that this grandiose figure of speech and the literary convention of exaggeration perpetuated the image of Assyria as "the rod of tyrants that smote peoples in wrath with stroke unceasing" and of her emperors as men "who shook the earth, who made realms tremble, who made the world like a waste and wrecked its towns, who never released his prisoners to their homes" (Isa. 14:5-6, 16-17).[6] Indeed, the royal Assyrian propagandistic literature has been successful beyond its own time limits and imposed itself on modern historiography as well.

In this paper, I shall not be concerned with the military aspect of the early Assyrian expansion. The aim is twofold: to delineate the goals and gains of Assyria in the West prior to the stage in which Tiglath-Pileser III inaugurated imperial annexation and deportation on a grand scale; and to examine the impact of the West on the culture of Assyria proper in the eighth and early seventh centuries.

The gains in the ninth century were predominantly economic: they consisted of raw materials, luxury items, and manpower for the urban and architectural enterprises of the homeland, especially for Calah, the new capital city.

In the past, mainly in the fourteenth and thirteenth centuries when the great empires controlled the trade routes and sources of raw materials, a Mesopotamian king was able to obtain the necessary commodities by means of international diplomacy, applying to an emperor of an equal rank, exchanging delegations and good-will gifts (=*šulmānu*).[7] But times had changed; the princes of the Neo-Hittite states, heirs of the great kings of Hatti-land, were apparently in no haste to establish a close trade relationship with Assyria. On the other hand, Assyria, having in the ninth century successfully repelled the Arameans, was now in a stage of military ascendancy when pillage practically replaced the regular trade exchange.

Hence the ever-increasing frequency of campaigns and the continuously widening horizon of Assyrian expansion. The most spectacular and immediate gain was the spoil and tribute rich in luxury items which were in great demand in the royal court and with the military elite.[8] The *tāmartu*, an early Assyrian term for occasional tribute, literally "a spectacular gift for display," was impressive and lavish. By comparison, the regular annual tribute–*maddattu*–was moderate, if not insignificant.[9] For example, in the year 857, the *maddattu* of Patina (this proves now to be the correct reading, not Hattina),[10] the largest of the north Syrian states, was 1 talent of gold, 2 of purple wool and 100 logs of cedar wood. The *tāmartu*, however, included 3 talents of gold, 100 of silver, 300 of copper, 300 of iron, 20 of purple wool, 1,000 copper bowls, 1,000 garments of linen with multicolored trimmings, 500 cattle, 5,000 sheep, and a king's daughter with her dowry for Shalmeneser's harem.[11]

In order to secure an uninterrupted flow of these items, both by means of the yearly tribute and by enforced, essentially unilateral "trade exchange,"[12] colonies were established in areas far away from the homeland and populated by Assyrians proper–not by foreign deportees as was the later practice under the empire. Their importance would be enhanced at the time when the king would not conduct the yearly campaign for plunder. They would also serve as supply bases for future military enterprises.

This early Assyrian colonization should be viewed as yet another aspect of the Assyrian expansion in the ninth century. An illuminating case is that of Aribua in Luhuti in northern Syria,[13] an Assyrian military colony established by Ashurnasirpal II in Patina (=Unqi, the Amuq) most probably in his ninth year, 875. "Into Aribua, the royal city of Lubarna the Patinean, I entered. The city I took for my own possession; grain and straw from the land of Luhuti I gathered and I heaped them up therein, and I held a feast in his palace. Men from Assyria I settled therein."[14]

Territorially Assyria did not extend yet to the Euphrates, so the new colony was separated from its motherland by the kingdoms of Bit-Agusi (Arpad) and Bit-Adini. Only much later, in 740, the Antioch valley was annexed to Assyria. The *raison d'être* of an outpost far in the West should be looked for in the sphere of the economic rather than the purely military. Aribua was apparently the western tip of a corridor leading to north

Syria and the Assyrian presence there emphasized her claim to hegemony in the West, which in the eighth century would become direct imperial rule.[15]

Assyrian colonists were also settled in fortresses (*birāti*) in Tushan, on the main road to Asia Minor, as well as in the cities of Sinabu and Tidu, established by Shalmaneser I in the thirteenth century in Na'iri, later abandoned and now restored and resettled by Ashurnasirpal.[16]

Two other cases of Assyrian colonization are from the days of Shalmaneser III: (1) Upon conquering Bit-Adini, he turned Til-Barsip and three other cities–among them Nanpiji, modern Membidj/Hieropolis–into his "royal cities." He gave them new Assyrian names and settled Assyrians in them.[17] (2) Farther to the north, on the Euphrates, he restored Pitru–Balaam's Pethor–and Mutkinu, two cities conquered and fortified by Tiglath-Pileser I and made Assyrian outposts, but subsequently lost to the Arameans.[18] Here, too, "men of Assyria" were settled.

The chief Assyrian outpost was undoubtedly Til-Barsip–renamed Kar-Šulmānu-ašarēdu. There, in the same year (856), Shalmaneser received the rich tribute of kings of the seacoast and kings of lands along the Euphrates: "silver, gold, lead, copper, copper vessels, cattle, sheep, brightly colored woolen and linen garments."[19]

The use of *kāru* (port, harbor, quay, trading station) as a component in the new name of Til-Barsip may not be accidental.[20] It was no doubt the economic center of the newly acquired western territories of Assyria. Similarly, when Esarhaddon destroyed Sidon in 677 and established a new port in its place, he called it Kar-Ashur-ah-iddina. In accordance with the imperial practice of the Sargonid empire, the new city was resettled not by men of Assyria but by "people of the mountains and the sea of the rising sun captured by my bow"–a general term for highlanders from the east and Chaldeans.[21]

The economic motivations underlying the Assyrian expansion in the West become more apparent in the reign of Shalmaneser III (859-824). His primary purpose, to judge from the order of his campaigns, was the domination of North Syria, southern Anatolia, and Cilicia, the principal source of iron and silver and later a key-point in the maritime trade, especially with Cyprus. These states, mostly governed by Neo-Hittite dynasts, formed an alliance, which was comprised of Carchemish, Patina, Bit-Adini, Bit Agusi (Arpad), Sam'al, Que, Hilakku, and two other small states. Rich as they were, these guardians of the ore and the major trade routes possessed little military strength. At a certain stage, the king of Carchemish, designated as "the king of Hatti," was probably the leader.[22] However, only four–the kings of Sam'al, Patina, Bit-Adini, and Carchemish–participated in the battle at Lutibu in Sam'al in Shalmaneser's first year (858). They were defeated,[23] and when, in the next year, the Assyrians came up once again, they hastily submitted and paid heavy tribute, mostly in the form of "spectacular gifts."[24]

Seventeen years later, in 839, after defeating Damascus and its allies, Que became Shalmaneser's main target. The Assyrians victoriously crossed the Cilician plain, reached Tarsus, and erected commemorative stelae on major roads at the borders of Que.[25] An almost similar feat was repeated in his twenty-fifth and twenty-sixth years. In these campaigns, Shalmaneser laid the groundwork for the Assyrian domination of Cilicia. From that time on Assyria had almost undisturbed access to Cilicia through Kummuh and Gurgum, or from the south through the Antioch valley. The vassalage of Que was resumed by Tiglath-Pileser III. Que was annexed by his son Shalmaneser V[26] and remained an Assyrian province until the fall of the empire.

The annexation of Bit-Adini (856) introduced a new stage in Assyrian domination of the

West. For the first time a major western state, a member of the "Northern Alliance," was subdued and became a regular Assyrian province, with imposed governor and feudal duties. The Euphrates was now Assyria's western border--and no state of military importance survived between Calah and Til-Barsip.[27]

It should be emphasized that at that stage direct annexation of states west of the Euphrates was not yet Assyria's goal in the West. No king until the days of Tiglath-Pileser III ever attempted to transform a vassal state west of the Euphrates into a regular province. Several times vassal kingdoms on the western borders of Assyria were heavily defeated (e.g., Arpad or Damascus). Yet this did not result in the loss of their independence. The frequent campaigns heavily damaged their economy, disrupted the overland trade, and brought havoc and devastation, while booty and tribute robbed the royal treasuries.

At this point enters the well-known league of the twelve states of central and southern Syria--"The Twelve Kings of Hatti and the Seacoast"--headed by Adad-idri (Ben-Hadad II) of Damascus and Irhuleni (Urhilina) of Hamath, which fought Shalmaneser at Qarqar[28] in 853, and again in 849, 848, and 845. The league of twelve--or actually eleven[29]--members could be classified as follows:

1. The three "Great Powers"--Damascus, Hamath, Israel.
2. North Phoenician ports--Usnu, Shiana, Arqa and Byblos.[30]
3. Egyptians (who apparently came to assist Byblos).[31]
4. Arabians of the Syrian desert.[32]
5. Beth Rehob, a small Aramean state at the foot of Anti-Lebanon (Amana).

The very participation of a token Egyptian contingent of 1,000 soldiers and one of 1,000 Arabian camels suggests that economic interests were underlying the political alliance or combination of alliances. It was in fact the most apparent common denominator that welded them together in spite of internal rivalry and intermittent local strife. It is also the only time in Syro-Palestine that a confederation of mutually opposing states was active for a considerable period, eventually to check, if not repel, the strongest military power of that age.

There is no indication in the sources as to when and how the league of the twelve was formed. Apparently it was not a product of a hasty alliance, accomplished in two or three years under the impact of the fall of Bit-Adini. If indeed the wars between Israel and Aram took place, not on the eve of the battle of Qarqar, as is often assumed, but as Morganstern had suggested,[33] at the early part of Ahab's reign, it would stand to reason that the league was formed a short time after Shalmaneser's accession to the throne and as a result of his raids against Cilicia. One wonders who was the architect of the alliance. It might have been Irhuleni, whose land was invaded, or Ben-Hadad II--Adad-idri--the founder of the greater Aram,[34] always listed as the first of the twelve kings. It might also have been Ahab the Israelite, who, having defeated Ben-Hadad, made him an ally of equal rank ("he is my brother," 1 Kings 20:32) with trade privileges (1 Kings 20:34). Although far from the center of Shalmaneser's campaigns, Ahab, who controlled the overland routes from Egypt to the north, must have felt economically threatened by Assyrian expansion.

The league of the twelve collapsed, not because it was defeated in battle, but mainly because Ben-Hadad its leader died or was killed and Hazael, his general, established a new dynasty in Damascus. Since ancient Near Eastern treaties were made for the duration of the dynasty, they dissolved with its cessation and with the accession of the usurper. And indeed Jehoram, Ahab's son, claimed the contested Ramoth-gilead and attacked Aram immediately upon Hazael's accession. But soon he and the rest of the Omrides were wiped out by Jehu, a general supported by the *b^{e}nē hann^{e}bī'īm*. Shalmaneser did not wait long. In 841, his eighteenth year, he invaded Aram for the first time, defeated Hazael, and captured his camp and his chariotry, though not Hazael himself, who retreated to Mt. Hermon (Senir). Shalmaneser devastated the oases of Damascus, but apparently Hazael did not yield, since no tribute of Damascus is recorded. Shalmaneser proceeded to the Hauran and from there to the Mediterranean coast and celebrated his victory by erecting a commemorative stela at Mt. Baali-Ra'si, a promontory opposite Tyre. In that campaign, as stated in Shalmaneser's Annals from his twentieth year,[35] he received the tribute of Ba'al-mazzer, king of Tyre, and of Jehu, "son of Omri," i.e., the king of the "House of Omri" (Bīt Ḫumri), the customary name of Israel in the Assyrian records. It is quite possible that Jehu accepted willingly the Assyrian suzerainty, which afforded protection for his new regime.[36] But, likewise, the subsequent campaign against Aram in 838[37] did not break Hazael. This was Shalmaneser's last intervention in central and southern Syria. Hazael, now relieved of the Assyrian pressure, gradually reduced Israel, defeated Jehu, and became the sole hegemon of southern Syria and Palestine.

When Adad-Nirari III resumed Assyrian penetration into Syria and especially when in 796 he defeated Ben-Hadad III (the son of Hazael) and invested Damascus, Joash (Jehu's grandson) paid tribute together with other kings of the countries formerly under Aramean hegemony.[38] Paradoxically Assyria was no longer a menace but a savior, a potential protector in the bitter struggle with Aram. Even in the first years of Tiglath-Pileser III, it was this heritage of the late ninth and early eighth centuries which prompted Menahem of Samaria to seek the help of Tiglath-Pileser in securing his throne and kingdom.[39] The conquest of Syria and Philistia which followed was indeed a sudden departure from Assyrian policy of the ninth century.

II

Having delineated some factors in the Assyrian political-economic expansion in the West of the ninth century, we come to consider its impact on Assyria proper. The ninth century witnessed the beginning of "enforced urbanization" in Assyria, which culminated in the building of Calah.[40] Ashurnasirpal II and Shalmaneser III transplanted scores of captives from the Neo-Hittite and Aramean states into Calah, and thus set a pattern for later deportations on a larger scale by Tiglath-Pileser III and Sargon II, who endeavored to resettle and revive those areas between the Habur and the Euphrates which had been devastated by their mighty predecessors.

In most cases the destination of these deportees was not stated explicitly, but many of them, no doubt, were taken to Calah. An illuminating source is the "Banquet Stele" of Ashurnasirpal,[41] which describes the official opening ceremony of the royal city and lists the number of people present at the banquet.

The text offers the following numbers, which are of prime importance for the study of Assyrian-enforced urbanization in the ninth century: 47,074 men and women "who were bid to come from all the districts of my land"; 5,000 envoys (*ṣirāni*, a new word, glossed by *šaprāte*);[42] 16,000 people of Calah and 1,500 palace officials. Altogether there were 69,574 people at the banquet, who were feasted for ten days, were wined, bathed, anointed, and then sent home "healthy and happy."[43]

The 47,074 men and women summoned to come (*qari'ūti*) did not stay in Calah, but as inferred from the text, were returned to their homes. Those who remained were the 16,000 inhabitants of Calah–mostly the new settlers–and the 1,500 palace officials (the population of Calah in the days of Ashurnasirpal seems to have been much smaller than has recently been assumed[44]). As stated in the Banquet Stele, in the somewhat later Annals, and in the "Standard Inscription" of Ashurnasirpal, these people came from the semi dependent and vassal states of Suhi and Laqe on the Middle Euphrates, Bit Zamani and Shupria on the Upper Tigris, Zamua in the East and Bit-Adini and Patina/Unqi in the West. In the course of years additional captives were deported to Calah. Shalmaneser III, who as he claims in the closing sentence of his annals from the twentieth year, carried off 110,610 captives,[45] did not indicate their destination. From the fact that he built excessively in Calah, one may well assume that some of these deportees were settled there. Calah served as Assyria's capital until 707 when Sargon transferred his seat to the newly built royal city of Dur-Šarrukin–Khorsabad. Here, too, the population of the city was formed of exiles mainly from the West. The same policy was repeated later by Sennacherib when he rebuilt Nineveh. His methods of populating his new capital could not have differed much from those of his predecessors. He does not state the origin of the new residents, but he claims, perhaps exaggeratedly, to have carried off about 200,000 Chaldeans and about 200,000 Judeans. The survivors must have formed the core of the builders of Nineveh and of its population. Naturally, craftsmen, artisans, and other skilled workers were preferred.

An additional profession was in great demand; it was an established practice already from the times of Tiglath-Pileser I that select troops of vanquished enemies were drafted into the Assyrian army. The population of Assyria was apparently too small to maintain a large standing army. Therefore it needed to be constantly replenished by foreign regiments. Units of chariotry were especially singled out. Thus Sargon drafted into the royal regiment –*kiṣir šarrūti*–a unit of 50 (or 200) chariots from Samaria and 50 chariots, 200 cavalry, and 300 foot-soldiers from Carchemish.

This policy of expanding the human resources of Assyria by means of deportation must have had far-reaching repercussions in every sphere of life. Soldiers, artists, craftsmen from the west were assimilated or were "regarded as Assyrians" according to the claims of the royal inscriptions, and gradually became a decisive factor in shaping the hybrid culture of the empire. The third and fourth generations of deportees did not differ much–as one may assume–from the native Assyrians. Still, we can recognize them by their foreign, Semitic personal names. That is, they did not change them to become, so to say, identified as fully "Assyrians". The personal names are our main, if not our sole, guide-mark. Using this guide-mark, we note that several provincial governors who reached the distinguished post of an eponym holder were Arameans, Phoenicians, or Israelites. The eponym for 763 was the governor of Gozan, Bur-Sagalē, i.e., "son of the god *ŠNGL'*,"[46] obviously an Aramean. The eponym for the year 764 was Sidki-ilu, the governor of Tushan, no doubt a Phoenician. In 701 the eponym was Hananu, the governor of Til-Barsip, an Aramean or Israelite. In 689 it was Gihilu or Gihil-ilu, the governor of Hatarikka, apparently an Aramean. In 673 it was Atar-Ili, the governor of Lahiru, a north Aramean, or an Arabian, and in 660 the eponym was Gir-ṣapūnu, that is, Gēr-Saphôn, the governor of Raṣapa, a Phoenician.

Let us look at some other evidence. It has already been noted that westerners identified by their foreign names became a common feature in Assyrian administrative documents from Nineveh, dating mainly to the reigns of Esarhaddon and Ashurbanipal. Now, the new adminstrative documents and contracts from Nimrud which have been published in the last twenty years have brought some evidence on the same phenomenon already during the reigns of Sargon and possibly Tiglath-Pileser. Thus, for example, an eighth-century document mentions several westerners, among them Hilqiya, who was in charge of seventy-six people, perhaps a military unit.[47] An Aramaic ostracon from Nimrud lists additional Israelites from about the same period.[48]

New and surprising evidence on westerners in the Assyrian court at Calah at an earlier period has just been published by J. V. Kinnier Wilson in *The Nimrud Wine-Lists* (London, 1972). The lists pertain to the reign of Adad-nirari III and the early years of Shalmaneser IV, i.e., the first quarter of the eighth century. These are wine allocations to the members of the court, mainly the queen, the princes, the highest state officials, as well as the technical personnel. They include a considerable number of foreigners, mostly westerners, some as professionals, others designated by their gentilics.

The professionals include (1) the scribes, consisting of three groups–Assyrians, Arameans, and surprisingly, Egyptians; (2) male singers–Assyrians, Babylonians ("Kassites"), Hittites, and Arameans; (3) diviners–from Babylon and from Kummuh (the latter are the *dāgil iṣṣurāte*, experts in ornithomancy); and (4) bakers–Chaldeans and Elamites. The texts mention a certain Abda', the Aramean expert in leather work, and Zakur, perhaps a goldsmith, as well as Adūni-Labiut, probably a Phoenician.[49] A similar text listing the distribution of bread rations mentions Salamanu and Hanunu.[50] The first was the commander of the guard of the queen mother; the second was commander of the guard of the chief of staff. Foreigners, without any professional definition, are also specified in several documents as recipients of wine rations. They include Samarians (three or four times), Egyptians, people from Sam'al, Carchemish, Melid as well as Manneans, Medians, and "Qutians" (i.e., highlanders from the northeast.

I doubt that all these people were captives as has been suggested.[51] It is unlikely that the court would feed captives. Moreover, Adad-nirari and his successor did not wage war with Sam'al, Carchemish, Melid, or Samaria. All these might have been professional soldiers, merchants, or–what is perhaps more likely–ambassadors of their countries to the Assyrian court. We should recall again that about one hundred years earlier, Ashurnasirpal entertained 5,000 foreign ambassadors (*ṣirāni*) in his famous banquet of inauguration at Calah.

Especially significant is the presence of Aramean and Egyptian scribes. As for the Arameans, there can be little doubt that the Assyrian administration employed Aramean alongside Assyrian scribes, and that they were evidently bilingual, as shown by the Aramaic dockets and notations on cuneiform documents from Nineveh from the seventh century. Still, it was not very clear how it came about that Aramaic emerged as an official language of the empire already in the reign of Tiglath-Pileser III, on whose monuments the Aramean scribe appears side by side with the Assyrian scribe. This is now better understood in the light of the new wine lists. We may well assume that it was, in the main, a need dictated by the ascendancy of the Aramean states and trade with the west.[52]

Not only scribes–the most famous of them was, no doubt, Ahiqar, Esarhaddon's *ummânu*[53]–but also certain western institutions became prominent in Assyria. First is the institution of the loyalty oath, the much-discussed *adê*.[54] Its earliest occurrence in Akkadian is in the vassal treaty imposed by Ashur-nirari V of Assyria upon Mati-ilu of Arpad in approximately 750.[55] From the same time is the Aramaic treaty between Mati-ilu and the elusive Bir-Ga'yian of KTK in which *'dn* (in cst. *'dy*), treaty, loyalty oath (lit. "oaths") is the key word.[56] There can be little doubt today that this Aramaic term (attested also in Hebrew as **'adim, 'edoth*)[57] is a loan word which supplanted the usual Akkadian terms *riksu, rikiltu* (pl. *riksāte*) = band, covenant.[58]

However, the issue is not merely philological. *Adê* is a concept and an institution. The relations between the Assyrian emperor and his vassal, especially under the Sargonids, are expressed in terms of–and are governed by–loyalty oaths. The royal inscriptions consistently enumerate the penalty imposed on whoever transgressed, "rebelled" in the imperial terminology, or despised an oath. Evidently, the Assyrians borrowed from the west the very concept of relationship between an overlord and his vassal, a situation well attested to in the Hittite and Akkadian vassal treaties of the second millenium.[59] The imposition of the vassal loyalty oath must have been the current way in Syria also in the first millenium to express the relationship between the hegemon and the minor state, like that of the great king of Damascus and all those who follow him, or that of the king of Israel and the small neighboring states.

The introduction of this new institution of *adê*-relationship corresponds to the growing element of bilingualism in Assyria. Apparently, vassal treaties with North Syrian countries were written in duplicate: in Aramaic and in Akkadian, in the Assyrian dialect.[60] That way the Aramaic treaty terminology was adopted by the Assyrians. But here the Assyrians went one step further. From the accession of Esarhaddon and especially from that of Ashurbanipal, numerous documents show that the populace of Assyria, rank and file, had to swear *adê*–the oath of allegiance to the new king.[61] Thus the concept of vassalage on which the relations between Assyrian kings and their vassals were based was extended into Assyria proper, and formed the very basis of the relationship between the king and his people, becoming a determining factor in the political structure of the seventh-century Sargonid empire.

Another western institution was court prophecy. Under Esarhaddon and Ashurbanipal, court prophets and prophetesses addressed the king in almost biblical fashion, unattested before in Mesopotamia. "Fear not O king! . . . I will not abandon you."[62] Still we should bear in mind that prophecy in Assyria of the seventh century is not necessarily a newly acquired Aramaic or Israelite institution. Perhaps it was an Assyrian, as versus a Babylonian, phenomenon, which Assyria shared with the West from the Amorite age.

Finally, western influence also penetrated one of the most specific Mesopotamian religious institutions: liver oracles.[63] In the oracular queries put before Shamash–through an act of extispicy, originally a Babylonian practice–one finds the use of Aramaic. It is repeatedly stated in the texts that the name of the petitioner (usually Esarhaddon) is written on papyrus (*niāru*)–obviously in Aramaic.[64] Of course, the Aramaic queries did not survive. Therefore, it is rather strange to find stated on a cuneiform tablet, "the man whose name is written on this *niāru*," instead of "on this *tuppu*." Moreover, one of the queries carries an Aramaic signature, apparently of one of the priests or scribes.[65]

The Arameo-Assyrian interconnections or even blending in what is usually designated as the "Assyrian civilization" of the later empire should be considered separately in greater detail.[66] I have attempted to trace its origins from the reign of Ashurnasirpal, the outstanding Assyrian nationalist. Ironically, it was he who, by his policy of deportation of westerners into Assyria proper, set the pattern for the future hybrid culture of the "Aramaic-Assyrian *koinê*." It was this *koinê* rather than the Assyro-Babylonian that clashed with the religious uniqueness of Israel[67] and which continued to exist in the ancient Near

East through the Persian period, becoming an underlying component in the *koinê* of the Hellenistic world.[68]

NOTES

*Editors' note: All the dates in this paper are B.C.E.

1 See K. H. Deller, *Or* 26 (1957) 144.

2 A. T. Olmstead, *JAOS* 38 (1918) 209-63; 41 (1921) 345-82.

3 See E. A. Speiser in *The Idea of History in the Ancient Near East,* American Oriental Series 38 (New Haven, 1955) 64-65.

4 See recently B. Albrektson, *History and the Gods* (Lund, 1967) 24ff.; 53ff.; and the review article of W. G. Lambert in *Or* 39 (1970) 172.

5 See A. L. Oppenheim, *JAOS* 63 (1943) 31-34.

6 Quoted from a new translation by the Jewish Publication Society of America, Philadelphia, 1973.

7 See recently P. Artzi, *Eretz Israel* 9 (1969) 26-28.

8 On the role of booty and tribute in the Assyrian empire, see N. B. Jankowska, *Vestnik Drevnei Istorii,* 1956, no. 1, 28-46. (Available now in English translation in *Ancient Mesopotamia,* ed. I. M. Diakonoff [Moscow, 1969] 253-76.) Most recently the question of tribute and booty in Assyria has been treated in extenso by Moshe Eilat in a Hebrew University Ph.D. dissertation to be published by the Bialik Foundation, Jerusalem.

9 On the Assyrian tribute terminology see W. J. Martin, *Tribut und Tributleistungen bei den Assyrern,* Studia Orientalia VIII/1 (1936).

10 The reading *Pa-ti-na* of early Assyriologists was correct after all. This comes out from a new fragment of a stele of Tiglath-Pileser III from Iran to be published by L. D. Levine and the present author. The name is written there *Pat-ti-nu.*

11 Kurkh Monolith II 21-24 (*ARAB* I, §601).

12 On the "forcible exchange," see now I. M. Diakonoff, "Main Features of the Economy in the Monarchies of Ancient Western Asia," in the *Proceedings of the Third International Conference of Economic History,* Munich, 1965, Congrès et Colloques X, 3 (Paris, 1969) 28-29.

13 On Aribua and Luhuti (Lu'aš), see J. Lewy, *Or* 21 (1959) 402-6.

14 *AKA,* 371, col. III, 81-83 (*ARAB* I, §478).

15 Shalmaneser III strengthened the hold of the "North Syrian Corridor" on his return from Que in his twenty-fifth year. He established an Assyrian fortress in the city of Muru in Bit-Agusi--apparently identical with Muru'a in the list of cities from the time of Tiglath-Pileser III (*ARAB* I, §821). It was against the greater Arpad, which succeeded Unqi as the major state in North Syria, that Adad-Nirari III fought for several years when he restored the Assyrian hold in the northwest, weakened since the death of Shalmaneser. See now A. R. Millard and H. Tadmor, *Iraq* 35 (1973) 57ff. Even during the bleak period usually referred to as the "Assyrian decline," 786-746 (see W. W. Hallo, *BA* 23 [1960] 44) the Eponym Chronicle records several expeditions undertaken to

reassert the Assyrian claim to that area.

[16]*AKA,* 237-39, *ARAB* I, §446, §501. Tushan and the district were annexed to Assyria by Ashurnasirpal II. Ishtar-emuqaya, the governor of Tushan, was the eponym for 867.

[17]Monolith II 30ff., *ARAB* I, §602. H. Genge, *Stelen neuassyrischer Könige* I (Freiburg im Breisgau, 1965) 92-93.

[18]See A. Malamat, *The Biblical Archaeologist Reader* 2 (1964) 97.

[19]Monolith II 39-40, *ARAB* I, §603; Genge, *Stelen,* 92.

[20]See J. Lewy in *HUCA* 27 (1956) 35ff.

[21]R. Borger, *Die Inschriften Asarhaddons Königs von Assyrien, AfO* Beiheft 9 (Graz, 1956) 48 (*ANET* 291[a]).

[22]B. Landsberger, *Sam'al* (Ankara, 1948) 30ff.

[23]In any case, the Assyrians did not proceed to Cilicia that year. Shalmaneser returned, ravaging Patina on his way, captured several fortresses (among them Hazazu) and set up a commemorative stele on Mt. Atalur in Northern Syria. (See K. Balkan, *Letter of King Anum-Hirbi of Mama to King Warshama of Kanish* [Ankara, 1957] 37).

[24]On this tribute list see J. M. Peñuela in *Sefarad* 9 (1949) 3-25.

[25]Fuad Safar, *Sumer* 7 (1951) 12, col. IV, 23-34; see A. Goetze, *JCS* 16 (1962) 51, n. 19.

[26]This was originally suggested by E. Forrer in *Die Provinzeinteilung des assyrischen Reiches* (Leipzig, 1920) 71, and I believe that this is still correct.

[27]Bit-Bahian, with its capital Gozan, must have been annexed prior to the fall of Til-Barsip, most likely in the later years of Ashurnasirpal. This would also place the Kapara period in Gozan/Tel-Halaf in the tenth century, as convincingly shown by Albright in *Anatolian Studies* 6 (1956) 75ff; see also D. Ussishkin, *Anatolian Studies* 19 (1969) 132. The historical evidence is not in favor of a late ninth century date as restated now by A. Moortgat, in *Festschrift für K. Galling* (1970) 211ff.

[28]For the location of Qarqar see recently M. Astour in *Or* 25 (1969) 412. The battle of Qarqar and the strength of the Assyrian army which faced the "Twelve Kings of Hatti" is discussed in a forthcoming paper of M. Eilat in *IEJ.*

[29]The explicit version of the Annals on the Monolith, the only text which gives a detailed list of the participants at Qarqar, enumerates eleven kings. The twelfth was apparently omitted by the rather careless scribe who incised the inscription in Kurkh on the upper Tigris and committed a considerable number of mistakes. Or is it the "amphictyonic formula of twelve" that imposed itself here, as in the case of the tribes of Israel, where the actual number always oscillated between eleven and thirteen?

[30]Written *Gu-<bal>-a-a,* a gentilic of *Gublu/i,* "Byblos"; see Tadmor, *IEJ* 11 (1941) 144ff.

[31]Muṣri here refers to Egypt--not to an Anatolian toponym (see most recently K. A. Kitchen, *The Third Intermediate Period in Egypt* [1973] 325). The main, if not the sole, evidence for the existence of a northern Muṣri is the present reference in the Monolith and the word *MṢR* in the Aramaic Treaty from Sefire (J. A. Fitzmeyer, *Biblica et*

Orientalia 19 [1967] 29-30). The latter, I submit, is not a geographical or personal name, but means "border." For details see my paper in *Samuel Yeivin Jubilee Volume* (1970) 397-401 (Hebrew). Paul Garelli could not have been aware of it when he wrote his valuable critical remarks on the question of Muṣri in *Hommages à André Dupont-Sommer* (1971) 37-48.

32 See *Scripta Hierosolymitana* 8 (1961) 246. The Arabian participation at Qarqar has been recently discussed in the Hebrew University dissertation of Israel Eph'al: "The Nomads on the Border of Palestine in the Assyrian, Babylonian and Persian Periods" (1971) 57-58; 21*-22* (in Hebrew).

33 J. Morgenstern, *JBL* 59 (1940) 385ff.

34 See B. Mazar, *The Biblical Archaeologist Reader* 2 (1964) 137ff.

35 Fuad Safar, *Sumer* 8 (1952) 11, col. IV, 10-11. See recently E. Lipiński, *RSO* 45 (1970) 60ff.

36 Cf. M. Astour, *JAOS* 91 (1971) 383ff.

37 J. Laessøe, *Iraq* 21 (1959) 154.

38 See now Millard and Tadmor, *Iraq* 35 (1973) 62-64.

39 *Scripta Hierosolymitana* 8 (1961) 249.

40 See A. L. Oppenheim, *Ancient Mesopotamia* (Chicago, 1964) 118-19; and especially D. Oates, *Studies in the Ancient History of Northern Mesopotamia* (London, 1968), chap. 3.

41 D. J. Wiseman, *Iraq* 14 (1952) 29-35.

42 Ibid., p. 35:143.

43 Ibid., p. 35:153-154.

44 Ibid., p. 28; and Oates, *Studies*, 43ff., 53.

45 Safar, *Sumer* 8 (1952) 13, 34-40.

46 See now A. R. Millard, *Ugarit Forschungen* 4 (1972), 161-62.

47 ND 2443 IV:4 (Barbara Parker, *Iraq* 23 [1961] 27).

48 See W. F. Albright, *BASOR* 149 (1958) 32ff.

49 No. 1 (p. 127); no. 10 (p. 139); no. 20 (p. 149).

50 K 1359 II, lines 10,31 (p. 102).

51 Ibid., pp. 91ff.

52 On the emergence of Aramaic as the main language of the Assyrian empire in the West see Mazar, *The Biblical Archaeologist Reader* 2 (1964) 140-42.

53 J. van Dijk, *Uruk Vorläufiger Bericht* 18 (1963/64) 45; and see J. C. Greenfield in *JAOS* 82 (1962) 293; and in *Hommages à André Dupont-Sommer* (1971) 49-50.

[54] See D. J. Wiseman, "The Vassal-Treaties of Esarhaddon," *Iraq* 20 (1958) 3, and esp. the review article of I. J. Gelb in *Bib Or* 19 (1962) 160-62; also R. Frankena, *OTS* 14 (1965) 134-40. (See also D. B. Weisberg, *Guild Structure and Political Allegiance in Early Achaemenid Mesopotamia* [1967] 32-42, and J. Renger, *JAOS* 91 [1971] 496.) This topic is now under constant discussion. For the latest treatment of the Biblical parallels see recently D. J. McCarthy, *Old Testament Covenant* (1972); and M. Weinfeld, *Deuteronomy and the Deuteronomic School* (1972) 101ff.

[55] Now in new translation by Erica Reiner in *ANET* supp., 96-97 (=532-33).

[56] Now in new translation by F. Rosenthal in *ANET* supp., 223-25 (=659-61).

[57] See D. R. Hillers, *HTR* 69 (1971), 257-59; Weinfeld, *Deuteronomy,* 111, n. 1.

[58] See V. Korošec, *Hethitische Staatsverträge* (1931) 24-35. Other terms for treaty, originating from the 2nd millennium, were elucidated by W. L. Moran, *JNES* 22 (1963) 173-76. (See now M. Weinfeld, *Leshonenu* 36 [1971/72] 85ff.)

[59] See A. Goetze in G. Waltzer (ed.), *Neuere Hethiterforschung,* 1964 (=Historia, Einzelschriften 7) 30-32; also M. Tzevat, *JBL* 77 (1959) 199-200.

[60] D. R. Hillers, *Treaty-Curses and the Old Testament Prophets* (1964) 80-81.

[61] See Wiseman, *Iraq* 20 (1958) 3-9. (See now M. Weinfeld, *VT* 23 [1973] 69-70).

[62] R. D. Biggs in *ANET* supp., 169^{b} (=605), and see now J. C. Greenfield in *Proceedings of the Fifth World Congress of Jewish Studies,* Jerusalem, 1969 (published 1972) 187-89.

[63] J. A. Knudtzon, *Assyrische Gebete an den Sonnengott* (1893); E. G. Klauber, *Politisch Religiöse Texte aus der Sargonidenzeit* (1913); and J. Aro in *La divination en Mésopotamie ancienne* (1966) 109-17.

[64] E.g., Knudtzon, *Assyrische Gebete,* nos. 106, 107, 116, 117, 126, 119; Klauber, *Politisch Religiöse Texte,* nos. 49, 50, 51, 56, 57.

[65] Knudtzon, *Assyrische Gebete,* no. 120.

[66] On the linguistic aspects of the "Aramaic-Assyrian Symbiosis," see recently Y. Muffs, *Studies in the Aramaic Legal Papyri from Elephantine* (1969) 189; and Stephen A. Kaufman, "The Akkadian Influence on Aramaic and the Development of the Aramaic Dialects" (Ph.D. diss., Yale University, 1970) 20ff.

[67] The religious aspects of this *koinê* are discussed now by Morton Cogan, *Imperialism and Religion: Assyria, Judah and Israel in the Eighth and Seventh Centuries B.C.,* SBL Monograph Series 19 (1973).

[68] On the role of the Arameans in the transmission of Mesopotamian lore and as an "interstratum" across the ancient Near East see now the new appraisal of A. L. Oppenheim in *Letters from Mesopotamia* (1967) 51-52.

My thanks are due to my colleague Jonas C. Greenfield for his helpful critical remarks.

PROPAGANDA AND POLITICAL JUSTIFICATION IN HITTITE HISTORIOGRAPHY

Harry A. Hoffner, Jr.

The term "apology" as a designation of a formal composition has most frequently been applied to texts from early Christian and pre-Christian times to denote a detailed defense against false attacks and accusations.[1] The most familiar examples of such apologies are that of Plato and those of the early Christian apologists. The late professor Edgar H. Sturtevant of Yale University, however, employed this term[2] to describe a lengthy text[3] composed in the first person for the Hittite emperor Ḫattušili III, a contemporary of the Egyptian pharaoh Ramesses II and the Assyrian kings Adad-nirari I and Shalmaneser I, who reigned about 1290-1265 B.C. Since Sturtevant's publications on this text the term "apology" has occasionally been employed by other Hittitologists[4] to describe Ḫattušili's remarkable composition, but the prevailing custom has been to call it either an "accession report" (German: *Thronbesteigungsbericht*),[5] an "aretalogy" or an "autobiography."[6] We will use the term "apology" in the ensuing discussion in the specialized sense of a document composed for a king who had usurped the throne, composed in order to defend or justify his assumption of the kingship by force. Since there is presently known no Hittite term or phrase with this meaning, by which scribes might have identified such texts in their colophons, we must identify surviving Hittite examples by formal criteria alone.

The Hittite kings exhibited in their official documents a remarkable sensitivity to rumors and accusations directed against the throne. Among the evils against which the kings must be protected were "evil words" (Hittite: *idalamuš memiyanuš*), which we should understand as "slander, defamation, malicious gossip." Hittite officials were instructed to denounce promptly anyone who directed defamatory remarks against the king, even if the offender were an intimate friend: "Or if a man hears an evil (plot) against His Majesty from a close friend, yet does not denounce (the friend before His Majesty),–let this (neglect of duty) be (forsworn) under oath!"[7] And again: "If you have a very close friend, and I, His Majesty, say to you: 'Have nothing more to do with him!' yet you do not break off with him,–let this (disobedience) be (forsworn) under oath!"[8] The thought and the wording of these instructions reminds one of the similar Deuteronomic command to denounce those who suggest the worship of gods other than Yahweh, even if the offender is a member of one's immediate family (Deut. 13:6-9). Hittite kings were always eager to root out any sign of potential treason against the crown, but the sense of insecurity and distrust of the lower echelons of civil servants shows itself in the official documents most intensely during the final half-century of the empire (c. 1250-1200 B.C.).

One can deal with incipient unrest in various ways. If the disaffection has not spread widely, one can arrest the discontents and either execute or intern them. This approach is certainly suggested by the above passages from King Tudḫaliya's protocol for the grandees (second half of the thirteenth century B.C.). But if the discontent has already spread too far, or if there is reason to believe that arrests will not put an end to it, one can counter the enemy propaganda with royal propaganda. Recently the noted East German author Stefan Heym in his book *Der König David Bericht* (Munich: Kindler Verlag, 1972) has drawn a modern parable from the supposed experience of a ninth-century Jewish official, Ethan ben Hoshaya, who was commissioned by King Solomon to draw up an elaborate explanation of the events surrounding the demise of the Saulids and the rise to the throne of David. That such a piece of royal propaganda may have had independent existence before portions of it were incorporated into the present canonical Book of Samuel has been long suspected by Old Testament scholars. I had occasion several years ago to call attention to the striking points of similarity between this "Apology of David" and the late thirteenth century Apology of Ḫattušili III. But what needs to be stressed here is that, although it may be impossible at present to prove any formal link between the Apology of Ḫattušili and the royal propaganda of David and Solomon, it is not impossible to speak of a tradition of royal apologies in the Hittite kingdom or even of a certain loose literary form, which several of them seem to assume. More than this one should not expect, since one would after all not expect usurpations to occur often enough in a stable society to justify the development of an elaborate traditional format.

Apologies in the above sense–defenses of usurpations–must be carefully distinguished from other defenses made by Hittite kings. A good example of another kind of defense can be found in the so-called "Ten-year (or "Decenniel") Annals of Muršili."[9] In paragraphs 3-4 of that text (KBo III 4 i 10-15), certain defamatory remarks against the young Muršili attributed to surrounding enemy lands are described: "His father," they said, "who was king of Ḫatti, was a valiant king and held the enemy lands in subjection. But he has died. The (older) son [Arnuwanda], who sat on the throne of his father, was also a mature man [Sum. LÚ.GURUŠ]. But he fell ill and died. [§4] He who now sits on the throne of his father is small and unable to defend the land of Ḫatti and its borders."[10] Although the words are attributed to the surrounding enemy lands, they surely reached the king's ears through his own subjects. And the king's concern must surely have been aroused by the possible effect which these words of enemy propaganda might have on the morale, indeed the loyalty, of his own subjects. This lengthy taunt or charge of incompetence was certainly cited for a purpose. Muršili does not answer the taunt immediately. Paragraphs 5-6 deal with the reasons for Muršili's delay in responding to this challenge by the surrounding enemies, namely, the pressing need to celebrate the long-neglected festivals of the sun goddess of Arinna. Midway through paragraph 6, however, the king returns to the subject of the taunts: "To the sun goddess of Arinna, my lady, I raised (my) hand and spoke: 'Oh sun goddess of Arinna, my lady! As regards the surrounding enemy lands, who keep calling me a child and keep belittling me and who keep trying to take (from me) your territories, oh sun goddess of Arinna, my lady, come here to me . . . and smite before me those surrounding enemy lands!' The sun goddess of Arinna heard my plea and came to my aid. Then after I had sat down on the throne of my father, I subjected these surrounding enemy lands in the course of ten years and slew them" (KBo III 4 i 22-29).[11] In other words on the occasion of the celebration of the festivals of the sun goddess the young Hittite king made a vow soliciting the aid of the sun goddess in the overthrow of those enemies who were presently taunting him. That the goddess achieved this vengeance for Muršili within the first ten years of his reign seems to be the clear import of these lines. And if so, then it was the celebration of this achievement which occasioned the drafting of this smaller,

Paragraphs 1-9 of the Telepinu Proclamation have often been discussed, but chiefly from the standpoint of what information they afford about the history of the reigns of Ḫattušili I and Muršili I. Yet far more important for our problem is the function which they seem to serve within the scheme of the document itself. As the historical prefaces in the treaty documents of the fourteenth century serve to justify the legal measures contained in the treaty proper, so the historical introduction in this text is intended as a basis for Telepinu's claims to kingship. The historical introduction to the narration of the coup d'état itself is intended to contrast the rightness of the first three kings (Labarna, Ḫattušili, and Muršili) with the wrongness of the following four (Ḫanteli, Zidanta, Ammuna, and Ḫuzziya). The rightness of the first three kings is underscored by the use of the same stereotyped phrases to describe their successes: "He became king. His sons, his brothers, and his relatives by marriage, the members of his family, and his soldiers were united . . . . And by his strength he kept the hostile country in subjection" (of Labarna in §§1-2, of Ḫattušili in §5, of Muršili in §8).[20] The common theme is unity and strength. These three monarchs could easily be called the "orthodox caliphs" of the Hittite Old Kingdom. Theirs was the golden age of harmony within and unmarred victory abroad. The only discordant note struck in this opening section (§§1-9) is in paragraph 7, where note is taken of the treacherous behavior of certain "subjects of the princes," who began to seize property holdings and conspired to kill their masters. Following as it does hard upon the description of paragraph 6, it would appear that this disorder occurred in the provinces and the large provincial cities assigned to the king's sons rather than in the Hittite heartland. Thus it does not constitute a contradiction of Telepinu's conception of the inner unity and tranquility of the capital. Even so, one should seek the positive contribution of this brief paragraph to the plan of the first nine sections. It is quite unlike the author to include extraneous information in his narrative just for the sake of historical completeness. Quite possibly he wishes to give here a brief allusion to the rebellion which even now seethes beneath the surface and later (§§11-12) boils up in regicide.

The crowning achievement of the Old Kingdom rulers in Telepinu's eyes was the sack of Aleppo and Babylon by Muršili (§9). Accordingly he diverges from his usual stereotyped phrases to describe that achievement. Aleppo had been the only Syrian thorn in the flesh for Muršili's predecessor Ḫattušili, who otherwise met with little effective resistance in North Syria. Another early Hittite text describes Muršili's conquest of Aleppo as avenging his father's blood upon that kingdom.[21] These twin military achievements and the rich harvest of booty which they yielded form the climax of that golden age.

Against the background of the glorious reigns of Labarna, Ḫattušili, and Muršili, the disgrace and ignominy of the reigns of Ḫanteli, Zidanta, Ammuna, and Ḫuzziya could not be more evident. It appears also that by the device of singling out the detail of the usurper married to his predecessor's sister the author wishes to bracket this period from Ḫanteli through Ḫuzziya. It is as though he would say, "Just as the brother-in-law Ḫanteli put an end to the golden age through his foul murder of Muršili, so the brother-in-law Telepinu put an end to the dark age of disgrace through the just and bloodless deposing of Ḫuzziya." Muršili did no harm to Ḫanteli, yet the latter killed him. Ḫuzziya tried to kill Telepinu, yet the latter spared his life (§22).[22] Through ruthlessness the age of disgrace began; through mercy the age of disgrace was ended and the golden age restored. The words which characterize the narrative of paragraphs 10-22 are "blood, killed, avenged." As the age of the first three kings was characterized by unity and success, so that of the following four kings was characterized by intrigue, murder, and defeat. Disaster at home is typified by the crop fail-

annals text at the end of the first ten years of the king's reign. In concluding tl
able document the Hittite king says: "Since I sat on the throne of my father, I
already been king ten years. These enemy lands I conquered with my own hanc
ten years. The enemy lands which the king's sons and the lords conquered are r
cluded (here). Whatever else the sun goddess of Arinna my lady gives to me (to
too I will execute and carry out" (KBo III 4 iv 44-48).[12] Note in particular th
concern here with only those military operations in which he was personally in
as well as his concern to carry out the commission of the goddess. The pattern
lows: (1) The young king is the object of vicious propaganda, not touching his l
his age and fitness to rule in the place of his father and older brother. (2) The
not defend himself against this propaganda by words, so he chooses to do so by
The deeds by which he must prove his manhood[13] must be performed in person
erations led by subordinates will do.[14] (3) Before beginning his ten-year quest
himself a man he seeks the aid of the sun goddess of Arinna and makes to her a
Muršili paid the vow is never stated, although it is possible that the composition
smaller ten-year annals text itself was at least partial payment. In that text in c
the longer, detailed annals the pride of place among the deities who aid Muršili i
always goes to the sun goddess.

Now the ten-year annals of Muršili may well be a defense of the young king's
But as noted above it must be kept distinct from the true apologies, which conc
king's right to the throne.

The two clearest examples of apologies among the official texts in the Hittite
are the Telepinu Proclamation[15] and the Apology of Ḫattušili III. Although dif
detail, these two texts share a general pattern, which once discerned demonstrate
or less traditional way in which Hittite usurpers defended their usurpation. The
outline reveals the essential structure of the two works:

1. Introduction: T §1, H §§1-2.
2. Historical survey: noble antecedents. T §§1-9, H §§3-10.
3. Historical survey: the unworthy predecessor. T §§10-22a, H §§10-12.
4. The coup d'état: T §22b, H §§12-13.
5. The merciful victor: T §§23 & 26, H §§12-13.
6. The edict: T §§27-50, H §§13-15.

Ḫattušili III begins his apology with a genealogy, for as a full blood brother of
talli he can lay claim to direct descent from the royal line of Šuppiluliuma and M
Furthermore, to bolster his claims to kingship he points to his remote namesake,
nasty founder Ḫattušili I, king of the city of Kuššara (Ḫatt. I 1-4, §1).[16] In this
though he was not the direct heir either of Muršili or Muwattalli, Ḫattušili could
a genealogical claim to kingship. In later years his descendents mindful of this plo
condemn its use by others (Ḫatt. XXVI 1 i 6-16, §2).[17]

Unlike Ḫattušili III, Telepinu could not lay claim to royal descent.[18] The nea
proached to a family connection with the preceding kings was in his marriage to
the eldest sister of his predecessor, Ḫuzziya (BoTU II 23A ii 9-10, §22).[19] But s
was hardly a legitimate claim to kingship, he does not adduce that fact in his ow
but only in passing as a kind of explanation for Ḫuzziya's alleged attempt upon h
Therefore, Telepinu's introduction is quite terse: "Thus (speaks) the Tabarna, Te
the Great King." It is clear that the defense of both usurpers had to rest upon g
other than descent.

ures mentioned in the reign of Ammuna (§20). Disaster abroad is illustrated by the defeats of the Hittite armies also in the reign of Ammuna (§21).

Telepinu attempts neither by an opening genealogy nor by any statement in connection with the description of his accession to link himself to the kings which preceded him.[23] It would not have served his purpose to mention it, even if, as Gurney believes, Telepinu was a son of Ammuna.[24] For the picture which he draws of that king is anything but complimentary, and it is clear that he regards himself as the spiritual heir of the first three monarchs. To him the reigns of the following four kings were a disastrous interlude, which it is his good fortune to end. Even the throne name Telepinu, as I have maintained elsewhere,[25] suggests that he conceived of himself at the very outset of his reign as the bringer of renewed prosperity and success. For the god Telepinu was the Ḫattian god whose disappearance signaled the failure of all that was good and whose reappearance signaled the restoration of the benevolent forces of nature.[26] That the new king did not choose for himself the name Ḫattušili or Muršili shows also that he had no pretension to an actual descent by blood from the first three kings.

The ground of Telepinu's removal of Ḫuzziya was of course not just the latter's unworthiness as king, but more specifically the king's attempt on Telepinu's own life (§11). Even a king might not murder with impunity, as Telepinu's own edict (§§30-31) later makes clear:

> Whoever hereafter becomes king and plans injury of brother or sister–you are his senate (*pankuš*)–speak to him frankly: "Read from the tablet(s) this tale of blood(shed)! Formerly in Ḫattuša blood(shed) became common. And at that time the gods exacted of the royal family the penalty for it."
>
> Whatever (king) does harm among (his) brothers and sisters risks (*šuwai-*) his royal head. Call the assembly (*tuliyan halzišten*)! If at that time he carries out his plan, let him make compensation with his head![27]

Similarly Ḫattušili III only takes action against Urḫitešub when the latter makes an attempt upon his life.

The coup itself is tersely described: "Ḫuzziya would have killed them (Telepinu and Ištapariya), but his plan became known,[28] and Telepinu drove them away" (*BoTU* II 23A ii 11-12, §22).[29] The reason for the plural object "them" is that the plot against Telepinu's life was shared by Ḫuzziya and his five brothers, all of whom with the ex-king were interned in houses built for them by the new king (§23).[30] There is no divine working on behalf of Telepinu as one sees in the Apology of Ḫattušili. He is not protected by a deity, or promised the kingship by one. The only direct references to the gods in this comparatively unreligious document are (1) in their avenging the murders of the kings (§§19, 20, 30) and (2) in the words of reproof spoken through the "men of the gods" (*siunan antuḫšiš*; *BoTU* II 23A ii 32, §27). It is interesting to note what form the gods' revenge assumed. In paragraph 19 the gods avenged the blood of Kaššeni, whom Zidanta had murdered, by prompting Zidanta's own son Ammuna to murder his father. In paragraph 20 the gods then avenge Zidanta's blood upon the young king Ammuna by withholding from the land increase of crops and cattle. Telepinu himself summarizes the matter in paragraph 30 as follows: "Formerly in Ḫattuša blood(shed) became common, and at that time the gods exacted of the royal family the penalty for it." Therefore, the chief role of the gods in this document is punishing the royal family for internecine strife. Telepinu makes no claim that they had designated him to rule. He even refrains from such an oblique claim to divine appointment as the phrase in Ḫattušili I's political testament: "In the place of a lion the gods will only put another lion" (§7; *HAB* II 39, §7).[31]

In the Ḫattušili Apology, on the other hand, the coup is described in terms borrowed from the courtroom. Archi has shown how throughout the text Ḫattušili the pious is contrasted with his evil foes. But at the moment of truth it is the confrontation between Urḫitešub and Ḫattušili which alone has importance.

As in the Telepinu Proclamation the question is raised as to which of the two is more fit to rule. And indeed Urḫitešub has been portrayed throughout the document as not only incompetent but also as an evil man who has recourse to witchcraft (*alwanzatar*) and other means which displease the gods. Ḫattušili has not neglected either to call attention to the young incumbent's mother's somewhat less than glorious state: he was "the son of an *esirtu*-woman" (*Ḫatt.* III 41).[32] But these factors were insufficient justification for the deposing of Urḫitešub. Telepinu based his swift, decisive coup on the alleged plot of Ḫuzziya to kill him and his wife. Ḫattušili, too, could and did accuse Urḫitešub of attempting to kill him, "But he at the command (lit. "word") of a god and the suggestion (lit. "word") of a man tried to destroy me" (*Ḫatt.* III 63-64). Yet it is not on the murder attempt of Urḫitešub that Ḫattušili bases his claim to kingship. It is true that he takes arms in self-defense (*Ḫatt.* III 65-66). His claim to kingship, however, rests upon the will of the gods, who have chosen him.[33] In the Apology it is the goddess whose name is written with the Ishtar sign and whose cult center was the town of Šamuḫa.[34] In other texts the deity who conferred kingship upon him was the sun goddess of Arinna.[35] In his final challenge to Urḫitešub, Ḫattušili in fact appeals to the Ishtar of Šamuḫa and the storm god of Nerik to decide the issue between the two of them by the ordeal of battle (*Ḫatt.* III 71-73, §11). The argument from the outcome of the ordeal of battle was unanswerable: "In truth would (the gods) have subjected a great king to a small king? Now because he started hostilities with me, they subjected him to me in the trial" (*Ḫatt.* III 78-79, §11). Ḫattušili's vindication as the king divinely chosen to depose Urḫitešub comes through the providence[36] of the goddess Ishtar, who reassures him in dreams (*Ḫatt.* IV 7-17, §12) and appears to others in dreams to enlist their support of Ḫattušili, saying, "On your own ye are weak,[37] but I, Ishtar, have turned all the Hittite lands to the side of Ḫattušili!" (*Ḫatt.* IV 21-23, §12). At the showdown the miraculous power of Ishtar supported Ḫattušili: (1) for the first time ever she refused to support Urḫitešub (*Ḫatt.* IV 24ff.) and (2) the Kaškeans who formerly had been Ḫattušili's enemies now appeared as his allies (*Ḫatt.* IV 26ff.). As ever more allies flocked to the side of Ḫattušili, Urḫitešub found himself trapped in the town of Šamuḫa "like a pig in a sty" (*Ḫatt.* IV 25-26) or "like a fish in a net" (*KBo* VI 29 ii 34).[38] Ḫattušili's victory and divine vindication was clear and complete.

A victor can afford to be generous, yet not all victors choose to be. Only when there is something to be gained from magnanimity do they make the effort.[39] Both Telepinu and Ḫattušili make the effort, because the situation was still delicate and the stakes for survival too high. Thus both documents are at pains to portray the new kings as men of mercy. Telepinu "built them houses (and said), 'Let them go (and) dwell (there). Let them eat (and) drink, and do not do them any harm. And I declare: "They did me harm, yet I will not do them harm"'" (*BoTU* II 23A ii 13-15, §23). And when the henchmen who were to carry out the murders were brought before him for judgment, he expressed his leniency as follows: "Why should they die? Let them rather hide their faces.[40] So I, the king, made them real[41] farmers. I took their weapons from their shoulder(s), and I gave them . . ." (*BoTU* II 23A ii 29-30, §26). Ḫattušili also dispensed favors upon his accession (§§12-13). He did not attempt to execute Urḫitešub, but publicly humiliated him,[42] bringing him from

Šamuḫa "like a captive" (*Ḫatt.* IV 31, §12), and interned him in the land of Nuḫašše in one of the fortified cities. Even the unsuccessful attempt of Urḫitešub to escape to Babylonia, where he could organize support for a return to power (*Ḫatt.* IV 33f., §12), did not lead Ḫattušili to the extreme measure of executing a son of Muwatalli. But additional precautions were taken in the selection of a new place of internment, which seems to have been a coastal area (A.AB.BA) *tapuša*, *Ḫatt.* IV 36). It is clear from the constant repetition of the phrase "out of respect for my brother (Muwattalli)"(three times in the main text: *Ḫatt.* III 62, IV 29, 61; twice in *KBo* VI 29: i 36, ii 38) that Muwattalli's line had many supporters still, and that Ḫattušili was resolved to win them over. As a gesture of good will to them he installed as a local king in the city of Tarḫuntašša,[43] where Muwatalli's capital had been situated,[44] the latter's son mKAL (to be read *Inara*?).[45] Still another party with which Ḫattušili dealt cautiously was Šippaziti, the son of his long-standing rival and opponent, Armadatta (*Ḫatt.* III 22; IV 3, 5, 6).[46] Once before (§10), when his father Armadatta had been convicted of unprovoked attacks on Ḫattušili, Šippaziti and his father had been spared harsh treatment and had only been sent to Alashiya for internment (verb: *uppa-*), while the crown awarded half of his estate to Ḫattušili for damages. The grounds for his lenient treatment then doubtless still called for lenient treatment after the defeat of Urḫitešup, despite the fact that this was a "second offense" by the family against Ḫattušili. *Ḫatt.* III 25 seems to read: *nu-mu* ᴵ*Ar-ma-*ᴰ*U-aš [ku-it...-w]a-aš an-tu-uḫ-ša-aš e-eš-ta* "and [because] Armadatta was a man [. . .] to me, . . . I let him off!" This seems to suggest that Ḫattušili and Armadatta were at least distantly related, a situation which is possible to explain, if we assume that Armadatta's father, Zida, was the same man as the Zida who was the brother of Šuppiluliuma, Ḫattušili's grandfather. If that Zida belonged to the same generation as Šuppiluliuma, Armadatta would have been roughly contemporary with Muršili, which fits with his being called "an old man and ill" by Ḫattušili shortly after his father, Muršili, had died (§10). Šippaziti would belong to Ḫattušili's own generation. As a great-grandson of the king who was Šuppiluliuma's father, Šippaziti was entitled to gentle treatment.

Both the Telepinu Proclamation and the Apology of Ḫattušili conclude with quasi-legal sections. This material fills quite a large amount of space in the Telepinu text, while in Ḫattušili it is brief. In Telepinu the regulations concern the conduct of justice as it affects the royal family. In Ḫattušili the regulations concern only the disposition of royal property to the cult of the goddess Ishtar of Šamuḫa. In both cases the narrative portions provide background for the legal portions, but since the Ḫattušili sections are few in number (§§13-15), one gains the impression that he perhaps only follows the documentary form in Telepinu's precedent and that his primary concern was the narrative itself and the justification of his usurpation.

The pattern of introducing legal reforms by historical narrative introductions is first attested in the Telepinu text. Thereafter one finds it in the probably "Middle Hittite" text describing the reforms of a king named Tudḫaliya (*KUB* XIII 9 and *KUB* XL 62; *CTH* 258 = Cat. 172, with unpublished dupl. 99/p).[47]

The reforms themselves focus on the restoration of the former unity and prosperity of the earliest monarchs. Thus Telepinu writes: "Whoever after me through all time shall become king, in those days let his brothers, his sons, his relatives-in-law, the members of his family, and his subjects (lit. "soldiers") be united! And you shall come (and) with (your) strength hold the hostile country in subjection" (*BoTU* II 23A ii 40ff., §29), harking back to his descriptions of the reigns of Labarna, Ḫattušili, and Muršili in paragraphs 1-2, 5, and

8. At the basis of this restored unity and strength should lie a clear and universally recognized order of royal succession, which Telepinu gives in paragraph 28: (1) son of the king's primary wife, (2) son of the king's secondary wife, and (3) husband of the daughter of the king's primary wife.[48] The aim was the elimination of ambiguity and unpredictable, unaccountable high-handed behavior of the sovereign. Therefore, in the future the king must not offer pardon and later rescind it (§29). He must neither himself instigate or tolerate among others plots to kill members of the royal family (§§30-31). With these words Telepinu renounces the dictum that "might makes right" and that "a king may do as he pleases."[49] The Hittite king, too, is accountable, in the first instance (as indeed previous to these reforms) to the gods who avenge bloodshed, but now also to the judicial body called the *pankuš*. The punishment meted out by the gods embraced not only the offender himself but his family as well.[50] The punishment decreed by the *pankuš*, on the contrary, must not extend beyond the person of the offending king or prince (§§31-32): "but let them not contrive harm for his house, his wife (and) his children!" This "limited liability" would seem also to emend the provisions of the Hittite laws,[51] whose main version dates to the reigns of Ḫattušili I and Muršili I (c. 1675-1600), which allowed in some cases that the deceased's heir appropriate the property of the convicted murderer, and in one other case actually prescribed that the murderer's son be handed over to the deceased's heir (law §44a).[52] Telepinu's reasoning was that, since the expropriation of the convicted man's property was often the principal motivation for falsely accusing him and engineering his death (§§31-32),[53] if one revised the law so as to eliminate the expropriation clause, it ought to reduce, if not eliminate, the plots to incriminate and have executed the Hittite princes.[54] Although superficially it might appear that the somewhat disorganized group of rulings at the end of Telepinu's text have no common theme, one can in fact relate all the rulings to the central concern of internecine strife and killings among the royal family! Thus even paragraph 50, which concerns persons in the royal family who practice sorcery, deals with the threat that the sorcerer poses to the lives of his relatives.

We mentioned at the outset that it was possible to speak of a tradition of Hittite apologies. Telepinu is the earliest usurper of whom we have certain evidence for a written defense. While it needs to be affirmed that no earlier such document can be proven, it should also be pointed out that a possible example of a still earlier written defense by a usurper exists in a lamentably fragmentary state. I refer to *KBo* III 54 (= *BoTU* II 16; *CTH* 10), whose recently discovered duplicate *KBo* XXII 7 adds almost no words not already contained in *KBo* III 45. A transliteration of this remarkable fragment follows:[55]

[ ] x *túḫ-ḫu-uš*[-

w[*a-*]*a*[!][56]*-tar-na-aḫ-ḫa-an ḫar-zi šu-uš-ká*[*n*

L[Ú].MEŠ URU*Ḫa-at-ti* KI ŠEŠ.MEŠ-*NI* x[

[*n*]*e-pi-ši* DINGIR.MEŠ *iš-tar-ni-in-ku-en* [*(ta)*

[UR]U KÁ.DINGIR.RA-*aš ku-e-az*[57]*-mi-it da-a*[-

[(GU)]D.ḪI.A-*NI*[58] UDU.ḪI.A-*NI*[58] *a-ap-pa-an ša-an*[-[59]...(*na*)]

[*(ku)*]*-en-ta ta e-eš-ḫar-še-et šu-up-pa*[-[60]

[ ]*-a-i-ú-en ta pa-a-i-ú-en ta ú*? [-[61]

[*ša-*] ⸢*a*⸣?*-li-ku-wa-aš-ta-ti ta-at-ra-an-t*[*a(-)*[58] . .*ŠA*? URU KÁ.DINGIR.RA)][62]

[*(u)t-n*]*e-e-az-ma tar-nu-mi-en* TÚG.SIG U[RU KÁ.DINGIR.RA??

[*nu ma*]*-a-an ša-la-i-iš at-ta-aš ut-tar p*[*é-eš-ši*-[63]

[x x x *me*]*-ma-a-i a-ni-ši-wa-at* m*Mur-ši-i*[*-li-*

[x x x x x] x *ŠUM-an-še-et le-e ku-iš[-ki te-ez-zi*[64]
[*ḫa-an*] *-te-ez-zi-i-aš-mi le-e*[
[*n*] *a?-an a-aš-ki-iš-ši k*[*ăn-kăn-du*[65]

[ ] x *ku-iš*[

Because of the fragmentary state of this text, certainty in its interpretation is in no way possible. Yet a few suggestions may be made here. In line 4′ the speaker includes himself or his readers among those who have "made the gods sick" by an evil deed. Line 5′ may explain what the deed was: "[We] took(?)[66] of Babylon their possessions."[67] In line 6′ cattle and sheep are mentioned, perhaps part of the booty taken from Babylon. The next verb is singular: "He killed/smote [. . .], and its blood. . .[he. . .-ed]." Line 8′ mentions "we went and their/your field [. . .]." The verb *šalikwaštati* means "we penetrated."[68] Lines 9′-10′ seem to refer to removing from the land of Babylon certain items of value, perhaps including "fine garments." Line 11′, the final line of the section which describes the evil deeds against Babylon which made the gods sick, seems to say: "[And w]hen he became rebellious(?),[69] the father's word [he(??)] c[ast off(?)]." That the final verb is third singular would seem to follow from the third singular verb "he became rebellious" in the protasis. The identity of the final verb ("cast off") is reasonably certain from the very similar passage in *KBo* III 27 obv 28ff., as well as from the interesting and relevant lines in paragraph 19 of the Political Testament of Ḫattušili (*KUB* I 16) addressed to Muršili. *If* this restoration is correct, who is the unidentified person who "became rebellious" and "c[ast off] his father's word"? Since the deed described in lines 1′-11′ is against the city of Babylon and is connected with penetrating its territory and taking its goods, it would seem highly probable that the person who cast off his father's word was Muršili himself, who led the Hittite armies against Babylon. As a consequence of Muršili's sin described in lines 1′-11′, the narrator proceeds in lines 12′ and following to draw consequences. The key word *anišiwat* in line 12′ is of uncertain meaning, since it is a hapax legomenon. Friedrich (*HWb,* 22, quoting Hrozný) translates it "today," but, although *šiwat* can be an endingless locative "on the day," *ani* can hardly be "this." If *ani* is the same as *anni-*, it would denote the more remote object "that." Thus one would translate *anišiwat* as "on that day." Because the end of Muršili's name is missing in the lacuna, one cannot determine its case, and therefore it is impossible to say if it is the subject or object of the sentence. Since the author of this text would hardly criticize Muršili in this fashion during the king's lifetime, it is possible that he says here: "On that day Murši[li died]." Yet since the narrator describes the Babylonian expedition as "we," either he or his readers must have taken part. Therefore, a date not long after the death of Muršili but within the next generation is probable. This would place the composition of this text during the reign of Ḫanteli or his immediate successor, a date which is not opposed by the archaic language of the text. Line 13′ adds: "His name let no on[e speak]!" I would assume that lines 15′-16′, although related to the preceding lines, do not refer to Muršili himself by the words "[Let them] h[ang] him in his gate!" although we have so little knowledge of the details of the death of that king that it is impossible to say.

In order to distinguish between what is fairly certain in this fragment and what is highly conjectural, let me review its contents and my interpretation. Lines 4′-11′ describe actions carried out against Babylon early in the Hittite Old Kingdom, therefore certainly by Muršili and his men. Some actions are attributed to the entire group, with which the narrator identifies either himself or his listeners by the use of "we" forms. Other actions he attributes to one man. In the final line, apparently summarizing, he attributes to the one man rebellion and the casting off of "(his) father's word." If the Babylonian raid itself displeased the gods, then the one man who could be singled out for censure would be the king who led that raid. I suggest then that this text was composed during the reign of Ḫanteli, and that he, through criticizing the final act of Muršili as displeasing to the gods, sought to remove all stigma from himself as Muršili's usurper. If this is so, the fragment forms a part of what was possibly the earliest bit of political propaganda used by a Hittite usurper and is a document which served as a precedent for Telepinu.

NOTES

[1]*Encyclopaedia Britannica* (1963 ed.), II, 124ff.; *Meyers Enzyklopädisches Lexikon,* 9. Aufl. (Mannheim, 1971), II, 404; *Der Kleine Pauly,* I, 455. For aretalogies see M. Nilsson, *Geschichte der griechischen Religion* (Munich, 1950), II, 216ff.

[2]E. H. Sturtevant and G. Bechtel, *A Hittite Chrestomathy* (1935) 42-99 (hereafter cited as *Chrest.*) (*CTH* 81).

[3]Original edition by A. Goetze in *MVAeG* XXIX/3 (1924) (hereafter cited as *Ḫatt.*). Additional joins and duplicates since Goetze's edition conveniently assembled in *CTH* 81, 15. A new edition by H. Otten will appear in a future volume of the series *StBoT* published by Otto Harrassowitz of Wiesbaden.

[4]A. Goetze, *CAH* II², fasc. 37, 45. See H. M. Wolf, *The Apology of Ḫattušiliš Compared* . . .(Ann Arbor, 1967) 12ff. for a review of evidence for the form of the document. See also O. R. Gurney, *The Hittites* (Baltimore, 1964) 175f.

[5]*MVAeG* XXIX/3 (1924).

[6]A. Goetze, *CAH* II², fasc. 37, 45.

[7]*KUB* XXVI 1 iv 7-10, §29; E. von Schuler, *Dienstanw.,* 8ff.

[8]*KUB* XXVI 8 ("B") i 33′-37′, §5; *CTH* 255.

[9]H. M. Wolf, *Apology of Ḫattušiliš Compared,* 16, lists similarities between the Annals of Muršili and the Apology of Ḫattušili.

[10]Translation in Goetze, *AM,* 16-21; and Ph. Houwink ten Cate, *Muršili . . . Karakter* [Dutch] (Leiden, 1966) n. 2.

[11]Translations in Goetze, *AM,* 21-23, and Gurney, *The Hittites,* 173-74; discussion in E. von Schuler, *Die Kaškäer,* 45, n. 282.

[12]Translations in Goetze, *AM,* 137, and Gurney, *The Hittites,* 174. See also Sommer, *AU,* 247; Friedrich, *Staatsv.,* I, 44; and Ph. Houwink ten Cate, *Numen* 16 (1969) 83, n. 12.

[13]Thus in the colophons (*KUB* XIX 30 iv 15; *KBo* V 8 iv 24) this text is called "the manly deeds of Muršili," on which concept see H. Hoffner, *JBL* 85 (1966) 327 with n. 4.

[14]See *Ḫatt.* II 37ff, §7, and H. Hoffner, *CBQ* 30 (1968) 220ff.; *KBo* III 4 iv 44-48, §42.

[15]*CTH* 19 (p. 5); Forrer, *BoTU* II 23; Sturtevant and Bechtel, *Chrest.,* 175ff.; O. R. Gurney, *CAH* II², fasc. 44, 3-10; Eiserle's Munich dissertation, which was a new edition of this text, has still not been published, as had been anticipated, in the series *Texte der Hethiter* (Carl Winter Verlag, Heidelberg).

[16]See H. Otten, *ZA* 61 (1971) 234.

[17]Von Schuler, *Dienstanw.,* 8-9, 17-18.

[18]See Gurney, *CAH* II², fasc. 44, 7 with n. 4, rebutting E. Menabde.

[19]Ibid., 7-8.

[20]On the grammar of §§2-3a (*BoTU* II 23A i 5-8) see H. Hoffner, in *Peoples of the Old Testament,* ed. D. J. Wiseman (Oxford, 1973) 207.

[21]*KBo* III 57 (*BoTU* II 20) obv. ii 10′-11′; Gurney, *CAH* II², fasc. 11, 24.

[22]See A. Archi, *Studi Micenei ed Egeo-Anatolici* 14 (1971) 186ff., for examples of this same use of contrasts in the propaganda of Ḫattušili III.

[23]Thus I cannot accept Gurney's second explanation of the events in §§21-22 (*CAH* II², fasc. 44, 7-8).

[24]That Telepinu did not, however, utterly disassociate his line from his immediate predecessors is shown by the name of his son Ammuna (*BoTU* II 23A ii 32, §27).

[25]Hoffner in *Peoples of the Old Testament,* ed. Wiseman, 208ff.

[26]See von Schuler in Röllig (ed.), *Wörterbuch der Mythologie* (Stuttgart, 1965), vol. 1, 201f.; and H. G. Güterbock in *Festschrift Joh. Friedrich* (1959) 207ff.

[27]*BoTU* II 23A ii 46-52, §§30-31; Sturtevant and Bechtel, *Chrest.,* 190-91; A. Goetze, *Kleinasien*², 87; H. G. Güterbock, *JAOS* supp. 17 (1954) 19; E. Laroche, *RHA,* fasc. 76 (1965) 35.

[28]The subjects of the verb (*arḫa*) *išduwa-* (J. Friedrich, *ZA* nF 3, 198 with n. 2; E. Neu, *StBoT* 5, 78f.) are usually evil thoughts or rebellious plans which the evil doer seeks to conceal (*šanna-).* Only once (*KUB* XXX 10 rev 19 and dupls.) is the subject something good (translation by A. Goetze, in *ANET*², 401).

[29]For the verbal construction *arḫa parḫ-* "to banish" (*HWb,* 159; A. Goetze, *JCS* 17, 99) the documentation is as follows: *KUB* XIII 7 i 12-13, "they will banish him, and he shall pay the judgement with his house"; *KUB* VIII 1 ii 7-8, "if on the 20th day the moon 'dies,' the prince, who has been banished, will return and occupy his father's throne"; *KUB* XIV 1 i 1, "Attariššiya of Aḫḫiya(wa) banished you [Madduwatta] from your land"; *KUB* XIII 2 iii 11ff., "As it has been from olden days, in the lands a regulation governing *hurkel* (incest) has been observed; in a town in which they have been accustomed to impose the death penalty, they shall continue to do so; but in a town where they have been accustomed to impose exile (or "banish") they shall continue that (custom)."

[30]Compare the internment of his disinherited son by Ḫattušili I in *KUB* I 16 (*HAB*), §6.

[31]*HAB,* 68. The prominent emphasis in the Old Hittite texts on the need for a king to be worthy or fit suggests that the apologies which justify deposing an unworthy king first arose in that atmosphere and fitted less well in the social and political climate of the empire period several centuries later. Perhaps this is why Ḫattušili III had to reinforce the argument of Urḫitešub's unfitness with claims of his own to divine revelations and divine designation.

[32]On Akkadian *esertu/esirtu* in Hittite texts, see A. Goetze, *ArOr* 2, 153ff. On this passage see Goetze, *CAH* II², fasc. 37, 44, n. 1.

[33]See Archi, *Studi Micenei ed Egeo-Anatolici* 14 (1971) 188ff.

[34]*Ibid.*

[35] *Ibid.*

[36] This translation seeks to express that combination of divine justice and effective power which seems to inhere in the Hittite term *parā ḫandantatar*. See *Ḫatt.*, 52ff.; Sommer and Ehelolf, *Pap.*, 30-31; Goetze, *Kleinasien*², 146; Sturtevant and Bechtel, *Chrest.*, 86 and 229; Wolf, *Apology of Ḫattušiliš Compared,* 28ff., 185; Hoffner, in *Peoples of the Old Testament,* ed. Wiseman; and A. Archi, *SMEA* 14 (1971) 188.

[37] See H. Hoffner, *JNES* 28 (1969) 228. Earlier translations by Goetze, *Ḫatt.,* 33; Sturtevant and Bechtel, *Chrest.,* 79; and H. G. Güterbock in Oppenheim, *TAPS* 46 (1956) 254.

[38] See Wolf, *Apology of Ḫattušiliš Compared,* 15.

[39] See Muršili's description of his father Šuppiluliuma's sparing of the acropolis and shrines of Carchemish in *KBo* V 6 iii 31ff.

[40] That is, not show their faces in the capital, but remain in seclusion. See *KUB* I 16 (*BoTU* II 8) ii 30-36, §6.

[41] *Karšauš* "real" as opposed to absentee landowners, whose serfs tilled the soil.

[42] For other instances of this practice see *KBo* III 22: 73-79 (Anitta text, §18), *KBo* X 2 iii 40-42 (Ḫattušili I annals, §20).

[43] URU.DU-*tašša* formerly read Dattašša.

[44] *Ḫatt.* II 52-53, §8.

[45] *Ḫatt.* IV 65, §13; also *ABoT* 57 (*CTH* 97) and 544/f (*CTH* 96).

[46] Šippaziti (*šippa-* LÚ), the son of Armadatta, is known aside from the passages cited in E. Laroche, *Les noms hittites* (Paris, 1966) 163; perhaps also from *KBo* XVI 83 iii 3; *KBo* XVI 60 rev. 6; *KBo* XVI 22 obv. 4. Possibly a third [mŠi-ip-]*pa*-LÚ, the son of Pulli, is known from *KBo* XVIII 89 obv. 4. Perhaps the grandfather (Zida) of the Šippaziti of the Ḫattušili text is the brother of Šuppiluliuma who held the office of GAL *MEŠEDI* and not a second Zida, as Laroche assumes (*Les noms hittites,* 211). *Ḫatt.* III 25 suggests Armadatta was related to Ḫattušili and was therefore a member of the royal family. If so, Šippaziti's royal descent (great-grandson of the king who was Šuppiluliuma's and Zida's father) would have influenced Ḫattušili's lenient treatment of him (*Ḫatt.* IV 36-40, §12).

[47] Aside from the literature cited in *CTH* 258, cf. E. von Schuler, *Die Kaškäer,* 60, n. 422; J. Friedrich, *JAOS* 88 (1968) 37; O. Carruba, *Die Sprache* 12 (1966) 84f.; and H. Otten in H. Schmökel, *Kulturgeschichte* (1961), 370.

[48] Goetze, *Kleinasien*², 87; Gurney, *CAH* II², fasc. 44 (1966) 10; E. Menabde, *Vestnik . . . Istorii* 4 (1969) 67-82; H. Hoffner, *JNES* 28 (1969) 228.

[49] For this *idaluš memiyaš*, compare: "Oh, the king [does] in secret what he pleases!" (*KUB* I 16 ii 53-54, §10; *RHA,* fasc. 67 [1960] 144), and for further examples see *BoTU* II 23A ii 5, 52; *BoTU* II 23C ii 1; *KBo* XIII 1 + *KBo* I 44, rev. 37-38.

[50] See Goetze, *Kleinasien*², 147 with text citations.

[51] Hittite laws §§6, 43-44a; see also *BoTU* II 23B iv 19-21, §49; and *KUB* XIII 9, ii 3-7.

[52] See also *KBo* XVI 25 (*CTH* 251) iii 10′ff.; and *KUB* XIII 7 (*CTH* 258, 2) i 17ff.

[53] I translate *BoTU* II 23A ii 56-58 as follows: "For what cause are princes destroyed? Is it not for the sake of (obtaining) their houses . . .?" See also ii 63-65.

[54] A good example of the abuse of such expropriation laws is seen in the story of Naboth and King Ahab of Israel (1 Kings 21).

[55] I should like to thank here Professors H. Otten and E. Laroche for their friendly suggestions regarding the transliteration and interpretation of this fragment. They are in no way to be held accountable, however, for my own interpretation of the lines.

[56] Reading suggested by Laroche.

[57] *KBo* XXII 7: 2′ *ku-it-šum-*[*mi-it*].

[58] Or perhaps *-ni*?

[59] Amount of space undetermined.

[60] Is this a form of the adjective *šuppi-* "holy" or the noun *šuppa* "flesh, meat"?

[61] Copy in *KBo* shows three vertical wedges, making LÍL possible. Forrer in *BoTU* read *ú*[-....] (assuming he saw four verticals?), but fails to draw the sign. *KBo* XXII 7: 5′ has *ku-e-ra-šum-m*[*a?-an?*], perhaps favoring LÍL, although the usual Hittite word corresponding to LÍL is *gimra-*. *kuera-* usually occurs in pairings with A.ŠÀ, so that the latter is certainly not its Sumerogram.

[62] *KBo* XXII 7 breaks off here.

[63] Restored following *KBo* III 27 obv 28ff. See Sommer, *HAB,* 154, n. 1 (reference courtesy of Laroche).

[64] Restored following *KBo* III 27 obv 7ff.

[65] Restored following *KBo* III 27 obv 9ff., 12, 22.

[66] Restoring *da-a*[*-ú-en*].

[67] Literally "their what" (*ku-e-az-mi-it, ku-it-šum-*[*mi-it*]). The booty from Babylon is mentioned prominently also in *BoTU* II 23A i 29, §9, on which see above.

[68] Or "we reached, touched, arrived at"; see *HWb,* 179, and Neu, *StBoT* 5, 147ff.

[69] The verb form is 3 sg. pret. *ḫi*-conjugation on the stem *šala(i)-*. Despite the single writing of the *l* one should consider it to be the same verb as is found in *KBo* I 45 ii 5 (*šallawar*), which translates the Akkadian word *za-ra-ru-u* (=*sarāru* "to rebel, rise up against"); see *Ḫatt.,* 87; *HWb,* 87; *MSL* III, 49-87; and Laroche, *RHA,* fasc. 79, 161. Alternatively, if the verb belongs with those medio-passive forms of the stem *šallai-/šalliya-* (Neu, *StBoT* 5, 146-47; Laroche, *RHA,* fasc. 79, 161: "etirer, tirailler"), then one would have to translate here "[wh]en he grew up/became great, his father's word [he] c[ast off]," and compare *KUB* I 16 iii 26-32, §19.

PART II: LITERATURE AND LANGUAGE

- 4 -

RELIGIOUS DRAMA IN ANCIENT MESOPOTAMIA

Thorkild Jacobsen

I. INTRODUCTION

Our subject this evening, Religious Drama in Ancient Mesopotamia,[1] is one that may very fairly claim the attention of philologists no less than students of ancient religions. It is also, however, in many ways a most elusive one, lavish with possibilities, sparing with certainties, abundant in all kinds of complexities, and with very few simple straightforward facts.

To get a hold on it--and to keep this paper within reasonable limits--we have therefore chosen to center attention on a single basic aspect of the problem only: what the religious drama was supposed to achieve, its meaning, and the ways in which that meaning changed with the times. We shall consider first, therefore, very briefly, the older materials down to Old Babylonian times and the fertility dramas--especially the Sacred Marriage Drama--with which they deal. Second, we shall then take up in slightly more leisurely fashion what we know about the religious drama in the first millennium: survivals of the fertility dramas and the appearance of a new type altogether, the Battle Drama.

II. THE OLDER MATERIALS

The existence of a ritual drama in Ancient Mesopotamia is most clearly attested to in the case of the Sacred Marriage Drama found in the cult of the various forms of Dumuzi or Tammuz and other fertility gods.[2] The rite is patterned after the normal Ancient Mesopotamian wedding ritual, which had the bridegroom appear with his wedding gifts of edibles at the door of the bride's paternal house asking to be let in. The bride, after she had bathed and dressed in all her finery, then opened the door to him and this opening of the door was the ritual act that concluded the marriage. Next, bride and bridegroom were escorted separately to the bridal chamber, where the marriage was consummated. The next morning the young couple presided at a feast of plenty.[3]

Our oldest evidence for the Sacred Marriage Rite dates back to late Proto-Literate times. The famous Uruk vase[4] of that date shows Dumuzi-Amaushumgalanna, the god who represented the power in the date-palm,[5] approaching the gate of Eanna followed by a long cortege of servants bearing his wedding gifts.[6] At the gate stands Inanna, the numen of the storehouse, ready to open it to him and thereby conclude their marriage. A later Old Babylonian text,[7] also belonging to the cult in Uruk, is styled as a blow-by-blow account by a well-placed observer keeping worshipers farther back informed about what is going on. This text tells first how Inanna dresses herself in jewels she finds on a heap of freshly harvested dates, then how she goes to the gate of the Giparu, identified by the text as the temple storehouse, to let in her bridegroom, Amaushumgalanna, and finally how she sends messengers to her father to have the bridal bed set up and Amaushumgalanna escorted to it.

A similar reporting style characterizes an Epithalamium published in *CT* 42 pl. 7-8.[8] That text, however, omits the encounter at the gate and has the bride, Inanna, proceed directly to the bridal chamber to see that the bed is well made up and comfortable. She then calls the bridegroom, who is represented by the king. Clearest of all is a direct description of the rite as rite which forms the last canto in the long Hymn to Inanna as the Evening Star.[9] This text also omits the encounter at the gate and begins by telling how the bridal bed is set up at New Year, how the king, Iddin-Dagan, who is a god since he incarnates Amaushumgalanna in the rite, goes to bed with her and consummates their marriage. The canto ends with a description of the feast next morning at which the divine couple presides.

Finally there is a long text dealing with Dumuzi, and clearly at home in a herding milieu,[10] which tells of Inanna's bathing herself and dressing for her bridegroom,[11] then, after a small lacuna which might have told of her opening the door to Dumuzi, of her being escorted to the bridal chamber. On this occasion she praises her young, barely nubile body and has the praise made into an erotic song.[12] After another small lacuna, we hear of the consummation of the marriage and of Inanna's request the next day for all kinds of milks and milk products, which her young husband gladly brings to her.

To give an impression of what these texts are like we shall quote a single one, the description in the Hymn to Inanna as the Evening Star mentioned above. In many ways it is our clearest and most informative piece of evidence.[13]

> In the palace, the house that administers the country--in the house that is the (disciplining) neck-stock for all lands,
> the house (called) "The River Ordeal"--has, in its entirety, the black-headed (people), the nation,
> founded a dais for (the divine) "Queen of the Palace" (Ninegalla),
> the king, being a god, will dwell with her on it.
>
> That she take care of the life of all lands,
> that on the day for her to lift the head and take a good look (at the bridegroom),
> on the day of going to bed together, the rites be performed to perfection,[14]
> has it (i.e., the nation) at New Year, the day of the ritual, set up a bed for Mylady.
>
> Halfa straw they have been purifying with cedar perfume,
> have been putting it on that bed for Mylady,
> over it a bedspread has been pulled straight for her,
> a bedspread of heart's delight to make the bed comfortable.
>
> Mylady bathes the holy loins in water,
> bathes them in water for the loins of the king,
> bathes them in water for the loins of Iddin-Dagan.
> Holy Inanna rubs (herself) with soap,
> sprinkles the floor with cedar perfume.
>
> The king goes with lifted head to the holy loins,
> goes with lifted head to the loins of Inanna,
> Amaushumgalanna goes to bed with her.
> In her holy loins he can but truly praise the woman:

"O my one of holy loins! O my holy Inanna!"[15]

After he on the bed, in the holy loins, has made the queen rejoice,
after he on the bed, in the holy loins, has made holy Inanna rejoice,
she in return soothes the heart for him there on her bed:
"Verily, I am the constant prolonger of Iddin-Dagan's days (of life)!"[16]

Beside the Sacred Marriage Drama there is reason to believe that three other fertility dramas existed, the Mourning Drama, the Road of No Return Drama, and the Search and Fetching Drama. In the case of the Mourning Drama we have entries in account texts of the Ur III period mentioning expenses in connection with the ú-sag̃-g̃á "the early grass" rite,[17] a rite which can be plausibly connected with the Dumuzi lament beginning edin-na ú-sag̃-g̃á "In the desert in the early grass (to her husband she drew near)", a lament for the dead Dumuzi in his raided fold.[18] Otherwise the existence of these dramas is conjectural, based on the style of the texts relating to them, a style which it is difficult to account for unless one assumes that they were "scripts" for a dramatic performance. Briefly stated the action of the three dramas is as follows.

The Mourning Drama consisted in a procession into the desert to Dumuzi's raided camp to mourn the slain god.[19] Chief mourners were his young widow, his mother, and his sister. One may surmise that they were represented by cult-statues or emblems carried in procession. Their laments would have been sung for them by singers accompanied by mournful music.

Similar to the Mourning Drama was the Road of No Return Drama[20] which would seem to have its roots in the cult of Damu–god of the sap that rises annually in trees and vegetation–on the lower Euphrates. It took in, though, almost every fertility god of the region as a form of Damu and also the dead kings of Ur III and later dynasties. The rite appears to have been a procession following the mother and sister–there is no widow in this case–in their search for the dead god.[21] Eventually the search leads them down into the Nether World, represented in the cult by a series of sacred tombs where lie various incarnations of the god.[22] The mother's decision to leave the realm of the living is reproved by her son in a song presenting the disembodied spirit of Damu as one with the wind spirits and unreachable.[23] The mother is not to be deterred, however,[24] and a curious set of dialogues based on the theme that the dead can hear the living, but the living cannot hear them, follows. Presumably different singers and musicians performed the laments of the different figures in the rite.[25] Toward the end of the "script" the theme of dialogue becomes a plea by the dead god for proper funerary offerings.[26] The end has the sister join him in the nether world, offering to be both sister and mother to him.[27]

The third such drama, the Search and Fetching Drama,[28] begins with a lament in Uruk expressing anxiety that the god may not come.[29] His mother then sets out to seek him from the nurse–a tree–with whom she left him.[30] Eventually he is found and escorted back to his father, the river-god Enki, in a joyous procession, his worshipers singing paeans of praise to him as the bringer of plenty.[31] Here again the god is identified with a variety of other fertility figures and with the departed kings of the Third Dynasty of Ur and the following Isin and Larsa dynasties.

1. Meaning

Having considered thus–albeit briefly–examples of the texts relating to the religious drama in Mesopotamia in Old Babylonian and earlier times, we may properly ask what the sense of that drama was: What was it meant to achieve?

The only scholar who has addressed himself specifically and at any length to that problem is, as far as we can see, Svend Aage Pallis, who devoted a good part of his book *The Babylonian Akitu Festival* to a general analysis of the Babylonian cult-drama on a broad comparative basis.[32]

Pallis saw the cult-drama as at home in what is generally termed "primitive" cultures, that is to say, "cultures which have their economic basis in hunting, herding, or incipient agriculture." In such cultures religion is generally characterized by "participation." Men identify themselves with the basic powers and elements in nature on which life depends, by way of sympathetic magic, by miming them. Thus, through a direct magical identification with them, and through acting as them, man is able to ensure that they will continue to be present and will function correctly at each transition to a new and untried time-period, each new year. "Men," says Pallis, "are the gods, to speak as Europeans, it is they who create all and through their mimic action of the drama ensure the prosperity of the coming year."[33]

Another scholar, Robert N. Bellah formulates the primitive attitude thus:[34] "In the ritual the participants become identified with the mythical beings they represent. The mythical beings are not addressed or propitiated or beseeched. The distance between man and mythical being, which was at best slight, disappears altogether in the moment of ritual when everywhen becomes now. There are no priests and no congregation, no mediating representative roles and no spectators. All present are involved in the ritual action itself and have become one with the myth."[35]

Between the meaning and function of the cult-drama in its original setting in primitive religions, and its role in more complex civilizations such as that of Ancient Mesopotamia–in the type of religions that Pallis calls "urban," Bellah "archaic"–lie a great many adjustments to more complex context, a great many reinterpretations that must be reckoned with.

Pallis says: "Between these cultures and the urban civilization a great gulf is fixed. The urban type is characterized by the introduction of anthropomorphism into all existence, into Nature and the divine powers, and by the steadily increasing differentiation of the individuals of the community into units having their own peculiar characteristics."[36]

Bellah notes: "The characteristic feature of archaic religion is the emergence of true cult with the complex of gods, priests, worship, sacrifice and in some cases divine or priestly kingship. The myth and ritual complex characteristic of primitive religion continues within the structure of archaic religion, but it is systematized and elaborated in new ways."[37]

Looking over our data for the Sacred Marriage Drama in Mesopotamia with an eye to the two ideal types here outlined, one will note that the "archaic" characteristics are well in evidence: representation rather than action by all; well-defined anthropomorph gods in sociomorph settings; and consonant with the anthropomorphic view, the desired benefits are sought through psychological and social motivation, not by *becoming* the power and *as it* doing what it should do. We have moved from magic to a psychological theurgy.

Besides these general features one notices also what would seem to be a shift in emphasis: from the god as source of all blessings, the goddess as receiving; to the goddess as the source, the god as recipient.

Closest to the drama as it is known in primitive cultures comes a description of the sexual union of the king as Dumuzi and his partner as Inanna, as they consummate their marriage in the Sacred Marriage Drama. The text is the herder's text mentioned above (Ni 9602). The passage which interests us here reads:

At its rising augustly, at its rising augustly,
Did the shoots and the buds rise up
The king's loins! At its rising augustly
Did the vines rise up, did the grains rise up
Did the desert fill (with verdure) like a pleasurable garden.[38]

There is here the same magic identification with the powers, and acting as them directly, that we met with in the primitive drama. The king and his partner "become" the powers to fertility in nature and by uniting when so identified have them function right, produce new life everywhere.

There are, however, also differences. Where a true primitive such drama would have the community participate as a whole--in Java, for instance,[39] we are told of ritual sexual intercourse in the rice fields to make them thrive--we have here already representation. The king and his partner act for the whole. Also, the powers with which they identify are personified, well-defined anthropomorph gods acting within a sociomorph pattern, that of marriage.

The following portions of the text--possibly originally an independent song--carries the anthropomorph mode further: Abundance and plenty is achieved through the allure of the young wife whose charm and rights to be properly maintained makes her wishes a command. Inanna asks, in line after line, for all conceivable milks and milk products, and her loving new husband is only too happy to provide them for her. Anthropomorphism thus imposes on the magically potent sex act the social form of marriage and makes of the abundance aimed at, a gift of love and duty by a new husband, a theurgy of enticement.

The view underlying the text we have just discussed, that the god--Dumuzi, Amaushumgalanna, or whatever--is the real source of the fertility and plenty on which the rite focuses, seems to be that of our oldest data. The long procession of bearers bringing produce as the god's wedding gifts on the Uruk Vase marks him as bringer of plenty, and in the abbreviated versions of the scene on contemporary roll-seals this role of his is indicated by his carrying a huge ear of grain.

The same view also appears in some of our younger sources. In the text in which Inanna dresses for her wedding in jewels she finds on a pile of freshly plucked date clusters, then goes to meet her bridegroom at the gate of the storehouse to take him to that pile, it is clear from many details that Inanna represents the storehouse; the groom, Dumuzi-Amaushumgalanna, the plenty of the incoming date harvest. Correspondingly, the mood is that of relief at having the harvest in, and the safety from want which it means: a young girl finding security in a good marriage.[40]

O that they put his hand in my hand for me,
O that they put his heart next to my heart for me,
Not only is it sweet to sleep hand in hand with him,
Very sweet is also the loveliness of joining heart to heart with him.

Lastly, we may mention the hailing of the king as Amaushumgalanna at the wedding banquet in the Hymn to Inanna as the Evening Star:[41]

The palace is celebrating, the king is joyous
the nation is spending the day amid plenty
Amaushumgal is come in joy
long may he live for us on the pure throne.

Alongside of this view, however, also a diametrically opposed one occurs, according to which the *goddess* is the source of the blessings envisaged, and the god, in the person of the king, the receiver.

The oldest attestation of this reversal of roles is in a hymn to Shulgi which tells how he paid a visit to Inanna in Uruk. The goddess was so delighted to see him that she composed a song about him in which she fondly and in detail recalled his prowess as a lover--presumably remembered from his performance in the Sacred Marriage Rite. In appreciation of this she in turn then blessed him at length, promising her help in battle and council, granting him prowess in all his pursuits and long life. Her motivation she stated as follows (ii. 34):

> as he did well by me on the couch,
> so be the lord done well by:
> let a good fate be decreed for him!
> So be the good shepherd Shulgi done well by:
> let a good fate be decreed for him!
> So be his stout arms truly done well by:
> let the shepherdship of all lands be decreed for them as fate![42]

We thus have here the same theurgy by allure that we met with in Ni 9602, only here it is the allure of the god in the person of the king that wins gifts from the goddess.

That in Isin-Larsa times such enticing of the goddess by his bodily charms actually *was* the role of the king in the Sacred Marriage, and that in fact the whole rite was thought to be enacted in order that he might successfully do so, comes out with remarkable clarity in both of the two explicit statements of the purpose of the rite that we possess.

In the Hymn to Inanna as the Evening Star the reasons for setting up the bridal bed of the rite were given as follows:

> That she take care of the life of all lands,
> that on the day for her to lift the head and take a good look (at the bridegroom),
> on the day of going to bed together, the rites be performed to perfection,
> has it (i.e., the nation) at New Year, the day of the ritual, set up a bed for Mylady.[43]

Even more specific is the Epithalamion (*CT* 42 pl. 4ff.) which says:

> The day has gone to rest--the day was the one ordained,
> the day to take a good look (at the bridegroom) on the (bridal) couch,
> the day for the lord to arouse (desire in) a woman,
> O grant life to the lord!
> Grant to the lord (to wield) all (shepherd's) crooks![44]

This latter text also has--listed by Inanna's handmaiden Ninshubura--the full catalogue of gifts of prosperity and thriving economy that Inanna is expected to grant her bridegroom; but both texts, characteristically, omit all mention of the wedding gifts of plenty brought by the divine bridegroom and the encounter at the gate.

Comparing the two contrary views we have here outlined, it must seem likely that they are not of an age but represent, rather, different understandings of the rite by different generations.

Oldest, it would appear, is the view of the god as ultimate source of the blessings sought, for not only is it the view that seems represented, as we have mentioned, in our older sources; but the god himself–whether Dumuzi or Amaushumgalanna–is inherently, in all we otherwise know about him, a god of fertility and yield, which cannot be said about the highly complex goddess, Inanna.

Younger, probably, is the view of the god as recipient, since that would appear to represent a gradual fading of the divine identity in favor of the human one of the king in whom he was incarnate in the rite. It is noteworthy how ready the texts we have are to recognize the king, even the person of the king, under his identity of Dumuzi-Amaushumgalanna in the rite. The human element appears to vie, apparently successfully, with the divine, and that being so it would have been natural to look to the goddess for the expected blessings rather than to him. A concomitant factor here may have been the dominant position Inanna came to occupy as city goddess of Uruk and in the pantheon of the country generally.

III. THE LATER MATERIALS

1. Survivals

The centuries after Old Babylonian times down to the first millennium have not left many data, so it is only with the first millennium itself that we can take up the story of the cult-drama once more. Our information comes to a large extent from two new types of texts: cultic calendars, which list cult-acts for each month of the year, and cult commentaries, which explain the meaning of individual rites. To a surprising extent the older dramas seem to have survived–at least as types–and in one case we even find that the "script" of such a drama was copied and recopied down to as late as Seleucid time. Specifically we can mention:

a. The Sacred Marriage Drama

The Sacred Marriage Drama survived in the cult of Nabû at Borsippa and quite possibly elsewhere. A cult-calendar published by Reisner in his *Sumerisch-babylonische Hymnen* as no. VIII tells how on the second of Ayyar (ca. May 1) Nabû is dressed in the garment of Anuship and conveyed during the night to the temple Ehurshaba, where he spends the night with his bride.[45] The verbal forms, predominantly passive, suggest strongly that Nabû in this rite was represented by his cult statue, which was carried around in the rite. Quite conceivably a number of erotic songs were performed to enhance the symbolic consummation of the marriage by the two statues. At any rate we possess one such late erotic composition in which Nanâ very childishly, but also very effectively, uses her wiles on Nabû to get him to unite with her.[46]

b. Other Fertility Dramas

Dramas continuing–though in variant forms–the dramatic rites of lament for a vanished god of fertility are attested from Assyria. An incantation[47] found in Assur and intended to persuade Dumuzi to take a troublesome ghost along with him on his journey to the Nether World informs us that the twenty-eighth of the month of Dumuzi (ca. Aug. 13) was called the day of the cattlepen. The twenty-ninth was the day of setting up the couch of Dumuzi, presumably for the dead god to lie in state. The form of the god is here, as shown by addresses to him as shepherd, very clearly that of Dumuzi the shepherd.

Other Assyrian texts seem to see the god rather in his variant form as Dumuzi of the grain.

We possess two letters[48] to the king which deal with the dates for the rites for Dumuzi in the various garrison towns of Assyria. The schedule for Assur, Nineveh, and Calah calls for a display–presumably a lying in state–on the twenty-sixth, twenty-seventh, and twenty-eighth of the month of Dumuzi. Arbela seems to be a day later with the twenty-seventh, twenty-eighth, and twenty-ninth. The first of these days, known as *killum* "the hue and cry" was probably the one when the god was pursued and fled, the second of them was the day of "dehulling (grain)" and should be the day on which he was caught and killed. This is confirmed by a cultic commentary,[49] also from Assur, which may be restored: "The 26th is the day of the hue and cry, on the 27th he is caught, Anu is . . . Dumuzi is interrogated. . . . His death is when they grind the roasted grain that has been thrown on Dumuzi on the millstones, The . . . of roasted grain that is placed there (means): He ascended to the upper regions according to what they say. . . . your brother which they moisten with beer (means): they install the brother in office according to what they say."[50] The last cryptic line reminds of Old Babylonian texts in which Dumuzi's sister Geshtinanna seeks him and is told by an official that he is being prepared for the high office of *enu*.[51] The text then gives a long list of honey, various woods, reed, grapes, silver, herbs, etc., which represent the various parts of "the kidnapped (*hablu*) god's body." Apparently that was the way it was represented in the rite.

The rite generally survived into medieval times, when, we are told, the women of Harran celebrated a rite called "the rattle" at which they wept for Ta'uz, i.e., Tammuz or Dumuzi, whose master cruelly ground his bones in a mill. The women during this celebration also abstain from all milled foods.[52] In reading this description one cannot but wonder at how closely the rite seems to have reverted to, or rather, locally has never left, the primitive form of the cult-drama, with no representatives and with minimal distance between men and mythical beings.

While the Dumuzi rites, as the evidence shows, were actually performed, there is more uncertainty whether the rite we called The Road of No Return did in fact continue to be performed, or survived as a literary document only. Any clear-cut answer is not possible on the evidence we have, but we tend to believe it was, since otherwise its popularity, attested to by the frequency with which it was copied to the latest times, would be hard to understand. As to Ishtaran, who is one of the incarnations of Damu, we are told in an Assyrian cultic commentary that at a given time Ishtar sets up a wailing for her brother Ishtaran and that something she is carrying into her temple is his body which she is interring.[53]

So far very unclear are lamentation rites for Enmesharra in Tebet (Feb.).[54] Except for the fact that he is an underworld deity and a remote ancestor of Enlil, little is known about him that could throw light on the rite. Often indeed, he seems to have been considered an enemy power.

2. The Battle Drama

New in the first millennium is a wholely different type of cult-dramas, the Battle Drama. It takes two recognizably different forms: The Battle of Ninurta against Anzu, the Asakku, or Enmeshara, and the Battle of Marduk against Tiāmat, Kingu and–oddly enough–Anu and Enlil.

a. Anzu and Enmeshara (Footrace and Chariot)

The curious text *KAR* 143 and duplicates–a text to which we shall return presently–states in lines 57-60 that "the footrace which they run in the month of Kislimu before

Bēl in all cult-centers is because Ashur sent Ninurta to capture Anzu. Nergal stated before Ashur: Anzu is captured. Ashur (said) to Nergal: 'Go! give the good news to all the gods. . . .'" A pictorial representation of the chase which this footrace reenacts is preserved for us on a relief from Ashurnasirpal's Ninurta Temple in Nimrūd.[55] It shows the god winged and armed with thunderbolts pursuing a winged lion, which represents Anzu.

Another form of dramatic presentation of this victory seems to be by means of a chariot returning from the wars. An entry in *LKA* 71 and 72, which replaces Ninurta with Nabû, says "The chariots that they have come with show of martial prowess from the desert and enter the center of the city: That is Nabû. He [has killed] Anzu,"[56] and with replacement of Anzu by Enlil *CT* XV 44 states "The chariots that they have come with great show of martial prowess. The third man on the chariot who [took] the goad (?) from (?) . . . . took his hand and leads him in before the goddess and is showing the goad to the goddess and the king, is because he is Nabû whom they sent against Enlil. He captured him. Nergal seized his hand and led him into Esagila and showed the weapon of his hand to Marduk, king of the gods, and Ṣarpanītu so that they were kissing him and blessing him."[57] Lastly *KAR* 307 mentions a chariot from Elam without its seat in which the king rides. It carries the body of Enmeshara. The king represented the victor, Ninurta. The horses drawing the chariot are the ghosts of Anzu. This chariot is driven up to the Temple of Enmeshara and the horses are tethered there.[58]

b. Kingu, Tiāmat, etc.

The Babylonian Epic of Creation, *Enûma elish*, which tells how Marduk "vanquished Tiāmat and assumed kingship" is generally–probably rightly–assumed to be a cult-myth corresponding to a dramatic ritual reenactment of this primordial battle each new year at the Akitu festival. However, our knowledge about that ritual itself is scant in the extreme. We know that, on the tenth of Nisan, Marduk--almost certainly represented by his cult-statue--was carried in procession down to the river where he was put on board his barge and conveyed to the Akitu house, E-shizkur, outside the city; that a feast during which he received gifts from all the gods was celebrated there, on the eleventh, and that then he returned to Babylon.[59] Professor Lambert has suggested that the battle with Tiamat was enacted symbolically by placing Marduk's statue on a dais in the Akitu house. He bases himself on a line in an ancient commentary stating that Marduk at the Akītu festival sits inside Tiāmat.[60] He may well be right. Perhaps, though, that seating of Marduk represents rather Marduk's establishing his abode, Esharra, on the body of Tiāmat. His victory could then have been symbolized by his boat ride over the waters out to the Akītu house. In support of such a suggestion one could quote his boatman-name Sirsir ". . . who crossed over the vast Tiāmat in his anger, passed over and over, as on a bridge the place of the duel with her" and the name Sirsir-malah: "Tiāmat was his vessel, he her boatman."[61]

Not usable for reconstructing what went on at the Akitu festival is, unfortunately, a lengthy cultic commentary known as The Death and Resurrection of Marduk. This text, as conclusively shown by von Soden,[62] cannot be taken at face value. It represents an Assyrian anti-Babylonian propaganda which reinterprets events during the Akitu as representing a trial of Marduk for rebelling against Ashur. *Enûma elish* is here an exhibit for the prosecution, and Marduk defends himself by saying that everything he did was for the glory of Ashur.[63] Actually the version of *Enûma elish* we have–based on Assyrian copies –blurs the story of Marduk's being elected king before the battle with Tiāmat, by having him act as a mere subordinate of "King Anshar" both when he challenges Tiāmat and when he reports back to him that his mission has been successful.[64] The cult-acts which the text subjects to its biased interpretations were, it is true, probably genuine parts of the rites in Babylon, but unhappily they do not in themselves constitute any recognizable or meaningful pattern.

A series of ritual acts that fairly closely reflect the story told in *Enûma elish* are recorded in Assyrian (*CT* XV 44). This text, after a lacuna of two lines, mentions a rite performed over a well. It represents "[Ea who] cast a spell over Enlil in the Apsû and entrusted him to the Anunnaki."[65] Clearly, except for the substitution of Enlil for Apsû, a reference to Ea's victory over Apsû. Next comes somebody, probably the king, lighting a fire. He represents Marduk who as a child . . . Then somebody, probably the *kurgaru,* play the *kiskilāti* instruments. They are the gods his father and brothers when they heard something, probably the news of his birth. Then something or someone is lifted up. That is Marduk whom Ninlil lifted up as a child and the gods kissed him.[66] We then jump to Marduk's championing the gods against the older powers. A brazier is lighted before Ninlil. A ram is placed on it and is burned in the fire. That is Kingu whom they burn in fire. "The torches which they light at the brazier are the unsparing arrows of the quiver of Bel which as they are shot off create surpassing fear, kill in their mighty striking home, are dyed in blood and gore."[67] After a cryptic line or two we hear that the king, wearing jewels on his pate, burns a sheep. He represents Marduk who carried firewood on his pate and burned the sons of Enlil and Anu in the fire. Next the king breaks open a *ḫariu* pot during a footrace. That is Marduk who in his onrush subdued Tiamat.[68]

While the killing of Kingu in this text is represented by the act of burning a ram, other symbolic representations of it are mentioned elsewhere. In *KAR* 307 a bull and a number of rams are cast down from the roof and thus killed. They represent Kingu and his seven sons whom they slay. A dove, which they cast down is Tiāmat, whom they cast down and kill.[69] This same rite is referred to in *LKA* 75, which says, "The 18th day which is called 'the silence' they cast Kingu together with his 40 sons down from the roof. The cream and honey that they put into the earthenware box they put as an image of their blood."[70]

c. Anu and Enlil

But not only Anzu, Enmeshara, Kingu, and Tiāmat are killed in these symbolic dramas, very often their place is taken by Anu and Enlil.

In the cultic calendar which mentions Nabû's sacred marriage in Ayyar that rite is followed on the seventh by his being taken to the garden of Anu, where he sits down in token of having taken the kingship from Anu. Later on he puts on Anu's crown.[71]

More explicit is *LKA* 73, which says, "The 18th, which is called 'The Silence,' is when they bind Anu and the Sibitti, the sons of Enmeshara." The next day is "The 19th, 'The Wrath,' the day the king binds Anu, the day Marduk binds Anu." On the twenty-first: "he tears out the eyes of the Enlils and puts them up on display."[72] The twenty-fourth is the day when "the king wears the crown, the lord severed the neck of Anu . . . as he assumed the kingship, bathed in water and dressed in a robe."[73] On this day they also dip a leper in the river, the leper is Anu (a play on the word *garabānu=garab Anu* "(the) leper Anu").[74]

No less ferocious is *CT* XV 44 which describes a ritual play with a loaf of bread by the king and the bishop (*sangu*). "The king who makes the bishop bounce a loaf baked in ashes with him. They are Marduk and Nabû. Marduk bound Anu and broke his . . . the loaf baked in ashes that they bounce is the heart of Anu as he pulled it out with his hands and . . ."[75]

A very similar rite is recorded in *LKA* 71: "The drinking bowl, in the opening of which is a *kakkusu* loaf, is the skull of the opponent of Anshar, in as much as Bel prevailed, bound Anu, dragged along his corpse, entrusted it to the Anunnaki (saying): 'Anu is in bonds with you!' As he flayed off his skin and clad his enemy Sipazianna (i.e., Orion) in it he also laid (?) Anu on top of the cut-off head."[76]

3. Meaning

If we ask, then, what happened to the ritual drama between Old Babylonian times and the first millennium, we can cite, of course, a great deal of survival and even some new examples of fertility dramas; but the fertility dramas no longer hold the center of the stage as before, nor is it always certain that they retain their earlier meaning, and have not been reinterpreted.

An example from *LKA* 72 may be quoted: "The woman of the city whom they lift up upon their heads and on their necks and then go into the fields and scatter seed corn–that is Bêl as he treads on the neck of those disobedient to him. They scatter seed corn as much as their hands (will hold) just as he is going to fill the desert (with corpses)."[77] The rite by itself could not more clearly identify itself as a rite of sowing. The interpretation given, however, rides roughshod over that original sense, makes the woman into Bêl, sees only that she is carried, and reinterprets the seed corn scattered as symbols of enemy corpses. A great deal of caution is indicated, therefore, and the fact that a rite survives does not guarantee that it preserves its original meaning.

What did survive was, as we have seen, the form of the Marriage Drama. As carried out with statues of Nabû and Nanâ as chief actors it is clear, however, that the old role of the king as vying for divine favors has disappeared. What took its place is not clear from our scant materials. Perhaps only a sense of sharing, as dependents, in the great events in the life of the divine master and mistress.

The death and lament drama of Dumuzi seems very likely to have retained its purpose of strengthening emotional ties with the god–especially in the case of Dumuzi of the grain where the death of the god has in fact been brought about by his worshipers and where the rite of lament is therefore one of great ambivalence and covert guilt.

The Road of No Return Drama survived in its script, which was faithfully copied and recopied. One can only guess, but a continuation of both performance and of the old aim of strengthening emotional ties would seem the most likely interpretation.

Turning from the survivals to look at the new form of drama that meets us in the first millennium, the Battle Drama, we may note to begin with that what would seem to be the earliest one attested, the battle of Ninurta with Anzu or the Asakku in January (Kislîmu) enacted as a footrace (*lismu*), appears to be in origin a fertility drama. Ninurta is the god of the thunderstorms of spring, and the relief from his temple at Calah actually shows him chasing–in a footrace high up in the air–Anzu or the Asakku, the hailstorm, throwing his lightening bolts as he is chasing away winter to issue in spring.[78]

As the footrace rite represents and recreates that chase for the new year, so does the other dramatic presentation: The return of the king, representing Ninurta, in his chariot after his victory. Since the chariot is known as a symbol of Ninurta and, indeed, because of its thundering noise, a symbol of most thundergods, the dramatic performance is clearly one representing the forces of spring, the thundershowers. However, when Nabû takes the place of Ninurta[79] and Enlil the place of Anzu (as in *CT* XV 44:24)[80] the link to forces in nature is lost, Nabû is no thundergod, nor has Enlil any connection with Spring.

While with Ninurta and Anzu an original base in a beneficent natural phenomenon can–or even must–be assumed, the case is different with the other form that the Battle Drama takes, that of Marduk and Tiāmat. Here, though the name Tiāmat means "the sea" and Marduk's attack on her in *Enûma elish* is clearly depicted as the onset of a thunderstorm, it is difficult to imagine any significant natural event in the Mesopotamian year that would pit the thundercloud against the sea; in fact it is even difficult to see what role the sea, far away to the south, could play in the consciousness of the average Babylonian.[81]

This being so, one should perhaps ask oneself whether such hostilities between divine powers as lie at the root of the Battle Drama as a form are necessarily limited to the realm of nature? Can they be found in other realms of existence also? Thus phrased the answer to the question is obvious: The realm of history has divine enmities and wars in abundance. For Mesopotamia in the first millennium it will be enough to point to Ashur and Marduk in Assyrian times as their rivalry finds expression, e.g., in the Assyrian commentary interpreting events at the New Year festival in Babylon as phases in a trial of Marduk for treason against Ashur, or in the statement of the commentary *KAR* 307 and its interpretation, "Meslamtaea is Marduk who goes down to the Nether World. He goes down because Anshar (i.e., Ashur) pursued him to the hole and he closed his door."[82] Nor can there be any doubt about the basis for the divine enmity. Ashur and Marduk, whatever they originally may have been, have become national gods and so bearers of the aspirations and enmities of the nations they represent.

If we return, with this in mind, to the battle between Marduk and Tiāmat and assume, accordingly, Marduk to represent Babylon, it would be natural to see in Tiāmat, or Tâmti as her name is often given, the "Sealand," the "land of Tâmti," *mat tâmti*, which was Babylon's chief opponent in the early half of the second millennium. The kingship Marduk achieved by his victory would then represent the kingship of the unified Babylonian world, such as it existed after the unification under Ulamburiash–but pushed back into mythical times.

If we may adopt such a political-historical view, a great many things become clearer. It has long been a *crux* why Enlil, one of the highest gods, is given no role to play in *Enûma elish*. As a political figure, however, Enlil represented Nippur and the South and was therefore on the enemy side. This role as enemy–puzzling without its historical context–comes to the fore in the ritual commentaries we have considered. Here both Enlil of Nippur and Anu of Uruk are enemies to be killed and tortured together with, or instead of, the other representatives of the South: Tiāmat and Kingu. In the material we also saw a shift replacing Ninurta as hero with Nabû, especially in materials of Babylonian origin. This again is understandable, since Ninurta as son of Enlil would be less acceptable than the son of Marduk, Nabû. Lastly we may perhaps point to the curious indefiniteness of the ritual of the New Year festival in Babylon, which does not at any point give us the clear-cut battle ritual one expects. Very likely, however, this festival was older than the battle theme. We know that as an Akītu festival it has its origins in an agricultural festival of seed-ploughing; so the battle theme, political in origin, may then well have been superimposed–as interpretations in abstract symbolic fashion–upon rites that originally had no such meaning.

With such interpretation superimposed the originally agricultural festival became a national festival: a reenactment–perhaps a recreation and reaffirmation–of the birth of the nation out of a battle for unification, but with the battle given cosmic scope and made primeval in a myth that was–in Malinowski's terms–a "charter" for Babylonia.

IV. CONCLUSION

To sum up then: We believe with Pallis that the cultic drama in Mesopotamia as elsewhere has its roots back in "primitive" society, that is, one based on hunting, herding, or incipient agriculture. Here the drama was a rite of direct sympathetic magic aiming to create fertility. Man as a group became one with the powers for fertility and did *as them* what should be done.

With the advent of Mesopotamian urban society anthropomorphism came to dominate the scene. Our fullest data are from a rather advanced phase early in the second millennium. The drama was now performed by representatives of the community such as the king, and the simple act of sexual congress was seen under the anthropomorphic and sociomorphic forms of love and marriage, binding the power for plenty to the community in strong psychological and social bonds. The same new theurgy through love underlies the sociomorphic rites of laments for the god's death, while the Search and Fetching Drama may well go back to, and retain the character of, original direct magic action.

The first millennium saw the survival of many of the earlier dramas of fertility, but the way they were now understood is not always clear. A new drama, the Battle Drama, came to dominate. Although in some cases rooted in older fertility dramas, this new form comes to be the preferred vehicle for a new *political* drama celebrating and reaffirming the birth of the nation as a divine achievement that was from the beginning, in mythical time.

It may be added in conclusion that this development is entirely on a line with the general trend of Mesopotamian religion in these millennia, from a nature religion to one of political cast: a democratic pluralism seeing the cosmos as a state ruled by a general assembly, and on from there to monarchy and exclusive and jealous nationalism.

NOTES

1 We use the term "religious drama" to denote cultic rituals which can be considered "drama" in that they "imitate or, to use a more modern term, 'represent' action by introducing the personages taking part in them as real, and as employed in the action itself" (A. W. Ward, *Encyclopaedia Britannica,* 11th ed., vol. 8, 475). In the data with which we are here concerned it may be considered axiomatic that the degree of "reality" accorded the acts involved was extremely high or even absolute.

2 For the Sacred Marriage Drama in Mesopotamia see Svend Aa. Pallis, *The Babylonian Akītu Festival,* Det Kgl. Danske Videnskabernes Selskab, Historisk-filologiske Meddelelsen XII, 1 (Copenhagen, 1926) 197-200, 247-48. Raymond Jestin, *Archiv Orientální* 17 (1949) 333-39; J. van Dijk, "La fête du nouvel an dans un texte de Šulgi," *Bibliotheca Orientalis* 11 (1954) 83ff.; and S. N. Kramer, *The Sacred Marriage Rite* (Bloomington, Ind., 1969). It is not possible for us to accept--even on major points of interpretation--all and everything in the views stated by these scholars, but we acknowledge gratefully the stimulus we have received from them.

3 A clear account of the Sumerian wedding ceremonies is offered in S. N. Kramer, *Sumerian Literary Texts from Nippur in the Museum of the Ancient Orient at Istanbul, AASOR* 23 (New Haven, 1944) no. 35, a myth about Inanna and Dumuzi. See my outline of its contents *BASOR* 102 (1946) 13-15. Also S. Greengus, "Old Babylonian Marriage Ceremonies and Rites," *JCS* 20 (1966) 55-72, esp. 69ff.; and "The Old-Babylonian Marriage Contract," *JAOS* 89 (1969) 505-32, esp. 522f. See also Kramer, *The Sacred Marriage Rite,* 76f. For the escorting to the bridal chamber and the banquet the next morning we have only the evidence of the ritual texts to go by.

4 H. Heinrich, *Kleinfunde aus den archaischen Tempelschichten in Uruk* (Leipzig, 1936) 15-16 and pls. 2-3, 38. For supplementary materials see E. Douglas van Buren, "The Ear of Corn," *Or* 12 (1935) 327-35.

5 Thorkild Jacobsen, "Early Political Development in Mesopotamia," *ZA* 52 (1957) 91-140, n. 32; reprinted in *TIT,* 376, n. 32.

6 Expenses in connection with the rite of the sacred marriage as it was celebrated in the cult of Dumuzi in Umma are listed in economic documents from that city of Ur III date. They include: 1 [udu] 1 máš/níĝ-mu(nus)-ús-sá ^{d}Dumu-zi-da "One sheep (and) one kid (for) the wedding gifts of Dumuzi" (Nikolskij, *Dokumenty chozjajstvennoj otčetnosti drevnej Chaldei iz sobranija N. P. Lichačeva, čast' II* [Moscow, 1915] no. 372) and 7 gu-niĝín ^{ĝiš}ma-nu/níĝ-mu(nus)-ús-sá ^{d}Dumu-zi "Seven cords of cornel (sticks) . . ." (ibid., 204). Very likely the entry 3 udu-ú 3 máš ^{d}Dumu-zi en-šè ĝen-na "3 grassfed sheep (and) 3 kids (for) Dumuzi going to the high priestess (*entu*)" in N. Schneider, *Die Geschäftsurkunden aus Drehem und Djoha in den staatlichen Museen (VAT) zu Berlin, Or* 47-49, no. 344 (1930) 18-19 also refers to Dumuzi–i.e., to the person incarnating him at Umma--bringing his wedding gift to Inanna, as incarnated in the high priestess (en:*entum*). All these texts are dated to the twelfth month which in Umma was named from the Festival of Dumuzi, i.e., the rite of his marriage.

Other deities whose sacred marriages were celebrated were Ningirsu and Baba of Girsu and Urukug in Lagash (al-Hiba). A tablet of the Agade Period (F. Thureau-Dangin,

Inventaire des Tablettes de Telloh [Paris, 1910] I, no. 1225; see A. Falkenstein, *Die neusumerischen Gerichtsurkunden* [Munich, 1956], vol. I, 104, n. 2) lists the wedding gifts which Ningirsu brought to Baba in Urukug at their "sacred marriage" each New Year. A little later Gudea lists these gifts in a statue inscription (St. E. v 1-vii 21) as ud-zag-mu ezen-^{d}Ba-ba$_6$ níg̃-mu(nus)-ús-sá-ak-da "the wedding gifts to be presented on New Year's day, the festival of Baba." He also tells how he increased them. In another statue inscription (St. G. ii 1-16) he tells how nig-mu(nus)-ús-sá šag$_4$-ḫúl-la ^{d}Nin-g̃ír-su-ke$_4$ ^{d}Ba-ba$_6$-dumu-an-na-dam-ki-ág̃a-ni-mu-na-ta-ak-ke$_4$ ding̃ir-ra-ni ^{d}Nin-g̃iš-zi-da egir-bi íb-ús Gù-dé-a ensi(k) Lagaša^{ki}-ke$_4$ G̃ír-su^{ki}-ta Uru-kug-šè silim-ma im-da-bé "he made his (personal) god Ningishzida escort the bridal gifts which Ningirsu in joy of heart presents to Baba child of An his beloved spouse. Gudea, ruler of Lagash was (vying) with him (in) offering (greetings of) peace (all the way) from Girsu (i.e., Tello) to Urukug (in Lagash = al Hiba)."

Since a man's personal god is normally present in his body, we may assume that what Gudea here tells us is that he himself, aided by his personal god Ningishzida, was bringing the wedding gifts to Baba. Moreover, since that task was the task of the bridegroom and the text explicitly states that Ningirsu brought them, it is perhaps not too bold to assume that Gudea, as ruler, represented and incarnated also Ningirsu on this occasion, particularly since all later sources consistently show the ruler–the king–in the role of divine bridegroom.

7 De Genouillac, *Textes religieux sumériens du Louvre*, *TCL* 15-16 (Paris, 1930) no. 70. See my n. 32 in "Early Political Development in Mesopotamia," *ZA* 52 (1957) 108 = *TIT*, 375. See also S. N. Kramer's study of the text in *Proceedings of the American Philosophical Society* 107 (Philadelphia, 1963) 495ff.

A few specific suggestions may be made. In lines 3-4, lú-zú-lum-ri-ri-ge mu-nim-mar an-[. . .]/kug ^{d}Inanna-ra lú-zú-lum-ri-ri-ge nu-nim-mar [an-. . .] "the dategatherer has . . .ed the datepalm/ the dategatherer has . . .ed the datepalm for holy Inanna," the missing verb was most likely one denoting "ascended" or "plucked." Accordingly, we would read the sign A of lines 5 and 6 as duru$_5$ "fresh ones"–the designation duru$_5$ = *raṭbu* is frequent with fresh dates (*u$_4$-ḫi-in-nu*)--and tentatively translate duru$_5$ ḫé-en-na-du duru$_5$ ḫé-en-na-du dúb (= *arḫānû*) g̃i$_6$-ga/^{d}Inanna-ra duru$_5$-da(?) ⌜sig$_7$⌝(?) ḫe-en-na-du dúb (= *arḫānû*) babbar-ra(!) as "May he take fresh ones to her! May he take fresh ones to her (namely) dark early ripened ones, may he take beside them fresh ones to Inanna (namely) light-colored early ripened ones." We see the verb in these lines as expressing a wish, the fulfillment of which is stated in lines 7-8 and read accordingly the sign DU as du, the "present future" and "plural" root of the verb for "take," "bring" (see *MSL* IV, 148.8). The sign which we restore ⌜sig$_7$⌝ is given as damaged in de Genouillac's copy; Kramer (after collation?) reads it as DU$_6$. If slightly damaged these two signs can look much alike. For the qualification of fresh dates (*uḫinnu*) as "light-colored" (babbar), "dark" (gi$_6$), and "ripened yellow" (sig$_7$-sig$_7$-al-se$_6$-ga), see *MSL* V, 121:335-36, and 340.

In lines 7-8, since du$_6$ "mound," "heap" seems to us awkward as direct object of de$_6$ (DU) "to take, bring," we prefer to read and translate: lú na-de$_6$ lú na-de$_6$ du$_6$-za-pàd-šè na-de$_6$/ki-sikil ^{d}Inanna<-ra> lú na-de$_6$ du$_6$-za-pàd-šè na-de$_6$ "The man has decided to take them to her, the man has decided to take them to her, has decided to take them to the gem-revealing heap. The man has decided to take them to the maiden Inanna, has decided to take them to the gem-revealing heap." The basic meaning of pàd is "find," "reveal" rather than "pick."

In lines 9-10 we assume that the full form of du$_6$ was dur. See *JNES* 12 (1953) 183 (=*TIT,* 347) n. 60.

Lines 26-33, which record the encounter of Inanna and Dumuzi at the gate, we would read and translate: lú-du$_6$-ra-^{na4}za-gìn-ri-ri-ga-ra en gaba-na mu-ri/ ^{d}Inanna-du$_6$-ra-^{na4}za-gìn-ri-ri-ga-ra ^{d}Dumu-zi-da mu-ri gab(a)!?<-na> mu-ri/ [PA] -⌜USAN⌝ An-na kuš$_8$ ^{d}En-líl-lá en gaba-na mu-ri/ É-an-na na-gada ^{d}En-líl-lá en gaba-na mu-ri/ $^{g̃iš}$ig-^{na4}za-gìn-na-g̃i$_6$-par$_4$-ra-gub-ba en gaba-na mu-ri/ $^{g̃iš}$ig-sal-é-uš-gíd-da-É-an-na-ka-gub-ba ^{d}Dumu-zi gaba-na mu-ri/ du$_6$-ra gaba-bi-a im-mi-in-gur-ru-a/ ^{d}Inanna-ke$_4$ du$_6$-ra gaba-bi-a im-mi-in-gur-ru-a/ mí-e níg̃-i-lu-lam-ma-na imi šu-tag-ba ḫé-⌜ku$_4$⌝(!?)-⌜ku$_4$⌝(!?) "The lord has met her of the lapis lazuli (gems) gathered on the heap, Dumuzi has met Inanna, her of the lapis lazuli (gems) gathered on the heap./ The shepherd of An, the herdsman of Enlil, the lord has met her,/ the herdsman of An, the cowherd of Enlil, Dumuzi, has met her,/ in the door (with ornaments) of lapis lazuli that stands in the Giparu the lord has met her,/ in the narrow door of the storehouse that stands in Eanna Dumuzi has met her,/ him whom she will bring back to the surface of the heap, him whom Inanna will bring back to the surface of the heap,/ (him) may she, caressing and crooning, take into its clay plaster (covering)."

Lines 34-36 tell how Inanna sends a messenger to her father. Read perhaps ki-sikil-e [...d]u$_{11}$-ga-ni-a (Thus Kramer after collation) a-a-ni-šè lú mu-un-gi$_4$/ ^{d}Inanna ki-e-ne-di-ba ⌜sud⌝(!?)-a a-a-ni-šè lú mu-un-gi$_4$ "The maiden amid shouts (of joy) sent a man to her father,/ Inanna, moving as in a dance (for joy) sent a man to her father." Her message—in eme-sal—covers lines 37-47: ma-mu ma-mu-a dè-ma-ab-bu-NE 38)ga-ša-an-mèn ma-mu ma-mu-a dè-ma-ab-bu-NE 39)ma-mi-par$_4$-ra-mu-a dè-ma-ab-bu-NE 40)$^{g̃iš}$ná-gi$_4$-rin-na-mu un-na-ab-gub-bu-uš(!?) (Text NE) 41)ú-za-gìn-dur$_5$-ru-[m]u dè-ma-ab-par$_4$-ge-NE 42)me-e mu-l[u] šà!-ba!-mu ⌜dè⌝(!)-ma-ni ib-ku$_4$-ku$_4$-NE 43)^{d}Ama!-ušum-gal-an-na-mu dè-ma-ni-ib-ku$_4$-ku$_4$-NE 44)šu-ni šu-mu-ta dè-ma-da-⌜mà⌝-ma-NE 45)šà-ba-ni! šà-ab-mu-ta dè-ma-da-ma-⌜ma⌝-NE 46)šu šu(!?)-⌜šè⌝ ⌜ma⌝-al-la-na ù-ku-bi zé-ba an-ga 47)šà-šà-ba-tab-ba-na ḫi-li-bi ku$_7$-ku$_7$-da an-ga "O that they rush into my house, my house for me!/ O that they rush into my house, my house for me who am the mistress!/ O that they rush into my Giparu house for me!/ When they have set up my pure couch for him,/ O that they spread for me my lustrous lapis lazuli (hued) straw!/ O that they have the man of my heart (lit. "my man of the heart") come in to me!/ O that they have my Ama-ushum-gal-anna come in to me!/ O that they put his hand in my hand for me!/ O that they put his heart next my heart for me!/ Not only is it sweet to sleep hand in hand(?) with him,/ very sweet is also the loveliness of joining heart to heart with him."

Reasons for reading the 3p. pl. durative mark NE as dè are given in *AS* 16, 99f., n. 19. To the passages there quoted add *CT* XVI pl. 14 iv. 36/37 nam-ba-gur-ru-da : *a-a i-tu-ru-ni* "may they not come back" (for de>da, see Poebel, *GSG*, §476). In line 40 we assume -bu-NE at the end of the line to be the dittography of the -bu-NE of the lines above and emend to -bu-uš!? The use of the signs G̃Á (MÀ) and MA as freely interchangeable ways of rendering the syllable ma as here in lines 44 and 45 is not infrequent in Emesal contexts. In line 46 emendation to šu-šu(!??)-⌜šè⌝ seems indicated by the parallelism of lines 44-45 with 46-47. The copy suggests a damaged KA with inscribed other sign, perhaps KA×ŠU : *ikribu*. If so the scribe could have misheard a dictated šu-šu-šè-ma-al-la-na as šu-šudi-šè-ma-al-la-na "(the sleep) of (i.e., after) his raising the hand for a blessing (is sweet)."

[8]See S. N. Kramer, *JCS* 18 (1964) 38-39; and 23 (1970) 11; *Proceedings of the American Philosophical Society* 107 (Philadelphia, 1963) 501ff.; and his *The Sacred Marriage Rite,* 81-84. The text begins with an address to Inanna describing the Temple Ezida in which the wedding is to take place. 1)["The . . . of the temple x]-⸢y⸣-g̃uru 2)The well orderedness of the temple of Eridu 3)The cleanness of the temple of Suen 4)and the (firmly) planted (protective) gateposts (urù-rú-a) of Eanna 5)were verily given (as gifts) into the hands of the house 6)my (dear) Ezida floats like a cloud (i.e., it is situated high up on a ziggurat on high terrace) 7)and is, too, a name of good omen (i.e., the name Ezida 'the good house' is a propitious one)."

Next the narrator reports to Inanna on the preparation of the bridal suite: 8)The pure (bridal) couch, being like unto lapis lazuli 9)which Gibil was (ritually) cleaning for you in Irigal 10)has someone greatly fit for (ministering to) queenship "filled with his seaweed (i.e., if umun$_5$ umuna:*alāpu* is meant; actually one expects šu!-mu-un-na-ni "his halfa straw") for you 12)In the house, which he has cleaned for you with his reed cuttings (see *MSL* VII, 55, line 362, gi-diri: MIN (*ḫu-ṣ*[*a-bu*]) he is setting up the laver for you."

At this point the narrator takes occasion to remind Inanna that the time to retire has come and that this is a very special occasion: ud ba-an-ná ud ba-an-dug$_{11}$/ ud-ki-nú-a-i-bí-kár-kár-dam/ ud-ù-mu-un-e-munus-zi-zi-i-dam ù-mu-un-ra nam-tìl zé-ém-mà-a 13)The day has gone to rest, the day is (the one) ordained (cf. ud-du$_{11}$-ga:*adannu*, e.g., *CAD* A.s.v. *adannu*), 14)The day for looking over (the bridegroom) on the (bridal couch) 15)the day for the king to arouse (desire in) a woman (zi corresponds to Akkadian *tebû* "to be sexually aroused"; see W. G. Lambert, *Babylonian Wisdom Literature* [Oxford, 1960] 218 rev. iv. 15) 16)(O) grant life to the king! (for the orthography cf. *MSL* IV, 44:176 which probably goes back to a Babylonian mà $^{\text{ma!}}$zé-èm)." In line 13 ná may be for original nà: "The day has been named."

In line 18 the narrator then reports that Inanna has indicated a wish to go to bed: al ba-an-dug$_4$ al ba-an-dug$_4$ ki-nú al ba-an-dug$_4$ "She has called for it, she has called for it, she has called for the couch," and in lines 19-22 the statement is repeated with the couch described as "the couch of heart's delight" (line 19), "the couch of the sweet loins" (line 20), "the royal couch" (line 21) and "the queenly couch" (line 22). As a good housekeeper the bride personally puts the finishing touches to the making of the bed. The narrator reports: 23)"Along with her making it comfortable (zé-ba-ni-da), along with her making it comfortable, along with her making the couch comfortable . . . 29)she spreads out [the bedding for the king] spreads out the bedding for him 30)spreads out [the bedding for the beloved] spreads out the bedding for him/ ii 1)[To the couch made comfortable by her she calls the] ki[ng] ii 2)To the couch made comfortable by her she calls the beloved/ ii 3)calls to him (with) promises of life, promises of long (life-)time." The bride's call is heeded by her trusty handmaiden Ninshubur who has been waiting for it to bring the bridegroom in/"ii 4)Ninshubura the trusty handmaiden of Eanna/ ii 5)staying awake (MES with gloss di-li-ib) has gone about her goodly office/ ii 6)has led him, bewigged, in to the loins of Inanna." The following lines, ii 7-iii 5, are taken up with Ninshubura's long list of blessings Inanna is to confer on the king. The consummation of the marriage is reported in the somewhat broken following section:

iii 6)"The king goes with lifted head to the holy loins/ iii 7)goes with lifted head to the ho[ly loins of Inan]na/ iii 8)the king going [with lif]ted head/ iii 9)going with lifted [he]ad to Mylady,/ iii 10)–after he has gone to bed with her and has done well by her (we read ki-nú! ù-[un-da-ak] mí ⸢un⸣-[n]a-dug$_4$-ta)/ iii 11)he puts [his arms] around the sacred one (⸢mu⸣-g[ib]) [Inanna]." The remainder of the text is badly broken.

9 See the careful edition by W. H. Ph. Römer in his *Sumerische 'Königshymnen' der Isin Zeit* (Leiden, 1965) no. 6. Römer gives a full bibliography (add now S. N. Kramer, *The Sacred Marriage Rite,* 64-66) and exhaustive notes. Our own suggestions are given in nn. 13-16 below.

10 Ni 9602 published by S. N. Kramer in *Proceedings of the American Philosophical Society* 107 (Philadelphia, 1963) 505-8 and 519-20; see his *The Sacred Marriage Rite,* 58-62.

11 We read col. i 27)a mu-ši-tu$_5$ na-ma mu-ši-su-ub 28)⸢šen⸣ a-tu$_5$-a lagar ù-mu-ši-tum 29)túg-mu túg-ám-kala-ga-dím si ba-sá-e 30)túg pala$_2$-maḫ mu-na-kala-ge-en and translate "27)I bathed myself and rubbed myself with soap (lit. "potash") 28)and when the servant had brought me the bathwater-ewer (for rinsing) 29)she was (helping) arranging my garment as a reinforcement garment 30)and I was reinforcing (thus) the large queenly robe (to look my best) to him." The term túg . . . . . kalag means literally "strengthen cloth," "to reinforce cloth," its Akkadian equivalent *gubbu* "to patch (cloth)." The underlying concept seems thus to be one of strengthening by providing a double thickness. We understand the passage to say that after the servant-girl has brought Inanna the water she needs to rinse off her well-soaped body, the girl stays to help her arrange her garment so that it will serve as undergarment for the queenly robe, thus adding fullness to the material in the latter. On large garments as typical of wealth, see my note in E. I. Gordon, *Sumerian Proverbs* (Philadelphia, 1959) 471, to line 176.

12 Col. ii 1-2, which resume the text after the lacuna are badly broken. In lines 3-13, if we understand them correctly, Inanna wishes that her self-praise be widely known, be made into a song for all to sing. We read and restore ii 3-13 as follows: 3)šà-⸢ab⸣-mu a-ra-zu-a mu-ni-[ib-kúš] 4)kug-a-ra-zu-a mi-⸢ri⸣-p[à-dè-en] 5)túg-maḫ túg-kalag-ga-ša-an-an-na-me-[en] 6)gala-e šèr-ra mu-ni-íb-[ra-ra] 7)nar-e èn-du-⸢a⸣ mu-ni-ib-[e$_{11}$-e] 8)mu-ut-na-mu mu-da-an-[ḫúl-le] 9)am ^{d}Dumu-zi mu-da-an-[ḫúl-le] 10)ka an-tuku-e inim ka-na(!?)-⸢a⸣ [mi-ni-ma-ma] 11)mu$_9$-ba-an-⸢tuku⸣ ⸢lú⸣-tur še-⸢er⸣-⸢ra⸣ [mi-ni-zu-zu] 12)⸢ù⸣-[ub]-zi-zi Nibru$^{k[i]}$ [ezen-àm] 13)ù-[ub]-⸢mar⸣-[m]ar TUR AN-[ ] and translate "3)my heart has pondered what I let you know. 4)What advisedly I have let you know I will have you disclose 5)I the lavishly gowned Inanna (lit. "the reinforcer [even] of large garments") 6)The elegist will weave it into a song 7)The singer will extoll it in a lay 8)My bridegroom will thereby rejoice in me 9)The shepherd (lit. "wild bull") Dumuzi will thereby rejoice in me 10)Whoever has a mouth will take the words into his mouth 11)Whoever hears it will teach the song to a youngster 12)When it has soared (to full chorus) it will be Nippur (celebrating) festival 13)When it falls (to diminuendo) it will be . . ."

The fashioning of Inanna's self-praise into a song, which she calls for, is the theme of lines ii 14-34. We read and restore: ii 14)⸢in⸣-nin$_9$-e s[al-l]a-ni de-e-e[š ba-ab-bé] 15)gala-e šìr-ra m[u-ni-ib-ra-ra] 16)^{d}Inanna-ke$_4$ de-e-eš [ba-ab-bé] 17)sal-la-ni šìr-ra mi-ni-[ib-e$_{11}$-e] 18)sal-la-mar-ra ne-en kak-⸢ra⸣-[a] 19)si-dím ^{mu_9}mar-gal-e kès[da-mu] 20)má-an-na ne-en eše-lá-[a] 21)ud-sakar-gibil-dím ḫi-li G̃Ù[R-ru-mu] 22)kislaḫ ne-en edin-na ⌜šub⌝(!?)-[ba-mu⌝ 23)a-šà us^{mušen} ne-en us^{mušen}-ma-[ra-m]u 24)a-šà-an-na ne-en a-ma-ra-mu 25)ma-a sal-la-⌜mu⌝ du$_6$-du$_8$-du$_8$-a a!-ma!-ra (text: ma-a-ra) 26)ki-sikil-mèn a-ba-a uru$_4$^{ru}-a-bi 27)sal-la-mu ki-duru$_5$ a-ma-ra 28)ga-ša-an-mèn gud a-ba-a bí-ib-gub-bé 29)in-nin$_9$ lugal-e ḫa-ra-an-uru$_4$^{ru} 30)^{d}Dumu-zi lugal-e ḫa-ra-uru$_4$^{ru} 31)[ša-ab]-mà uru$_4$^{ru} mu-lu-šà-ab-mà-kam 32)[a]úr-kù-ge a-ba-an-⌜tu$_5$⌝ 33)[úr-k]ù-ga-àm um-ši-⌜di⌝ 34)[na-ma úr-kù]-⌜ge⌝ [a-ba-an-su-ub] 35)[úr-kù-ga-àm um-ši-di] (lacuna). For the restorations in lines ii 15 and ii 17, see van Dijk, *TLB* II no. 2 i. 12-13. For the restoration [di] (Emesal, preterite for EmeKU g̃en) see *MSL* IV, 27, col. i 3. We translate: "14)The young lady was praising her parts 15)and the elegist was weaving it into a song, 16)Inanna was praising them 17)and he was extolling her parts in the song (as follows:) 18)'My enchased parts so nailed down 19)as (with) linchpins attached to a big cart, 20)my boat of heaven so (well) belayed, 21)full of loveliness like the new moon, 22)my unworked plot, left so fallow in the desert, 23)my duck-field (i.e., stubblefield on which ducks are fattened) so studded with ducks 24)my highlying field so (well) watered 25)my parts, piled up with levees, (well) watered, 26)Who--I being a maiden--will be its ploughman? 27)my parts, (well) watered lowlands, 28)who--I being a lady--will put ploughing oxen to it?' 29) 'Young lady, may the king plough them for you, 30)May Dumuzi, the king plough them for you!' 31)'The ploughman is the man of my heart, of my heart! 32)When I have bathed the pure loins in water, 33)and when--the loins pure--he comes to me, 34)when I have rubbed the pure loins with soap (lit. "potash") 35)and when--the loins pure--he comes to me . . .' (lacuna)."

The point of Inanna's--richly extravagant--metaphors, the fact on which she prides herself, is that her parts are sprouting hairs, indicative that she has become nubile. These still scant hairs are compared to the studs or rivets in an enchasement, the linchpins on cartwheels, the stakes to which a boat is moored and to ducks dotting a field. Much the same point, attainment to nubility, is stressed in a song to the goddess Baba, sung by her girlfriends as they escort her to the bridal chamber during her sacred marriage to Ningirsu/Ninurta. The passage in question (Chiera, *Sumerian Religious Texts* [Upland, Pa., 1924] no 5, 39-44) reads 39)i-da-lam gaba-me ba-gub-gub 40)i-da-lam sal-la-me síg ba-an-mú 41)úr-mu-ti-in-na-šè di-di-dè Ba-ba ga-ba-ḫúl-ḫúl-le-en-dè-en 42)^{d}Ba-ba$_6$ sal-la-mà-ke$_4$-eš ga-ba-ḫúl-ḫúl-le-en-dè-en 44)gu$_4$-ud-an-zé-en gu$_4$-ud-an-zé-en 45)egir-bi in-na-sa$_6$ in-na-sa$_6$ "39)Now our breasts stand up! 40)Now our parts have sprouted hairs! 41)Going to the loins of the bridegroom, Baba, let us rejoice! 42)Dance ye! Dance ye! 43)Baba, let us rejoice on account of our parts! 44)Dance ye! Dance ye! 45)At last it will please him, will please him." Similar erotically oriented songs etc. as part of wedding ceremonies are, of course, found in many other cultures.

13 See the edition by Römer cited above in note 9. The section here translated corresponds to lines 167-92 of Römer's edition. The major versions on which the text is based are Römer's A=*SRT* no. 1, B=*ISET* I pls. 91-94, C=*HiA V* no. 2, and F=*HiA V* pl. 1 no. 2, variants from CBS 11391. The relation between them seems to be roughly

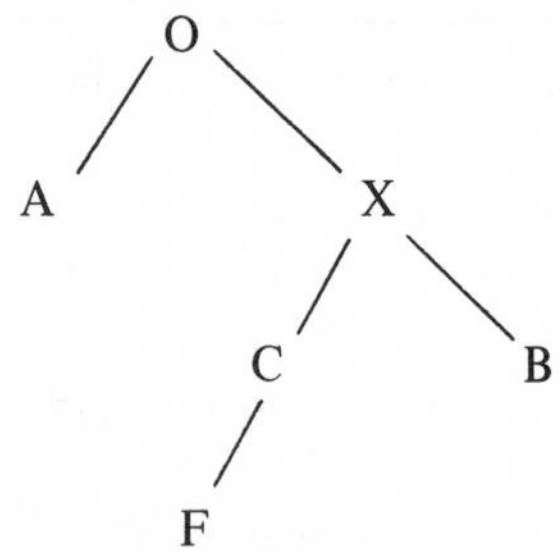

The text of A is much superior to that of the descendants of X. X appears to have mechanically restored a badly broken text reading a stereotype nam-kur-kur-ra tar-re-da-ni for a damaged zi-kur-kur-ra èn tar-re-dè in line 171, restoring sag̃-íl-le mu-un-du for a im-ma-tu_5-tu_5 in line 182 and adding a senseless line 186a úr-^{d}I-din-^{d}Da-gan-šè sag̃-íl-la mu-un-du. Only on two points does the X tradition appear preferable to that represented by A: Reading the two short lines 174 and 175 as one line only and preserving a line, 188a after 188. In favor of X on these two points is the apparent logical division of the passage into stanzas of four lines each (167-70, 171-74+75, 176-79) down to the climactic section leading up to the congress of the divine couple where a five-line stanza (3 and 2) is used (180-84, 185-89) after which the four-line stanza is resumed (189-92). In addition it may be argued that line 188 naturally calls for a further line of elaboration and specification.

14 For the meaning of lines 171-73 as looking to a "theurgy by allure," see below pp. 69ff. The verb igi-kár "to take a good look at" "to examine" would seem to constitute an old technical term for a girl choosing her mate, surviving in expressions dealing with the demoness Kiskil-lilla's choosing her lover-victim. In ud-ná-a we assume that the participle corresponds to use of the root with infix -da- in the finite form.

15 As noted by Römer (*Sumerische 'Königshymnen'*, 193, to line 188) a variant mí–i-i to mí–e/dug_4 is nowhere attested. We read, therefore, munus zi àm-i-i-dè "he can but truly praise the woman." Our rendering "can but" seeks to express the force of the prefix a- before present/future form as "conditioning of the subject by a *coming* occurrence: inclination toward it, obligation toward it, being destined to it." *AS* 16, 17f., n. 5. Line 188a we restore on the bases of B and F as úr-kù-ga-$g̃u_{10}$ kug ^{d}[Inanna]-$g̃u_{10}$. Our translation assumes that úr-kù-ga represents a genitive without regens ú-kug-a(k) (on such genitives see my "Notes on the Sumerian Genitive," *JNES* 32 (1973) 62, n. 6) so that the reference is the same as that of the following kug ^{d}[Inanna]-$g̃u_{10}$. It is also possible, of course, to see kuga as a simple adjective (i.e., intransitive participle) and to translate "O my holy loins!" still as referring to Inanna.

16 For mi-ni-in-sù-ga-ta of lines 190 and 191, see sù(-g): *rêšû* "rejoice," *ŠL* 373.8, 373.25, and 373.26. The infix -ni- we consider a causative infix resuming the adessive -e after nin and ^{d}Inanna. See *AS* 16, 93f., n. 16. Our rendering "in return" of the profix ša- of $šag_4$ ša-mu-di-ni-ib-kúš-ù seeks to express the force of "contrapuntive," "counterpart occurrence" of that profix see *AS* 16, 73. For $šag_4$-kúš-ù: *nâḫu ša libbi*, see *ŠL* 384 152 d. Line 192 we restore on the basis of A and C as [ud] ^{d}I-din-^{d}Da-gan-na [su-ud]-su-⌜ud⌝ ḫé-me-en.

17 One such group of texts comes from Umma and dates to the first month of the year (ŠE-GUR$_{10}$-KUD), that is to say, to the month after the month of Dumuzi for which the texts show expenditures connected with Dumuzi's wedding, e.g., for his "wedding gifts" (NÍG-SAL-ÚS-SÁ [d]Dumu-zi Nik. IV 204 and 372). The ú-sag̃(-g̃á) ritual seems to have taken place, not in Umma itself, but in nearby Zabalam, for parallel with the notation ú-sag̃-šè g̃en-na "going to the ú-sag̃(-g̃á) one finds Zabalam[ki]-šè g̃en-na "going to Zabalam" (cf. the various entries in Boson, *TC* s. 346; Jean, *ŠA* CLXI: 129; *TCL* 5, 5672. iii 22; and Keiser, *STD* 207 ii. 46-47). The deities involved are Nin-gipar "The Lady of the Giparu," i.e., Inanna, and Nin-ibgal, another form of Inanna. Present was also the goddess Igi-zi-bar-ra, known to be the personified harp of Inanna. The most natural way to interpret these entries would seem to be that they relate to a ritual procession with statues of the goddesses in question–in the case of Igi-zi-bar-ra she presumably came in her form as sacred harp–out into the desert to lament the dead Dumuzi.

Beside the ritual of the ú-sag̃(-g̃á) in Umma there was one in Ur presided over by Ningal at about the same time of year. Since Nanna and Ningal in many ways resemble Dumuzi and Inanna, it seems likely that also here a lament for a slain or vanished husband is involved. Of such texts may be mentioned *UET* III 273 ú-sag̃ [d]Nin-[gal] and ú-sag [d]Nin-AN-[ ]. Note also ír-ú-sag̃-g̃á "the early grass lament" in *UET* III 242. See further *UET* V 749: 19; 766 rev. 3′; 779:18; and 783:25.

18 IV *R* 21.1. Line 1 restored from subscript on *SBH* 37 rev. 17. See also below n. 20.

19 See "Toward the Image of Tammuz," *History of Religions* (1961) 199-201 (=*TIT,* 83-87, see also 102-3).

20 The basic texts for this ritual are *SK* nos. 26, 27, 45; de Genouillac, *Premières récherches archéologiques à Kich* (Paris, 1924-25) vol. II, D 41, C 108, C8; and Cros, *Nouvelles fouilles de Tello,* p. 206 (AO 4328). In the course of time a good deal of material derived from the cult of Dumuzi the shepherd, i.e., from the Mourning Drama just discussed, was added to the composition, notably the new beginning edin-na ú-sag̃-g̃á. In this expanded form the composition is attested to in IV *R* 27.1 (tablet I), *OECT* VI pl. XV (K 5208), *TCL* VI 54 (AO 6462), *BA* V, 681 (K 6849), K 4954 (unpublished copy made available to us by F. Geers), *ASKT,* p. 118 no. 16 (Sm. 1366), *ZAnF* 6, 86 (Rm. 220), IV *R* 30.2 (K 4903, Sm. 2148, tablet IV), *SBH* no. 37 (2-NT 358), *BA* V, 674f., no. xxx (K 3479), *BA* X, 112 no. 30 (K3311), *SBH* no. 80. Our designation of it as the Road of No Return Drama–admittedly provisional only–is taken from the beginning lines of the second lament in tablet IV.

21 After a lament addressing Damu and his many incarnations under dendral images, "(O you) my tamarisk that drank not water in its garden bed, whose top formed no foliage in the plain, my poplar that rejoiced not at its water conduit, my poplar that was uprooted . . . etc." (IV *R* 27.1, 16ff), there is a gap in which *SK* 26 i and *OECT* VI pl. XV (K 5208) obv. probably belong. Then we follow the mother and sister: The mother curses the day when a nether-world deputy came to her for her son in Girsu on the Euphrates (K 5208 rev.). In her anguish, and lowing like a cow for its calf, she sets out to find him, telling how he was taken from her by the deputy (*TCL* VI 54 obv), she wanders from canebrake to canebrake hoping to be shown where her son is, only to be told that her search is in vain, the sheriff of the nether world will not return him to her (*TCL* VI 54 rev.; *LKU* 11 rev.; *BA* V, 687 [K6849]). While in the case of the mother,

Damu's death is seen under the image of an arrest or impressment by the nether-world authorities, it is in the case of his sister, the physician Gunura, given form as a natural death after illness. She has sat with him tending him in the G̃iparu houses at the various sacred tomb sites of the rite "since yesterday." (Read ša-kab-kà-ba-⸢ta⸣ with kap as a gloss that got into the line. The Sumerian word for "yesterday" seems to have been ša-ka-ga in eme-KU, še-še-ge-ba in emesal with an intermediate form ša-k/ga-ba common to both. See the materials given in *CAD* A/II, 79 s.v. *amšāli*.) But now she leaves to ask for him "who has left the G̃iparu" (*SK* 26 ii). After another gap we hear the dead god warning his mother--but not heard by her--not to come to him, she cannot eat such food and such water as he has eaten and drunk since yesterday--a reference to the funeral offerings of food and water left in the grave--it has turned bad (K 4954 obv.). The mother, unaware, continues her lament and search and is again told by someone--perhaps still the canebrake--that the nether-world sheriff will not give her son back to her. She then threatens that she will stand in the sheriff's gateway wailing, hoping thus to force his hand (*SK* 26 iii and later duplicate *ASKT* 16, Rm 220).

22 "If it is required, o lad, let me walk with you, the road of no return!/ Woe the lad! The lad my Damu!/ She goes, she goes toward the breast of the mountains./ The daylight waning, the daylight waning, toward the mountains (still) bright, to him who lies in blood and water, the sleeping lord./ To him who knows no healing lustration,/ to 'The Road that Destroys Him Who Walks it' / To 'The Traces of the Kings,'/ To 'The Threshing Floor of the Anointed Ones'/ *SK* 26 iv 1-9. The localities mentioned are stations on the road of the procession, tombs in which various forms of Damu are buried. In the later version of IV *R* 30, 2: 11-35, the text of the passage has suffered a good deal, it assumes Damu to be the subject rather than his mother, reads kur-ug$_5$-na-š[è] in line 3 (=IV *R* 30, 2: 28) for kur-dal[la-šè] and interprets it as kur-ug(a·e)n(e)·a(k)·še: *ana er-ṣe-tim mi-tu-ti*; in the following line 4 (=IV *R* 30, 2: 26) e$_4$-urin(ŠEŠ)-a-šub-ba ù-mu-un-na-šè has become i-si-iš-na-šè ud-šub-ba-na-šè translated as *ni-is-sà-tam ma-li i-na u$_4$-um im-qu-tu ina i-dir-tim*, which looks like a conflation of two damaged manuscripts, one providing e$_4$-šeš [....]-na-šè, the other [....]-a (interpreted as [u]d)-šub-ba [....]-na-šè. In line 5 (=IV *R* 30, 2: 28) e$_4$-tu$_5$ was heard as itu and e$_4$-silim-ma-nu-zu-šè was read--from a broken text?--as nu-silim-ma mu-zu-šè and translated as the cryptic *ina ar-ḫi la mu-šal-li-mu šat-ti-šu* (reading mu-ba for mu-zu?). In line 6 (=IV *R* 30, 2: 30) kaskal-àm-ma-an-rá-til-til-le-eš comes out as kaskal-la ba-an-da-til mu-lu-u$_x$-lu-zu-šè, perhaps over a broken manuscript offering kaskal a[-AN]-⸢ma⸣ (read as ba-)-an-⸢DU⸣ (read as ⸢da⸣)til-[til-le-eš]. The origin of the last half of line 30 in IV *R* 30, 2 eludes us. Line 6 (=IV *R* 30, 2: 32) sìr-da ù-mu-un-nini-šè is fairly well preserved in sìr-da-mu-u-na-šè but was misunderstood by the translator, who rendered it as *a-na ṣir-ḫi ša be-lí*. In line 7 (=IV *R* 30, 2: 34) maš-g̃á-gudu-ge$_{18}$-ne-⸢šè⸣ is hardly recognizable in mes-ki-a-na-sù (*maškan* misheard as mes-ki-a-na?, gudu misread as *sù*?) nu-mu-un-da-pà-da (free emendation *ad sensum*?).

23 "The wind blew off a pure reed from the G̃iparu./ The wind blew off a pure reed, the lad, from the G̃iparu/ 'Since I am lying in the South-wind, lying in all North-winds, since I am lying in all the little ones sinking the ships,/ Since I am lying in all the big ones drowning the harvest,/ Since I am lying in all the North-winds and the tornados,/ She should not get to where (I) the lad am--why does she follow me?/ She should not get to where (I) Dumuzi am--why does she follow me?'" (*SK* 26 iv 10-17). We read the

first sign of line 11 as guruš rather than as e because a particularizing stanza (see *JNES* 12 [1953] 162, n. 5 = *TIT*, 334f.) is expected. This reading also has a measure of support from IV *R* 30, 2: 42. The final -a of lines 12-15 we take to represent -à(m) "it being that," "since." The na- of negative wish in lines 16 and 17 "may she not" we render as "she should not." For the concept of spirits of the dead as "reeds," see "Descent of Inanna" 279-80 where the deputies of the nether world are compared to reeds, and also the word gidim:*eṭemmu* "ghost" if its basic meaning is "as (frail, unsubstantial, as) a reed." For the concept of the disembodied spirit as "wind," see Thureau-Dangin "Passion du dieu Lillu," *RA* 19, 184-85, line 55 im-bi ba-bar-g̃u$_{10}$ un-nà (glossed na) "when she has pronounced my 'its (i.e., the corpse's) spirit (lit. "wind") has blown away'" glossed in Akkadian as *ša-ar-šu i-di-ip* (see *Nabnītu* F a 26, [i]m-bar-ra-mu-un nà: *e-de-pu ša eṭemmi* "to pronounce: 'spirit (lit. "wind") blow out toward me!'"), which refers to the funerary formula for releasing the spirit from the body. See also my comments on líl:*zaqīqu* in *AS* 16, 96, n. 17 first column and note besides "spirit," related to *spirare* "to breathe," "blow," also "ghost" from Anglosaxon *gast* "breath," "spirit," "soul." The same theme--the mother chasing the disembodied spirit of her son as it is borne away on the winds--is treated in the Dumuzi lament *CT* XV 20-24 in lines 10-19: im-íb-bé nam-da-an-si-ig kur-díb-bé g̃ar-⌜ra⌝-[da] / gi-ge$_{18}$ ì-sìg-ge sag̃-šè im-mi-ib-s[ul-sul] / guruš-e a šà-ba-ni a bar-ra-ni/ su$_8$-ba ^{d}Dumu-zi-dè a su-mu-ug-ga-ni/ ama-ni ér-re e-ne-er dùg mu-un-na-ka[r-kar] / ér-re a-še-re e-ne-er dùg mu-un-na-ka[r-kar] / ì-du-du ér-gig ì-šéš-šéš/ ì-ku-ub(!?) šu šà-bé-eš im-lá/ ér im-me ér-bi gig-ga-kam/ sìr im-me sìr-bi gig-ga-kam/: "The raging winds chose to blow off with him to set him down in the grasping Nether World (lit. "mountains")/ As a reed he is swaying, is rushed ahead./ The lad--woe (for) his heart, woe (for) his body!/ The shepherd Dumuzi--woe (for) his frailty./ His mother, weeping, is running to him/ is running to him weeping and lamenting/ She keeps going, sorely she cries and cries . . . she halts, puts a hand to (her) heart./ She weeps--those are tears of anguish!/ She wails--those are wails of anguish!/" For dùg-kar-kar, see kar: *lasāmu* as also the Akkadian phrase *birkē lāsimūte*.

The younger text form of *SK* 26 iv 10-17 as witnessed to by IV *R* 30, 2 obv. 41-rev. 19 and *SBH* 37 obv. deviates considerably. In lines 10-11 (=IV *R* 30, 2 obv. 41-42, *SBH* 37 obv. 9-11) it has e-gi$_6$-pàr-ta im-ma-ra-⌜è⌝ (var. ba-ra-è with gloss im. Presumably ba-ra-è developed by way of a broken text [im]-⌜ma⌝-ra-è in which -ma- was read as ba- while the gloss im- came from another text available to the copyist which had im-[ma-ra-è]): [*ištu bīt Gi-p*]*a-ri it-ta-ṣi*/ guruš-me-en G̃i$_6$-par-ta im-[ma-ra-è] (var. ba-ra-è with gloss im-). The third person *it-ta-ṣi* seems to disregard -me-en of the Sumerian line unless the translator considered guruš-me-en a vocative "O you lad, it went out of the G̃iparu." After the standard litany the younger text form continues--omitting line 12--with line 13 of *SK* 26 iv, which it gives as di$_4$-di$_4$-bi $^{g̃iš}$má-sù-sù in-nú rather than as di$_4$-di$_4$-lá má-sù-sù nu-me-en-na and cryptically translates as *ṣe-eḫ-ḫe-ru-tu-šú ina e-lip-pi ṭi-bi-tim* [*ṣal-lu*$_4$] "all its/his small ones sleep in a sunken ship" (IV *R* 30, 2 rev. 12 f. and *SBH* 37 obv. 21 f.). Line 14 (=IV *R* 30, 2 rev. 12 f. and *SBH* 37 obv. 23f.) is rendered as gal-gal-bi buru$_x$-sù-sù i[n-nú] and translated--equally cryptically--as *rab-bu-tu-šú ina e-bu-ri šal-lu-ma* MIN "all its/his big ones are immersed (Assyrian Perm. 3m.pl. II of *šalû*) in the harvest." For mer-mer of *SK* 26 iv 15 the later texts have tu$_{15}$-u$_x$-lu "the South wind," and in line 16 a damaged copy with n[a]-mu-un-⌜ma-al⌝ may be responsible for the reading nu-mu-un-kúš-⌜ù⌝-[dè] (var. nu-mu-un-kúš-ù-d[è]) in IV *R* 30, 2 rev. 16 and *SBH* 37 obv.

27. How ki-guruš-a-ka of *SK* 26 iv 16 came to develop into a lection translatable as [*ina*] *nu-bat-ti* is not clear to us.

24 In *SK* 26 iv 19-21 Damu complains about the bonds with which he is bound and the cloth put over his head, and the mother (?) states her readiness to share the insubstantial fare of Hades with him, eating food that is not food, drinking milk that is not milk. A large lacuna sets in here.

25 When the text resumes with *SK* 26 v, Damu meets–if we understand the difficult text correctly--a group of travelers and, not realizing that they are ghosts like himself, he tries to send a message back with them to his mother: (*Damu:*) "Let me instruct you about (the road to) the city of my father who engendered me, (that) my compassionate father may enquire about me,/ Let me instruct you about (the road to) the city of my mother who may enquire about me,/ Let me instruct you about the (personal) god who engendered me, (that) my compassionate (personal) god may enquire about me./ Let me instruct you about Ninsuna who conceived me, (that) my compassionate mother may enquire about me./ O you man, let me instruct you! O you lad, let me instruct you!/ Let me instruct you about (the road to) Tummal and the chariots of the highway (that) my mother may enquire about me/–O you lad, let me instruct you!"/ (*Spirit:*) "O you lad, please do not instruct me about anything!/ At what you instruct me, O you lad, your mother will not come to you,/ At your cry that resounds in the desert, O you lad, your mother will not come to you!/ 'Alas,' she cries, 'alas'/ Your 'wake up!' is said, 'Woe! Alas!'"/ (*Spirits:*) "I was a man!" "I was a lad!"/ "I was a maiden!" "I was a woman!"/ "We were children (lost) in the streets in an unknown place!"/ (*Damu:*) "Little one, little one, why come you to me!"/ (*Spirit woman:*) "Setting up the harp (of) counsel I tarry with you/ My setting up a ghostly harp in the wind--what (good) is it (now)?/ (Mere) ghostly messages! I was one versed in songs–what (good) are (now) my messages?"/ (*Spirit man:*) "I was a man, I am treading the mourning measure to the (strains) of the harp,/ waiting for sunset I pass the day with you, am treading the mourning measure."/ (*Damu:*) "O that afflati would occur to my mother,/ O that my passing afflatus--that afflati–would command her!/ I am another petitioning lad,–may she demand my release!/ May she petition the deputy, the one who is my undoing!"/ (*Narrator:*) "He cries in the desert, the cry resounds!"

We read and restore line 1 as ⌜uru⌝-⌜ad⌝-d[a-g̃á-šè na ga-di$_5$ ad-da š]à-l[á]-⌜sù⌝-g̃[u$_{10}$ èn-g̃u ḫa-a-tar] see lines 4: . . .-⌜g̃u$_{10}$⌝ èn-⌜g̃u$_{10}$⌝ ⌜ḫa⌝-⌜a⌝-[tar] and line 7 en-g̃[u$_{10}$. . .] and assume that the part of the line to be repeated was indicated with blank space by the scribe in lines 2 and 3. For the writing Tum-lá for Tum-ma-al, see above col. ii 10 e Tum-lá; for $^{g̃iš}$gigi[r ḫa-ra-an-na] rather than ḫar-ra-an $^{g̃iš}$gigir-ra, see below col. vi 8 [$^{g̃iš}$gigir ḫa]-ra-an-na ab-ba-te and duplicate *SK* 27 i 12′ gi-gi-ra ḫa-ra-ni um-ma-te. In line 8 we read ám na n[a-mu-di$_5$-ge-en] and in line 9 ám n[a] [g̃á]-ra i-im-⌜di$_5$⌝-[ge-na-za]. In lines 9 and 10 we read -zu! for -ba which makes no sense. The term ù-ri-àm-zu "Your 'Wake up'" in line 12 we take to refer to a traditional test to establish that death had occurred. The writing an-du in the same line we assume to be phonetical for an-du$_{11}$. In lines 13-14 the inverted parallelism shows that mu-tin here represents *zikarum* "man" (*ŠL* 61.178). We have so translated it also above in line 5. At the end of line 14 read mu-un-sá-me-en for munus-men. In line 15 -me-en is probably dittography from the preceding lines. The plural di$_4$-di$_4$-lá suggests that the original had -me-en-dè "we (exclusive)." In line 17 we read balag-ad-ša(!) as phonetic for ad-ša$_4$. In line 18 ám-li-la we interpret as Emesal for níg-líl-a(k) "a thing of (mere) wind" and translate it "ghostly" since Sumerian shows the same semantic development from "wind," "breath" to "spirit" as Latin and Anglosaxon (ghost<AS *gāst* "breath," "spirit," "soul"). We read TÚG in lines 19 and 23 as umuš: *ṭēmu*. In line 22 ám-líl-líl-la and ám-líl-la "a thing of (mere) wind" seems to have the same specific sense as Akkadian *zaqīqu*: "afflatus," "inspiration," "dream image." We read dè-ma!-ma-da at the end of the line and umuš-g̃ar da-an-na-an-g̃á-[g̃á] in line 23. In line 24 šu-du-de is phonetic for šudu-dè and the end of the line seems to have šu!-ba(?)-àm-mu ḫé-im-me. The second half of line 25 we read as šu-du ḫu-mu-⌈un⌉-ši-ib-ta with -ta representing rá, i.e., ĩra. Line 26 we restore as gù edin-na ba-ni-in-[dé gù-mu]-⌈un⌉-ra-r[a]. The section ends with the beginning lines of a song deploring Damu's plight. After a lacuna follows *SK* 27 i and duplicates *SK* 26 vi and *PRAK* II D 41.1. Since the latter text begins its count of cantos (ki-ru-gú "place at which to counter," i.e., sing the antiphone) here, there must have been a tradition that considered this a new beginning. Damu is told that his mother is approaching the "Threshing-floor of the Anointed ones" (⌈gu⌉-da-ge$_{18}$-e-ne ma-aš-ka-ba. We assume ta-a stands for te-a. The final -ŠÈ(?) is not clear to us) and that she is brewing beer (kaš i-šur) while calling to him. The speaker hopes that Damu will drink that beer when his mother will have served it (ù-pa-ku-uš ḫa-pa-nag̃-nag̃ for ù-ba-kuš$_x$(PÉŠ)ḫa-ba-nag̃-nag̃). After a few cryptic lines he is told that "when your sister has drawn near to the 'Road of the Chariot' . . ." The continuation is lost. (We assume that *SK* 26 vi 8 ([g̃išgigir ḫa]-ra-an-na and *SK* 27 i 12 gi-gi-ra ḫa-ra-ni derive from an original gigir.a(k) ḫarran.b(i.)a) for *SK* 26 vi 8-9 "woe mother who gave birth, woe for your son etc." can hardly have followed directly in the original.) The next song expresses Damu's frustration at not being able to answer his mother's call: ". . .I am not one who can answer my mother who cries for me in the desert,/ who makes the cry echo for me in the desert,/ she will not be answered!/ I am not the grass–may not come up for her (again)/ I am not the waters–may not rise for her again,/ I am not the grass sprouting in the desert,/ I am not the new grass coming up in the desert!" (*SK* 26 vi 13-19). There follows then a long litany listing the various forms of Damu and the tombs in which they are interred. It begins "Flowing waters, pure waters have come pouring out (lit. "have come out pouringly"),/ Since amidst flowing waters of the font, amidst the water pails of the young anointed ones/ In Enegir, the city of the young anointed ones/ the warrior Ninazu is laid to rest/ since in Gishbanda, the mountain of laments, the child Ningishzida is laid to rest,/ Since in Girsu, the house (?) of sheep shearings (?), the lad Damu is laid to rest/ Since etc. etc." (*SK* 26 vi 19-28; *PRAK* D 41.19′; we follow the latter) and continues the list of Damu figures through the dead kings of Ur III and into those of the Dynasty of Isin (*SK* 26 vi-vii; *SK* 27 ii; *PRAK* D 41 kirugu 2).

26 The following section is extremely difficult. It seems to lead into an offer by Damu to bring *urinnu*-plants to his mother and sister for them to brew beer so that, when he has drunk that beer, he may experience a sense of well-being; it ends with complaints about his pains. The following song (*SK* 27 iii 10ff.; *PRAK* D 45 ii 29ff.) seems to be a lament by Gunura. It begins "Let me roam around, in the city for you. What, what, has been done to the lad?" The following songs *SK* 27 iv we do not understand. At one point the dead god plaintively asks to put his head in his mother's lap. *SK* 27 v and *PRAK* 41 iv begin with a lament for Damu and his untimely demise. That of *PRAK* iv

is fairly extensive (reminding of *SK* 26 i) while that of *SK* v 2-6 is much abbreviated. It seems related to *CT* XV pl. 19.

27 *SK* 27 v 7-16 (*Sister:*) "O my chubby faced brother my lovely faced one!" (*Damu:*) "O my sister who must also be mother for me,/ O Ama-^{d}Geshtin, who must also be a mother for me,/ Tears like a child I weep,/ Sobs like a child I sob to you."/ (*Sister:*) "Who is your sister?--I am your sister!/ Who is your mother?--I am your mother!/ The day that dawns for you will also dawn for me,/ The day you see, I shall also see . . ."

28 The basic text is de Genouillac, *Textes religieux sumériens du Louvre,* no 8 and duplicates *CT* XV pls. 26-27, 30.

29 See *PAPS* 107/6 (1963) 477 f. (=*TIT* 41f.) "For him of the faraways--the wailing for (fear) that he may not come,/ For my child of the faraways--the wailing for (fear) that he may not come/ For my Damu of the faraways--the wailing for (fear) that he may not come,/ For my anointed one of the faraways--the wailing for (fear) that he may not come,/ From the holy cedar tree where I, the mother gave birth to him,/ From Eanna above and below--the wailing for (fear) that he may not come,/ The wailing of the lord's house for (fear) that he may not come,/ The wailing of the lord's town for (fear) that he may not come/–That wailing is verily a wailing for the vines, the vegetable beds may not give birth to them/ That wailing is verily a wailing for the grains, the furrows may not give birth to them/ . . . / . . . / That wailing is verily for the great river, it may not give birth to its waters/ That wailing is verily for the acres, they may not give birth to mottled barley/ etc. etc." *CT* XV 26.1-14 with Kramer's collations *RA* 65 [1972] 26; and *TCL* XV 8.64-75. The latter text writes ki-bé-da-ke$_{4}$ (lines 64 and 65) for ki-bad-rá (i.e., dìra)-ke$_{4}$ of *CT* XV 26 and nam-mir-ra for na-ám-ir-ra throughout. In lines 66-69, it has a longer litany than *CT* XV 26.3-4 but omits line 4 gudu-mu ki-bad-rá-ke$_{4}$. In line 7, it reads eri$_{4}$-kug ki-eri$_{4}$-ma du$_{8}$-⌈u$_{4}$⌉(?)-da-ra "out of the pure storehouse the place where stores are to be piled up" instead of *CT* XV 26.5 $^{\text{g̃iš}}$eren-kug ki-ama-ni-dú-da-ke$_{4}$(!) (with -ni- *sandhi* for -ni ì-). In line 71, read (eia-an(!)-na, phonetic for É-an-na, phonetic orthography is also an-na-ši-ki-aš-ta for ana-šè-ki-éš-ta of *CT* XV 26.6. Lines 7-8 of *CT* XV 26 are omitted. Lines 72-73 of *TCL* XV 8 seem to correspond in reverse order to *CT* XV 26.9-10 but 72 has gú for gu (old mistake for še!) in *CT* XV 26.10 and áb-zi-né for its ab-sín, while 73 reads ⌈šar⌉ "vegetables" for gu "vines" of *CT* XV 26.9 and šár-šár-re for its šar-šar(!?)-e(!?). Line 74 has i-lu-bi a-gud^{ku_6} na-nam kar-zé-be$_{5}$ ní-im-màl "That wailing is surely for the carp-flood, it may not come to be at the good quay" varying notably with *CT* XV 26.11 erìm-ma-bi ám-ma-al-e na-nam MIN(=erìm-bé) MIN(=ám-ma-al-e) na-ù-dú "Is verily for its storehouse and the goods,--its storehouse may not give birth to goods." Line 75 has dam-ti-la-[dumu]-tìl na-nam "It is verily for the living spouse, the living child" for correct dam-til-la dumu-til-la na-nam "It is verily for the spouse finished off, the child finished off" of *CT* XV 26. The end of the line, níg̃-sag̃-⌈e⌉ na-ù-dú in *TCL* 15, 8 and me-sag̃-e na-ù-dú is not clear to us.

30 "O my (good) nurse from whom I was separated--I had a child dwell with you,/ a child engendered by An,/ I had a child dwell with you/ had the lord Ningishzida dwell with you/ I had a child dwell with you/ had the lad my Damu dwell with you/ I had children dwell with you/ had Ishtaran and Ibishuba dwell with you/ I had a child dwell with you/ I have adorned my eyes with eyeblack for him/ have adorned my forearms

with cedar perfume for him,/ have adorned my back with embroidered cloth and embroidered (?) linen (see *MSL* X 135.273 túg-du$_8$-du$_8$: *tap-šu-ú*; the translation "embroidered" follows a suggestion by Landsberger)/ have adorned my head with a resplendent turban for him!/--You were having that child sleep in your core, sleep in your bark/ I had a child dwell with you/ you were having the lad Ususu sleep in your core, sleep in your bark/ . . . / I had a child dwell with you,/ with that child I would eat in my turn, would drink in my turn/ etc" (*TCL* XV 8.67-102). ". . .I had a child dwell with you/ 'Woe!' she says to her, 'Woe!' she says to her, the (cry of) 'Ah!' descending into the Nether World (i-lu mu-un-dab-bé[=mun-da-b-e)i-lu mu-un.dab-bé [ù ki-šè] -e (=ki-šè e$_{11}$)/ 'My provider who is gone from me!' she says to her--the (cry of) 'Ah!' rising to Heaven (*TCL* XV 8.111-113; *CT* XV 26ff. apparently omits this section)." In the seventh canto the mother continues telling the nurse how she has dressed up for the meeting with her son, adding that he will be coming out of the river: "To gladden him who comes out of the river,/ I, to gladden the child who comes out of the river,/ to gladden the lad who comes out of the river,/ . . . . I have adorned my eyes with eyeblack for him/ adorned my back with embroidered (?) cloth, and embroidered (?) linen for him/ adorned my head with a resplendent turban for him/ The wild bull (or "shepherd") who lay down to (sleep) the treacherous sleep/ Ususu who lay down to sleep the treacherous sleep/ . . . / My child was lying in the *shuppatu* rush and the *shuppatu* rush hushed,/ My child was lying in the halfa grass and the halfa grass hushed/ He was lying in the tamarisk and the tamarisk rustled to him./ He was lying in the poplar and the poplar sang lullabies to him/ I am the sappy cedar of the Hashur (range)/ I am a woman, my arms and fingers, are sappy cedar/ He will come to me to the desert where I am/ Like a deputy to his place of drawing water he will come along to me/ Like a shepherd to his place of drawing water he will come along to me" (*TCL* XV 8.118-44; see *CT* XV 26f 22-48 and 30.2′-25′ which vary not inconsiderably. At the beginning of the canto *CT* XV 26.22 has a line omitted in *TCL* XV 8: a-ù-a ì-al-lá-ré-da which is repeated at the end of the canto, *CT* XV 27:48 as a-ù-a i-lu-a-re-da. We assume it to be phonetic for a-u$_5$-a illu (A-KAL) re-da. The corresponding line *CT* XV 30:2′ seems to have a-e[l-lu] and, after a break, ù-a ù-a. In the following line, *TCL* XV 8:119 has íd-ta-íd-ta [è] ḫúl-le-da while *CT* XV 26:23 offers íd-da-íd-da-é-sìg-ge-da and *CT* XV 30:3′ ì-da-ì-[da] -ì-sìg-ge-da. We assume these orthographies to be phonetic for íd-ta-íd-ta-è-sig$_5$-e-da and would translate *CT* XV 26:22-23 as "(To please) him who sails the high waters, the flood,/ To please him who comes out of the river/." Line 2′ of *CT* XV 30 seems to have understood e$_4$ illu (A.KAL) of a broken text as the cry e-el-lu and to have filled in the remainder of the line as ù-a ù-a "Woe!, Woe!" In the lines corresponding to *TCL* XV 8:119-25 and *CT* XV 27:24-26 the latter text consistently writes é-da for íd-ta é for è and sìg-ge-dam for ḫúl-le-dè of the former. *CT* XV 30:4′ has ma-a ṭu-mu for me-e dumu of the other texts and writes ì-da for íd-ta, é for è, and sìg-ge-da for ḫúl-le-dè. The litany mentions "the lad," Ususu, Umunmu (for Umun-mu-<zi-da>, i.e., Ningishzida), Damu, Ishtaran, and Igishuba in *TCL* XV 8:121-24; *CT* XV 27 has Damu and "The anointed one"; *CT* XV 30 has the same two but adds Ishtaran. *TCL* XV 8 waits with two lines which the other texts have here until its lines 140-41 ^{giš}erin dur$_5$-ru-ḫa-šu-úr-ra-ka/ munus-me-en da-si-mu ^{giš}eren-duru$_5$-àm. The form they take in *CT* XV 27:27-30 is zag-mu ^{giš}eren-àm gaba-mu ^{giš}šu-úr-men$_5$-àm/ e-me-da zag-si-mu ^{giš}eren-duru$_5$-àm/ ^{giš}erin-duru$_5$-àm ḫa-šu-úr-ra-ka/ mu-gi$_6$-ge Dilmun^{ki}-a-ka/ "My sides are cedar, my breast is cypress/ O nurse, my limbs are sappy cedar/ are sappy cedar, are of the Hashur range/ are black wood of (the island) Tilmun." *CT* XV 30.8′-10′ reads zag-mu $^{\text{g̃iš}}$eren-na gaba-mu $^{\text{g̃iš}}$šu-úr-men$_5$-na/ umme(da)-da zag-si-mu $^{\text{g̃iš}}$eren-duru$_5$-àm/ $^{\text{g̃iš}}$eren-duru$_5$-àm ḫa-šu-úr-ra-kam. To *TCL* XV 8:126-29 corresponds *CT* XV 27: 31-34. It writes i-bí for igi, omits -da of šim-bi-zi-da, and has mí im-ma-ni-dug$_4$ for mí mu-na-ni-dug$_4$ in line 31, omits -mu after á-l-kúš and again writes mí im-ma-ni-dug$_4$ in its line 33, which corresponds to *TCL* XV 8:127 as also in 34 which corresponds to *TCL* XV 8:128. In line 32 corresponding to *TCL* XV 8:129 it reads sag̃-ki-mu "my brow" for simple sag̃ in the latter, omits è-a after dalla and writes mí im-ma-ni-dug$_4$ as in the preceding lines. *CT* XV 30:11′-14′ follows generally *CT* XV 27 but has šim-bi-zi-da in line 11′, reads mí um-ma-ni-dug$_4$ "when I shall have adorned for him" throughout, adds è after dalla in line 12′, reads zu rather than -ka after $^{\text{g̃iš}}$erin-na in line 13′, and gada-dù-a for gada-dug$_8$-a in line 14′, before *CT* XV 27:36 which corresponds to *TCL* XV 8:130. The former has an extra line: ma ṭu-mu-mu i-ne-éš ná-da which *CT* XV 30 writes me-e ṭu-mu-bi-ne-eš ne-da "My child (*CT* XV 30: '[as for] me–that child') asleep until now." The term am "wild bull" is also a standard epithet for "shepherd." For u$_8$-lu-lu-uš of *TCL* XV 8:130ff., *CT* XV 26:36ff. has ù-lul-la which *CT* XV 30:16′ff. writes ú-lu-lu. We assume these writings to represent ù-lul-šè. To ú-GUG$_4$-e- ú-nú of *TCL* XV 8:126 and 137 corresponds ú-GUG$_4$ i-ni-in-nú in *CT* XV 27:39 and 40, while *CT* XV 30:18 has ú-ú-SAR (i.e. ú-GUG$_4$(?))-a ì-nú after which it reads šu-mu-e, šu-mu-a, and šu-mu-e, all phonetic for šumun. We assume that as in *SBH* 4[4].127f. the first ú-GUG$_4$ corresponds to Akkadian *šuppatu*, the second, to be read šumun, to Akkadian *elpetu*. In *TCL* XX 8:142-44 the text seems badly corrupt. *CT* XV 27:43-47 has ṭu-mu-bi-ra-an-edin-na šu-mu-un--na-ni-in-bar/ an-edin-ki-edin-na šu-mu-un-na-ni-in-bar/ edin-ki-en-nu-un-mà mu-un-da-ab-dù mu-nu$_{10}$-dím ki-áb-lu-a$^!$-na$^!$ (thus Kramer's collation) en-nu-un mu-un-da-ab-ab-dù/ su$_8$-ba-dím e-zé-lu-a-na en-nu-un mu-un-da-ab-dù/ "That child it (i.e., the *elpetu*-rush) released into the high desert/ released him into the high desert and the low desert/ The desert kept watch over him at the place like a cowherd over the place of his numerous cows, it kept watch over him/ Like a shepherd over (the place) of his numerous sheep it kept watch over him/ *CT* XV 30.22′-26′ has much the same text but writes ṭu-mu-bi-ir without *sandhi*, the verb in line 22′ and line 23′ is šu mu-un-na-ni-ib-bar$^!$-e$^!$ according to Kramer's collation. In line 24 it omits -ma after en-nu-un and writes the verbal root du$_{11}$ rather than du. In line 25′ it omits lu after áb and in 26′ it adds ki before e-zé; both lines omit en-nu-un (presumably it is to be understood) and have dè-mu-un-da-ab-du$_{11}$ "May it keep it (i.e., watch) over him." The text of *TCL* XV 8:142-44 may be read: idim-ki mu na mu-un-díb-bé/ múl-lá-dím ki-a-bala-a-na na-mu-un-díb-bé/ su-ba-dím ki a-bala-a-na na-mu-un-díb-bé/. The line corresponding to *CT* XV 27:43 seems to have been lost,idim-ki looks like a misheard edin-ki, mu-na–perhaps over earlier numun-na–misheard for ennumma, while mu-un-díb-bé probably derives from a variant *mu-un-da-ab-e of mu-un-da-ab-dù/du$_{11}$. The writing múl-lá-dím for mu-nu$_9$-dím probably reflects a misunderstanding of the Emesal variant mu-lu for mu-nu$_9$ ABxKU. For this variant, see Landsberger, *MSL* IV, note to 1.13f. ki-a-bal-a-na, finally, seems to be a misheard ki-áb-lu-a-na (over *kiablana); it was repeated mechanically in the following line.

31 *TCL* XV 8:146-87, the eighth canto begins šèr-mà̃l šèr-mà̃l ù-mu-un-bi šèr-mà̃l "Noble! Noble! that lord is noble!" and goes on to praise Damu as son of Urash and Enki and

as of attractive appearance. With line 158 the refrain becomes "O that you be appeased toward us." *CT* XV 30:28′ has the variant maḫ-àm maḫ-àm ù-mu-un maḫ-àm "August, august, the lord is august" and presents a slightly different text. It also divides off *TCL* XV lines 158ff. as a separate canto and writes its refrain as te mu-e-dè-en-ḫug̃-e "What will appease him toward us," for *TCL* XV 8:158ff. dè-mà-e-dè-ḫug̃-en. The ninth canto *TCL* XV 8:183-89 begins gud [d]Da-mu ⌈am⌉ [d]Da-mu gud [d]I[štaran-na/ e-la-⌈lu⌉ ⌈gud⌉ [d]⌈Da⌉-mu gud [d]Išt[aran-na] "Bull of Damu, wild bull of Damu, bull of Ishtaran/ Hiya! (e-la-lu) bull of Damu bull of Ishtaran" and may be directed to the oxen pulling Damu's boat along. The remainder of the canto is not clear to us. The tenth canto begins: [i-i] m(!?)-dè-du-na mu-e-ḫúl-le-na/ šul-la mul-an-na silim-ma-g̃en-na/ [d]Ù-sù-sù aia-šè i-im-dè-g̃en-na mu-e-ḫúl-le-na/ "You whom I accompany, in whom I rejoice/ walking with speed under the stars in peace, O Ususu whom I accompany to the father, in whom I rejoice, etc." and continues through the standard Damu names through the dead kings of Ur III and Isin. The character of the rite as a fertility rite comes out clearly in lines 209ff. "The lord of food and drink whom I accompany, in whom I rejoice/ The lord of food and drink whom I accompany, in whom I rejoice." It continues, unfortunately much damaged, with references to cattlepens, sheepfolds, vines, and canals. The three last songs are similar processional hymns. The eleventh begins "Great Lord could I but rival you in awe and glory (ù-mu-un gu-la i-ši me-lám-ma nu-uš-mu-e-ši-sá-sá). The twelfth repeats the seventh canto verbatim, "To gladden him who comes out of the river"; and the thirteenth elaborates on the theme "You come to us laden with all your loads, you come laden/ O Ususu you come to us laden, you come laden" etc. ([ág-g̃úr]-⌈g̃uru⌉-zu mu-e-en-da-kára mu-kára/ [[d]Ù-sù]-sù mu-e-en-da-kára mu-kára/). The things he brings are restoration ([k] i-bi-gi$_4$-a) presumably of temples and cities, [food] and [water] of life etc. The composition ends with a traditional [[d]Ù-sù]-sù zag-[mí]-zu maḫ-àm "O Ususu, your praise is august!"

32 Svend Aa. Pallis, *The Babylonian Akitu Festival,* 268-306.

33 Ibid., 274f.

34 Robert N. Bellah, "Religious Evolution," in W. A. Lessa and E. Z. Vogt, *Reader in Comparative Religion* (New York, 1965) 77.

35 Ibid.

36 Pallis, *The Babylonian Akitu Festival,* 269.

37 Bellah, "Religious Evolution," 78.

38 See above n. 10. The passage here translated is rev. col. iii 7-11. We read maḫ-[b] i [zi-ga-bi maḫ-bi zi-ga-bi] / [g̃i] š-bí[l] pa-pa-al m[u-un-da-z] i/ úr-lugal-la ⌈maḫ⌉-zi-ga-⌈bi⌉/ gu mu-un-da-zi še mu-un-da-zi/ edin giri$_6$-kìri-zal-gim mu-un-da-ab-si/.

39 See G. van der Leeuw, *Religion in Essence and Manifestation* (Gloucester, Mass., 1963), vol. I, 99.

40 See end of n. 7, above. The passage here quoted is lines 44-47.

41 See nn. 9 and 13-17, above. The passage here translated is lines 210-13 as presented by Chiera, *Sumerian Religious Texts* (Upland, Pa., 1924) no. 1 col. vi 19-21 é-gal ezen-àm lugal ḫúl-àm/ un-e nam-ḫé-a ud zal-zal-e-dè/ [d]Ama-ušum.gal-an-na ḫúl-ḫúl-e àm-DU/ [g̃iš]gu-za

gi-rin-ba ud ḫa-ma(!?)-ni-ib-sù-dè/ The reading ḫa-ma- for ḫa-ba- in the last line follows Kramer's collation in *ZA* 52, 78. The parallel texts, *HiAV.* no. 2 and *ISET* pls. 33-36 (read thus for 91-94) omit all but the last line and both give it with gi-rin-na for gi-rin-ba.

42 J. van Dijk, *Tabulae cuneiformes a F. M. Böhl collectae* II (Leiden, 1957) no. 2. The passage here translated is lines 34-41, ii 7-14. See J. van Dijk, *Bibliotheca Orientalis* 11, 83ff.; and Kramer, *The Sacred Marriage Rite,* 63-64. The passage reads: ki-nú-a mí mà ì-du$_{11}$-ga-a-dí/ ù-mu-un-ra mí da-an-dug$_4$/ na-ám-zé-éb ḫe-mu-ni-íb-ta(r)-ar/ subad(SIPA)-zi ^{d}Šul-gi-ra mí-da-an-dug$_4$/ na-am-zé-éb ḫe-mu-ni-íb-ta(r)-ar/ á-gú-ra-na mí zid da-an-dug$_4$/ na-ám-subad(SIPAD)-kur-kur-ra/ na-ám-šè ḫe-mu-ni-íb-ta(r)-ar/. The orthography is unusual using íb for eb in zé-éb, ḫe- for ḫé and, apparently, zíd (or zì) for zi(d).

43 See above p. 67 with n. 15. The passage, Chiera *SRT* 1, 171-75 (= col 5.18-22) reads zi-kur-kur-ra èn-tar-re-dè/ ud sag̃-zi-dè igi-kár-kár-dè/ ud-ná-a me šu-du$_7$-du$_7$-da/ zag-mu ud garza(PA-AN)-ka/ nin-g̃u$_{10}$-ra ki-nú mu-na-an-g̃ar/. We follow *SRT* 1 which generally seems the better text. For zi kur-kur-ra èn-tar-re-dè, preferable as *lectio difficilior*, *HiA V* no 2 and *ISET* pls. 33-36 have nam-kur-kur-ra tar-re-da-ni "When she is to make (administrative) decisions concerning all lands." Thus apparently also *HiA V* pl. 1 no. 2. For igi-kár-kár-dè, *HiA V* 2 and *ISET* pls. 33-36 have igi-kár-ak-dè. *HiA V* pl. 1 no. 2 may follow *SRT* 1; for me šu-du$_7$-du$_7$-da, *HiA V* 2 and *ISET* 33-36 have me šu-du$_7$-du$_7$-dè. So presumably also *HiA V* pl. 1 no. 2. In the next line, *HiA V* no 2 has AN-PA for PA-AN of *SRT* 1, *HiA V* pl. 1 no 2, and *ISET* 33-36. For ki-nú mu-na-an-g̃ar, *HiA V* no 2 has an unclear broken sign instead of ki-nú and follows it with mu-da-g̃ar, while *ISET* 33-36 omits ki-nú and writes ba-an-da-g̃ar. Both of these texts write *SRT* 1, 174-75 on one line only. As to the translation, igi-kár-kár was discussed above in n. 15, the term ud-ná-a is most naturally to be connected with the ki-nú of the rite and the sexual congress in which it centers. Note that the comitative relation "to lie with (-da) someone" cannot be made explicit in the verbal noun but must be understood.

44 See above n. 8. The passage here quoted is *CT* 40 ii pl. 7 no. 4 col. i. 13-17.

45 *SBH* 145.12ff., esp. lines 14-21.

46 J. van Dijk, *Sumer* 13, 119-212 (IM 3233).

47 E. Ebeling, *Tod und Leben* (Leipzig, 1931) 47-56.

48 R. F. Harper, *Assyrian and Babylonian Letters* (London and Chicago, 1892-1914) nos. 35 and 1097. See W. von Soden, *ZA* 43 (1936) 256.

49 E. Ebeling and F. Köcher, *Literarische Keilschrifttexte aus Assur* (Berlin, 1953) no 72.

50 [UD-*26*-KAM] ⌜*u*$_4$⌝*-um ik-ki-li ina u*$_4$*-u*[*m 27-*KAM *iṣ-ṣa*]*-bat* ^{d}*a-nu-um*/ [....] ^{d}*Dumu-zi iš-ša-a'-li* [.......] *e-li*/ [....*mu*]*-ú-su* ŠE-SA-A *ša ina* U-GÙ ^{d}*Dumu-zi* ŠUB-ŠUB *ina* NA$_4$ MEŠ *ki-i qa-mu-*[*šú*]/ ⌜....*qa-*⌝*la-a-te ša* G̃AR*-nu* DUL-DU *a-na* AN-TA-MEŠ *ki-i qa-bu-*[*ú-ni*]/ [ ] ŠEŠ*-ka ša ina* KAŠ.MEŠ *ú-la-ba-ku-*⌜*šu*⌝(?) ŠEŠ ÍL*-ni ki-i qa-b*[*u-ú-ni*]/.

51 See *UET* VI no 22.16-20.

52 See Ebeling, *Tod und Leben,* 45.

53 Ebeling and Köcher, *Literarische Keilschrifttexte aus Assur,* no 71 obv. 3-4; see van Dijk,

Sumer 13, 117.

54 *ZA* VI (1891) 241-42 Sp. I 131 rev. line 3.

55 See E. A. W. Budge, *Assyrian Sculptures in the British Museum* (London, 1914) pls. XXXVI-XXXVII; and C. J. Gadd, *The Stones of Assyria* (London, 1936) 138.

56 *LKA* 71 obv 7 and *Sumer* 13, 117. IM 3252 obv. 8'-9' [^{giš}GIGIR^{meš} *ša* TA EDIN *ú-š*]*ú-úš-ka-tu-nim-ma a-na* SAG$_4$ URU KU$_4$ ^{d}AK *šu-*⌜*ú*⌝-⌜*ma*⌝ *An-*⌜*za*⌝-[*a i-né* (?)-*er*(?)]. The form *ušaškatunimma* would seem to be a Š. Pres. 3 pl. m. ventive of *šakādu*, a synonym of *qitrudu* (*AHw* 924). For the alternation *d/t* see *GAG* 29c.

57 *CT* XV 44:24-28 [^{giš}GIGIR]^{meš} [*ša*] *ti-iš-kad-*⌜*da*⌝ *ú-ša-úš-kad-u-ni-ni* LÚ-3-U$_5$ *ša* ^{giš}*ma-hi-tú ina* ⌜*la*⌝(?)[-*har*(?)-*uš*(?)-*ka*(?)]/ [ ]-*ša* ŠU-*su* LU-*bat ina* IGI DINGIR *u-še-rab-šu* ^{giš}*ma-hi-tú ana* DINGIR *u* LUGAL *ú-kal-lam* ⌜*ki*⌝-[*i*]/ [^{d}A]K *šu-ma ša ana* ^{d}BAD *i-tar-ra-du-šu* LÁ-*šu* ^{d}U-GUR ŠU-*su iṣ-*[*bat*]/ [*ana* É-*s*]*ag-kil* KU$_4$-*ma* ^{giš}TUKUL ŠU^{II}-*šu a-na* ^{d}AMAR-UD LUGAL DINGIR^{meš} *u Ṣar-pa-n*[*i-tum*]/ [*ú*]-*kal-lim-ma ú-na-úš-šú-qu-šu-ma i-kar-ra-b*[*u-šu*].

58 *KAR* 307 obv 24-29 ^{giš}GIGIR *ša* KUR-ELAM-MA^{ki} *ša* ^{giš}GU-ZA-*šú ia-a'-nu* LÚ-BAD ^{d}*En-me-šár-ra ina* SAG$_4$ ÍL-*ši*/ ANŠE-KUR-RA^{meš} *ša ina* SAG$_4$ *ṣa-an-du* GI[DIM] *ša An-zi-i* LUGAL *ša ina* SAG$_4$ ^{giš}GIGIR GUB-*zu*/ LUGAL *qar-ra-du* EN ⌜^{d}⌝MAŠ *šu-u*/ *ša še-hi ša* KI-*šu* GUB-*zu* EME^{meš} *ša An-z*[*i-i k*]*i-i iš-du-dam-ma ina* ŠU^{II}-*šu ú-kal*/ ^{giš}I-LU *bīt* ^{d}*En-me-šár-ra ina* ⌜É⌝-SIG$_4$ *i-lul*/ Ì-UDU *it-qi* NÍG-GIG ^{d}*En-me-šár-ra* "The chariot from Elam without its seat carries in it the body of Enmesharra./ The horses that are harnessed to it are the ghost of Anzu. The king who stands in the chariot:/ he is the king, the warrior, the lord Ninurta./ The one (in charge) of (leading the horses by) the bridle-strap, who stands with him: because it pulled at the tongues of Anzu he carries (it) in his hands./ The sill of the temple of Enmesharra: he hitched up at the wall,/ the tallow of a fleece is taboo for Enmesharra." We assume that *še-hi* is a variant form of *šīhu*, which denotes an attachment of leather on the bit of a horse. See Salonen, *Hippologica Accadica* (Helsinki, 1956) 117. In the first millennium Anzu--probably via its form as winged lion--came to be seen as a horse. See V *R* 46.20 a.b. MUL-ANŠE-KUR-RA:^{d} IM-DUGUD^{mušen}. The last lines of the section may indicate that the chariot had paddings or covers of sheepskin and so could not enter the temple.

59 See Pallis, *The Babylonian Akitu Festival*, 124f.

60 W. G. Lambert, *AfO* 17, 315 Commentary 4, see 318; and *AfO* 19, 118, nn. F. 4.

61 *Enūma elish,* tablet VII 74-77.

62 W. von Soden, "Gibt es ein Zeugnis dafür, dass die Babylonier an die Widererstehung Marduk's geglaubt haben?" *ZA* 51 (1955) 130ff.; cf. *ZA* 52 (1959) 224ff.

63 See von Soden's edition in *ZA* 51, 136.34-36. Basis is *KAR* 143, restorations from *KAR* 219 are in round parentheses. (We read the traces in *KAR* 219 for line 36 as *ina* IGI ^{d}UTU.) 34)(*E-n*)*u-ma e-liš* (*ša da-bi-ib-u-ni ina pān* ^{d}*Bē*)*l ina* ^{ITU}*Nisanni*(BAR) *i-za-mur-ú-šú-ni ina muhhi ša ṣa-bit-u-ni* [*šu-u*]/ 35)(*ṣ*)*u-ul-l*(*e-e-šú-nu ú-ṣal-la*) *su-ra-re-šú-nu ú-sa-r*[*a-ar*]/ 36)(*ina pān* ^{d})*Šamaš šu*(-*tú i-da-bu-ub ma-a dam-qa-a-te š*)*a* ^{d}*Aš-šur ši-na e-ta-pa-áš ma-a mi-i-nu hi-*[*iṭ-ṭi*] "Enūma elish which is pleaded, which they chant before Bēl in Nisan, that is against the prisoner. He implores them, he entreats them, before Shamash he pleads: 'These were favors to Ashur, I did them, what is my crime?'"

64 *Enûma elish,* tablet IV 83 *a-na An-šár* LUGAL DINGIR-DINGIR *lim-né-e-ti te-eš-e-ma* "Against Anshar the king of the gods you sought evil!" and tablet V 79 *[i-di]-ir-šum-ma An-šár šarru*(LUGAL) *šul-ma u-šá-pi-šu* "Anshar embraced him (and) he proclaimed (conditions of) peace to the king."

65 *CT* XV 44.3-4 [...........] UD DU-*ku ina* U-GÙ ⸢TÚL⸣ GUB-*zu dul-lu ina* X [. . .]/ [^{d}*É-a ša* T]U$_{6}$ *ana* ^{d}*En-líl ina* ZU-AB ŠUB-*su ana* ^{d}*A-nun-na-ki ip-qí-i*[*s-su*].

66 *CT* XV 44.5-9 [LUGAL *i-š*]*a-tu ša i-qa-du-ni* ^{d}AMAR-UD *šu-ú ša ina* TUR-*i-šu* X [....]/ [....] *šá kis-ki-la-te i-maḫ-ḫa-ṣu* DINGIR^{mes} AD^{mes}-*šá* ŠEŠ^{mes}-*šá šu-nu ki iš-mu-u* [....] [....*u-ša*]*q-qí-ma* DINGIR^{mes} *ú-na-áš-šá-qu* ^{d}AMAR-UD *šu-*[*ú*]/ [*ša* ^{d}*N*]*in-líl ina* TUR-*i-šu* ÍL-*ma ú-na-šá-qu-šu*/.

67 *CT* XV 44.9-10 [KI-N]E *ša ina* IGI ^{d}*Nin-líl* KUR-*ḫa* UDU-NITAḪ *ina* U-GÙ KI-NE ŠUB-*u*/ *ina* BIL-GI *i-qa-mu-šá* ^{d}*Kin-gu šu-ú ki-i ina* NE *i-qa-mu-*⸢*šu*⸣/ ^{gis}*zi-qa-a-te ša* TA ŠAG$_{4}$ KI-NE *ú-ša-an-ma-ru mul-mul-li la pa-du-*[*te*]/ *ša* ^{gis}*iš-pat* ^{d}EN *ša ina sa-la-'i-šá-nu* DIRI-*ú pu-luḫ-*[*tú*]/ *ina ma-ḫa-ṣi-šá-nu dan-nu i-ni-ru* BAD^{mes} *ú par-šu ṣe-bu* . . ./

68 *CT* XV 44.16-18: LUGAL *ša du-ma-qí ina muḫ-ḫi-šu* ÍL-*u* UDU-SAL-ÁŠ-QAR^{mes} *i-qa-lu-*⸢*ú*⸣/ ^{d}AMAR-UD *šu-u ša* GIŠ.BAD^{mes}-*šu ina muḫ-ḫi-šá* ÍL-*u* DUMU^{mes} ^{d}BAD ^{d}DIŠ *ina* GIŠ-BAR *iq-*[*mu-ú*]/ LUGAL *ša ḫa-ri-ú ina li-is-ni i-pát-tu-u* ^{d}AMAR-UD *šá ina ú-ša-ri-šá Ti*(!?)-*amat*(!?) *ik-*[*mu-ú*].

69 *KAR* 307 rev. 17-19: *1* GUD *u* UDU-NITAḪ^{mes} *šá q*[*u*]-⸢*li*⸣ *šá* [T]A ÙR-*ri* TÍL-*su-nu i-na-sa-ku-u-ni*/ ^{d}*Kin-gu* EN *7* DUMU^{mes}-[*šu k*]*i-i* SIG$_{7}$^{mes}-*ṣu*/ TU^{musen} *šá i-na-*⸢*su*⸣*-ku Ti-amat i-na-sa-ku-nim-ma* GAZ^{mes}-*u*. "The one bull and the rams of the '(Day of) Silence' which they cast down alive from the roof: (It is) Kingu together with his seven sons as they are slain (SIG$_{7}$=*maḫaṣu*?) The dove which they cast down: they are casting down and killing Tiāmat."

70 *LKA* 73:3-4: UD-*18*-KAM *ša qu-li* DU$_{11}$-GA-⸢*ú*⸣ ^{d}*Kin-gu* EN *40* DUMU^{mes}-*šá* TA ÙR ŠUB^{mes}-*ni* Í LÁL *ša ina* ŠAG$_{4}$ ^{gis}GÁ ŠUB^{mes}-*ni a-na* NU BAD^{mes}-*šu-nu* ŠUB^{mes}-*ni*.

71 *SBH* VIII 145 ii 23-26 UD-*7*-KAM *ana É-me-ur-ur uš-te-šir ana É-an-na el-*[*li*]/ *ana* GIŠ-SAR *uṣ-ṣa-a: ana* GIŠ-SAR ^{d}*A-nim i-ru-um-ma uš-šá-*[*ab*]/ *áš-šú* LUGAL-*ut* ^{d}*A-nim il-qu-ú ú gam mi ri* [....]/ *šipat*(?) LÚ-MAŠ^{mes} *ḫi-im-šá-at* ^{gis}GISIMMAR AGA ^{d}*a-nim i-te-ed-*[*di-iq*] "On the 7th day (of Aiaru) he proceeds to Emeurur, goes up to Eanna (and) comes out toward the garden: He enters the garden and sits down. (This is) because he assumed Anu's kingship. . . .he puts on the crown of Anu."

72 *LKA* 73.5-8: UD-*18*-KAM *ša qu-li* DU$_{11}$-GA-*u* ⸢d⸣ *A-num* ^{d}IMIN-BI DUMU^{mes} ^{d}*En-me-šár-ra ki-i* LÁ-*u*/ UD-*20*-LÁ-*1*-KAM *ib-bu-u u*$_{4}$-*mu* ^{d}*A-num* LUGAL LÁ-*ú u*$_{4}$-*mu* ^{d}AMAR-UD LUGAL ^{d}*A-num* LÁ-*ú*/ UD-*21*-KAM ^{d}*En-líl-e* IGI^{II}-*šá-nu ú-na-saḫ-ḫa-am-ma a-na dag-gil-ti ú-še-li-šá-nu-ti.*

73 *LKA* 73.11: ⸢UD⸣-*24*(!)-KAM *ša* LUGAL AGA ÍL-*u be-lum* GÚ ^{d}*A-nim ik-ki-su* ⸢X⸣-⸢X⸣ [....] LUGAL-*tu ki-i il-qu-ú* A^{mes} *ir-muk na-al-ba-šá* [*it*]-*t*[*a-al-ba-áš*].

74 Ibid., line 13: *ga-ra-ba-a-nu ša ina* ÍD *ú-ṭa-bu-u ga-*⸢*rab*⸣ ^{d}*A-num š*[*u-ú*].

75 *CT* XV 44.20-24: [L]UGAL *ša* NINDA. *ka-ma-nu* LÚ-SANGA *it-ti-šá ú-šar-qa-du* ^{d}AMAR-UD ^{d}AK *šu-*[*nu*]/ [^{d}AMAR-U]D ^{d}*A-num* LÁ-*šá-ma iš-bir-šá* ..... [NINDA *ka-m*]*a-*⸢*nu*⸣*-ú ša ú-šar-qa-du* ŠAG$_{4}$ ^{d}DIŠ *šu-ma ki-i iš-du-du ina* ŠU^{II}-*šá i-*[...].

[76]*Sumer* 13, 117 (IM 3252) 13′-18′ and *LKA* 71 obv.: ⌜DUK⌝-GÚ-ZI *ša kak-ûs ina* ŠAG$_4$ KA-*su* U-GÙ SI *An-*[*šár*]/ MU ^{d}EN GUB-*ma* ^{d}*A-nu-um ik-mu-*⌜*ú*⌝/ *iš-du-du* LÚ-BAD-*šú ana* ^{d}*A-nun-na-ki ip-qid*/ *it-ti-ku-nu-ma* (*LKA* 71: KI-*ka-nu-ma*) *ka-me* ^{d}*A-n*[*u-um*]/ SU-*šu ki-i i-ku-ṣu* MUL-SIPA-ZI-AN-NA [KÚR-*šu*]/ *ki-i ú-lab-bi-šú u* ^{d}*A-nu-um ina* U-GÙ SAG-DU *nak-si* ⌜*i*⌝*-mid*. Instead of reading KÚR as *nakru* "enemy" one might consider a reading *palāmu* "royal robe" and translate: "and clad Orion in his (i.e., Anu's) royal robe."

[77]*LKA* 72 obv. 9-11: MUNUS *šú* URU *ina* SAĜ-DU-*šú*-[*nu*]/ [*ù*] *ina* GÚ-*šú-n i-na-ûš-šú-ši-ma*/ *ina* A-ŠÀ DU-*ku* ŠE-NUMUN *ú-sà-pa-ḫu* ^{d}⌜EN⌝ *šu-ú* GÚ ⌜*la*⌝-[*ma-gi-re-šu*]/ [*ú-k*]*a-bi-is-su* ŠE-NUMUN *ú-sà-pa-ḫu ma-ṣi qa-te-šú-nu ki-i a-na ṣe-re-e ûm*[*a-al-lu*].

[78]See above n. 56.

[79]As in *LKA* 71 obv 7 and *Sumer* 13, 117. obv 8′-9′. See above n. 57.

[80]See above n. 58.

[81]Reasons to assume that this mythical motif entered Babylonia from the west were given by us in *JAOS* 88 (1968) 104-8.

[82]*KAR* 307 rev. 7-8: ^{d}*Mes-lam-ta-è-a* ^{d}AMAR-UD *šú a-na* KI-*tim* DU$_6$-DU-*ú* DU$_6$-DU *ûš-šu An-šár a-na* ḪABRUD *ir-du-du-šú-ma* ⌜KÁ⌝-*šu* BAD-*ú*.

- 5 -

THE PROBLEM OF THE LOVE LYRICS

W. G. Lambert

The present paper is not of the usual type in that it presents for discussion, not some modern ideas on the ancient Near East, but some ancient texts. And extraordinary ones at that. The matter began some fifteen years ago when the late Benno Landsberger and the present writer independently noted the similarities of three fragments of Late Assyrian cuneiform tablets inscribed with Babylonian literary texts of a very distinctive flavor. This material is divided into paragraphs, though no development of ideas is discernible in the sequence of paragraphs. The present writer published the then known pieces in the *Journal of Semitic Studies* 4 (1959) 1-15, and concluded that the text was of first-millenium date and included love lyrics between Marduk, city god of Babylon, and Ištar of Babylon, his concubine.

Since 1959 the present writer has identified thirteen further fragments, both Assyrian and Babylonian, and in addition, two pieces of a very important related Ritual Tablet. This proves that the pieces connected previously on purely internal evidence do really belong to a single corpus, and that the paragraphs were for recitation in rituals of Ištar of Babylon. It might seem, then, that the problem is solved, but in fact the texts remain some of the most enigmatic in cuneiform. First, the Ritual Tablet. This consists largely of the incipits of the paragraphs for recitation interspersed with the briefest statements of movements of the actors within Babylon. Usually it is not even said that the particular paragraph will be recited: the incipit alone has to convey all that. Thus much is left unsaid–one presumes that the ancient participants had learned the procedures by experience and needed only a few hints and reminders--and no clear and detailed picture of the actions emerges. The framework of the Ritual Tablet is a little more revealing. Every so often a pair of lines across the column indicates the end of one day's rites, and a rubric between these rulings tells when and where the action took place. These rubrics are mostly incomplete, since the two pieces of the tablet are broken, but from what remains it appears that most events at least took place either at midday or in the evening in "the street of Eturkalamma." This is the name of the temple of Ištar of Babylon. The fourth day of the month seems to have been the favored day. The colophon of the Ritual Tablet, also broken, describes the text as "Regular rites . [. . .]" (The word *kīnajātu* in the *Chicago Assyrian Dictionary*, *qinajjātu* in von Soden's *Akkadisches Handwörterbuch*, has in this corpus the meaning just given, ultimately based on the Akkadian loan in Sumerian, gina.) The Ritual Tablet is clearly only one of a series, which presumably covered the whole year.

The surviving portions of the tablets with the full text of the paragraphs do indeed offer in many cases those cited by incipit in the Ritual Tablet. The order does not always agree, but since in many cases use of the same paragraph is prescribed at several points in the Ritual Tablet, a collection of these paragraphs could only give them in correct order by a most improbable frequent repetition. However, there may have been different editions with variant order circulating, since "You are the mother, Ištar of Babylon" occurs in different contexts in the Assyrian as compared with a Babylonian tablet. The much greater problem is the content of the paragraphs, and its interpretation. The main actors are named occasionally as Marduk, his consort Zarpānîtum, and Ištar of Babylon, his "girlfriend" (*tappattu*) or "concubine" (*k/qinītu*). More often names are not given, though changes in person and gender of grammatical elements give hints but not explicit information. Cultic matters of a conventional kind are alluded to from time to time but more frequently a highly individualistic style and thought manifests itself. The text seems definitely to be poetry in most parts, and is always literary, but literary in first-millenium style, which was a style rarely employed, so that there are very considerable problems of translation, quite apart from the fragmentary state of some of the paragraphs. The results, when these problems have been overcome, are often most baffling. In places there is something like the work of those modern poets who try to create word pictures without grammar. Imagery of the boldest kind is commonplace, and the eroticism is the most explicit for ancient Mesopotamia. Parallels are hard to find. There are, indeed, a few paragraphs in the state ritual for Babylon from this source, but the only other similar text known to the writer is II *R* 60, translated, though in places inadequately, by E. Ebeling in his *Tod und Leben* (Berlin, 1931), 13-19. Thus little help can be got from other ancient sources so that we are left to form our own judgment. How should we take it? As factual record merely, as jest, as innuendo, or as something else?

THE FRAGMENTS AND THEIR ARRANGEMENT

Late Assyrian: Nineveh	*Copy on plate*
83-1-18, 464	3-4
K 6082 + 81-7-27, 241	6
K 6606+9944+Sm 1891+82-5-22, 569	5

(A copy of K 6082 is given by Winckler, *SKT* II 67; and of K 6606+9944+Sm 1891 by the present writer in *JSS* 4 [1959] 2.)

K 4247+8492+13760+15375	3-4
81-2-4, 294	6

(A previous copy of the latter piece is given by King in *CT* 15, 38.)

K 7924	3

(A previous copy of this piece is that of Macmillan, *BA* V, 694.)

Rm II 385	6

Assur

LKA 92 (Photo K 212a)

Late Babylonian

BM 46336+46371 (81-7-28, 61+97)		7-8
BM 67554 (82-9-18, 7552)		6
BM 33879 (Rm IV 441), an exercise tablet		4
BM 41107 (81-4-28, 654)	Ritual tablet	1-2
BM 41005 (81-4-28, 552)	Ritual tablet	1-2

(Due to the condition of the surface of BM 46336+ the copy is given with some reserve, and only those parts duplicated elsewhere are edited here.)

It is at present impossible to arrange all the fragments of text in sequence. The first three Ashurbanipal pieces, from Nineveh, seem to come from the same hand, and possibly from the same tablet, but if there was a series of tablets containing these paragraphs written by the same scribe, pieces of different tablets of the series would of course look very similar. The following two pieces from Nineveh as given above also appear to be the work of one scribe, though not the one who wrote the first three. Of these two groups of fragments K 4247+ and 83-1-18, 464 are very important in that both have some remains of obverse and reverse, and both are from the left-hand edge of their respective tablets. They duplicate each other in both first and last columns, so it is almost certain that they belong to the same edition. The pieces of the first group show that this edition was of tablets with small writing and at least four columns of script each side. Thus there was plenty of room to put all the text of K 6082+, K 6606+ and 81-2-4, 294 between the first and last columns of K 4247+ and its duplicate 83-1-18, 464. Unfortunately it is not clear if K 6082+ and K 6606+ are obverse or reverse pieces. K 4247+ happens to have the first line preserved, and something of each line of the whole paragraph, and in addition the beginning of the second paragraph. Thus it provides the beginning for a reconstruction.

K 7924 is a fragment from near the top of its original complete state: not many lines are missing from the first. The left-hand column, though lacking the left-hand edge, can be seen from the shape to have been the first column on the tablet (and, in reverse, the last). The first preserved lines on the obverse are the ending of the first paragraph on K 4247+ and duplicate. Thus K 7924 began with the same paragraph. The second paragraph was also common to all three copies. Thus it seems that K 7924 may have had the same material as K 4247+ and 83-1-18, 464 when complete. What remains of its second column and reverse is not duplicated elsewhere, so the matter cannot yet be settled. However, in one important respect K 7924 differs from K 4247+ and 83-1-18, 464. It writes each two lines of the other copies in the space of one. Thus to have contained the same amount of text as its two Assyrian duplicates it will have needed only half the number of lines, assuming of course that this doubling-up was consistently done. The shape suggests that it may have had two columns a side only. Another textual witness with the same double lines is the Late Babylonian exercise tablet BM 33879. In this case the lines were so long for the format of the tablet that they run around the right-hand edge on to the reverse, and the completion of the paragraph being written had to be put vertically on the left edge and left-hand side of the reverse. The paragraph is the same as the first one on the three witnesses just discussed, and the catch-line of the following paragraph is added, the first line of the second paragraph on the same three witnesses. Thus K 4247+ and its duplicates do provide the basis for beginning a textual reconstruction, though more pieces will have to be found before it can be completed. One further duplicate is the Assur fragment LKA 92, which restores 81-2-4, 294, obverse.

The remaining two fragments are Rm II 385 and BM 46336+46371. The former is a bottom left-hand corner of a smallish tablet, written in rather large script, so quite unlike the other Late Assyrian fragments. Too little survives to say more about its arrangement, though one of its paragraphs, that on the obverse, duplicates the last paragraph on BM 46336+. This is also written in big script, and it is the left-hand side of what was probably a tablet of four columns in all. As mentioned above, it gives the paragraph "You are the mother, Ištar of Babylon" in a different context from the Late Assyrian fragments. The whole surface of what is left of this tablet is damaged, so it is not given in full here.

Thus one incidental result of the scribal arrangement is to draw attention to the structural arrangement of the text. Much of it is certainly composed in couplets, and the first paragraph on K 4247+ is arranged in the translation so as to bring this out. It may be noted as a matter of curiosity that the third preserved paragraph on *LKA* 92 and duplicate begins with two double lines, followed by four single lines, the "repeat" sign and the final line.

For practical reference the related fragments are referred to as numbered "Groups" in the following editions.

RITUAL TABLET

BM 41107 obv.: beginning of tablet, column i

1) [*rik-su rik-s*]*u šá si-pit-ti* aš mu ú ma *in-ni-kan-*[*nu*]
2) [*ú-nam-bi*] ^{d}*zar-pa-ni-tum ina pa-pa-ḫi ṣal-la-a-tú* ^{d}*bēl ina ūrim*(ùr)*-ma šá* ^{d}*bēl* [. . .]
3) . . .] x-*na-a-a-ni-tum at-ta ku-ri-ti-iá šá kaspi ana* x x [. . .]
4) . . .] x-*tú a-di šāri ṭa-a-bi at-ta-man-nu at-ta-m*[*an-nu*]
5) [*at-ti um-m*]*e-e* ^{d}*ištar*(mùš) *bābili*(tin.tir)^{ki} *ù* x x x (x) *ina lìb-bi e-*[. . .]

---

6) . . . *kīm*]*a šá ina* ^{iti}*dùzi*(šu) ud.o.k[am ....] x x [. . .
7) . . .] x x [. . .

* * * * *

BM 41005 obv. i: continuation of column i

1) . . .] x
2) . . .] x u_4*-mu*
3) . . .]*-nu*
4) . . . *bīt qu-l*]*e-e te-ba-ku al-lak*
5) . . . *-n*]*a-a-a-ni-tum*
6) . . . *-k*]*a*? *kur-ban-nu*
7) . . . *ā*]*l banâte*(dù)^{te}
8) . . .] x *parak* ^{d}*a-nun-na-ki*
9) . . .] *adi é-tùr-kalam-ma*
10) . . . *é-tùr*]*-kalam-ma ina kisalli šap-li-i*
11) . . .] x *adi e-reb* ^{d}*bēlti*(gašan)*-iá*
12) . . .] x-*ti-šú*
13) . . .] x *ri-gim-šú*
14) . . . *te-ba-ku*] *al-lak ultu né-reb* ^{d}*madānu*(di.ku$_5$) *adi pān*/*maḫar bēli-iá*
15) . . .] x *ba*/*ma šá* ^{d}*bēl ṣal-la*
16) . . .] x *a-lik* ^{d}*bēl ultu pān*/*maḫar* ^{d}*bēlti*(gašan)-⸢*iá*⸣ *adi é* sal sukkal
17) . . . *ú-p*]*al-làḫ-an-ni*(! tablet *-šú*) *ia-a-ši ma-a-ri*
18) . . . ^{l}]^{ú}*nakri-ka* ^{i}*up-ta-na-làḫ-an-na*
19) . . . *m*]*a-a-ri ú-ta-na-làḫ-an*
20) . . . *kī*] *ma ḫa-ri-ṣu*
21) . . .] x *ú-nam-bi*

---

22) . . .] *ina muṣlāli*(an.bir$_x$(NE))

(End of column i)

* * * * *

BM 41005 obv. ii: lower portion of column ii

1) [x x (x)] x x [. . .
2) *ù*? *ki-ni-tum mê*^{m} [^{eš} *ši-qa-a* . . .
3) ^{lu}šu.du$_8$.a^{meš} *ù* sal *šá* x [. . .
4) *ištēn*(diš) *kan-nu šá kur-gar-ra* i-x [. . .
5) ^{d}*zar-pa-ni-tum šarra i-kar-rab*? x x x [. . .
6) *a-di*/*ki*-KUR *pu-šá-ni-tum ultu bīt qu-le-e adi* ⸢*é-ká*⸣-[*gu-la* . . .]

RITUAL TABLET

Beginning of tablet, column i

1) "[The ritual], ritual of lament." . . . . [.]
2) [I bemoaned]." "Zarpānītum is sleeping in the cella, Bel is on the roof," of Bel [. .]
3) . . .] . . . . . . "You are my short silvery girl." To . . [. .]
4) . . .] . . "Together with the pleasant breeze." "You, whoever you are, you, whoever you
5) "[You are the] mother, Ištar of Babylon" and " . . . . in . [...] are."

---

6) . .] as in the month Tammuz, the .th day [. . .

(odd words and phrases only preserved until the middle of column ii)

2) and "Give the concubine water [to drink" . . .
3) . . . . . and . . . [. . .
4) one potstand which the Kurgarrû-priest will . [. . .
5) Zarpānītum will bless the king . . . [. . .
6) . . . Pûšanītum." From the Bīt Qulê to Ekagula [. . .]

7) *ultu é-ká-gu-la ḫur-sag-kalam-ma āl ba-na-a-*[*te* . . . .]
8) *ḫarrānu*^{II} *šá kutî*(gú.du$_8$.a) *te-ba-ku al-lak bābili*(*E*)<^{ki}> ^{na4}*kunukku lu da-a* [. . . .]
9) *at-ta um-me-e* ^{d}*ištar*(mùš) *bābili*(tin.tir)^{ki} *ana kirî ra-mi-ki ki-i ú-*[. . . .]
10) ^{d}*zar-pa-ni-tum ki-i iq-nu-ú i-te-lu ana ziq-qur-ra-ti* x [. . .]
11) *múl-di parak* ^{d}*a-nun-na-ki pi-rik sūqi*(sila) *é-tùr-kalam-ma adi kir*[*î* . . .]
12) *ina bāb* ^{d}*bēlti*(gašan)-*iá* ^{d}*bēltu*(gašan) *ittiq*(dib) ^{iq}-*ma ú-ta-am-*x[-(x)]
13) ^{d}*zar-pa-ni-tum ana kirî ur*(! tablet šu)-*rad ana nukarribi*(nu.kiri$_6$) *il-ta-na-as-s*[*i-*(*ma*)]
14) ^{lú}*nukarribu*(nu.kiri$_6$) ^{lú}*nukarribu*(nu.kiri$_6$) ^{lú}*rāb banî*(dù) *šá la i'-ma-lu-*[x-(x)]
15) *mi-nu-ú šam-mu-ka šá ru-u*$_8$*-ú-a* ^{d}*zar-pa-ni-tú ana kirî ma* x [. . . . . . . gu]b-*az*
16) ^{lú}*nukarribu*(nu.kiri$_6$) ^{lú}*nukarribu*(nu.kiri$_6$)-*ma* ^{lú}*rāb banî*(dù) *šá āli-ia lu-ú* [*at-ta*]
17) *i-šam-ma* KA X KU *si-in-da-ak-ku su-uḫ-su šá tap-pat-ti-i it*[*tú*? . . .]
18) *šu-ri-da-a i-da-a a-di šāri ṭa-a-bi múl-di kirî pap i*[*b*? . . .]
19) *áš-šu-ut ḫa-da-a-tum áš-šú-ut qal-la-a-tú ù al-lak* ^{íd}[. . .]
20) *kīma* ^{d}*bēltu*(gašan) *i-te-eb-ru rik-su ina bāb* x *ana tar-ṣa né-bé-ri* [. . . .]
21) áš mu ú ma *in-ni-kan-nu ú-nam-bi u ki-ni-tú mê*^{meš} *ši-qa-*⌜*a*⌝ [. . .]

---

22) *an-nu-u šá* ud.4.kam *ina muṣlāli*(an.bir$_x$(NE)) *u li-lat sūq*(sila) *é-tùr-kalam-ma u* ^{íd}x [. . .]

---

23) *rik-su rik-su šá si-pit-tum e-ka-a-ni li-mu-ra-a-ku*
24) *ana bīt qu-le-e te-ba-ku al-lak kīma šá* ud.4.kam

BM 41005 obv. iii: top portion of column iii

1) *ultu bīt si-pit-te-e adi bīt qu-le-e ina pān* ^{d}*ni-nú-a-a-tum izzazza*(gub)^{za}-*ma*
2) *at-ta ku-ri-ti-iá šá kaspi ina bīt qu-le-e ki-i a-mur-ru-ka*
3) *ḫur-sag-kalam-ma āl ba-na-a-tum ultu múl-di bīt qu-le-e adi é-ká-gu-la*
4) *kīma šá* ud.4.kam *ultu é-ká-gu-la adi bīt ilāni*^{meš} *šá é-ḫur-sag-ti-la*
5) *ḫarrānu*^{II} *šá kutî*(gú.du$_8$.a) *te-ba-ku al-lak ana tar-ṣa ú-ki-it šá* ^{d}*šarrat*(gašan)-*nippuri*^{ki} *izzâz*(gub)^{az}-*ma*
6) an da aš mi ri šá ú sa lak *ultu ú-ki-it adi abul* ^{d}*uraš*
7) *ana bi-iṣ-ṣu-ri-ka šá tak-la-a-tú kalba ú-še-reb bāba a-rak-kás*
8) *ana bi-iṣ-ṣu-ri-ka šá tak-la-a-tú kīma abni-ka aq-ri ina pāni-ka*
9) *bi-iṣ-ṣu-ru-ú šá tap-pat-ti-i am-me-ni ki-ki-i te-te-né-pu-uš*
10) *bi-iṣ-ṣu-ru-ú šá tap-pat-ti-i pi-rik bābili*(E)^{ki} *šin-gu i-saḫ-ḫur*
11) *bi-iṣ-ṣu-ru-ú šá šitta*(min)^{ta} *ubānāti*(šu?.si)^{meš} *am-me-ni ṣa-la-a-tú tug-da-nar-ri* TAR-*as ma*
12) *abulla uṣṣi*(è)-*ma ana tar-ṣa ḫur-sag-kalam-ma* ^{lú}*kur-gar-ra ina kin-ṣi-šú ik-kam-mi-iṣ-ma*
13) *te-nin-di inaddi*^{di} *in-ḫi in-na-ḫu i-te-bi-ma kiš*^{ki} *ra-ba-a lu-mur*
14) *bābili*(E)^{ki} *šú-qa-a lud-gul-ma i-za-am-mur ḫur-sag-kalam-ma āl ba-na-a-tú*
15) *ana tar-ṣa* ^{d}*nin-líl ú-kan-nu ana tar-ṣa é-sa-bad ru-u*$_8$*-ú-a ru-*⌜*u*$_8$*-ú*⌝-<*a*>
16) *al-ka e-ṣi ba-ni* im me tum *ù me-li-li qab-lu me-*[*li-li*] *tāḫazu*(mè)
17) *iqabbi*(dug$_4$.ga)-*ma* ^{lú}*assinnu*(ur.sal) *ana qab-lu ur-rad gu-uš-tum i-za-*x [. . . .]
18) ^{d}*zar-pa-ni-tum ki iq-nu-ú i-te-lu*(! tablet IB) *ana ziq-qur-ra-ti* x [. . . .]
19) *ki-ni-tum mê*^{meš} *ši-qa-a i-qab-bi bi* ⌈(. . .)]

---

20) *ana é-tùr-kalam-ma i-tar-ma ana kisalli e-li il-li* [. . . .]
21) *ki-na-a-a-tum šá bīt-a-ni ki-ma šá* ud.4.kam *ina* ká x [. . .]
22) *bābi bīt-a-ni* ká dib *kisallu šap-li-i* x x [. . . . .]
23) (traces)

*   *   *   *   *

7) from Ekagula "Ḫursagkalamma, city of beauty [. . . .]
8) "I will arise to take the road to Kutha," "Babylon, seal . . . [. . . .]
9) "You are the mother, Ištar of Babylon." "To the garden of your lover when I/he/she [. . . .]
10) "When Zarpānītum became angry she went up to the ziggurat . [...]
11) At the side of the dais of the Anunnaki, in the district of the Street of Eturkalamma up to
12) The Lady will pass through the Gate of My Lady and will . . . [.] the garden [. . . .]
13) Zarpānītum will go down to the garden and will keep crying to the gardener,
14) "Gardener, gardener, *building inspector* . . . . . [. .]
15) What is the plant you have that belongs to my friend?" Zarpānītum to the garden . . [. . .
16) "Gardener, gardener, be the *building inspector* of my city!" . . . .] will stand,
17) . . . . the bed of my girl-friend . [. . .]
18) "Bring down and place." "Together with the pleasant breeze." At the side of the garden..[...]
19) "The wifehood of happy women, the wifehood of slave-girls," and "I will go when the Lady
20) has crossed over the river [. . .]" The ritual at the . . gate facing the river crossing [. . . .]
21) . . . . I bemoaned," and "Give the concubine water to drink," [. . .]

---

22) This is (what takes place) on the 4th day at noon and in the evening in the street of Etur-kalamma and at the river . [. . .]

---

23) "The ritual, ritual of lament." "Where will they see you?"
24) "I will arise and go to the Bīt Qulê" as on the 4th day.

(column iii continues without a break)

1) From the House of Lament to the Bīt Qulê he/she will stand in front of Ninayītum.
2) "You are my short silvery girl." "When I saw you in the Bīt Qulê."
3) "Ḫursagkalamma, city of beauty." From the side of the Bīt Qulê to Ekagula,
4) as on the 4th day. From Ekagula to the temple of the gods of Eḫursagtila.
5) I will arise and take the road to Kutha." Facing the Akītu of Šarrat-Nippuri he/she will
6) . . . . from the Akītu to the city-gate of Uraš. stand and
7) "Into your genitals in which you trust I will make a dog enter and will tie shut the door."
8) "Into your genitals in which you trust, like your precious stone before you."
9) "Genitals of my girl-friend, why do you constantly so do?"
10) "Genitals of my girl-friend, the district of Babylon is seeking a rag."
11) "Genitals with two fingers(?), why do you constantly provoke quarrels?" He/She will . . and
12) will depart from the city gate and facing Ḫursagkalamma the Kurgarrû-priest will kneel on
13) recite prayers and utter his chants. He will arise and sing, his knees and
14) "Let me see great Kish, let me look on lofty Babylon." "Ḫursagkalamma, city of beauty."
15) Facing Ninlil they will set up. Facing Esabad, "My friend, my friend,
16) go, go out . . . . ," and "Battle is my game, warfare is my game,"
17) he/she will utter and the Assinnu-priest will go down to battle, he will . . a jig [. . . .]
18) "When Zarpānītum became angry she went up to the ziggurat . [. . . .]
19) "Give the concubine water to drink," he/she will utter . [. . .]

---

20) He/She will return to Eturkalamma and will go up to the upper court [. . . .]
21) The regular rites inside as on the 4th day. In the gate . [. . .]
22) the inside gate, he/she will *pass through* the gate to the lower court . [. . . . .]

(odd signs and phrases only preserved up to the end of column iv and the colophon)

BM 41005 rev. iv: column iv upper portion

1) . . . *ê*]-*tùr-kalam-ma izzâz*(gub)^{az}-*ma*
2) . . .] x *bēli-iá*
3) . . .]-*ma*
4) . . .] *ṣal-lu*
5) . . .] i di
6) . . .] x *ūri*(ùr) *lu-ú-lu*
7) . . .] *ú-kan-nu*
8) . . .] x i bu gar an
9) . . .]-*ka*
10) . . .] *kar-bēl-mātāti*(kur.kur)
11) . . . *ú*]*š-pur-ki*
12) . . .] x mur
13) . . .] lu
14) . . .] ur ni *gu-uš-tú*
15) . . .] *ú-nam-bi kam izammur*(šìr)^{mur}
16) . . .]-*ma*
17) . . . *kin-na*]-*a-a-tú kīma šá bīt-a-nu*
18) . . . *a-n*]*a kisalli šap-li-i ur-rad-ma*
19) . . .] mud? bi *bāb bīt* ^{d}*sin*
20) . . .] x-*ma ú-nam-bi*
21) . . . *r*]*e-ḫe-et ki-iṣ-ṣi*
22) . . . -*i*]*m-ma*
23) . . . *k*]*i-na-a-a-tú*
24) . . .] x

* * * * *

BM 41107 rev. iv: end of tablet, column iv

1) . . . *ni*]*šī*^{meš} x x x [. . .
2) . . .] x *ilāni*^{meš} *a-pa-a-tú* x x [. . .
3) . . . *ina muṣlāl*]*i*(an.bi]r$_{\text{x}}$(N]E)) *u li-lat sūq*(sila! tablet: BE) *ê-tùr-kalam-ma* [. . .
4) . . . +]7/8^{àm} mu.šid.bi *ki-na-a-a-tú* x [. . .
mu x [. . .
5) igi.tab igi.x [(. . .)]

Notes on the Ritual Tablet:

BM 41107 obv. 1: see *ri-kis si-pit-t*[*i*] : *SBH* 145 ii 15. The second incipit, which also occurs in ii 21 below and in Group III C 3, is consistently written aš mu ú ma. Read *ina mu-šam-ma* "by night" or *rum-mu-ú-ma* "they are/were released."

II 10: for *qenû* "become angry" see *Or* 40 (1971) 95 and H. Otten and W. von Soden, *StBoT* 7 (1968) 10-12, I 36, to which K. K. Riemschneider has kindly drawn attention.

II 14, 16: curiously Langdon in *JRAS* (1933) 857 gave evidence that ^{lú}GAL.KAK (though not *rab banî*) may mean "chief gardener." The meaning of *rab banî* still needs thorough investigation.

II 17: for *suḫsu* see A. Boissier, *DA* 19:8 apud *CAD* I, 230a.

III 9-10: for the writing *tap-pat-ti-i* = *tap-pat-ti-ia* cf. Group IV 4, where *tap-pat-ti-ia* occurs, and see *Or* 40 (1971) 95.

1) . . .] people . . . [. . .
2) . . .] . gods, windows . . [. . .
3) [This (is what takes place . . .] at noon and in the evening in the street of Eturkalam-
4) . . .] (so many) lines, the regular rites . [. . . . . . .] ma [. . .
. . [. . .
5) collated and checked [. . .

GROUP I

Section I

A = K 4247+8492+13760+15375 obv. i: lines 1-38.
B = K 7924 obv. i: lines 14-49.
C = 83-1-18, 464 obv.: lines 32-44.
d = BM 33879 (Rm IV 441): lines 1-33.

1) *rik-si rik-si šá ^{d}zar-p[a]-ni-tú*
2) *mi-lul-a-ti ša ^{d}marduk*
3) *mi-lul-a-ti ša ^{d}marduk*
4) *kin-na-a-a-ti ša ^{d}zar-pa-ni-tum*
5) *i-na lìb-bi rik-si ša ^{d}zar-pa-ni-tum*
6) *mu-šu e-muq-ti la i-ba-áš-ši*
7) *mu-šu e-muq-ti la i-ba-áš-ši*
8) *mu-šú alti amēli la i-par-rik*
9) *in-du-*x *a-na-ku a-na ^{d}zar-pa-ni-tum*
10) *pir-ti muš-šu-rat ù*? ⸢*ed*⸣*-bat qa*?-[*t*]*ú*?
11) *i-na šá-ni-ti-ia a-na ^{d}ištar*(m[ù]š) *bābili*(tin.tir)^{ki}
12) *a-na ṣilli*(gissu) *u ṣēti*(ud.da) *e*(! tablet d: KAL)*-te-rim ṣēli*(ti)
13) *a-ga-nê-ti a-*⸢*di-i*⸣ *ḫa-ṭu-ú*?*-šú*
14) *pir-ti muš-šu-rat ù*? *ed-bat qātu*^{II}
15) *a-ga-n*[*ê*]*-ti a-di-*⸢*i*⸣ *qa-la-li-šú*
16) *a-na ṣilli*(gissu) *ù ṣēti*(ud.da) *te-te-rim ṣēli*(ti)
17) ⸢*a*⸣*-šib-*[*t*]*úm* giš/ud gar nu *pa-as-sa*
18) *tu-ma-aq ka-la-ma la šal-ma*
19) *at-ti e-muq-ti b*[*ī*]*ta ep-ši*
20) *at-ti l*[*i*]*l-lat šipāti*$^{\text{ḫi.a}}$ *ep-ši*

Variants:

1) A: *rik-su rik-s*[*u, -t*]*i*
2) d: *me-lul-e-t*[*i*
3) d: *me-lul-e-ti šá*
4) d: [*k*]*i-na-a-ti šá*
5) d: *šá ^{d}za*[*r*]*-pa-ni-tú*
6) d: *mu-šá e-muq-tum+la* gál*-ši*
7) d: *mu-šá e-muq-tum,* gál*-ši*
8) d: *mu-šá al-ti*
10) A: *pi*[-
12) d: om. *a-na*
14) A: *pi-ir-*[
16) d: om. *a-na*; *u*
18) d: *ka-li-ma*
19) d: [*at-t*]*a*
20) d: *at-ta* B: *up-ši*

1) Ritual, ritual of Zarpānītum,
2) Games of Marduk,
3) Games of Marduk,
4) Regular rites of Zarpānītum.
5) In the ritual of Zarpānītum
6) By night there is not a good housewife,
7) By night there is not a good housewife,
8) By night a married woman creates no difficulty.
9) I am a . . . for Zarpānītum,
10) My hair is flowing and my hands *hang loose*.
11) In my hostility to Ištar of Babylon
12) For shade or open air I have covered my side.
13) These women–so long as he does wrong–
14) My hair is flowing and my hands *hang loose*.
15) These women–so long as he is despised–
16) For shade or open air you have covered my side.
17) She who is present . . . a doll,
18) You (masc. sing.) hold back in everything that is not sound.
19) You are the good housewife–create a family;
20) You are the fool–process wool.

21) *ku-um ta-ṭ[u-u]p-pu qé-e* ^{d}*bēli-iá*
22) *ku-um tal-tam-ma-ri šipāti*$^{ḫi.a}$ *ep-ši*
23) *ku-um [te?-e]p?-pu-š[u]* na x x x (x) *libbi-šú*
24) *ep-ši bīta a-na mu-ti-ki*
25) *a-šib-tùm* [. . .
26) *sap-pa* x // x *ma-li-ma-ku lut-tu*
27) *e-muq-ti* x x da x [. . .
28) *ṭè-ma-ni-t[u]-ia ú-šad-ba-ab-ki*
29) *a-na ka-a-ši um-*x [. . .
30) *lubār*(LU!$^{ḫi.a}$)*-ki i-na šin-na-ti ú-šá-aṣ-bat-ki*
31) *ul-tu a-gan-ni-ia* [. . .
32) *lu-bar-ki i-na šin-na-ti ú-šá-aṣ-bat-ki*

---

33) *e-ka-a-ni li-mu-ra-*⌜*ku*⌝ x-*šú a-a maš maš-a-te*
34) *e-me kalbu* x [. . .
35) *ba-qa-an iṣ-ṣu-[r]u-um-ma lu-ub-qu-un-ki*
36) *ki-iz-za-ni-iš* [. . .
37) *ia-a-ši [i]š-ta-na-al-an-ni*
38) *e-me* x [. . .
39) *ba-qa-a[n* . .] x-*mi-na-a-a-ti*
40) *e-me* [. . .
41) *ba-qa-[an* . .] x-*ni mi-ig-ri*
42) *ba-qa-a[n* . . .
43) *mi-šil a-[kal?-la? m]i-šil ú-maš-šar*

---

44) *a-na* a x [. . .
45) . . .] x ^{lú}*bābilû*(tin.tir)^{meš}
46) [. . . . .]
47) . . .] x$^{ki.meš}$
48-49) (trace)

Variants:

21) d: *[a-na k]u-mu*
22) d: *ana* ⌜*ku-mu*⌝ *tal-te-*⌜*mi*⌝-IA B: *up-ši*
24) d: ⌜*mu-ti-ka*⌝
29) d: *k[a-a-š]ú*
30) d: ⌜*lu-bar-ki*⌝
31) A: *a-ga-*⌜*a*⌝-[
32) A(C): TÚG$^{ḫi.a}$-*ki*
33) d: *e-ka-nu*, *maš ma-*⌜*ša-a*⌝-[

21) Instead of twisting the threads of My Lord,
22) Instead of staying respectful--process wool.
23) Instead of *making* . . . . . of his heart,
24) Create a family for your husband.
25) She who is present [. . .
26) A dish . . the vessel might be full,
27) The good housewife . . . . [. . .
28) I will make my intelligent one(s) speak to you (fem. sing.)
29) To you (fem. sing.) . . [. . .
30) I will make you hold your clothes in (your) teeth.
31) From my bowl [. . .
32) I will make you hold your clothes in (your) teeth.

---

33) Where will they see you? . . . .
34) A dog is like . [. . .
35) With the plucking of a bird will I pluck you.
36) Like a goat(?) [. . .
37) He keeps on asking me!
38) [. .] is like . [. . .
39) With the plucking [. .] . . . . . .
40) [. .] is like [. . .
41) With the plucking [. .] , . . my favorite.
42) With the plucking [. . .
43) Half I [will hold back], half I will let go.

---

44) To . . [. . .
45) . . .] the Babylonians

Section II: K 7924 obv. ii

1) *a-di šàr*[*i ṭa-a-bi* . . .
2) *ba-ti-iq* ma x [. . .
3) *ina re-mi-ki lal-l*[*a-ru*? . . .
4) *ina tub-qa-a-ti-šá* x [. . .
5) *it-tu-ú-a* ni giš x [. . .
6) *la ṭa-a-bi šá re-m*[*i-ki* . . .
7) ^{lú}*má-laḫ*$_4$ *šá re-m*[*i-ki* . . .
8) ^{lú}*nuḫatimmu*(MU) *šá re-m*[*i-ki* . . .
9) ^{lú}*atkuppu*(ad.KID) *šá re-mi-*[*ki* . . .
10) *ṣu-ra-ru-u šá re-mi-k*[*i* . . .
11) *pi-ṣal-lu-ru šá re-mi-*[*ki* . . .
12) *mu-ra-šu-u šá re-mi-k*[*i* . . .
13) *ḫa-ma-ṣi-ru šá re-mi-ki* [. . .
14) *tu-ma-nu-u šá re-mi-k*[*i* . . .
15) *ul-tu tam-tim pu-uḫ-*[*ḫi*?*-ri*? . . .
16) *ina muḫḫi bal-*x [. . .

* * * * *

Section III

A = K 4247+ rev. iv or vi; lines 6-35
C = 83-1-18, 464 rev.; lines 1-15

1) x [. . .
2) be x [. . .
3) *ṣu-ub-*[. . .
4) *mut-tab-bil-t*[*um* . . .
5) *ša-di-du ú-*[. . .
6) *mu-še-lu-ú-*⸢*a*⸣ [. . .] x x x [. . .]
7) ^{giš}*gi-šal-li-ia šá* $^{\text{na4}}$*mušgarri*(muš.gír)
8) *ša* $^{\text{na4}}$*pappardilî*(babbar.dili) *par-ri-sa-a-ti*
9) *ul-tu il-lu-ur-ti a-di il-lu-ur-ti*
10) $^{\text{na4}}$*pappardilâ*(babbar.dili) *ma-la-ku di-ig-li*
11) *pir'i*(nunuz) ^{giš}*erīni sik-ka-tu-u-a eb-li mar-kas kitû nam-ru*
12) *ak-kul-le-ti šá* $^{\text{na4}}$*aš-pú-u*
13) x x mu *uḫ-ḫu-zu ḫurāṣu liq-tú*
14) [^{giš}]*nar-da-ma-a-a šá* ^{giš}*erīni*
15) ⸢*ú*⸣ *ša-di-du šá* ^{síg}*ta-kil-ti*
16) [x *a*]*-ram-mu-u-a ina* ^{giš}*a-su* x x
17) [x]*-ur-ru bāb-šá-nu* x x x x (x)
18) x *a-ram-me-ia* x [. . .
19) *ṭa-bu-ti il-l*[*a-ku šá na-pi-šu*]
20) ^{giš}*maqurri*(má.gur$_8$) *ṣi-ḫa-a*[*t* . . .

Variant:

12) A: *ak-kul-le-ia*

1) Together with the [pleasant] breeze [. . .
2) It is cut off . . [. . .
3) In your vulva is honey(?) [. . .
4) In its recesses . [. . .
5) My seeder plough . . . [. . .
6) That which is not pleasant of [your] vulva [. . .
7) The sailor of [your] vulva [. . .
8) The cook of [your] vulva [. . .
9) The basket-maker of [your] vulva [. . .
10) The lizard of [your] vulva [. . .
11) The gecko of [your] vulva [. . .
12) The cat of [your] vulva [. . .
13) The mouse of your vulva [. . .
14) The .... of [your] vulva [. . .
15) Gather(?) from the sea [. . .
16) Upon . . [. . .

* * * * *

4) The equipment(?) [. . .
5) The lanyards . [. . .
6) My "lifters" . [. . .] . . . [. . .]
7) My oars are of serpentine(?),
8) my punting poles are of pappardilû-stone.
9) From oarlock(?) to oarlock(?)
10) I am filled with gems of pappardilû-stone.
11) My pegs are offshoots of cedar, the girding ropes are shining linen,
12) my . . . . are of jasper.
13) The . . . are overlaid with choice gold,
14) my clamps(?) are of cedar,
15) and the lanyards are of purple wool.
16) My [. .] . . . . . in myrtle wood
17) [.] . . their gate . . . . .
18) . of my . . . . [. . .
19) Pleasant things [of (good) aroma] go
20) the boat of pleasure [. . .

21) *tu-ul-lu-la-ku ina* ì.g[iš?
22) *šal-*[*ṭ*]*u ina lìb-bi* [. . .
23) *mār š*[*ar*]*ri mar-kás* [. . .
24) *šá l*[*ú* x (x)] x ḫa [. . .
25) di x [. . .
26) *am-me-n*[*i* . . .
27) *ina* ^giš^*maqurri*(má.g[ur₈)[. . .
28) *ša-ia-'-*[. . .
29) *la i-ba-áš-*[*ši* . . .
30) [^gi^]^š^*nár-da-ma-*⌜*a*⌝*-*[*a* . . .
31) [*z*]*i?-i*[*b?* . . .
32) ⌜*ù*⌝ [. . .
33) ⌜*ù*⌝ x [. . .
34) x a [. . .
35) [x] x x [. . .

Section IV: K 7924 rev. iii(?)

1) *ina ṣilli*(giss[u)[. . .
2) *ina ṣilli*(gi[ssu)[. . .
3) ki [. . .
4) k[i . . .

Section V: K 7924 rev. iv(?)

1) . . .] x x x x
2) . . .]*-bi šaptā*^meš^*-šá*
3) . . .] x*-bi pa-ni-šá*
4) . . .] x *ut* ^giš^*erši*

---

5) . . . .] x x x *a-ka*

Notes on Group I:

I 10, 14 Until the sign following *-rat* is certainly identified, *ed-bat*, from *edēpu*, will remain doubtful.

I 11 For *šanîtu* see *AfO* 19 (1959-60) 63 note on 64.

I 20, 22 The reading of B *up-ši* is obscure, though it could be emended to *up-pi-ši*.

I 21 See *CAD dâpu* and the Arabic root *ṭwp* 'walk around,' 'turn.'

I 33 For the interrogative use of *lū* + preterite, see *JCS* 21 (1967) 131, n. on 30.

II 5 Perhaps restore *šamna*(ì.giš) *l*[*u-up-pi-ti* "[rub] my seeder plough with oil."

III Many of the names of parts of the boat are not certainly understood, and the translations, where these are given, are to be treated accordingly.

III 21 The verb here is certainly *talālu*, though its meaning is uncertain. In addition to the verb used with the bow in the Zû Epic (*RA* 48 [1954] 148[2]), which may be connected with *alālu* "hang" (see *CAD* A/1, 331), other meanings occur (see *Or* N.S. 22 [1953] 260-61).

21) I am . . . . . with oil(?) [. . .
22) The victor in [. . .
23) The crown prince [. . .] the girding [. . .]
24) . . [. .] . . [. . .
25) . . [. . .
26) Why [. . .
27) In the boat [. . .
28) . . . [. . .
29) There is not [. . .
30) My clamps(?) [. . .

1) In the shadow [. . .
2) In the shadow [. . .

2) . . .] . her lips
3) . . .] . . her face
4) . . .] . . the bed.

GROUP II: K 6606 + 9944 + Sm 1891 + 82-5-22, 569

Column A

1) [. . .] x *lìb-bi ú-*[. . .
2) x-*ba-a-a ana* ^{giš}*maqurri*(má.gur$_8$) *us-*[. . . .]
3) *a-teb-bi-ma a-na* ^{giš}*maqurri*(má.gur$_8$) [. . . .]
4) *a-ra-aḫ-tu ana bābili*^{ki} [. . . .]
5) *mu-de-e nāri* ^{giš}*sikkāna*(zi.gan) x [. . . .]
6) *mu-de-e ta-ba-li áš-lu ú-šá-á*[*š-da-ad*]
7) *mu-de-e šá raq-qat nāri ú-šá-aṣ-ba-ta pa-ri-šá-a-te*
8) a li ki ma *ina ka-ri-šú a-gíl-li*
9) *šú bēli ri-mi-ni-i* ^{d}*marduk*
10) *ina ku-tal bīti-šú a-gíl-li šá bēltim*(gašan)*-ma šá é-tùr-kalam-ma*
11) *el-li-ma a-na muḫḫi ka-a-ri az-za-a-zi*
12) *ik-kil-li a-nam-di ana* ^{lú}*bābilāiē*$^{ki.e}$
13) *šàr šarrāni*^{meš} ^{lú}*bābilāiē*$^{ki.e}$
14) ^{d}*nabû*(nà) *ana bābili*^{ki} *i-te-lam-ma*
15) *ú-pur-ku-nu šú ṣi-ḫa-a-ti*
16) ^{d}*na-bi-ia-a-ni ana* ⌜*bābili*⌝ [^{ki} . . .]
17) *ti-bi* e x [. . .
18) x x [. . .

Note: A 8, 10 For the interpretation *a-gíl-li* see *CAD āgīlu*.

Column B

1) (traces)
2) . . .]*-ú ana pit-ri i-ga-r*[*i*]
3) . . .] *la ṭè-ma-ni-t*[*u*]
4) . . .] x x *pa-ni-ia am-mar*
5) . . .] *ki-ma* ^{na4}*parūti*(giš.ŠIR. gal)
6) . . .] *ki-ma ḫurāṣi*
7) . . .] x *uḫ-taš-šá-áš*
8) *-t*]*i ana eṣ-ṣer āli*
9) . . .] *ma-a-ri al-lak*
10) . . .] x *a-na bīt* ^{giš}*erši*(ná)
11) . . .]*-še-ki li-bil*
12) . . .] *e-mu-ru-k*[*i*]
13) . . .] *e-mu-ru-k*[*i*]
14) . . .] x *mê*^{meš} *ul i-man-*[*ni*]
15) . . .] x-*e ul i-nam-din*
16) . . .] x-x-*su a-na ḫa-la-ṣi*
17) . . .] x ne *É ul it-ti-iq*
18) [x x] x ti ul x x x x na *pi-ti*
19) x x-*ia* x x [. . .] x x
20) *ša* x x x [. . . . .] x
21) *ša* en ṣ[i]? x x [. . . . .] x
22) *ša* x x x [. . . . .] x-*šú*

Column A

1)[. . .] . . . . [. . .
2) . . . . to the boat . [. . . .]
3) I will arise and [. . . .] to the boat.
4) The Araḫtu-canal to Babylon [. . . .]
5) Him who is familiar with the river [I will make handle] the paddle,
6) Him who is familiar with dry ground I will make [drag] the towing-rope,
7) Him who is familiar with the marshy parts of the river I will make handle the punting-poles.
8) . . . . on its quay is the *towman*
9) Of Marduk, the merciful lord.
10) Behind his temple is the *towman* of the Lady of Eturkalamma.
11) I will climb up on to the quay and will stand,
12) I will utter a cry to the men of Babylon,
13) The King of Kings, O men of Babylon!
14) Nabû has come up to Babylon!
15) Your festive hair style.
16) Our dear Nabû [. . .] to Babylon.
17) Arise . . [. . .

Column B

2) . . .] . . . wall . . .
3) . . .] she who is not intelligent
4) . . .] . . . I will see my face
5) . . .] like alabaster
6) . . .] like gold
7) . . .] he/she is made happy
8) . . .] to design(?) the city
9) . . .] my boy-friend I will go
10) . . .] to the bed chamber
11) . . .] . . . let him/her bring
12) . . .] they have seen you
13) . . .] they have seen you
14) . . .] will not count . . .
15) . . .] . . . will not give
16) . . .] . . . to press out
17) . . .] . . . will not pass over
18) . . . . is open
19) [. . .] . . . [. . .]
20) [. . .] . . . [. . .]
21) . . . . . [. . . . .] . . .
22) . . . . . [. . . . .] . . .

23) *ana* x x x [. . . .] x x ⌜*tu*⌝-*ḫal-laq*
24) *mār ba-né-e ma-a-*[*t*]*i il-li-ku*
25) ^{na4}*uqnû ša* [. . .] x *ina pi-til-ti*

---

26) *at-ti man-nu šùm-ki man-nu šá ana šu-b*[*at*] *bēli-ia tan-da-ni-ri*
27) *al-kim-ma ki-i šá a-qab-ba-ki ep-ši*
28) *ul-tu muḫḫi ú-ri ana muḫḫi patri*(gír) *muq-ti*
29) [^{giš}]*sikkat*(gag) *parzilli muḫ-ri a-na ṣi-*[*l*]*i-ki*
30) [*šil*]-*ta-ḫu še-qu-ti* [*muḫ-r*]*i*
31) [x]-*ri-ia-ma* na ki šu x [. . .] x
32) . . .] ⌜^{lú}*nappāḫu*⌝ [. . .

Column C

1-2) (traces)
3) *akla*(ninda$^{ḫi.⌜a⌝}$) [. . .
4) KI+MIN bi? x [. . .
5) *akla*(ninda$^{ḫi.a}$) ib x [. . .
6) *šikaru rēštû na-áš-*[*pu* . . .
7) ^{d}*bēl šá taš-ši-*x [. . .
8) *bal-ta* nu? šá? ta x [. . .
9) *er-bi-i-ma* x [. . .
10) *šu-ṣi-i lil-li* x [. . .
11) *pi-i-ki-ma* ud zi [. . .
12) *ša ina lìb-bi taš-ši-*[. . .
13) *a-ḫi-ki ina zēr ma-a-t*[*i*? . . .
14) *ša ina lìb-bi taḫ-ṣi-ni* [. . .
15) *šēpī*^{II}*-ki ina* ^{giš}*mar-ri* x [. . .
16) *ša ina lìb-bi* ti x x [. . .
17) *šá ú* x x x [. . .

GROUP III: K 6082 + 81-7-27, 241

Column A

1) x [. . .
2) *i-*x [. . .
3) *su-u*[*ḫ*?- . . .

---

4) *šu-ri-da-ma* [*i-da-a* . . .
5) *šá* ^{d}*bēl bābili*^{ki} x [. . .
6) *a-šar a-mur-šá-nu qin-nu qa-a*[*n-nu*]
7) tu.gur$_4$^{mušen} *ma-lu-ú ga-ap-nu*
8) *li-da-né-e šá ḫar-ba-qa-ni*
9) *la-mu-ú* ^{d}*bēl ki-ma ki-li-li*
10) *ina muḫḫi bēl bābili*^{ki} *it-ta-na-at-ba-ku-ni*
11) ^{giš}*ḫas-ḫas-tu* ^{giš}*šurmēnu*(šur.mìn) *ù bu-ra-ši*

---

12) *e ba-ru-ú ina libbi e-bé-eḫ*
13) *ak-ka-a-a-i áš-kun-ka ṭe-e-mu*
14) *ina šá-pa-ḫu-ti-ka ina libbi uznī*^{II}*-ka ú-làḫ-ḫiš*

23) . . . . [. . . .] . . you will destroy
24) The aristocrats of the land went
25) Lapis lazuli which [. . .] . in a sling.

---

26) You, whoever you are, whatever your name is, who always go to the dwelling of my lord,
27) Come and do as I tell you!
28) Fall from the roof on to a dagger,
29) Get an iron spike in your side,
30) Get sharp arrows.
31) [.] . my . . . . . [. . .] .
32) . . .] the smith [. . .

Column C

3) Food [. . .
4) Ditto . . . [. . .
5) Food . . [. . .
6) Strained "first" beer [. . .
7) Bel, whom you . . [. . .
8) Vigor . . . . [. . .
9) Enter and . [. . .
10) Put out the fools . [. . .
11) Your mouth . . [. . .
12) In which you . . [. . .
13) Your arms from the seed of the *land* [. . .
14) Wherein you sought protection [. . .
15) Your feet on a spade . [. . .
16) Wherein . . . [. . .

Column A

4) Bring down and [place . . .
5) Of the Lord of Babylon . . [. . .
6) Where the wild doves nest,
7) The pigeons fill the trees,
8) And the fledglings of the . . . . bird
9) Surround Bel like a crown,
10) The needles of cypress and fir
11) Pour down upon the Lord of Babylon.

---

12) Oh, seer, on (mount) Ebeḫ
13) What were the instructions I gave you?
14) In your . . . . I whispered in your ears,

15) *ana ekurrāti*(é.kur)^{meš} *šá māti šá ta-ma-ku-ú mi-ki-ma*
16) *ana šá-a-šú la ta-me-ka-a-šú ana é-kur é-tùr-kalam-ma*
17) *é-kur ìl-šú ma-gir-šú bēl-šú ana lìb-bi-šú mit-gur*
18) KI+MIN *šu-tu-ma bēl bābili*^{ki} ^{d}*marduk*

Column B

1) [. .] x x [. . .
2) [x] x x *a-na* x [. . .

---

3) *in-di ana ú-ri lu-ú* x [. . .
4) *ul-tu* lu ka ni x [. . .
5) *šá ṣi-in-di it-*[. . .
6) *ina pa-ni-šá ar-ra-b*[*u* . . .]
7) *ina ar-ki-šá ḫa-m*[*a-ṣi-ru*]
8) *si-si-ke-ti-šú i-bi-i*[*ḫ*]
9) *šu-ú ḫu-lu-ú mār ḫa-ma-ṣ*[*i-ri*]
10) *tap-pat-ti a-na* ^{uru}*kār-bēl-mātāti*(kur.kur) *áš-pur*(-)[*ki*?]
11) *am-me-ni ta-aṣ-ru-ti-ma ta-ba-š*[*i*]
12) ^{giš}*saparra*(kak.liš.lá) *ša bēli-šú am-me-ni taš-ku-ni ni-piš ri-*[x]

---

13) *ina né-bé-ri* ^{uru}*kār-bēl-mātāti*(kur.kur)
14) *tap-pat-ti a-mur-ma ḫa-ma-ku dan-niš*
15) *pe-ṣa-ti-ma ki-i pi-ṣal-lu-ur-t*[*i*]
16) *maš-ku naq-lat ki-ma di-q*[*a-ri*]
17) *tu-uḫ-tan-nab tu-uḫ-ta*[*š-šá-áš*]

Column C

1) [x] x [. . .
2) *amtu* x [. . .

---

3) aš mu ú [ma *in-ni-kan-na ú-nam-bi*]
4) *šal-šu* x [. . .
5) *aš-ta-at-*x [. . .
6) *ul alap* ku gi [. . .
7) *ul imēr šá bīt* ^{lú}x [. . .

Notes:

A 4-11 See Landsberger, *MSL* VIII/2 135-37.

A 17 Note the use of the I/2 *mitgur* in the sense of the Sumerian prefix inga. See *ta-am-gu-ur-ma šar-ra-am ù ka-lu-šu-nu im-ta-ag-ru*: *JRAS* cent. supp. (1924) pl. 6 ii 1.

C 6-7 See 81-2-4, 294 rev.:] x [; *ul immer r*[*e*]*-e-šú* x [; *bīt be-lí-šú re-es-su* x x.

15) Neglect whichever of the temples of the land you wish,
16) But do not neglect this one, the temple Eturkalamma,
17) The god of the temple is favourable to it, and its lord is also favourable to it.
18) Ditto. He is Marduk, lord of Babylon.

Column B

3) May my support . [. . .] to the roof.
4) From . . . . [. . .
5) Of the yoke . [. . .
6) Before her a dormouse [. . .]
7) Behind her a rat.
8) He girded his garments:
9) He is a shrew mouse, born of a mouse.
10) I sent [you(?)], my girl-friend, to Kār-bēl-mātāti.
11) Why did you break wind and become embarrassed?
12) Why did you make the wagon of her lord a . [.] smell?

---

13) At the river crossing of Kār-bēl-mātāti
14) I saw my girl-friend and was completely overwhelmed.
15) You are white like a gecko,
16) Your skin is dusky like a pot,
17) You are exhuberant, you are made [happy].

Column C

3) . . . [. . . . . I bemoaned].
4) . . . [. . .
5) . . . . [. . .
6) He is not an ox . . [. . .
7) He is not a donkey belonging to the house of a . [. . .

GROUP IV

LKA 92 (photo K 212a): lines 1-23.
81-2-4, 294 obv.: lines 12-23.
Lines 18-22 have been restored from BM 46336 + 46371 obv. 9-11.

1) . . .] *ip-pu-uš ṣi-ib-tum* x [. . .
2) . . .] x-*li-ma ú-šaq-qa-ma ina qaqqadi-šú* [. . .
3) . . .]-*nak-kar-ma*(! text LA) *elī-šú* [x x]

---

4) [*bi-iṣ-ṣu-ru šú*] *tap-pa-ti-ia pi-rik bābi-lí sin-gu i-saḫ-ḫ*[*ur*]
5) [*a-na ka*]-*pa-ri šú re-mi-ki a-na ka-pa-ri šú li-biš-šú-ti-ki*
6) [*ú*] *a-na* ^{sal}*bābilāiāti*(tin.tir)$^{ki.meš}$ *li-iq-bi sin-gu la i-nam-di-na-a-ni-iš-ši*
7) [*a*]-*na ka-pa-ri šú re-mi-šú a-na ka-pa-ri šú li-biš-šú-ti-šú*

---

8) [*a-na bi-iṣ*]-*ṣu-ri-ki šú tak-la-te* [*k*]*i-i abni-ka-ma aq-ra ina pa-ni-ki*
9) [x (x)]-*ki a-na pa-ni-ki šu-uk-ni bu-ul-im-ma ni-pi-is-su eṣ-ni*
10) [(..)] ⌜*ki-i*⌝ *la bu-ú-ku ka-bé-e ki-i la ri-is-ni šú* ^{lú}*ašlākī*(TÚG.BABBAR)^{meš}

---

11) *a-na* [*bi-iṣ*]-*ṣu-ri-ki šú tak-la-te kal-bi ú-še-er-re-eb bāba a-rak-kas*
12) *kalba ú-še-*[*er-r*]*e-eb bāba a-rak-kas ḫa-aḫ-ḫu-ru ú-še-er-re-eb qin-na i-qan-na-an*
13) *it-ti a-ṣe-ia it-ti e-re-bi-ia*
14) *ḫa-aḫ-ḫu-re-ti-ia ṭè-mu a-šak-kan*
15) *ad-da-ni-ka ḫa-aḫ-ḫur-ti-ia*
16) *ina muḫḫi kamūni*(uzu.dir) *la te-qer-ru-ub*
17) KI+MIN *šú su-ḫa-ti ni-pi-is-su*

---

18) *at-ti um-me-e* ^{d}*ištar*(mùš) *bābili*(tin.tir)^{ki}
19) *banīti*(dù)^{ti} *šar-rat* <^{lú}>*bābilāiē*(tin.tir)$^{ki.meš}$
20) *at-ti um-me-e* ^{giš}*gišimmar* ^{na4}*sāndi*(gug)
21) *banīti*(dù)^{ti} *ša a-na ma-gal ba-na-a-tú*
22) *šú ana ma-gal be-lu-ú šú a-na ma-gal ba-nu-ú la-an-šú*
23) (traces)

Variants:

11) *LKA* om. *bi-iṣ-*
12) 81-2-4, 294: *ú-še-ra*[*b*]
14) *LKA*: *ṭe*]-*ma*
17) 81-2-4, 294: *ša*
18) BM: [*at-t*]*a*, tin.tir^{ki}-*im*
 81-2-4, 294: om. d
19) BM: *ba-ni-tú*
 LKA:]-*ni-tum*, tin.tir^{ki}.ke$_4$
 81-2-4, 294: *šar-rat* mùš tin.ti[r$^{ki.x}$]
20) BM: [*at-t*]*a*
21) BM: AN *ba-ni-tum šá ana*
 LKA: -*t*]*um šá*, -*n*]*a*?-*at*?
22) 81-2-4, 294: [*a-n*]*a ma-gal be*-x[
 LKA: -*n*]*i-šú*

1) . . .] will make, seizure . [. . .
2) . . .] . . . he will raise and on his head [. . .
3) . . .] . . . upon him [. .]

---

4) [Genitals of] my girl-friend, the district of Babylon is seeking a rag,
5) [To] wipe your vulva, to wipe your vagina.
6) [Now] let him/her say to the women of Babylon, "The women will not give her a rag
7) To wipe her vulva, to wipe her vagina."

---

8) [Into] your genitals in which you trust, like your precious stone before you,
9) Set your [. .] before you, sniff the smell of the cattle
10) Like something not mended by the tailor, like something not soaked by the laundrymen.

---

11) Into your genitals in which you trust I will make a dog enter and will tie shut the door;
12) I will make a dog enter and will tie shut the door; I will make a ḫaḫḫuru-bird enter and it will nest.
13) Whenever I leave or enter
14) I will give orders to my (fem.) ḫaḫḫuru-birds,
15) "Please, my dear ḫaḫḫuru-bird,
16) Do not approach the mushrooms."
17) Ditto. The smell of the armpits.

---

18) You are the mother, Ištar of Babylon,
19) The beautiful one, the queen of the Babylonians.
20) You are the mother, a palm of carnelian,
21) The beautiful one, who is beautiful to a superlative degree,
22) Whose figure is red to a superlative degree, is beautiful to a superlative degree,
23) (traces)

Rm II 385, DUPLICATED IN THE OBVERSE BY BM 46336 + 46371 rev. 8-18

Obverse

8) *i*[*a-a-ši ma*]*-a-ri ú-pal-làḫ-an-ni* KI.[MIN]
9) *ú-šaq-q*[*é*]-⌜*e*⌝*-ki ki-i dūri ú-šap-pal-ki ki-i ḫi-ri-*[*ṣi*]
10) *a-ḫe-ep-pe-e-ki kī*(gim) ib? ḫab? x du *pi-rik* giš bir [x]
11) *ú-šag-ra-ár-ki ki-i* x-x-*ru-rat a-raḫ-*[*ḫi*] x (x) [. .]
12) *a-si-ir-ki ki-i ba-*⌜*na*⌝*-tum pi-rik* giš ḫi [x x]
13) *al-kam-ma bēl ba-na-tu-ú a-ma/ba-la*?-[. . .]
14) *tu-šaq-qan-ni ki-i dūri ina ṣilli*(g[iss]u)*-ia nišī*^{m}[^{eš} . . .]
15) *tu-šap-*<*pa*>*-la-an-ni k*[*i-i* . . . .]
16) *ta-ḫe-ep-pan-ni* x x [. . . . .]
17) *tu-šag-ra-ra-ni ki-ma* x [. . . .]
18) *ta-si-ir-ra-an-ni ki-i* x x [. . .]

Variants (all BM):

14) *tu-šaq-qa-nu*
15) *tu-šap*-x-x *ḫ*[$^{e\text{-}pí}$]
16) [*t*]*a-ḫe-ep-pa-nu*
17) [*ta-* z]I-*ra-an-ni*

Reverse

1) *ia-a-ši ma-a-ri* [. . .
2) MIN *ta-aḫ-ḫa-za ú*-x [. . .
3) *ku-um* MIN ta x x [. . .
4) *at-ta lu-u* x [. . .
5) *at-ta* x [. . .
6) *at-ta* [. . .
7) ab x [. . .
8) tar [. . .
9) x [. . .

Notes:

Obv. 11 The tempting reading *i*[*s-q*]*â-ru-rat* "revolving harrow(?)" seems impossible from the traces.

8) As for me, my boy-friend scares me, As for me, my boy-friend scares me: (he says)
9) "I will lift you up like a wall, I will bring you down like a ditch.
10) I will break you like a . . . . [.]
11) I will roll you over like a . . . . from the store . . [. .]
12) I will plaster you over like beauty . . . . [. ."]
13) Come, my lord of beauty, I will . . [. . .]
14) Should you lift me up like a wall, people [will . . .] in my shade.
15) Should you bring me down like [. . . . . . .]
16) Should you break me . . [. . . . .]
17) Should you roll me over like . [. . . .]
18) Should you plaster me over like . . [. . .]

BM 67554

1) . . . *q*]*a-at-nu* ⸢*bīt sa*⸣-*á*[*r-ru-tum* . . .
2) . . .]-*qa ṣu-ma-m*[*i-tum* . . .
3) . . .] x-*di ap-pa-ri mer-di u* x [. . .
4) . . . *ḫur-sag*]-*kalam-ma*^{ki} *āl ba-na-a-ti ana-ku u* x [. . .
5) . . .] mud x lum *bīti-šá* dù^{meš} KI+MIN KI+M[IN . . .
6) . . .] x *qa-at-nu bīt sa-ár-ru-tum* KI+MIN K[I+MIN . . .
7) . . .] x *ṣu-ma-mi-tum* KI+MIN K[I+MIN . . .
8) . . . *a*]*p-pa-ri mer-di u er-šú* KI+MIN KI+[MIN . . .

---

9) [*ḫar-ra-nu šá kutî t*]*e-ba-ku al-lak ḫar-ra-n*[*u* . . .
10) . . .] x *ḫal-lu-ri-ia* x [. . .
11) . . .] x-*nu a-na muḫḫi kiš-k*[*i*?- . . .
12) . . .] *ḫa-ri-ṣi āl*[*i* . . .
13) . . .] *mar*?-*ri-ia* [. . .
14) . . .] NI-*ti-i*[*a* . . .
15) . . . *a*]*l*?-*ti* x [. . .

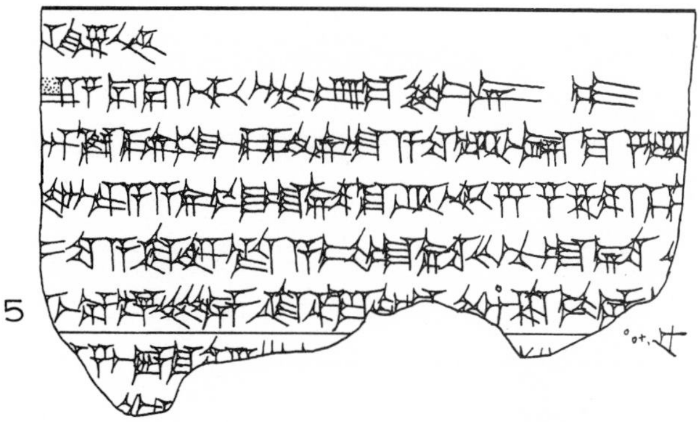

BM 41107
Obv.

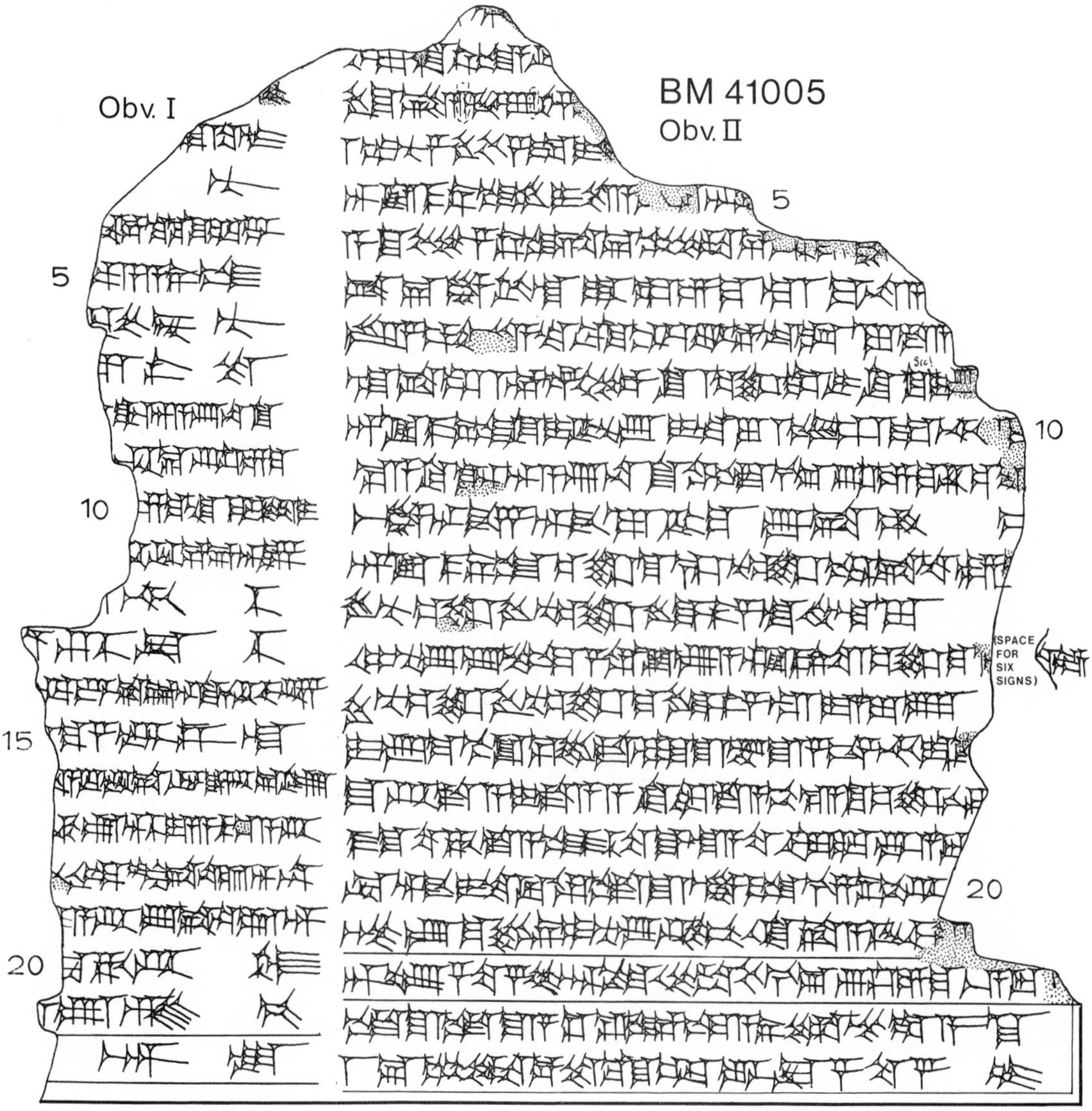

BM 41005
Obv. II

Obv. I

Sic!

(SPACE FOR SIX SIGNS)

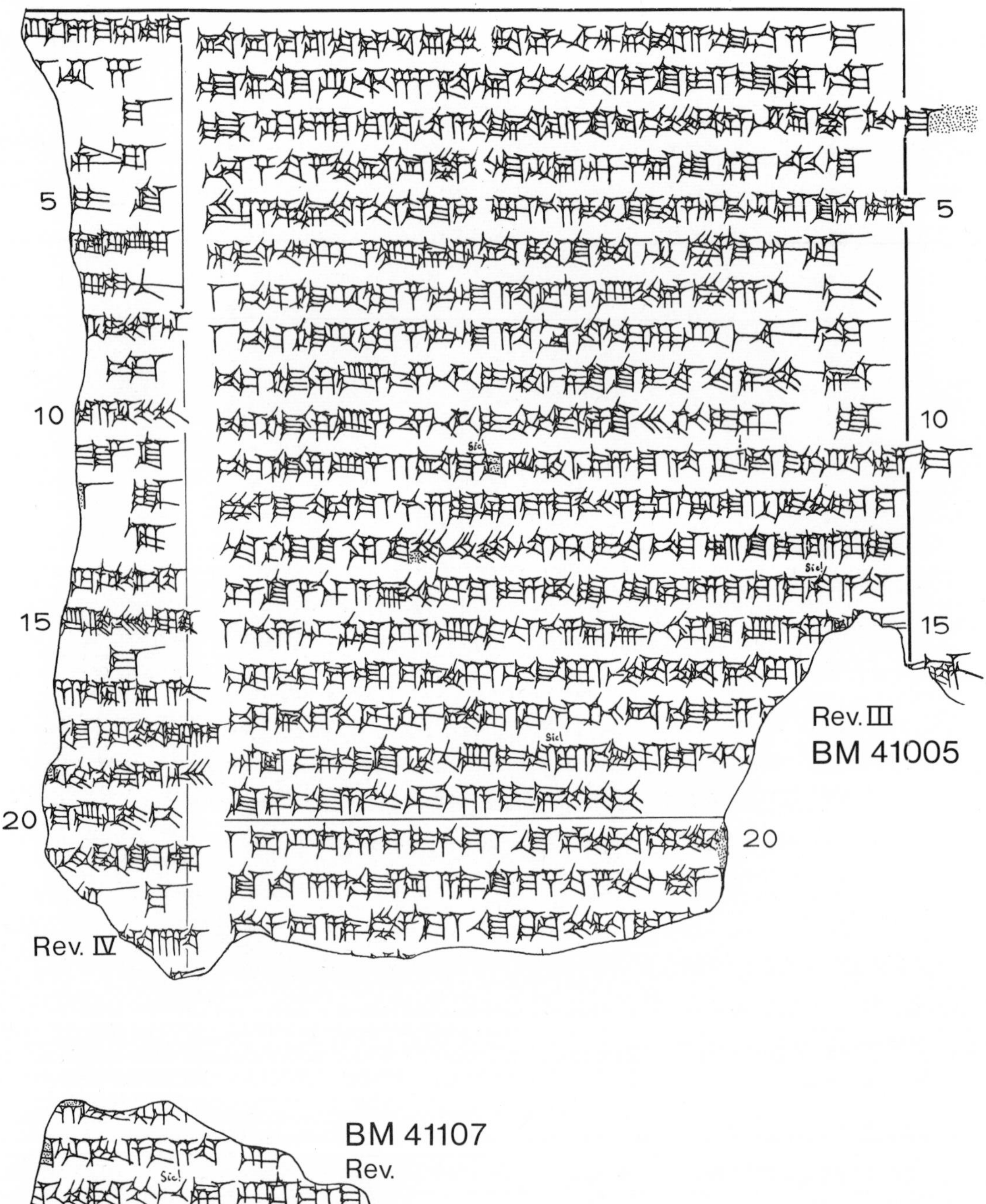

Sic!

Sic!

Sic!

Rev. IV

Rev. III
BM 41005

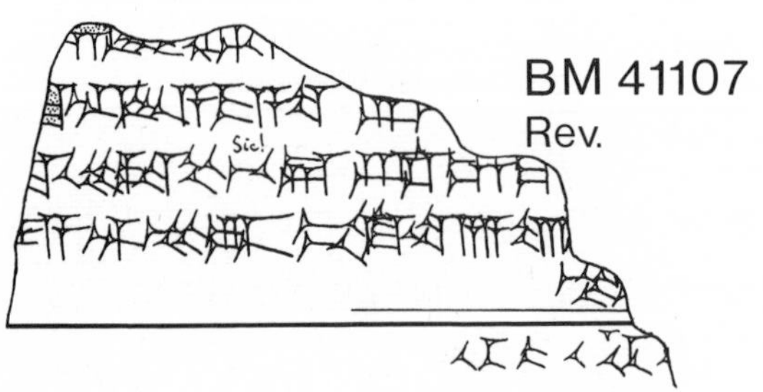

BM 41107
Rev.

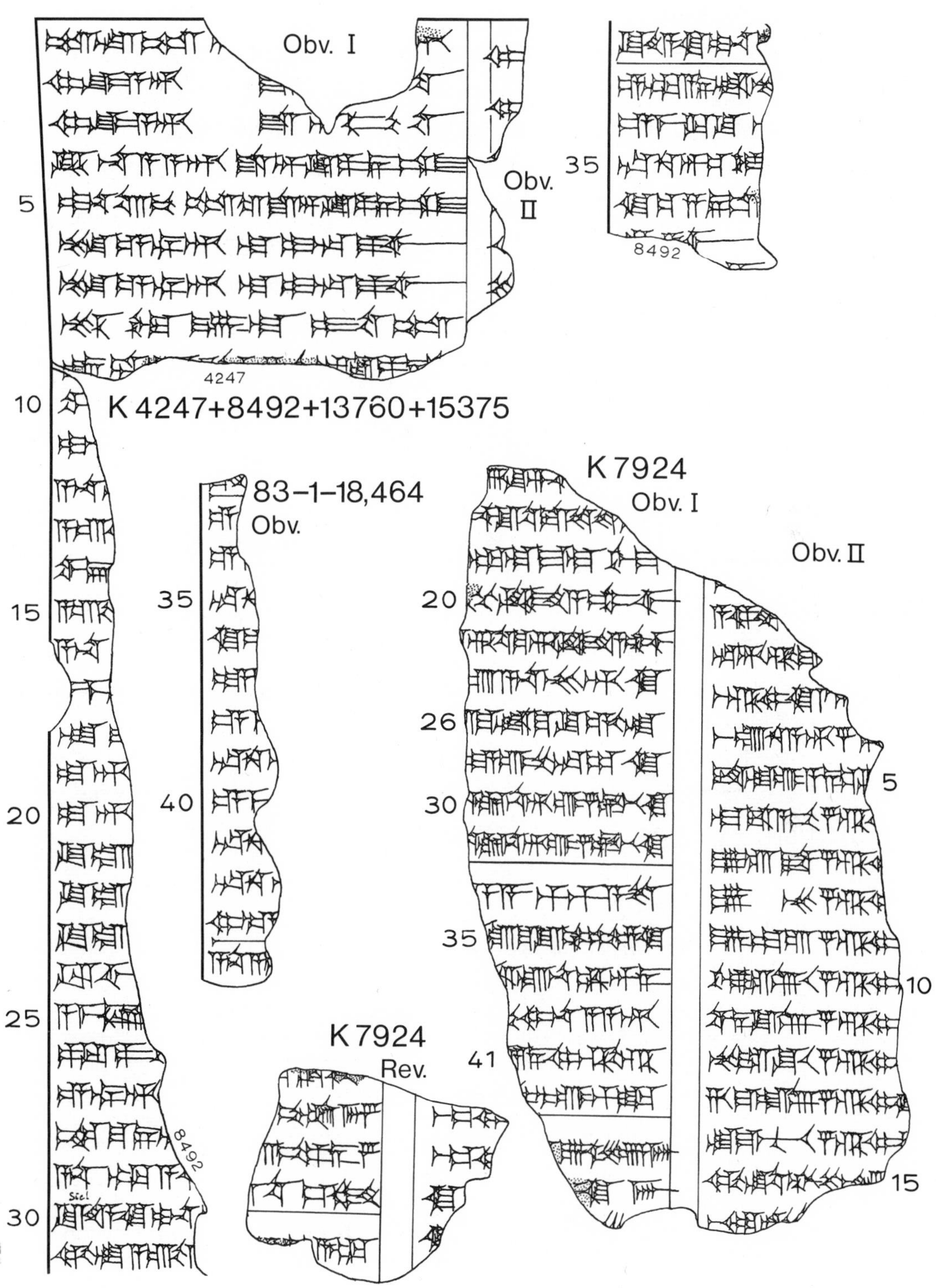

Obv. I
Obv. II
4247
K 4247+8492+13760+15375
8492
Sic!
83–1–18,464
Obv.
K 7924
Obv. I
Obv. II
K 7924
Rev.

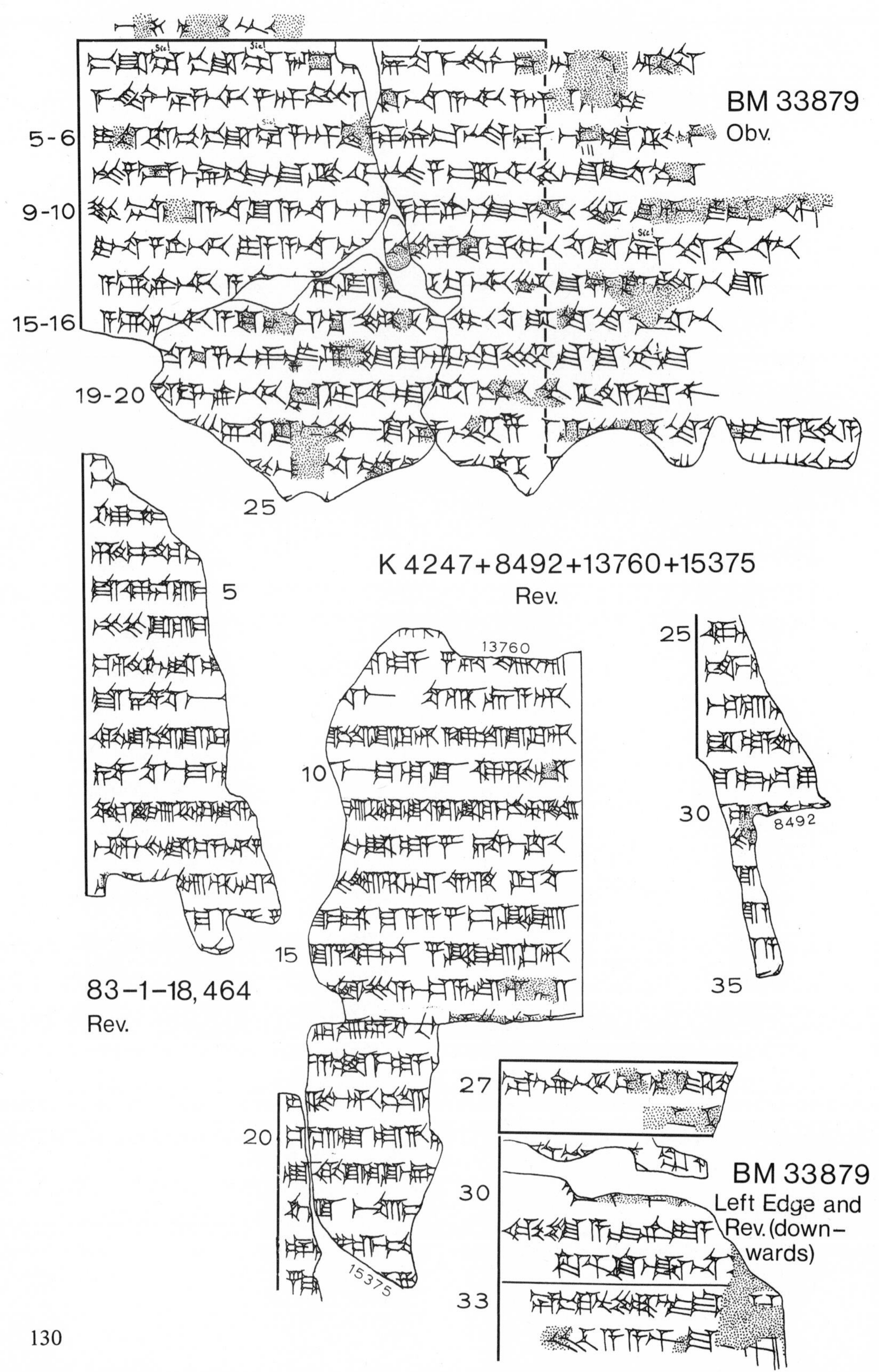
BM 33879
Obv.
K 4247+8492+13760+15375
Rev.
83–1–18, 464
Rev.
BM 33879
Left Edge and
Rev. (down-
wards)

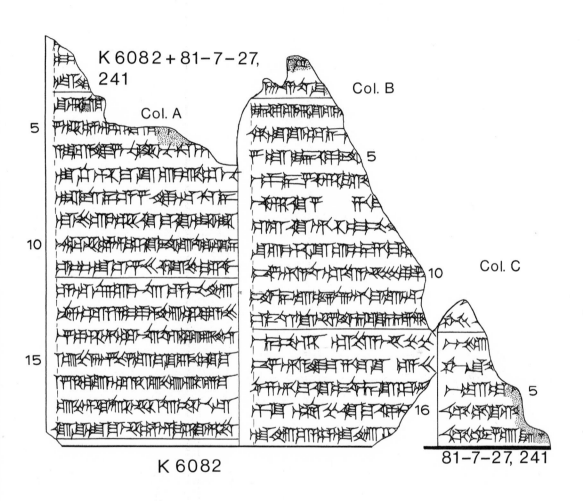

K 6082 + 81–7–27, 241

Col. A

Col. B

Col. C

K 6082

81–7–27, 241

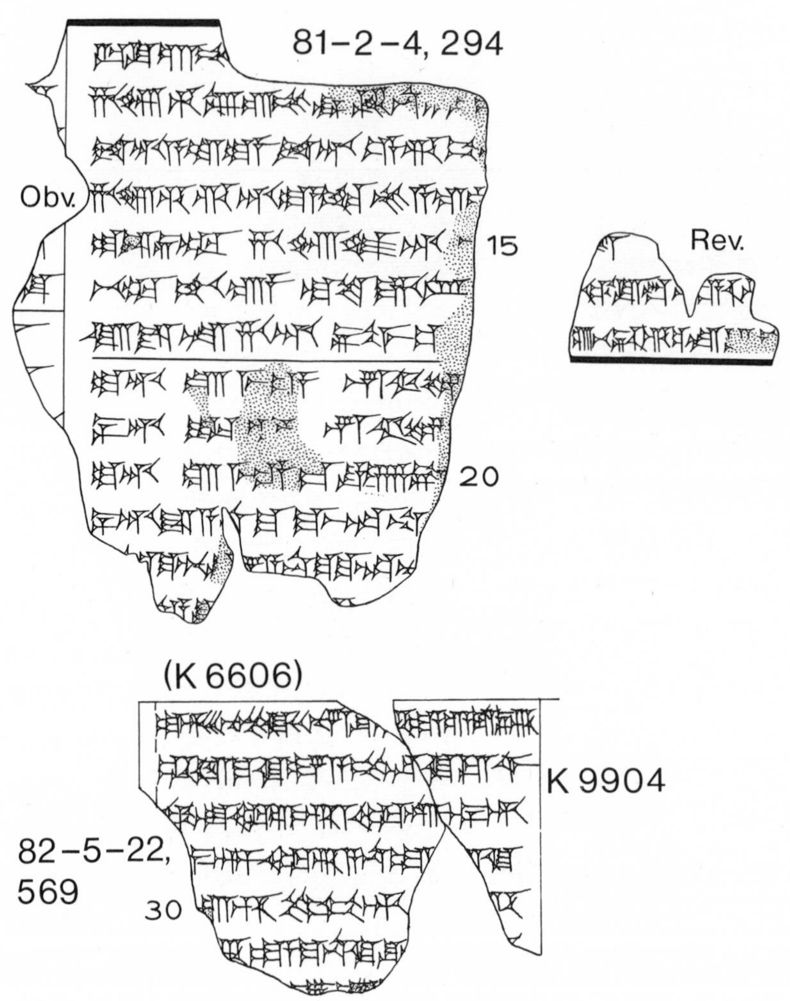
81-2-4, 294
Obv.
15
20
Rev.
(K 6606)
K 9904
82-5-22,
569
30

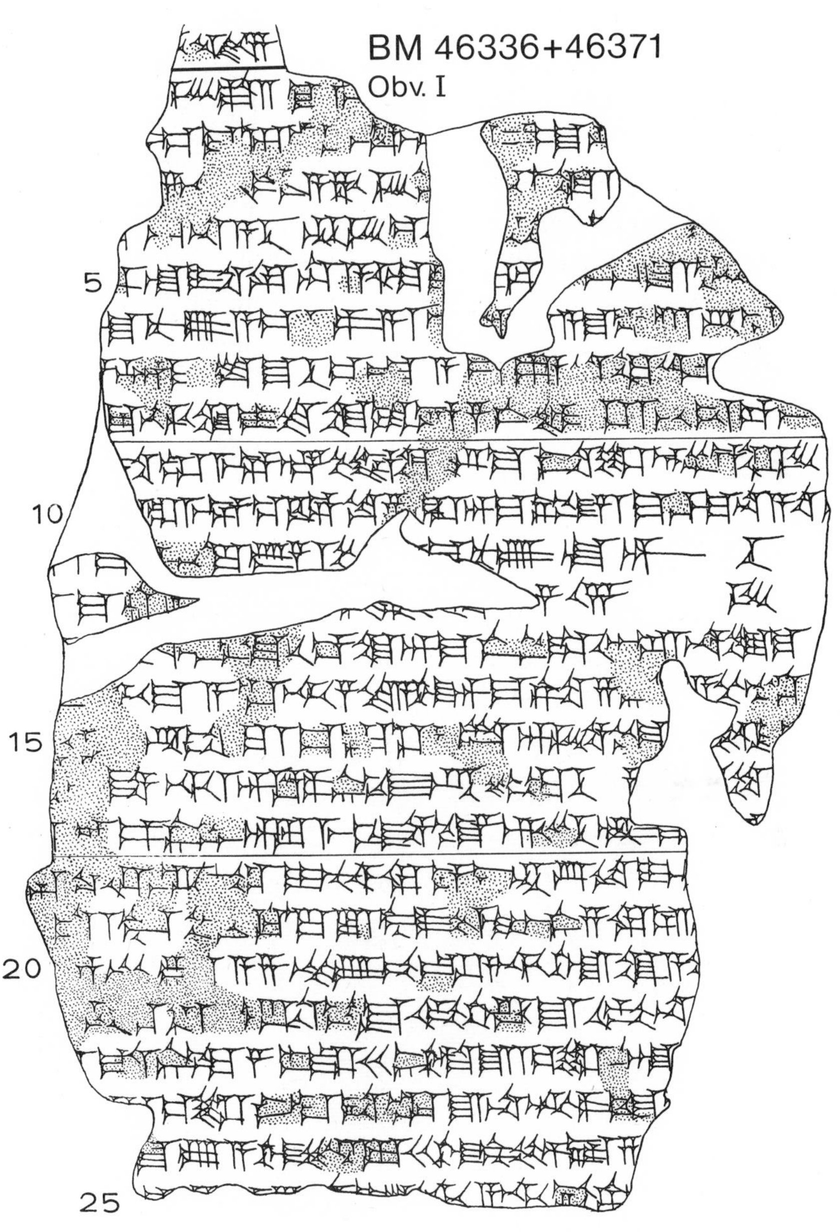
BM 46336+46371
Obv. I

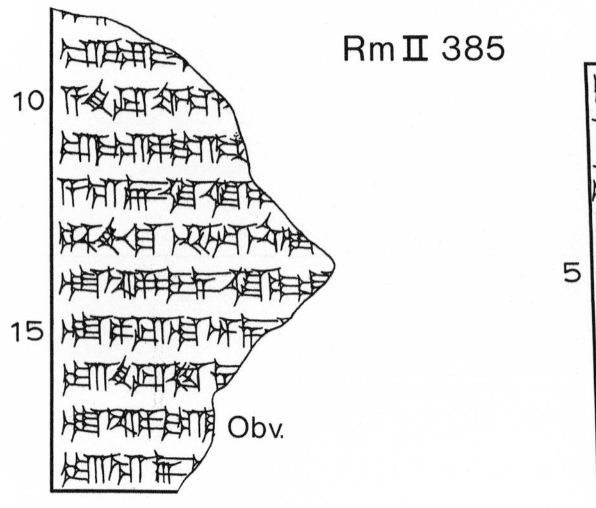
Rm II 385
Obv.

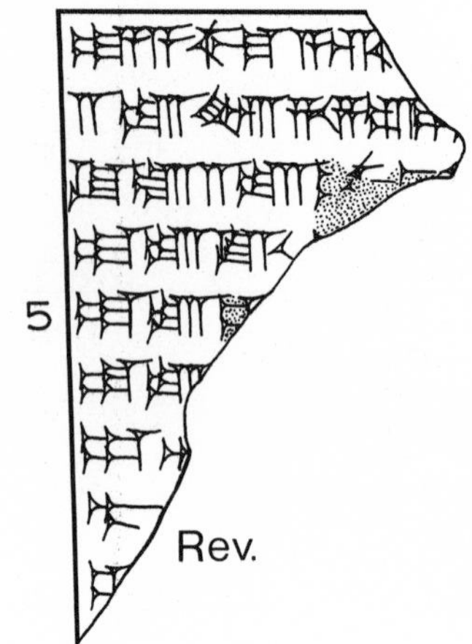
Rev.

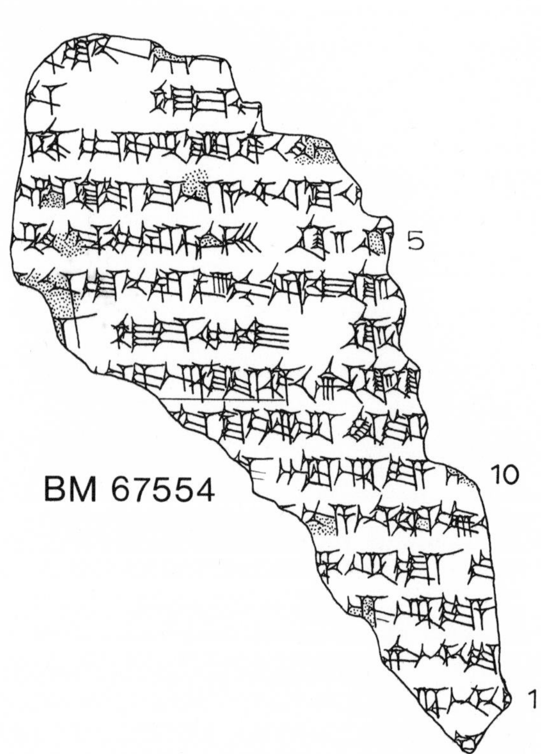
BM 67554

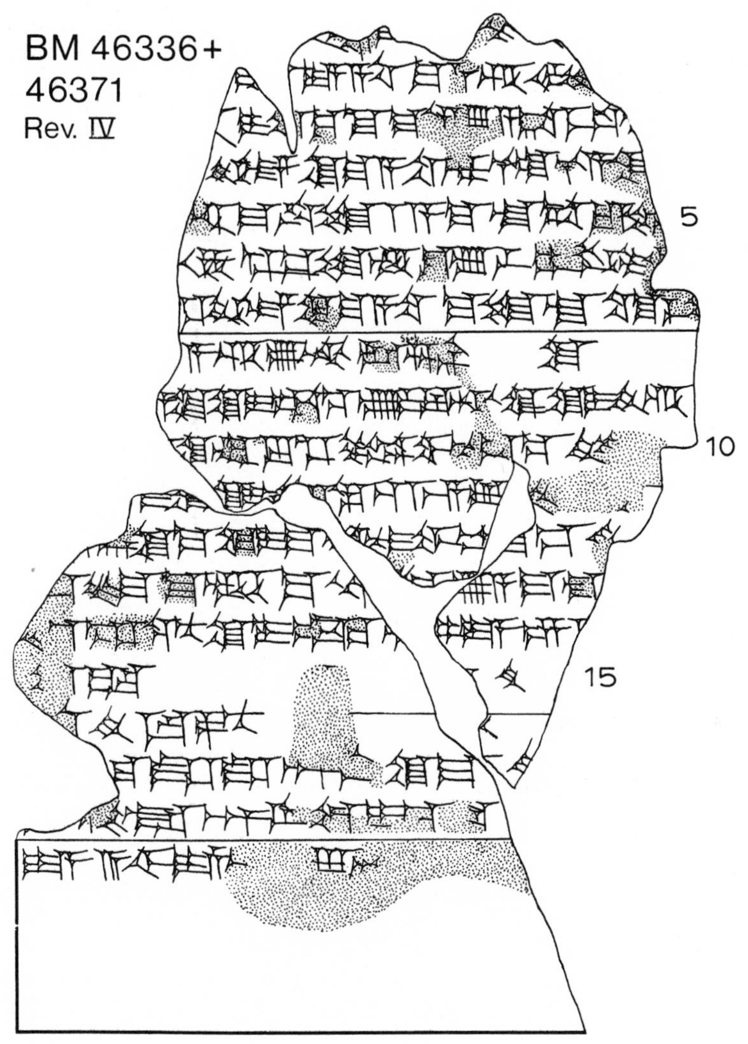
BM 46336+
46371
Rev. IV

- 6 -

HITTITE MYTHOLOGICAL TEXTS: A SURVEY

Harry A. Hoffner, Jr.

What the nonspecialist may call "Hittite myths" and what is listed under that term in the English translations in Pritchard's *Ancient Near Eastern Texts* actually consists, as has often been noted,[1] of tales which the Hittites learned from several ethno-linguistic groups: the non-Indo-European Ḫattians, the non-Indo-European Ḫurrians, and other groups (Luwians, Palaeans). In fact, strange as it may seem, it is difficult to identify a single mythological tale in the corpus of myths from Boğazköy which one may attribute to the Indo-European Hittites themselves with any certainty.[2]

The group of tales about the exploits of the gods which came into Hittite hands first after their arrival in Anatolia was doubtless the Ḫattian group. Only tales from this group have so far been found in Old Hittite versions. Unlike myths derived from the Ḫurrians, these Ḫattian myths were committed to writing only in connection with rituals.[3] They are therefore probably not to be thought of as real literary compositions. Yet this should not blind the reader to genuine literary values in these sometimes deceptively simple stories. For elsewhere in the ancient Near East we know of truly great literary works, which were recited in connection with festivals. The fact that their plots were suited to the festival occasion or to the ritual being performed detracts in no way from their value as literary creations. We have no way of knowing the oral prehistory of these Ḫattian stories. Nor can we say that they were only employed in connection with those rituals in which they are transmitted in writing. It is quite clear that they lack the elaborate formulae and the stereotyped metaphors, similes, and kennings of the Ḫurrian tales.[4] It is also clear that several are etiologic. The fact that several are well adapted to more than one use speaks for multipurpose employment of the stories. In fact, it is noteworthy that already in the earliest known periods of the Hittite kingdom a collection of tales about the deeds of historical persons was codified as a repository of admonitory examples.[5] Other stories which must have been transmitted orally, were occasionally used to reinforce the commands of the king in the protocols, state treaties, and other official documents.[6] Did the Hittites derive this custom from the Ḫattians preceding them? Did the Ḫattians also use tales about the activities of the gods for admonitory purposes?

Many of the myths of Ḫattian origin share a similar plot structure. The myths of the Telepinu type and the Illuyanka myth in particular tell of a crisis which results from the disappearance or defeat and incapacitation of a deity important to the welfare of the land. The crisis leads to a general meeting of the gods to find means of remedying the situation. The deity chosen to restore the former order has to seek the aid of either a mortal[7] or some other lower creature (in Telepinu, the bee). Success is eventually achieved, but the Illuyanka story (in both versions) includes a casualty in the person of the mortal who assists the god.

In several of the Ḫattian myths prominent use is made in the plot of marriage customs.[8] In particular in the Illuyanka myth and in the story of Telepinu and the Daughter of the Sea God (*CTH* 322) the role played by the husbands corresponds to that of the person who in Hittite laws is called the *antiyanza*.[9] This kind of husband enters the home of his bride's parents and, in lieu of title to his wife's dowry during her lifetime or after her decease, receives a payment at the time of the marriage. This payment is described by the word which denotes the bride-price,[10] which the husband pays to the bride's parents in the more usual patrilocal marriage. In the Illuyanka myth and the tale of Telepinu and the Daughter of the Sea God this institution is presupposed and indeed its procedures are utilized to achieve the principal goals in the action of the plot. Thus in Illuyanka version two[11] the goal of the storm god is to recover his eyes and heart, which the dragon Illuyanka has taken from him. In order to avoid direct confrontation with his former conqueror before he has retrieved them, he must devise a plan to obtain them indirectly in a manner which will not arouse suspicion. So the storm god begets a mortal child and orders the boy to offer himself to the dragon as a son-in-law. That the boy is to be an *antiyanza* is clear, although the specific term is not used. For he "goes to the house of his wife" to take up residence there, and when entering his wife's house is entitled to ask for a gift or payment (in this case the storm god's heart and eyes), and when at the end the storm god is about to destroy the dragon and his family, the young man is bound by the mores of his society to say, "Include me with (them)! Spare me not!" and to die together with his new family. The ties with his own father and mother were severed, and the new relationship superseded the former. The new relationship was what the Hittites called *andayantatar*,[12] the status of the *antiyanza*.

In the myth of Telepinu and the Daughter of the Sea God[13] the same type of marriage must be understood as underlying the plot. The story is set in primeval days, when the various spheres of influence (sky, earth, nether world, mankind) were allotted to the various deities.[14] At that time the sea god, perhaps unhappy with his lot, became angry and carried off the sun god from the sky and hid him. Conditions deteriorated on earth because of the sun's absence. Yet, no god could stand against the sea god. So the storm god summoned his son Telepinu and contrived a plan. Telepinu went to the sea god, who became afraid and gave him his daughter in marriage. He also gave him the sun god. This could be understood in the same way as the second version of Illuyanka: the god Telepinu married into the sea god's family and received the sun god as his marriage price, just as the mortal son of the storm god received the eyes and heart of his father. But Telepinu did not stay with the sea god. He took his wife and the sun god and returned to the residence of the storm god. This gave the sea god reasons for complaint. As long as Telepinu remained with him, Telepinu needed to make no payment; on the contrary he could request a payment for himself. After he had departed, he was no longer entitled to keep the daughter or the sun god, unless he made good the bride-price. Thus the sea god sent a message to the storm god: "Your son Telepinu [has taken] my daughter as his wife. He has taken her away (to his home)." (This second statement is an unnecessary addition unless the marriage was first conceived as of the *antiyanza* type.) "Now [what] will you give me?"[15] The storm god asked the advice of the goddess DINGIR.MAḪ, who advised him to pay. Thereupon the items to be paid are listed[16] until the text breaks off.

At this point an explanation is necessary as to why the term *antiyanza* is not used in either text. In the second text one could point to the fragmentary nature of the text. Perhaps, one could argue, the word did occur in one of the long breaks. But surely no such excuse can be offered for version two of Illuyanka, which is in good textual order. It seems to me that the answer is obvious. One needs a special term only for a kind of marriage which is uncommon. The Hittites, to whom this type of marriage was a novelty, coined the term *antiyanza*, which is a Hittite–not a Ḫattian–word to describe it. If the arrangement was new to the Hittites, it must have been a survival of a practice among the autochthonous peoples, the Ḫattians. And if this type of marriage was common among the Ḫattians, perhaps even the prevailing type, then it needed no special name. Indeed, the very fact that in the Illuyanka myth the institution seems so clearly to underlie and explain the plot, yet no special mention is made of any unusual type of marriage, would be *prima facie* evidence that this was the normal type of marriage among the Ḫattians.

In the first version of Illuyanka there are also certain parts of the plot which seem extraneous to the central theme of the vanquished storm god aided by a goddess and a mortal finally overcoming his erstwhile conqueror. The role of the goddess and the mortal fits into the common framework for the plots of these Ḫattian myths, as I have already discussed above. What seems extraneous is the final episode in which the mortal man Ḫupašiya, who although he is already married, has become the goddess Inara's captive husband, and longs for home like Odysseus' on Circe's island. Although he is warned he must never look out of Inara's window in her absence, he does so, catches sight of his wife, and longs to leave. When Inara discovers what he has done, she kills him. Since the lovers' retreat was a house on a cliff in the region of Tarukka, it is possible that the episode grew up to explain the presence of the ruins of that house, which, according to the text, eventually came into the hands of the king.

Both versions of the Illuyanka myth are said to form the cult-legend of the Purulli Festival, which was performed in the spring to celebrate the renewal of plant life.[17] According to the ritual at the end of the second version the festival witnessed a gathering of all the gods (that is, their statues) and a competition. We know of other examples of competitions or games held at festivals by the Hittites, including pugilism.[18] However, if, as is possible, the Hittite expression *pul tiyanzi* (which Goetze translated "they compete") really means "they cast lots," then this festival is the determining of primacy among the gods of the Nerik circle by lot-throwing. About this first celebration of Purulli the text records that the god Zašḫapuna of the city of Kaštama was the greatest.

Among the myths which reached the Hittites through Ḫurrian intermediacy was the so-called Kumarbi cycle, which includes the Kingship in Heaven myth, the myth of the Kingship of the God KAL, and the Ullikummi myth.[19] Of these, the first and third have already received detailed treatment by a number of Hittitologists, and both are available to English-speaking scholars in good translations by Albrecht Goetze[20] and Hans Güterbock.[21] Exceedingly interesting similarities between the Kumarbi cycle and the early Greek myths about Ouranos, Kronos, and Zeus have been pointed out first by Emil Forrer and then in much greater detail and precision by Güterbock.[22] The similarity concerns primarily the generations of gods who held divine kingship, that is, ruled the other gods, and the events attending the passing of the throne from one generation to the next. Meriggi[23] has added the important observation that in one of the poorly preserved lines of column II of Kingship in Heaven the birth of a god identified by the Sumerian word KIRI_4.ZAL (or KA.ZAL) meaning literally "shining nose, shining face"[24] is described in a manner which strikingly parallels the birth of "bright-eyed" (*glaukōpis*) Athena. One god splits open the skull of Kumarbi and the deity KA.ZAL emerges from the skull. Of some importance to the proper understanding of Kingship in Heaven is the relationship between the deities who succeed to the kingship. That they are not father and son has been stressed by others. It is my opinion that the kingship is passed back and forth between two competing lines of gods. Those lines can be seen most clearly in the following table:

Alalu	Anu
Kumarbi	Storm god (Teshub)
Ullikummi	

The filiation between Alalu and Kumarbi is made most explicitly in col. I, line 19, where Kumarbi is called Alalu's NUMUN "seed."[25] The filiation between Kumarbi and Ullikummi is also explicit in the Song of Ullikummi, where Kumarbi copulates with a gigantic rock and begets thereby the stone monster Ullikummi. As for the other line, the text tells us that Anu's genitals were swallowed by Kumarbi and impregnated him with three gods, one of whom was the storm god Teshub. Thus it is indisputable that we have two rival dynasties here with the kingship alternating between them in their struggles. Each deposed father is avenged by his son, who then becomes the new ruler. Of course, this alternation from generation to generation proceeds no further, for from the preserved portions of the end of the Song of Ullikummi it is clear that the storm god Teshub himself, not his son, will defeat Ullikummi in their second encounter, now that the latter's firm hold on the shoulder of Upelluri has been severed.

The characters in the Kumarbi cycle can easily be compared with figures in other mythologies. It has long been noted that Anu, whose name harks back to the Sumerian sky god's name, compares in his role in Kingship in Heaven with the god Ouranos ("heaven") in Greek myths. Anu is deposed and at the same time emasculated by Kumarbi, just as Ouranos is emasculated by his son Kronos. The correspondence between the Greek Kronos and the Ḫurrian Kumarbi has recently become even more striking with the discovery by E. Laroche that the god depicted holding the stalk of grain on the Yazilikaya relief is none other than Kumarbi, who at Ras Shamra/Ugarit was identified with the West Semitic god Dagan.[26] Thus both the Greek Kronos and the Ḫurrian Kumarbi were grain gods, which, of course, makes it quite appropriate that Kronos "reaped" his father's genitals with a sickle! Ullikummi has been compared with the monster Typhon of the Greek legends. Ubelluri, who holds heaven and earth, is an obvious Atlas figure and matches his Greek counterpart in stupidity as well. For as Atlas was dim-witted enough to be outwitted even by the muscle-bound Hercules in the episode of the golden apples of the Hesperides, so Ubelluri is not even aware of the attaching to his shoulder of the stone monster Ullikummi, who grows so big that he reaches from the nether world all the way to heaven.[27]

The myths of the Kumarbi cycle are much better known to the general public than the so-called "minor" Ḫurrian myths. Yet among these are some with not only highly interesting plots--they remain very fragmentary--but also points comparable with other myths and legends in the ancient Near East. Most of these minor Ḫurrian myths and legends were first edited by H. G. Güterbock or Johannes Friedrich in the 1940s and 1950s.[28] Two--the myths of Appu and Ḫedammu--have recently been reedited with additional fragments by Jana Siegelová.[29]

A unique feature of the Appu myth is that it seems to illustrate or substantiate a moral, which, although in a fragmentary state of preservation, can just be made out in the first preserved lines of the text. I understand it to say: "He (a deity, perhaps the sun god) is the one who always vindicates just men, but evil men he repeatedly bends like a GIŠ.RU (or GIŠ-*ru* "tree"?),[30] evil men he repeatedly strikes on their skulls (like) *šakšakiluš* until he brings them to ruin." The story which immediately follows was obviously intended to bear out the truth of this statement. Its interpretation should therefore proceed from these lines. The man, whose name identifies this myth, Appu, is important only as the father of two boys, whom he names respectively "bad" (*idaluš*, once in variant *ḫuwappaš*) and "good, just" (*ḫandanza*). The names may also make reference to some circumstances attending their births, but it is also clear from what follows that the names accurately reflect their characters.[31] Idalu is greedy and dishonest, while Ḫandanza (like Abraham in the story of his dividing the promised land with Lot)[32] is quiet and willing to allow himself to be swindled, as well as impeccably honest. As in the Abraham-Lot story, the god allows Idalu apparently to get away with his dishonesty. Idalu takes the best share of his father's inheritance and gives to Ḫandanza the worst. Yet the sun god causes Ḫandanza's inferior cow to outstrip Idalu's healthier and more valuable plow ox. The old, worn-out cow the sun god caused to bear calves. At this point the text becomes almost entirely illegible. Siegelová's newly found fragments provide only tantalizing disconnected bits of what may have been the intervening narrative. One fragment seems to repeat the words of the proem with specific reference to brother Idalu:[33]

] ᴰUTU-*uš* *IŠ-ME nu-k*[*ân*
-]*y̌a-at nu* LÚ.ḪUL[-
GI]ˢ̌ḪAŠḪUR-*lu-ma-wa-za-kân* [GIM-*an li-la-ak-ki*
-*d*]*a*? -*an* SAG.DU-*an* [*ša-ak-ša-ki-lu-uš wa-al-ḫa-an-na-i*

"[. . .] the sun god heard and [. . .] and Idalu [. . .] '[like] an apple tree [he repeatedly bends . . . .] the head [(like) *šakšakiluš* he repeatedly strikes].'"

Eventually the two brothers begin a series of appearances before various deities to consider their case. It would seem that brother Idalu, angered at the prosperity of Ḫandanza despite all his own tricks, wishes to charge Ḫandanza before the gods. It is here where the appropriateness of the iterative forms of the verbs in the proem appears.[34] At each successive trial the verdict goes in favor of Ḫandanza. Thus the just man is vindicated "repeatedly" and the unjust man is bent "repeatedly" like an (apple?) tree and struck on the head until he is brought to ruin. The sun god (Shamash) at Sippar is the first to hear the suit and awards the verdict to Ḫandanza, using the same verb (*šarlai-*) as was employed in the proem. Whereupon Idalu begins to curse, and when the sun god hears the cursing, he refuses to make the final decision, and urges them instead to go to Nineveh, where Ishtar will hear their case. They go to Nineveh, but here the text breaks off again, so that we can only suppose on the basis of the proem that Ishtar too vindicates Ḫandanza. Since earlier in the tale brother Idalu had enumerated six prominent Mesopotamian deities: Shamash, Sin, Adad, Ishtar of Nineveh, Nanaya of Kiššina, and Marduk of Babylon,[35] one wonders if the case was eventually appealed at all of these six Mesopotamian courts. At any rate, there is nothing in the proem which would lead one to expect any other major turn of events in the tale such as that assumed by the theory of Güterbock that the tale of the Sun God and the Cow was a continuation of the Appu story.[36]

The Ḫedammu myth in its preserved portions (even with Siegelová's additions) yields little in the way of an intelligent plot. The goddess Ishtar is confronted with a sea monster named Ḫedammu, who is described as having a voracious appetite. Wishing to destroy him, the goddess first attempts to lure him through her feminine charms and then to do him in through violence. In this activity she not only resembles the Mesopotamian Ishtar known from Sumerian and Akkadian texts, but also the goddess Inara as portrayed in the first version of the Illuyanka myth.[37]

In the myth called the Sun God and the Cow (*CTH* 363; *KUB* XXIV 7 ii 45ff.),[38] the story opens with the sun god contracting a great sexual desire for a cow, which grazes in his meadow. He apparently tries first to threaten her to leave his meadow and then takes her sexually.[39] The offspring of this union is anthropomorphic, a fact which intensely angers the cow. She tries to kill her two-legged child, but the sun god rescues him and leaves him on a mountainside under the protection of the wild animals. There he is found by a childless fisherman, who thanks the sun god for leading him to this foundling.[40] The child is brought home by the fisherman, who presents it to his wife and asks her to feign birth pangs, so as to make it appear to the neighbors that the child is their own newly born infant. This the woman does, and the ruse apparently succeeds. At this point the text breaks off. Güterbock has suggested that the cow at the beginning of this story is the same cow which appeared in the Appu myth and that this is therefore a continuation of the Appu myth. As stated above, I cannot concur with this interpretation of either story.

Another Ḫurrian tale concerns a hunter named Keššši,[41] who takes a lovely young wife. The girl so entrances him that he neglects his hunting and even his widowed mother who has been depending on him to this point. The mother cajoles him into going hunting again. But in the mountains he finds no game. His preoccupation with his new wife also causes him to neglect the gods' cult, and for this reason they hide all the game from him. After a long and fruitless hunt, Keššši falls ill. Most of the rest of the story has not survived, but in a final fragment we read of dreams which Keššši has and which his mother seeks to interpret for him. These contain interesting symbolism, mostly concerning feminine attire.[42] The mother offers an interpretation for each dream, but the broken condition of the text does not allow us to reconstruct her interpretations with any certainty. Other Keššši stories, or alternatively other parts of this story, are found among the El Amarna tablets and in Ḫurrian texts from Boğazköy.

A myth of Canaanite origin in Hittite translation concerns the god Elkuniršа (probably West Semitic *'ēl qônē' 'ereṣ* "El, creator of the earth") and his wife Asherah, here written Ašertu.[43] The goddess Asherah propositions the young god Ba'al (name written ᴰU "storm god") through her maidens, whom she sends to him. "Come, sleep with me!" she urges him. When, however, Baal refuses her, she becomes enraged and threatens him: "Get behind me, and I will get behind you! With my word I will press you down! With my . . . I will . . . you!" The leaders indicate words of unclear reading or interpretation. The verb[44] in other contexts is to be translated "to send, write." Here it must fit into the context of a threat. Thus H. Otten translated it "pierce" or "prick." If he is right, then the uncertain noun must be a sharp implement. Otten read the signs which represent the implement as [ᴳᴵŠBA]L?.TUR-*az* "with the spindle." Since the spindle is the feminine implement par excellence, as I have tried to show elsewhere,[45] I accepted this reading in my 1965 interpretation of this passage. Recently, however, Professor H. G. Güterbock suggested to E. Laroche that the half-broken sign read [BA]L? by Otten was [GÍ]R "knife."[46] I have checked the traces on the tablet and found that Otten's KUB XXXVI copy is correct, and that these traces cannot be reconciled with the sign [GÍ]R, although they are possible for [BA]L, as well as for several other signs. Therefore I would tentatively retain Otten's reading because it fits the traces as well as the womanly context better. It is likely that some misunderstanding of the underlying West Semitic original of this passage has obscured the meaning for us. When Baal has left Asherah, he goes to her husband Elkuniršа and reports the incident. Elkuniršа instructs him to go, sleep(?) with her, and humble her. We are not told that Baal slept with Asherah, so that it is feasable that the *hapax legomenon šaššumai* does not mean that. Perhaps it is a synonym of "humble" on the order of "threaten, reprimand(??)." If so, then Baal did precisely as he was told. He reported to her that he had slain her children. Whereupon the goddess is stunned and begins mourning for her children. At this point is a lacuna of undetermined length. When the story resumes, Asherah is persuading her husband Elkuniršа to allow her to punish Baal. She coaxes him by holding out the prospect of sleeping with her again. I restore the broken context as follows:[47]

[*ma-a-an-wa* ᴰ]U-*an* [*am-mi-ta-az me-mi-ya-na-az* . .]
[*kat-ta t*]*a-ma-aš-mi a*[*m-mi-ta-az-ma-wa-ra-an* ᴳᴵŠ X.TUR-*az ḫa-at-ta-ra-a-mi*]
[*nu*]-*wa-du-za kat-ta še-eš-m*[*i* . . . . .] . . . .

"[If] I may [p]ress [down] the storm god [with my 'word' and may pierce? him with] m[y . . .], I will sleep with you." The text then says: "Elkuniršа hearkened (i.e., agreed to her conditions) and said to his wife: 'The storm god [I hand over to you.] Treat him as you like!'"[48] Then the couple goes to bed.

But while they are talking, the goddess Anat is listening in in the form of a bird. And when they retire to the bed, she flies off across the steppes to find Baal and warn him. She finds him in the steppes and warns him: "Oh Baal! [The food] of Ashertu [do not eat!] The wine do not dri[nk! . . .] . . . [. . .] she is seeking [to harm you.]"[49] Now follows another large lacuna. From two larger fragments which belong to the same text, it appears that Asherah succeeds in injuring Baal, for he must be purified from the evils which she inflicted upon him. Instrumental in the purification are Anat (written Ishtar) and the "sons of the Anunnakki."[50]

From the foregoing survey it is evident that the Hittites collected tales from various sources. Very few were purely literary works. It has been noted that the Ḫattian myths were transmitted only in connection with rituals. Even the Ḫurrian myth of the Sun God, the Cow and the Fisherman (*KUB* XXIV 7 ii 45ff.) follows a ritual and hymn to Ishtar on the same tablet, and the Appu tale, which begins with the hymn-like dedication to the sun god, may have followed a lengthy hymn to the sun god. We have just seen how the tale of Elkuniršа, Asherah, and Baal leads into a rather lengthy ritual description, whose application must surely have gone beyond the mere needs of the narrative. Considering how few of the smaller Ḫurrian myths we possess in complete texts, it is perhaps difficult to claim the status of real literary works for more than the great narratives of the Kumarbi cycle, and for Gilgamesh translations. Aside from these it seems that the Hittites regarded their myths as of a piece with the genres of prayer and ritual. In other words, they employed their myths in acts of worship and magical treatment.

NOTES

[1]H. G. Güterbock, in *MAW,* 141-43; O. R. Gurney, *The Hittites* (Baltimore, 1964), 177ff.

[2]I do not consider the *Siege of Uršum* (*KBo* I 11; *CTH* 7) a myth, although as in many other quasi-historical texts legendary elements are found therein (see H. G. Güterbock, *ZA* 44 [1938] 114ff.). Thus it is no example of a purely Hittite mythological tale (con. Gurney, *The Hittites,* 178).

[3]Güterbock, in *MAW,* 143.

[4]See on this subject the Brandeis University dissertation of my former student Bert DeVries, "The Style of Hittite Epic and Mythology" (1967).

[5]*KBo* III 34 and duplicates (*BoTU* II 12, and so forth), *CTH* 8. See Güterbock, *ZA* 44 (1938) 100ff.; Kammenhuber, *Saeculum* 9 (1958) 139.

[6]*KBo* V 3+12 iii 53, 65; iv 42, 51, 59; Friedrich, *Staatsv.,* II, 128, 134ff.

[7]In the Illuyanka myth it is Ḫupašiya in version one and the mortal son of the storm god in version two.

[8]For a sketch of these customs, see A. Goetze, *Kleinasien*[2] (Munich, 1957) 111-13; Gurney, *The Hittites,* 99ff.; and for the principal sources, see Hittite laws §§27-37 (English translation by Goetze in *ANET*[2], 190).

[9]Hittite law §36. K. Balkan, *Dergi* 6, 147ff. first explained the meaning of this term in the Hittite law. Güterbock first suggested the relevance to Illuyanka (*MAW,* 152), but did not develop the idea to the details of the story.

[10]Hittite *kušāta*.

[11]See English translation by Goetze in *ANET*[2], 126.

[12]*Hwb,* 23; see Balkan, *Dergi* 6, 147ff.

[13]*CTH* 322, composed of *KUB* XII 60 and its duplicate *KUB* XXXIII 81. Transliteration: Laroche, *Textes mythologiques hittites* (*RHA* 77:79) 19f. At present no translation is available, although a French one is being prepared by E. Laroche to appear in a volume of the series Littératures anciennes du Proche-Orient (Éditions du Cerf, Paris), and an English translation has been prepared by the writer to appear within the next two years in a volume of Hittite texts in English translation.

[14]*KUB* XII 60 i 1-4. See Gulšeš myth (Otten, *AfO* 23 [1970] 32f., lines 8-19).

[15]*KUB* XII 60 i 16-19.

[16]Here the items which constitute a *kušāta* are listed. In *KUB* XLI 11 rev. 13ff. one finds the items which constituted an *iwaru* "dowry." For the latter passage, see now H. Hoffner, Jr., *AOAT* 22 (1973).

[17]Güterbock in G. Walser (ed.), *Neuere Hethiterforschung* (Historia, Einzelschriften, Heft 7, 1964) 61, 69; Hoffner, *Alimenta Hethaeorum* (New Haven, Conn.: American Oriental Society, 1973).

[18]Güterbock, in Walser (ed.), *Neuere Hethiterforschung,* 72.

19 See *CTH* 343-45 and E. Laroche, *Textes mythologiques hittites, RHA* 82, 145ff. with citation of previous literature.

20 *ANET*², 120ff.

21 *JCS* 5 (1951) 135ff.; 6 (1952) 8ff.

22 E. Forrer in *Mélanges Franz Cumont,* Annuaire de l'institut de philologie et d'histoire orientales, IV (1936) 687-783; H. G. Güterbock, *Kumarbi Efsanesi* (Istanbul, 1945); idem, *AJA* 52 (1948) 123ff.

23 *Athenaeum* 31 (1953) 104, n. 11; see E. Laroche, *RHA* fasc. 79, 162. The passage is *KUB* XXXIII 120 ii 37-38.

24 For the Sumerian, see B. Landsberger, *JCS* 8 (1954) 132; A. Sjöberg, *ZA* 55, 1ff.; *AS* 16, 69; the Akkadian translation of the god's name would seem to have been *muttellu* "princely" (*AHw,* 690).

25 The reading NUMUN had not yet been established for this line in time for Goetze to employ it in his translation in *ANET*², 120.

26 E. Laroche, *RHA* fasc. 84/85 (1969) 70; *Ugaritica V,* 523ff.; *JAOS* 88 (1968) 149ff.

27 *ANET*², 125 (left-hand column).

28 Güterbock, *Kumarbi Efsanesi,* 116ff.; J. Friedrich, *ArOr* 17/1 (1949) 232ff.

29 "Appu-Märchen und Ḫedammu-Mythus," *StBoT* 14 (1971). See also H. A. Hoffner, Jr., *Tyndale Bulletin* 20 (1969) 52-55, an article unfortunately unknown by Siegelová.

30 See below, where, if my understanding and restoration of *KBo* XIX 105: 4'-7' (*StBoT* 14, 14) is correct, the more specific GIŠḪAŠḪUR-*lu* "apple tree" would make the reading GIŠ-*ru* "tree" here certain.

31 H. A. Hoffner, Jr., "Birth and Name-giving in Hittite Texts," *JNES* 27 (1968) 198ff.; see also Siegelová, *StBoT* 14 (1971) 28ff.

32 Gen. 13:8ff.

33 *KBo* XIX 105: 4'-7' (*StBoT* 14, 14), on which see n. 30 above.

34 *šarliškizzi, lilakki, walḫannai.*

35 *KUB* XXIV 8 + *KUB* XXXVI 60, iv 13-20 (*StBoT* 14, 12-13).

36 Advanced first in *Kumarbi Efsanesi* (1945) 119-22, still apparently held in *MAW,* 154-55.

37 *ANET*², 125 (bottom of right-hand column).

38 J. Friedrich, *ZA* 49 (1950) 224ff., prepared a transliteration, German translation, and commentary.

39 Comparable is the tale of the Syrian god Baal mating with a heifer (*ANET*², 142, left-hand column). On the broader question of bestiality in Near Eastern mythological and legal texts see H. A. Hoffner, Jr., *AOAT* 22 (1973).

40 The child sired by a god, abandoned, found, and adopted by a humble couple is a theme which can be found frequently in ancient Near Eastern legend. Compare the Sargon

Legend (*ANET*², 119).

[41] Friedrich, *ZA* 49 (1950) 234ff., prepared transliteration, German translation, and commentary.

[42] Such motifs in a man's dreams must have been ominous; see H. A. Hoffner, Jr., *JBL* 85 (1966) 326ff., and Delbert Hillers in *AOAT* 22 (1973).

[43] *CTH* 342; H. Otten, *MIO* 1 (1953) 125ff.; H. A. Hoffner, Jr., *RHA* fasc. 76 (1965) 5ff.; Goetze, *ANET*³, 519. Goetze's translation is far too cautious and obscures many of the gains in interpreting the myth since 1953.

[44] *ḫat(ta)rai-*, on which see *HWb*, 66.

[45] *JBL* 85 (1966) 326ff.; see Delbert Hillers in *AOAT* 22 (1973) 71-80.

[46] Laroche, *Textes mythologiques hittites*, 140, n. 1.

[47] *KUB* XII 61 ii! 1′-3′ (Laroche, *Textes mythologiques hittites*, 141).

[48] For the situation of El surrendering Baal to one who would harm him, compare *ANET*², 130 (right-hand column) in the Baal-Anat cycle from Ugarit.

[49] *KUB* XXXVI 37 + *KUB* XXXI 118 ii 13-14, as I would restore them.

[50] Laroche, *Textes mythologiques hittites*, 142-43.

- 7 -

THE SYRIAN SCRIBE OF THE JERUSALEM AMARNA LETTERS

William L. Moran

This paper draws on the Albright legacy of problems he did not solve but, with characteristic insight, pointed to and left for others to work out.* Almost thirty years ago, in the course of his famous series of articles on western peripheral Akkadian, he mentioned in passing that the Jerusalem Amarna letters should not be included in a description of normal scribal practice in Palestine.[1] He gave no arguments to support this statement, and though both before and since that time others, the writer among them, have noted certain idiosyncrasies of the Jerusalem scribe, no one has offered evidence that could be said to justify the broad implications of his remark.[2] It has remained to this day simply an *obiter dictum*, unchallenged and unproven.

It will be our contention that Albright was right, and in fact more right than he could have known with the sources then available to him. Compared with the scribes in Palestine and along the southern Phoenician littoral, the Jerusalem scribe is indeed constantly *extra chorum*.[3] But this is only part of the problem. Compared with other scribes in a wider setting, he is no longer simply an anomaly; he is an alien. For, by and large, what sets him apart in Palestine is paralleled in the writing and language we find as we move northward along the lines of the several Syrian traditions. And what remains unparalleled even there is for the most part more readily understandable in this general area. In short, the Amarna letters from Jerusalem have a large component which we may call northern, and this is their central problem. A description of this component and an explanation of its presence are the subject of this paper.

WRITING

Paleography

Though paleography has never been brought into the discussion of the Jerusalem scribe's background, it yields perhaps the clearest evidence. In Schroeder's list (*VAS* XII 73-94) there are 120 signs in the Jerusalem column, with a total of 175 different forms.[4] Comparison with the adjacent columns, with no attempt to distinguish or evaluate types or degrees of similarity or difference, reveals the following distribution: 8 Jerusalem forms, the same everywhere; 63, no geographical pattern, identical forms in both north and south;[5] 45, forms either unattested elsewhere or too rare for meaningful comparison;[6] 10, same forms only in Palestine or Phoenicia; 46, same forms only in the north;[7] 3, same forms only in Egypt.[8] Admittedly, this is only a general picture. A more comprehensive list based on more than the Berlin collection would certainly introduce some modifications.[9]

It is also true that the comparison depends in part on the consideration of minute details, and coincidence and divergence may at times be fortuitous and evidence difference of hands rather than traditions; a larger sampling would require additional adjustments of the distributional pattern. But all this granted, the preponderance of northern forms in the Jerusalem column remains and requires explanation.[10]

Decisive in establishing the northern character of the script is the comparison of signs in which the differences regard more or less sharply defined distinctive features. In such a comparison the correspondences with southern forms virtually disappear, whereas those with northern forms still make up a long list (see Figure 1).[11] It consists, moreover, mostly of signs of high frequency. We may thus rule out chance as a relevant factor.

Figure 1 speaks for itself, and we restrict our comments mainly to supplementary evidence:[12]

No. 23 LI (see n. 4, above), parallels: Mitanni (second form), with variations in Mitanni (first form) and Tyre.[13] Also: Ḫatti (*BoTU* I no. 158; *Ugar.* V no. 169); Ugarit (*VAS* XI 17 = *EA* 45; *VAS* XI 19 = *EA* 47; *VAS* XI 20 = *EA* 48; *PRU* III, RŠ 15.14; 15.86; 15.89; 15.Z, and passim);[14] Alalakh (*AT* 70; 447 iv 18-19 [Level II]; rare);[15] Nuḫašše (*VAS* XI 22 = *EA* 51);[16] Qatna (*BB* 37 = *EA* 53; *BB* 36 = *EA* 55; *VAS* XI 23 = *EA* 54).

No. 26 QA (second form), parallels: Mitanni, Egypt, Babylonia. Also: Ḫatti (*BoTU* I no. 219); Ugarit (*PRU* III, RŠ 15.155; 15.173; 15.A and passim); Qadeš (*VAS* XI 108 = *EA* 189); Ḫazi (*VAS* XI 106 = *EA* 186).[17]

No. 33 TI, parallels: Amurru. Also: Mitanni (*VAS* XII 201: i 21ff. = *EA* 25; *BB* 11 = *EA* 26); Ḫatti (*BoTU* I no. 275; *Ugar.* V no. 169); Ugarit (*VAS* XI 17 = *EA* 45; *PRU* IV, RŠ 17.42; 17.129; 17.158 and passim); Alalakh region (*AT* 108).[18]

No. 38 IG, parallels: Mitanni,[19] Babylonia, Tyre. Also: Ḫatti (*BoTU* I no. 117; *Ugar.* V no. 169); Ugarit (*VAS* XI 17 = *EA* 45; *PRU* III, RŠ 15.109; 16.144; 16.249; 16.368 and passim); Alalakh (*AT* 49, but very rare; see 47, 132, 202, 248, etc.); Nuḫašše (*VAS* XI 22 = *EA* 51); Qatna area (*VAS* XI 24 = *EA* 56; see *BB* 36 = *EA* 55:26, Qatna).[20]

No. 45 KAB (first form), parallels: Mitanni, Alašia,[21] Amurru. Also: Ugarit (*VAS* XI 19 = *EA* 47; *PRU* III, RŠ 16.138; 16.295; *PRU* VI 49, etc.); Amurru (? *VAS* XI 31 = *EA* 67).[22]

No. 50 EN, parallels: Mitanni. Also: Ḫatti (*BoTU* I no. 65); Alašia (*BB* 7 = *EA* 37); Ugarit (*VAS* XI 19 = *EA* 47; *PRU* III, RŠ 15.85; 15.A; 16.174, etc.); Alalakh (*AT* 70, 132 [but see line 24], 181 [but see lines 9, 14], 440 [Level I], rare); Beirut (*BB* 16 = *EA* 136, Rib-Addi writing from Beirut; *BB* 26 = *EA* 141); Byblos (*BB* 45 = *EA* 139).[23]

No. 64 ŠUM, parallels: Mitanni,[24] Ḫatti, Alašia, Egypt. Also: Ugarit (*VAS* XI 19 = *EA* 47; *PRU* III, RŠ 16.129; 16.141; 16.200 and passim); region of Alalakh (*AT* 112); Gezer letter.[25]

No. 72 UM (third form, slightly aberrant), parallels: Mitanni, Alašia, Babylonia, Amurru.[26] Also: Ḫatti (*BoTU* I no. 296); Ugarit (*PRU* III, RŠ 15.139; 16.154, etc.); Tyre (*BB* 28 = *EA* 149; *BB* 30 = *EA* 151); Qadeš (*VAS* XI 108 = *EA* 189).

No. 74 TA, parallels: Mitanni, Ḫatti, Alašia. Also: Ugarit (*VAS* XI 17 = *EA* 45; *VAS* XI 19 = *EA* 47); Alalakh (*AT* 5 = *JCS* 8, 5).

No. 77 TUR (see n. 4, above), parallels: Mitanni, Ḫatti, Alašia. Also: Ugarit (*VAS* XI 19 = *EA* 47; passim in *PRU* III, IV, VI, *Ugar.* V, with variations between Jerusalem first form and Alašia third form); Alalakh (*AT* 49, very rare); Qatna area (*VAS* XI 24 = *EA* 56).

No. 95 TUM (first form), parallels: Mitanni, and for the distinctive feature of the vertical, see Alašia and Babylonia. Also: Ḫatti (*BoTU* I no. 283); Ugarit (*PRU* III, RŠ 15.86; 15.89; 16.189; 16.287); Alalakh (*AT* 3, 4, but very rare); Qadeš (*VAS* XI 108 = *EA* 189).

Figure 1

	Mitanni	Hatti Z	Alašia	Ägypten	Babylonien	Phönizien: Gebal	Phönizien: B. S. T	Jerusalem	Amurru	Andere Formen
95. tum, ×tù				Nr. 198, III 16			S		Auch = tù Nr. 88,34 89,39. 41 usw.	
117. al							T, S	[Nr. 163,43: alu! mit Zus. al.]		
124. ù, šam		Z		Nr. 198 III 17.18	Nr. 38 (6 Senkrechte!)		S, T			Nr. 177, 7.19.25. Hier und auch sonst (z.B. 187,24) für „und" gebraucht.
125. ga Id. H! GA; KAL.GA. und GA.KAL			häufig für Kà (als Suffix „dein")		Nr. 1,5					
130. amêlu (Id/Det.)		Z, Z.							S	
136. da, ṭa						Nr. 27,30 Nr. 68,66	B, S.T., T			Nr. 177, 2 124 Nr. 183, 20
138. ma		Z					B.S., T			
142. ša		Z.					B.S., T.			
175. GIR šêpu Id. ^{ilu}GIR., ^{ilu}GIR.DU							S., T			Nr. 143,3
201. ib/p Id. ^{ilu}NIN.IB ^{ilu}IB						Nr. 68,1 Nr. 27,X			doch: S ^{ilu}IB Nr. 94,36	Nr. 143,10.
222. ḫa							S., T			

No. 117 AL (see n. 4, above), parallels: Mitanni, Ḫatti, Babylonia, Tyre. Also: Ugarit (passim); Alalakh (*AT* 4, etc., but rare).[27]

No. 124 Ú (second form), parallels: Mitanni, Ḫatti, Alašia, Babylonia. Also: Ugarit (*Ugar.* V no. 41; p. 487, RŠ 15.30+; *PRU* VI 50, etc.); Egypt (C. H. Gordon, *Or* NS 16 [1947] 5 = *EA* 370).

No. 125 GA (see n. 4, above; first form), parallels: Mitanni; (second form), parallels: Alašia. Also: Ugarit (passim); Alalakh (*AT* 361, very rare).

No. 130 LÚ, parallels: Mitanni, Ḫatti, Alašia. Also: Ugarit (*VAS* XI 17 = *EA* 45, etc.); southern Syria (*VAS* XI 113 = *EA* 200).

No. 136 DA (second form), parallels: Mitanni, Ḫatti, and see Tyre.

No. 138 MA, parallels: Mitanni, Ḫatti, Alašia, Tyre, Amurru. Also: Ugarit (passim); Nuḫašše (*VAS* XI 22 = *EA* 51); Qatna (*VAS* XI 23 = *EA* 54); Damascene (*VAS* XI 111-112 = *EA* 196, 194) and in the same general area (*VAS* XI 113 = *EA* 200).

No. 142 ŠA (with four horizontals, see n. 4, above), parallels: Mitanni, Ḫatti, Tyre, and see Amurru. Also: Amurru (? *VAS* XI 136 = *EA* 238),[28] Nuḫašše, Qatna, etc. (as in previous entry).

No. 175 GÌR (see n. 4, above), parallels: Mitanni. Also: Ugarit (*Ugar.* V no. 48; also, *PRU* VI 6 in anše.gìr.nun.na; *Ugar.* V no. 163 iv 14′ in alim$_x$); Amurru (? *VAS* XI 136 = *EA* 238); Syria (*VAS* XI 177 = *EA* 317).[29]

No. 201 IB, parallels: Mitanni, Egypt, Babylonia, Amurru. Also: Ḫatti (*BoTU* I no. 113); Ugarit (*PRU* III, RŠ 15.132; *PRU* IV, RŠ 17.334 and passim); Alalakh (*AT* 182, 269, but very rare); Nuḫašše (*VAS* XI 22 = *EA* 51).

No. 222 ḪA (first form), parallels: Mitanni, Egypt, Babylonia, Tyre, Amurru. Also: Ḫatti (*BoTU* I no. 99); Ugarit (passim); Alalakh (*AT* 435, but very rare); Nuḫašše (*VAS* XI 22 = *EA* 51); Amurru (? *VAS* XI 135-136 = *EA* 237-38).

To sum up: in the Jerusalem letters the forms of twenty signs--those of LI, IG, KAB, EN, ŠUM, TUR, GÌR, IB are especially important--have no parallels in Palestine, and only occasional, sporadic ones in southern Phoenicia, whereas beginning in southern Syria and northward they have numerous correspondences and are often the rule. From the viewpoint of paleography, it is a northern hand that wrote these letters.[30]

Syllabary

Noteworthy are the following:

*AS*² 114 IA = *a͡ia* in URU *a͡ia-lu-na*^{ki} (*EA* 287:57). Reference is to biblical Aijalon, which in *EA* 273:20 appears in a conventional spelling, URU *a-ia-lu-na*. In view of *a͡ia-nu-um-ma* (*Ugar.* V 27:49) *a͡ia* is established for the northwest periphery.[31]

*AS*² 129 KUM = *qu* in *ḫal-qu-mi* (*EA* 286:51), *ḫal-qu* (*EA* 288:40, 52). Common in MA (note *li-il-qu-ú* and *il-qu-ú-ni*, *EA* 16:34, 40) and MB (*AS*²), this value is unattested at Nuzi or Alalakh, but is found, though rarely, in the northwest periphery (*PRU* IV RŠ 17.252; 17.393; 18.54A–all forms of *ḫalāqu*, provenience of last unknown, language Assyrian or strongly Assyrianizing).[32]

*AS*² 184 SAR = *šir*$_9$ in *lu-ma-šir*$_9$ (*EA* 290:20); see *lu-ma-še-er* (*EA* 288:58; 289:42), *lu-ma-še-ra* (*EA* 285:28; 286:45; 287:18). *AS*² restricts this value to a single instance at Nuzi, but R. Biggs, *JNES* 29 (1970) 138 cites a probable MB example (same verb, *uuššuru*). Add (all forms of *u͡uššuru*): Alalakh (<*ú*>*-wa-šir*$_9$*-šu*, *AT* 15:4); Ugarit (*Ugar.* V no. 44), Amurru (*PRU* IV 180; *EA* 156:13; *EA* 171:5 *ú-wa-aš-šir*$_9$*-an-ni*, see line 5 *ú-wa-aš-ši-ra-an-ni*), Qatna (*EA* 55:20, [49]), Tunip (*EA* 59:33), Tyre (*EA* 149:17, 76), Alašia (*EA* 34:14,

16), Egypt (*EA* 162:42, 51, 56), and possibly Byblos (*EA* 131:32). Note also the equation at Boghazköy of *e-şír* = *e-şir*$_9$ (*MSL* XIII 260:5′-8′).[33]

AS[2] 218 TE = *de*$_4$ in *li-de*$_4$ (*EA* 289:46), *li-de*$_4$*-mi* (*EA* 286:25; 287:11, 48, 57), *i-de*$_4$*-mi* (*EA* 289:35), *ša-de*$_4$*-e* (*EA* 287:56), *la-ma-de*$_4$*-ka* (*EA* 287:59), *d*[*e*$_4$*-k*]*a* (*EA* 288:41), *de*$_4$*-k*[*a*] (*EA* 288:45), and *de*$_4$ *-ka-ti* (*EA* 287:73). In the Amarna archive, with the exception of *ir-de*$_4$*-e* (*EA* 359 rev. 27, Egypt), all occurrences of TE = *de*$_4$ are confined to forms of *idû*, and these are found in letters from Mitanni, Qatna, Amurru, Tyre, Alašia, and two northern sites (*EA* 260, 317).[34]

AS[2] 223 PI = *pi* in all thirteen cases of *piṭat(t)u*.[35] In the Amarna archive, this value is confined to texts from Assyria (*EA* 16:10, 14), Mitanni (PN in *EA* 27:89, 93; 28:12; and passim in the Hurrian letter *EA* 24), Alašia (*EA* 36:15[?], *EA* 37:17), Syria (*EA* 368:1, 4, 5, 14, rev. 5; on provenience, see n. 3), and possibly Byblos (*EA* 138:8, if Edel's reading and explanation, *JNES* 7 [1948] 23, are correct). Aside from occasional occurrences at Boghazköy, these are the only instances we know of for this value in the western periphery.[36]

AS[2] 223 PI = *ŭ* in *ŭ-qa-bi* (*EA* 286:22),[37] and perhaps *ú-ša-ŭ-ru* (*EA* 286:21, 24),[38] possibly *an-ni-ŭ* (*EA* 289:9).[39] According to *AS*[2], this value is OB, rare in MA and later, unattested in MB; R. Biggs, *JNES* 29 (1970) 138, adds an occurrence at Boghazköy.

AS[2] 238 ḪAR = *kín* in *li-is-kín* (*EA* 286:38; 287:13, 40; 288:48) and *gin*$_x$ in URU *gin*$_x$*-ti-ki-ir-mi-il* (*EA* 288:26; 289:18, +KI) and *gin*$_x$*-ti* (*EA* 289:19; 290:28). *AS*[2] finds this value in the Mari liver models (add PN *Me-kín-nu-um*, *TIM* V 23:2, 9, and seal, Gungunum), MA, Am (= Jerusalem!), Ugaritic (see also *Ugar.* V no. 20:18, no. 38:3), and Boghazköy, to which add Egypt (see Goetze, *JCS* 1 [1947] 250, n. 7).[40]

The Syrian, non-Palestinian cast of the Jerusalem scribe's syllabary is clear. The use of *de*$_4$ in forms of *idû* and of *pi* seems particularly significant.

Orthography

The Jerusalem scribe exhibits a number of orthographic peculiarities pertinent to the problem at hand:

1. /ṷ/, initial and intervocalic, is very often written with the *m*-series: (a) all forms (16) of *ṷuššuru*, following the practice in Babylonia, Mitanni, Ugarit, the Alalakh region (*AT* 108), Ḫatti, and Egypt, in contrast with the older spelling with the *ṷ*-series maintained at Gezer, Pella, Tyre, Byblos, Qatna, Tunip, Upe, Alalakh, etc.;[41] (b) *mu-ʾi-ru* (*EA* 290:8).[42]

2. In the formulaic *ana* PN *qibīma umma* . . ., where it is preserved in the Jerusalem letters, we find *qí-bi-ma* (*EA* 286:1; 287:65; 290:2) rather than the traditional and archaic *qí-bí-ma*.[43] The latter is used exclusively in the Amarna correspondence, with only five or six exceptions: *EA* 132 and 362 (both Byblos), 200, 207 (probably), and 230 (Syrian provenience of all three probable), 28 (Mitanni), and 15 (Assyria). The Jerusalem spelling is the rule in the letters found at Ugarit,[44] in MA and Nuzi letters, and is well attested in MB.[45]

3. Six times we meet the spelling KUR.URU GN(.KI): *EA* 287:14-15, 25, 46; 289:18; 290: 11.[46] In all the Amarna letters, despite their almost innumerable namings of towns and villages, to our knowledge there are only two instances of the sequence KUR.URU: KUR.URU *ḫa-at-ti* (*EA* 44:8) and KUR.URU *ú-g*[*a*]*-r*[*i-it*] (*EA* 45:35). In these letters from Boghazköy and Ugarit, respectively, we meet the practice long known as typical of Hittite scribes and, now with the discoveries of Ugarit, seen to be also quite common elsewhere in the north.[47]

4. In the Amarna archive, in 121 references to the ʿApiru, with the possible exception of *EA* 207:21, only the Jerusalem letters have a syllabic spelling (8x), and this exclusively. Syllabic spellings elsewhere in roughly contemporary texts: Ḫatti and Ugarit.[48]

5. The use of the *din*-sign, with orthographic doubling of the *n*, in *i-din-nu* (*EA* 287:15; 289:23), is paralleled by *i-na-an-din-nu-nim* (*EA* 155:13, Tyre), *id-din-nu* (*EA* 155:38, Tyre; 171:9, probably Amurru), *i-din-nu-nim* (*EA* 161:22, Amurru), and possibly *i-din-*[*nu*] (*EA* 40:9, Alašia; see Knudtzon's remarks, *EA* 40:9).[49] Note the cluster: Amurru, Alašia, Tyre, Jerusalem.

6. The representation of the sibilants in the Jerusalem letters is an old problem, which cannot be discussed here.[50] Suffice it to indicate what seem the two most likely solutions. With Goetze, one may dismiss vacillations (KUR *ka-si/ši*, *EA* 287:72, 74) and anomalies (a Jerusalem scribe representing Proto-Semitic /ṯ/ and /ś/ by the same sign: KUR *ša-ak-mi* [*EA* 289:23], *ša-de₄-e* = Hebrew *śāde* [*EA* 287:56]) as a matter of "syllabary," i.e., an orthographic tradition which does not distinguish the sibilants and which, though to some extent perceptible almost everywhere in western peripheral Akkadian, is typical of "Reichsakkadisch."[51] Or one may take the evidence at face value and accept a binary opposition of /ṯ-ś/ versus /š/, with the support of Egyptian transcriptions of Canaanite. This opposition, however, hardly obtained in the dialect of Jerusalem, for on the evidence of biblical Hebrew, at Jerusalem /ṯ/ and /ś/ never fell together. In either solution we are once again probably confronted with the intrusiveness of the Jerusalem letters in their local setting.[52]

Punctuation

The "Glossenkeil" is employed quite frequently (19x) by the Jerusalem scribe. Some of its uses are quite normal: (1) West Semitic gloss to Akkadian word or expression (*EA* 286:6 [if *ú-ša-a-ru* is West Semitic]; 287:37, 56); (2) West Semitic gloss to Sumerogram (*EA* 287:27 [second "Glossenkeil"], 73, and perhaps 7); and (3) marker of following word as non-Akkadian (*EA* 287:16, 41[?]; 290:24[?]). Where it appears at the beginning of a line (*EA* 286:15; 288:53; 290:24[?]), it may serve to mark the line as a run-over of the preceding, with which it constitutes a sense-unit. But this still leaves many instances without explanation. In the latter, the only purpose we can suggest is to punctuate the text and mark major and minor "pauses": major, before new sentences (*EA* 286:47, 62; 287:27 [first "Glossenkeil"], 41[?], 75); minor, either before relative clauses (*EA* 287:6; 290:5), or between subject and verb (*EA* 286:10), verb and adverb (*EA* 287:52), verb and object (*EA* 287:58). If this proposal is pertinent, then the occasional use at Boghazköy of the "Glossenkeil" as a punctuation mark seems the relevant comparison.[53]

LANGUAGE

Assyrianisms

Certainly the most striking feature of the Jerusalem scribe's language, though so far it has not been recognized, is its large Assyrian component. The peripheral Akkadian of the west, it is true, exhibits a number of Assyrianisms, some fairly standard, others sporadic and unpatterned.[54] Being neither, those of the Jerusalem letters are unique.

1. Demonstrative Pronoun-Adjective

Nom. *anni'u (anniu̯u)*	*an-ni-ú epši* PN . . . "This is the deed of PN" (*EA* 287:29).
	epšu māti an-ni-ú, "This deed against the *land*" (*EA* 290:25).

epšu ša ēpušū an-ni-iû, "This is the deed they committed" (*EA* 289:12).

Gen. *anni'e* — *ina ašri an-ni-e* (*EA* 286:11).

Acc. *anni'a (anniia?)* — *haziānu ša eppaš epša an-ni-â*, "as for a governor who commits such a deed" (*EA* 289:9).

Uncontracted forms, which are the rule without exception in the Jerusalem letters, have no parallel in the entire Amarna archive.[55] The paradigm is pure MA.[56]

2. Noun

The only clear--and correct--Assyrian form is *û-re-e*, "roof" (*EA* 287:37), which reflects the MA shift /im/ > /e/. In *la-ma-de₄-ka* (*EA* 287:59) the bound-form before a pronominal suffix is also, and erroneously, [e] rather than [i].[57]

3. Verb

Here Assyrian influence is especially strong:[58]

(a) Where there is a distinction between Babylonian and Assyrian in forms of the precative, the latter is the rule (10x) without exception:

1 p. *lāmur*, Babylonian *lūmur* (*la-mur-mi*, *EA* 286:40; *la-mu-ur*, 286:46).
lērub, Babylonian *lūrub* (*le-lu-ub*, *EA* 286:46).[59]

3 p. *lūṣi*, Babylonian *līṣi* (*lu-ṣi-mi*, *EA* 286:56).
lūmaššer/lūmaššera, Babylonian *līmaššer/līmaššera* (*lu-ma-še-er*, *EA* 288:58; 289:42; *lu-ma-šir₉*, 290:20; *lu-ma-še-ra*, 285:28; 287:18).
lūtirra, Babylonian *līterra* (*lu-ti-ra*, *EA* 290:21).

(b) Verbs primae aleph$_{3\text{-}5}$ are consistently (13x) treated as in Assyrian:

G inf., *erāba*, Babylonian *erēba* (*e-ra-ba*, *EA* 286:43); *ezābi*, Babylonian *ezēbi* (*e-za-bi-ša*, *EA* 287:62).[60]

G present, *tippaša* (for *teppaša*), Babylonian *teppuša* (*ti-ip-pa-ša*, *EA* 287:71);[61] *eppaš*, Babylonian *ippuš* (*e-pa-aš*, *EA* 289:9); *eppušū*, Babylonian *ippušū* (*ep-pu-šū*, *EA* 287:19--obviously the writing is ambiguous, but in view of the other forms the assumption of vowel harmony, *eppašū* > *eppušū*, seems legitimate).

G preterite, *ēpušū*, Babylonian *īpušū* (*e-pu-šu*, *EA* 289:12); *ēpušūne*, Babylonian *īpušūni* (*e-pu-šu-nê*, *EA* 290:5); prec. *lērub* (see above).

Gt present, *ētelli*, Babylonian *ītelli* (*e-tel-li*, *EA* 287:45).

Š imperative *šērib*, Babylonian *šūrib* (*še-ri-ib*, *EA* 286:62; 287:67; 288:64).

Š present *ušerrubū*, Babylonian *ušerrebū* (*û-še-ru-bu*, *EA* 287:11, vowel harmony).

Babylonian forms (4x or 2x) of verbs *primae aleph*: *ikkalū*, Assyrian *ekkulū* (*i-ka-lu*, *EA* 286:6); *errub*, Assyrian *errab* (*e-ru-ub*, *EA* 286:39; perhaps *ērub* with volitive force intended, interference from Canaanite volitive *'aqtul*), *erēši*, Assyrian *erāše* (*e-re-š*[*i*], *EA* 289:7); perhaps *eppuš*, Assyrian *eppaš* (*e-pu-uš*, *EA* 286:14), but see above on *errub*.

(c) Verbs *mediae infirmae*. Above, under *Syllabary*, we have already noted the writings *d*[*e₄-k*]*a* (*EA* 288:41), *de₄-k*[*a*] (*EA* 288:45), and *de₄-ka-ti* (*EA* 287:73). Since all other instances of *de₄* are to be explained in terms of contrast with /di/,[62] and since when the latter is in place the *di*-sign is used (*a-di*, *EA* 287:45, 47; 288:60), it follows that we must interpret the forms of *dâku* as reflecting Assyrian *dēk* (plus Canaanite morphs) rather than Babylonian *dīk*.

(d) Verbs *tertiae infirmae*. Only twice do verbs of this class exhibit Babylonian vowel contraction (*i-ba-šu-û*, *EA* 285:23; *it-ta-ṣû-û*, *EA* 286:48), whereas lack of contraction characteristic of Assyrian is found five times: *ta-ša-mi-û* (*EA* 286:50), *te-le-qê-û* (*EA* 288:

38), *i-qa-bi-ú* (*EA* 288:54), *li-il-qé-a-ni* (*EA* 288:59), IG-GI-*ú-šu*. To our knowledge, with the exception of the very obscure *i-te-e-i-ú* (*EA* 162:74, Egypt; *īde'u* according to *AHw* 321 sub *ḫannipu*), the hardly less obscure *e-ma-e* (*EA* 136:14), and *a-ṣa-i* (*EA* 195:21), nowhere in the Amarna archive are verbs of this class–and it includes some of the most frequently attested, such as *šemû*, *leqû*, *qabû*–written with cv-v that does not represent cv_1-v_1 = cv̂.[63]

Under this heading it should perhaps be mentioned that, except in *EA* 285:23, *ibašši* is uninflected and is used with subjects in the plural: KUR.ḪI.A *ù* LÚ *ḫa-zi-a-nu-*<*ti*> (*EA* 287:21); LÚ.MEŠ GN (*EA* 289:19).[64] Here again there may be MA influence, but of course with only two examples we cannot be sure.[65]

4. Lexicon

(a) *lamnu* (*EA* 287:71), elsewhere in Amarna Babylonian *lemnu* (6x), except *EA* 189:7 (Qadeš, see *ú-la-mu-nu-ni*, lines 6, 8) and *EA* 97:5 (resembles Byblos tablets; see Knudtzon's observations, *EA* II, 1192, n. 1).

(b) *ḫaziānu* (*EA* 286:52; 287:22; 288:9), plural **ḫaziānūtu* (*EA* 285:19; 286:19; 287:24; 288:56), unparalleled in Amarna despite the frequency of the term.[66] According to *AHw* 338b-339a, *ḫaziānu* MA and NA(PN); add *ARM* XIII 143:5′ (*ḫa-zi-ia-nu-*[*um*]), 18′ (*ḫa-zi-ia-an*); *AHw* 339a, abstract *ḫaziānuttu* MA; add *ARM* XIII 143:8 (*ḫa-zi-ia-nu-tam*).

(c) *a-la-'e-e* (*EA* 286:42; 287:58) reflects Assyrian *la'ā'u* rather than Babylonian *le'û* (*i-le-'e-e*, *EA* 287:62).[67]

(d) *ištu* = *itti* (*EA* 286:43; see line 40). For this there are a number of parallels in the periphery,[68] which are perhaps based on MA usage (see *AHw* 401).

There is, then, no denying a rather strong Assyrian influence on the language of the Jerusalem letters.[69] And, if we look in the west for examples of a comparably Assyrianizing language, we find them at Amurru, Alašia, Ugarit, and Boghazköy, all sources which would seem immediately to furnish an additional argument for the case we have been gradually building up for the northern background of the Jerusalem letters.[70] Caution, however, is in place. The Assyrian component in these latter documents is understandable and is probably to be explained as ultimately reflecting the expansion of Assyrian political power,[71] whereas at the time of the Jerusalem letters, however late we may date them within the possible limits of the Amarna archive, such an explanation is most improbable.[72] Hence the different political (and cultural) context diminishes somewhat the force of the apparent parallels.

However, if we ask ourselves where--in Syria or in southern Palestine--even prior to the rise of Assyrian political power, the influence of the Assyrian language seems more likely, the answer seems pretty clear; and if other evidence points in the same direction, only one answer is possible: Syria.

Miscellaneous

1. Lexicon

(a) *adi*, "(together) with, besides" (*EA* 287:47; 288:60), is not clearly attested elsewhere in the Amarna archive, in which *qādu* is the rule. However, *adi* is so used in MA and MB, and see *adu* in *PRU* IV 49:17; *adu kinanna* in *EA* 357:88 is a special case which we will discuss elsewhere.

(b) *an-ni-ka-nu* (*EA* 287:52) is certainly the same word as *an-ni-ka-nu* "here" in *PRU* IV 216:12 and 227:21 (see *AHw* 52, *CAD* A/2, 132 sub *annikī'am*).[73]

(c) The adjective *banû*, which is attested four times (A.WA.TÚ.MEŠ *ba-na-ta* [*EA* 286:62-63; 287:67; 289:49], A.WA.TÚ.MEŠ [. . .*b*]*a-na-ti* [*EA* 288:65]), emerges in MB as a replacement for *damqu* (see *CAD* B, sub voce), and is found elsewhere in Amarna in letters from Babylonia, Assyria (*EA* 16), Mitanni, Ḫatti, Amurru, Egypt; to this list we may also add occurrences at Ugarit (see *CAD*). The expression *aṷatu banītu*, *aṷâtu banâtu*, etc., is attested in Babylonia, Mitanni, Ḫatti, Ugarit.

(d) *dāriš* in *ana dāriš* (*EA* 287:61). The only strict parallel in peripheral Akkadian is *ana dārišma* at Nuzi (*JEN* 620:10), but *adi dāriš* (exclusively peripheral: Egypt, Ugarit, Amurru) should also be compared. Standard western peripheral: *ana dārīti* and *adi dārīti*.

(e) *enūma* (12x), which has a number of meanings in the Jerusalem letters, including the extraordinary one of a preposition meaning "like,"[74] is used exclusively, and *inūma* does not occur. The standard MB form is noteworthy in the south, where *inūma* is the rule. Aside from a sporadic occurrence in a letter from Hazor and its consistent use in the letters from Tyre--once more Tyre!--*enūma* belongs in Amurru (? *EA* 237, see n. 28), Mitanni, Nuḫašše, Qatna, Alašia, Alalakh (very rare), Ugarit, and Ḫatti.

(f) *ḫamuttam* "quickly" (*EA* 285:29) is attested once in OB, passim in MB letters, and in the periphery, at Nuzi, Mitanni, Ḫatti, Ugarit, Alašia (see *EA* and *CAD*). It tends to replace *arḫiš*, which is standard in Phoenicia and Palestine.

(g) *maḫru* with *ina* in *ina maḫrīia* (*EA* 289:39). The only parallels in the Amarna archive are *EA* 16:8 (Assyria), *EA* 29:38 (Mitanni).

2. Typology

A rather unusual feature of the Jerusalem letters is the four postscripts which Abdi-Ḫeba addresses to "the scribe of the king, my lord" (*EA* 286-289). In the Amarna archive, comparable additions to the main text of the letter are found in *EA* 12 (Babylonia), 32 (Egypt), 42 (? Boghazköy), 170 (Amurru), and 316 (southern Palestine).[75] Other parallels are to be found at Boghazköy and Ugarit.[76]

CONCLUSION

So far we have seen various lines of evidence all converge and form a rather consistent pattern.[77] They not only confirm Albright's insight on the individuality of the Jerusalem scribe in a Palestinian setting, but they agree in pointing to its source--a profound influence of northern scribal practices on the exercise of his craft.

However, before speculating on how this might have come about, consideration must be given to two other lines of evidence, the first of which in some sense runs counter to those we have followed so far. This is the absence in the language of the Jerusalem letters of the truly distinctive features of "Reichsakkadisch," and the presence of a large West Semitic component.[78] For this combination there is nothing comparable in the sources from Alašia, Amurru, Ugarit, or Alalakh, not to mention Egypt, Boghazköy, or Mitanni. If we may define the Jerusalem scribe in geographical terms as a "northerner," he is no less a "southerner" too.

The various hypotheses that this curious mélange might suggest must also take into account the evidence on the background of the Jerusalem scribe's master, Abdi-Ḫeba, a question of considerable interest in itself. In *EA* 286:9ff., 287:25ff., and 288:13ff., Abdi-Ḫeba acknowledges that he owes his position in Jerusalem to neither his father nor his mother, but only to the strong arm of the king. With this debt to the pharaoh he also associates the fact that he is not a governor but a soldier (*EA* 288:9-10), a distinction of titles which he makes again at the beginning of another letter (*EA* 285:5-6). Similarly, on another occasion (*EA* 289:69) he reaffirms his membership in the military, with its implications for him of absolute loyalty. In short, running through the correspondence like a theme is a concern for origins of authority, title, and status that is without parallel in the letters of other vassals, and it requires explanation.

In our opinion the main crux is the interpretation of the claim to be a soldier and not a governor.[79] It should not be understood simply as a statement of loyalty. For Abdi-Ḫeba, governors are not synonymous with treachery; rather, he sees in them the faithful and often suffering opposition to the perfidious 'Apiru (*EA* 288:36-46). Nor may we take his claim to mean that his authority is exclusively military, for example, that of a garrison commander. For not only do the other local princes speak of him simply as one of their number (see *EA* 280), but in taking office he "enters his father's house" (*EA* 286:13; 288:15), a long-established expression for accession to the throne.[80]

What would make sense of this apparent contradiction of a governor who is also not a governor but a soldier, and at the same time explain the unparalleled insistence on the pharaoh's personal intervention in Abdi-Ḫeba's coming to power, would be the assumption that unlike most of his peers he did not come to the throne in an established line of succession, but rather, after belonging to the military, had been brought into Jerusalem by "the strong arm of the king." On this reading of the passages in question, Abdi-Ḫeba would in some sense be a *novus homo* on the Jerusalem scene, though perhaps not entirely so, if the reference to his father's house is to be given its full weight. He may have belonged to the old royal house, or a branch of it, which, for reasons we can only guess at, lost Jerusalem but not the pharaoh's favor.

This seems to us the most plausible interpretation, apart from any concern for the scribe's background. However, as is clear, it is also very relevant to this question and, in the light of all the other evidence for the intrusiveness of the writing and language of the letters, gives strong support to the view that the scribe was truly an outsider and not a native Hierosolymitan open to outside influences.

Where, then, did he come from? Since to some extent Egypt belongs under the designation "northern," one could consider looking in that direction, especially when the history of political refugees like his master is recalled. However, there is absolutely nothing in the language of the Egyptian scribes that even remotely resembles the interference-component, both West Semitic and Assyrian, we find in the Jerusalem letters. On the evidence at hand, therefore, we must turn elsewhere, and only Syria, somewhere along the border between "Reichsakkadisch" and "Canaanite-Akkadian," remains as a likely place of origin. And if we may join the scribe's history with that of his master, we would propose that it was in the latter's company, as part of a new royal entourage, that he came south to the Judaean stronghold.

NOTES

*This paper is a slightly revised version (Jan. 1974) of the one presented to the Albright Colloquium in Jan. 1973. Besides updating the bibliography, it incorporates some of the results of a collation (Aug. 1973-Jan. 1974) of the Amarna tablets in the Ashmolean Museum, British Museum, Musées Royaux d'Art et d'Histoire, Louvre, and Vorderasiatisches Museum. (We gratefully acknowledge the courtesy of the various museum authorities, and the grants of the American Philosophical Society and the American Council of Learned Societies in support of our inquiry.) First-hand study of the Jerusalem letters (four of six; *VAT* 1643 [*EA* 288] and *VAT* 1644 [*EA* 287] missing) and comparison with the other letters have only confirmed, in our opinion, the conclusions we had reached earlier.

1 *BASOR* 94 (1944) 26.

2 For various distinctive features of the Jerusalem letters, see H. Zimmern, *ZA* 6 (1891) 246, n. 6; 250, n. 1; F. M. Th. Böhl, *Die Sprache der Amarna Briefe, LSS* V/2, 2; 24; 47, n. 1; O. Schroeder, *OLZ* 18, 295f.; A. Goetze, *Language* 17 (1941) 128, n. 15; W. L. Moran, *The Bible and the Ancient Near East,* ed. G. Ernest Wright (Garden City, N. Y., 1961) 59; 68, n. 42 = Anchor Book 66; 79, n. 42; A. F. Rainey, *El Amarna Tablets, AOAT* 8, 75; Ichiro Nakata, *Jour. Anc. Near East. Soc. Columbia Univ.* 2 (1969) 19-24. Only the last study, in the style of "friendly amendments" to the present writer's earlier remarks, purports to be a full treatment of the subject.

3 A frequent exception to this contrast is the scribe from Tyre. Albright's opinion, *JEA* 23 (1937) 190ff., that the scribe was an Egyptian is both very questionable and, even if correct, would provide no explanation of the peculiarities of the script. S. Gervitz, *Or* NS 42 (1973) 176f., has shown how fragile Albright's arguments were, and he might also have pointed to the Egyptian-Akkadian vocabulary (*EA* 368), which Smith and Gadd, *JEA* 11 (1925) 231, on paleographic grounds (note also PI = *pi* 5x), rightly argued could not have been written in Egypt, but rather somewhere in Syria; it is therefore evidence outside of Egypt of the kind of knowledge displayed by the Tyrian scribe's glosses. Certainly the latter was not trained in Egypt. His script exhibits no typically Egyptian features, but in general is that of the scribes from Byblos to Sidon, with its relatively small signs and light impressions. The Tyrian scribe seems, therefore, to reflect a local tradition subject to strong northern influences. P. Artzi, *Bar-Ilan Annual* 1 (1963) 24ff., has already noted the northern "Glossenkeil" notation (like the GAM-sign) at Tyre and Byblos; see chart, 34, and conclusions, 49 (English summary, XV).

4 This list is not complete and must be used with some caution. To confine ourselves to the major omissions in the Jerusalem column: no. 11 KA, add forms in *VAS* XI 162:2, 6; no. 23 LI, add form in *VAS* XI 164:23, and see n. 13, below; no. 77 TUR, add form in *VAS* XI 163:30; 164:66; 165:31; no. 81 LUGAL, add form with three verticals passim; no. 117 AL, add form in *VAS* XI 164: 47 (variant of form in *VAS* XI 163:43, which is not, as Schroeder proposes, URU = al_x; note that the alleged URU never appears before city-names but only with a syllabic value); no. 125 GA, add form in *VAS* XI 162:12, 42; no. 128 É, add form in *VAS* XI 162:13; no. 138 MA, add form in *VAS* XI 162:2; no. 171 NIM, add (conventional) form in *VAS* XI 161:7; 162:14, 18; no. 142 ŠA, add form with four horizontals in *VAS* XI 161:27, 163:6, 19, 31, 71; no. 204 KIN, add form in *VAS* XI

161:7. Also, correct copy in *VAS* XI 161:3 of GÌR, and add form to no. 175; both the upper and lower horizontals slant downward and upward, respectively.

[5] By north we mean, roughly, above a line from Ṣumur on the coast to Qatna inland, within which area further distinctions are possible (see J. Nougayrol, *Ugar.* V, 76). This line more or less corresponds to the southern limits of the diffusion of Landsberger's "Reichsakkadisch" (*JCS* 8 [1954] 58; see also 48). The data of paleography are not unrelated to those of language. Note, for example, the contrast in both script and language between the letters of Abdi-Aširta (*VAS* XI 27-29, not included in Schroeder's Amurru column) and Aziru and his sons (*VAS* XI 83-85, 88-93, 95; on 94, see M. Dietrich and O. Loretz, *Beiträge zur Alten Geschichte and deren Nachleben,* Festschrift F. Altheim, ed. R. Stiehl and H. E. Stier [Berlin, 1970] 14ff.). Paleographically and linguistically, the former should be classified with the Byblos letters, whereas the latter are northern in script and typical examples of "Reichsakkadisch."

[6] It should be noted that this relatively high number reflects both the limited range of comparison on which the list is based (e.g., no. 179 "unattested" Ú [second form] is found in *PRU* VI 7, 10, etc., and *AT* 4) and differentiation on the basis of minor details (see, e.g., no. 60 MÁ, which we also list as unattested despite its obvious and very close resemblance to the third and fourth forms in the Byblos column). The only real idiosyncracies are no. 93 IL (to Schroeder's reference add *VAS* XI 164:26; 166:10, 18), concerning which Professor Sachs has suggested to the writer that the excessive number of verticals at the end represents simply a conflation of the wedges in the conventional forms; no. 79 ṢI (second form), actually either UNU or $MURUB_4$, a confusion that is based on the close similarity of ṢI with variant forms of the latter (see *BoTU* I, no. 298, and p. 20, 19); note also the TA+A ligature in TA.ÀM (no. 74).

[7] On the exception Tyre, see n. 3, above.

[8] Despite its location, Egypt is not to be classified with the south, neither in script nor in language. In both respects its closest affinity is with the north. Under the former, see F. Thureau-Dangin, *Le Syllabaire Accadien* (Paris, 1926) v; distinctive logograms such as KAxUD = *šinnu* (see B. Landsberger and H. G. Güterbock, *AfO* 12 [1937-39] 57) and UGU = *elû* (adjective); and in addition to our remarks below on Figure 1, note LA, UŠ, SAL, etc., as paleographical correspondences with northern forms. See also Knudtzon's remarks, *EA* I 17-18. The language of the letters from Egypt is almost entirely free of the profound Northwest Semitic interference characteristic of the south, and despite certain differences (see R. Labat, *L'akkadien de Boghaz-Köi* [Bordeaux, 1932] 76) closely resembles "Reichsakkadisch"; note, too, lexical rarities like *appūnana* and *mamīnu* (Bog. OB).

[9] The principal modifications based on our collations will be noted below. N.B.: the BM collection now includes both the four "Rostovitz" tablets (purchased in 1903) and the eight tablets formerly in the possession of the Egyptian Exploration Society (*EA* 370-77, acquired in 1966, now numbered BM 13864-13871).

[10] It might be objected that the northern corpus is somewhat larger than that of the letters from Phoenicia, and hence the northern character of the Jerusalem sign-forms may only reflect this imbalance. However, the Phoenician forms are, in general, also those of Palestine and southern Syria, and this means that the real imbalance weighs rather heavily on

the side of the southern corpus. And this imbalance is only increased if one also includes the pertinent material from Shechem, Taanach (here see the small sign-list of A. E. Glock, *BASOR* 204 [1971] 24-25), and Megiddo (here see the sign-list of A. Goetze-S. Levy, *'Atiqot* 2 [1959] 125-27; corrections: no. 213 EL is really no. 93 IL, and the first form of no. 143 ŠA in the Byblos column has an extra horizontal wedge).

[11]Only no. 160 AḪ and no. 162 ḪAR exhibit distinctively southern features, which in this case, as is generally true, means more archaic.

[12]The purpose of the supplement is the very modest one of underscoring the strongly provincial character of the south and thereby the individuality of the Jerusalem scribe. Hence the additional parallels cited are not meant to be exhaustive, nor do they imply that "southern" forms are without correspondence in the north. N.B.: Except for the Babylonian column, which is part of Schroeder's list, we restrict ourselves to the western peripheral sites. Hence we do not adduce Assyrian or Nuzi forms, though they are instructive and an exhaustive paleographical study would have to consider them (see, e.g., the "northern" forms of TUR, IB, MA, ŠEŠ, ŠA, IB, ŠUM in *WA* 9 = *EA* 16, of EN and LI in *KAV* 209, etc.; at Nuzi, EN in *HSS* V/2, 3, 8, etc.; IB ibid. 8, 29, etc.).

[13]The variation should be added to the Jerusalem column; see *VAS* XI 163 = *EA* 287:11. Though we do not cite additional parallels for this form, it could be amply documented. N.B.: Tyre = T in the B(eirut).S(idon).T(yre) column.

[14]Most of the evidence we possess from Ugarit is later than the Amarna period, but what we do possess from this time (*EA* 45, 47, and probably 46, 48; see Albright, *BASOR* 95 [1944] 30ff.; J. Nougayrol, *PRU* III xxvii; M. Liverani, *Storia di Ugarit,* 23), suggests that, paleographically, the post-Amarna age at Ugarit was not one of great innovation. (It is to the south, along the Phoenician coast [also in Palestine?], where considerable change seems to have taken place and the writing assumed many features formerly characteristic of the north; see the letters from Beirut [*PRU* III 12] and Sidon [*PRU* III 9].)

[15]Even when allowance is made for the pre-Amarna date of Alalakh Level IV, *AT* gives the impression of a quite conservative tradition and of a surprising independence from the great center of Waššukanni, the contemporary practices of which are illustrated in a few texts at Alalakh and Nuzi (see B. Landsberger, *JCS* 8 [1954] 58, n. 119; 54, n. 95). And again language goes along with the writing; e.g., the absence of *uperris/upterris* (contrast *EA* Mitanni and Nuzi, for which see Gernot Wilhelm, *Untersuchungen zum Ḫurro-Akkadischen von Nuzi, AOAT* 9, 25-26).

[16]On the provenience of this letter, see J. Nougayrol, *PRU* IV 32.

[17]The location of Ḫazi is not established (see W. Helck, *Die Beziehungen Ägyptens zu Vorderasien im 3. und 2. Jahrtausend v. Chr.,* 195, n. 67), but along with *VAS* XI 135-136 = *EA* 237-238 (see n. 28 below), it is certainly one of the southernmost sites to exhibit northern forms.

[18]On *AT* 108, see B. Landsberger, *JCS* 8 (1954) 54, n. 95 (contradicted by 58, n. 119).

[19]See also *AT* 13.

[20]On the provenience of this letter, see *EA* II 1121.

[21] The designation "Alašia" is of itself not a satisfactory term, for the letters of this provenience are, in writing and language, a very heterogeneous group. They deserve special study, and here we can only state our opinion that we must distinguish, certainly two, and probably three, scribes: the first wrote *EA* 33-34; the second, *EA* 35, 38-40; the third, if not the same as the second, *EA* 36-37. Only the latter two scribes exhibit northern forms–C. Kühne, *Die Chronologie der internationalen Korrespondenz von El-Amarna, AOAT* 17, 5, n. 33, refers briefly to the influence in both the Jerusalem and Alašia letters of "eine auswärtige Schultradition." In the case of Alašia, it seems difficult to speak of a *foreign* tradition when there is no evidence for what we might call native.

[22] On the provenience of this letter, see *EA* II 1144f.

[23] These few occurrences of northern forms of EN at Beirut and Byblos should not obscure the striking contrast between Jerusalem and the rest of the south, which is especially noteworthy because of the extremely high frequency of EN as a logogram for *bēlu*. In *VAS* XI 42 = *EA* 85:25, it is difficult to decide whether under the horizontal there are traces of a small vertical or simply a slight break; see Schroeder's copy. The latter seems to us more likely.

[24] Also *AT* 13-14.

[25] R. A. S. Macalister, *The Excavation of Gezer* I, 30. The provenience of this letter is unknown; Albright, *BASOR* 92 (1943) 28ff., suggested Egypt.

[26] The same form appears in *BB* 27 = *EA* 142 (Beirut) but with the value DUB, not UM, from which it is distinguished. At Jerusalem, as in the north in general (except Alalakh) and Egypt (except *EA* 369:2), UM and DUB coalesce, whereas in the south (except Tyre) they are kept distinct (besides Byblos passim, see *EA* 193, 237, 253).

[27] *VAS* XI 111 = *EA* 196:16 (Biryawaza of Upe), AL with oblique wedge but preceded by two verticals (see Babylonia, third and fourth forms).

[28] On the provenience of *EA* 237-38, see *EA* II 1304, n. 1.

[29] P. Artzi, *JNES* 27 (1968) 163ff., has demonstrated the Syrian provenience of *EA* 317.

[30] See also the form of SA (no. 53).

[31] On the values of the PI-sign, see I. J. Gelb, *Or* NS 39 (1970) 537-39; he is reluctant to admit PI = *aia*, but allows that it may turn up in the periphery.

[32] On RŠ 18.54A see Walter Mayer, *Untersuchungen zur Grammatik des Mittelassyrischen, AOAT* Sonderreihe 2, 3, and note specifically: *-mā* introducing direct discourse; *ētamrū* (Babylonian *ītamrū*), *iṣabbutū* (Babylonian *iṣabbatū*), *iḫṭi'uni* (3 singular subjunctive, Babylonian *iḫṭû*; for the reading see J. Aro *AfO* 18 [1958] 423); *kunāšunu* (2 plural independent pronoun; see Mayer, *Untersuchungen,* 28); *gab-bu-ru-ti* = *kabburūti* < *kabbarūti*(?). Since the Jerusalem scribe does not confuse stops, *qu* may not be interpreted simply as a graphic variant of *ku*. If one reads *bat-⌜qû-û⌝* in *EA* 287:36 (so Albright; see *ANET* 488, "they breached"), the restriction of *qu* to forms of *ḫalāqu* is still no difficulty; see below on $\check{s}ir_9$, and note ṢI = *zê*, *zî* (in the periphery) only in forms of *zêru* (to the references in *AS*[2] add *Ugar.* V no. 30:30, 32′; we thus disagree with Nougayrol, in *Ugar.* V 72, n. 3), etc.

33 The list of occurrences of *šir*$_9$ in various forms of *uuššuru* does not claim to be exhaustive, nor do we deny the possibility that the scribes may have confused present, preterite and perfect. We do insist that *šir*$_9$ in *lu-ma-šir*$_9$ is a valid inference from five writings with *-še-er* or *-še-ra*, and if confirmation were needed, *e-šír* = *e-šir*$_9$ would be sufficient.

34 On the provenience of *EA* 260 and 317, see n. 29, above. It should be noted that TE = *de*$_4$ is not "Hurrian" (*ARM* XV 49; P. Artzi, *JNES* 27 [1968] 167), nor is it a peripheral development from the confusion of voiced and voiceless stops. Rather, it is an archaic survival like *bí* in *qí-bí-ma* and goes back to a syllabary which distinguished between *di* and *de*. The existence of such a syllabary, which Gelb seems to postulate for the OAkk. period (see *MAD* II², 97, no. 218), Jacobsen (to whom we express our thanks for making his work available to us) has shown in an unpublished study of the Tell Asmar letters. Thus, in the early Isin-Larsa period, we find *ti-de*$_4$ (AS 31-T 299) "you know," and *lu-úr-de*$_4$ (AS 30-T 399) "I will conduct." The use of *de*$_4$, therefore, and its virtual confinement in the west to forms of *idû* is just one more archaic feature of western peripheral Akkadian.

35 As noted by Böhl, *LSS* V/2, 2; see also Rainey, *AOAT* 8, 75. Note, too, that DA = *ṭa*, not only here, but in all writings of /ṭa/ (9 forms of *paṭāru*); this is the standard MA/MB orthography.

36 See R. Labat, *L'akkadien de Boghaz-Köi* 7, to which a number of references might be added.

37 The usual reading is with Canaanite verbal preformative {ia} or {iu}, but one difficulty is that this would be a unique instance in the Jerusalem letters of such a form. Moreover, the one who is quoted in what immediately follows (*ḫalqat māt šarri bēlīia* "Lost is the land of the king, my lord") is certainly Abdi-Ḫeba: (1) *aqabbi ḫalqat māt šarri,* "I say, 'Lost is the land of the king'" (line 49); (2) the "good word" the pharaoh's scribe is to present to his master is *ḫalqat gabbi māt šarri bēlīia* (lines 64-65); (3) in the lines immediately preceding the passage in question (17-21) we have *aqabbi* followed by a direct quotation, and then *u kinanna ušāru ina pānī šarri bēlīia* "and as a result I am lied about before the king, my lord"; in lines 22-24 we have *enūma* (since) PI-*qa-bi* followed by a direct quotation, and then *kinanna ušāru ana šarri bēlīia* "as a result I am lied about to the king, my lord." Hence there is no question that the speaker in lines 22-24 is Abdi-Ḫeba; to credit anyone else with the speech runs counter not only to the clear parallelism with the immediately preceding lines, but also to the tenor of the entire letter–only Abdi-Ḫeba has the courage to tell the pharaoh how parlous the situation around Jerusalem really is. Why, then, assume a periphrastic "it is said" or the like? To which it may be asked, "Why assume such a rare value of the PI-sign?" We suspect the answer to be that we are dealing with a "learned" provincial scribe (see Šarruwa of the Idrimi inscription) who is displaying his learning, probably in the hope of impressing his colleague in Egypt. This would be not the only example of his pedantry.

38 Favoring *ú-ša-à-ru* is the writing *ú-ša-a-ru* in line 6. Etymology remains a moot point, but for the issue at hand it is not crucial, since the orthography makes it clear that there is question of a hollow root (*šwr/šyr*) or possibly a *mediae aleph* verb (*š'r*). (We interpret the form in question as reflecting a West Semitic qal passive, with indicative present-future {u}; see qal passive perfect *šīrtī* in *EA* 252:14, and *ši-ir*$^!$*-te* in *EA* 180:19.) With

either etymology *ú-šà-ia*$_8$*-ru* also remains a possibility. For *mediae aleph* verbs, note in the same letter *ta-ra-ia-mu* (18) and *ta-za-ia-ru* (20), and of course hollow verbs may exhibit a similar orthography (*GAG* §22i, §104k-l), with parallels elsewhere in the periphery (see *ta-ba-ia-aš*, *Ugar.* V no. 162:32; *iq-ta-na-ia-al*, *KUB* 37, 210:6).

39 But *an-ni-ia*$_8$ is more likely (see peripheral *ki-ia-am*, etc.), in view of *an-ni-*PI (*EA* 289:12) = *an-ni-i̯ú* (u_{17} in *AT* 2:34, 36 needs collation; *ut-ta-šu*?).

40 We hesitate to follow Rainey, *AOAT* 8, 92, and to read URU *gin*$_x$*-ti-e-ti* in *EA* 295 rev. 7; the stance of the apparent *gam* is not right for the end of ḪAR.

41 First noted by Böhl, *LSS* V/2, 47, n. 1. For the classification of these forms under orthography rather than phonology, see A. Goetze, *Language* 14 (1938) 135, n. 3.

42 From *u̯u''uru*, stative used as West Semitic perfect, imperative form extended to stative (perfect) on analogy *qattil* (imperative) : *qattil(a,* perfect) : : *u̯u''ir* (imperative) : x = *u̯u''ir(a)*. In view of I. Nakata's difficulties, *ANES* 2 (1969) 21 (see n. 1, above), we should perhaps add that many older orthographies survived, in peripheral Akkadian especially, along side the new ones, so that there could be considerable fluctuation between writings with the *u̯*- and *m*-series, even in the same letter (e.g., both writings, *au̯atu* and *amatu*, are found in *EA* 38; for the Nuzi evidence, see Gernot Wilhelm, *AOAT* 9, 15-16). Thus there is nothing really noteworthy in the Jerusalem scribe's writing *au̯atu* with the *u̯*-series and *u̯uššuru* with the *m*-series. Were the reading *lu-ú a-mi-la-tu-nu* (so *AHw* 90b) in *EA* 289:26 correct, then *au̯īlātunu* should also be listed here. However, it is extremely dubious: (1) as Knudtzon already remarked (*EA* I 874, n. 3), before *mi* there is "ein kleiner Zwischenraum," which does not appear in Schroeder's copy, and this strongly favors *mi* introducing a new word; (2) not only are the two verticals (Knudtzon *2*, *AHw a*) quite clear (ligature with previous putative *ú*, with Knudtzon, Autogr. no. 156; against Schroeder's copy), but had the scribe intended to write *a*, he would have drawn a smaller first vertical; and (3) it is not clear what, in context, "be ye men" means. Perhaps, with considerable reservation, *lu-ú 2 ṣíl-la-tu-nu*, "The two of you *must* be a protection."

43 First noted by I Nakata, *ANES* 2 (1969) 23-24, though his list of *EA* occurrences is incomplete, and no reference is made to extra-Amarna practice.

44 Exceptions are so rare that they require comment; see J. Nougayrol, *PRU* VI 2, n. 1.

45 It also appears as an Akkadogram in the Hittite letter *AT* 125 (Levels I-II). Its occasional occurrence in OA and the writing *q*[ì]*-bi-ma* in an Ur III letter (David I. Owen, *Or* NS 40 [1971] 398:3) may also be mentioned.

46 Probably to be included here is KUR.ḪI.A URU *Urusalim*^{ki} (*EA* 287:63), since KUR.ḪI.A seems to be a mere variant of KUR: (1) note the singular suffix in the previous line, *ezābiša* "abandon *it*"; (2) KUR.ḪI.A is always used with singular predicates (*ḫalqat, EA* 286:23, 49, 60, 64-65; *paṭarat*, 286:35; *ibašši*, but see below); (3) see [KU]R.ḪI.A LUGAL EN *gab-*<*ba*>*-ša* (*EA* 286:36) and KUR LUGAL*-ri gab-ba-ša* (*EA* 288:24). (The writer is unable to present the distribution of otiose ḪI.A, and can only point to a comparable use of MEŠ. For a further extension of MEŠ, see J. Nougayrol, *PRU* IV 138, n. 1; *Ugar.* V 146, n. 2) The writings KUR.URU, to which we called attention previously, are dismissed by Nakata, *ANES* 2 (1969) 22, n. 21, as irrelevant in a discussion of the Jerusalem scribe's peculiarities.

47 For Boghazköy, see Labat, *L'akkadien de Boghaz-Köi*, 14f.; for the Ugarit archives, see J. Nougayrol, *PRU* III 2, n. 14. The existence of other writings in the Jerusalem letters –KUR GN$^{(ki)}$ and URU GN$^{(ki)}$–in no way diminishes the significance of the northern parallels; see Nougayrol's remarks, ibid.

48 See J. Bottéro, *Le problème des ḫabiru à la 4e Rencontre Assyriologique Internationale* (Paris, 1954) 71-129.

49 Same writing in MA; see Walter Mayer, *AOAT* Sonderreihe 2, 11. In the south the only writing at all comparable is *ti-id-*[*di-i*]*n-na* (*EA* 244:19, Megiddo).

50 The problem has been thoroughly discussed by Dr. Lamia A. Rustam Shehadeh in her dissertation, "The Sibilants in the West Semitic Languages of the Second Millenium B.C." (Harvard University, 1968).

51 A. Goetze, *Language* 17 (1941) 128, n. 15. We are inclined to this view, but it should be noted that all the problematic cases concerned place-names and possibly one or two Canaanite words; there is no confusion of the sibilants in the writing of Akkadian. In other words, the scribe seems to have drawn on a tradition of the spelling of individual *words* (see n. 32, above), and only where such a tradition is lacking do the ambiguities of the syllabary make themselves felt.

52 A few other idiosyncrasies of the Jerusalem scribe may be mentioned, though they are hard to interpret in terms of background: (1) Formulaic "seven times and seven times (I have fallen)" is always (5x) written 7 TA.ÀM *ù* 7 TA.ÀM, a spelling which in the repetition of TA.ÀM is unparalleled among the many attested for this extremely common phrase. (2) In *EA* 286:7, 15, 32, the logogram EN(*bēlu*) seems to have a phonetic complement *-ri*, which is still without a convincing explanation; Schroeder, *OLZ* 18, 295f., lists the various solutions, to which we might add that EN.RI could be a Hurrogram reflecting Hurr. *ibri* "lord" (see *Ugar.* V no. 161:20). (3) AD.DA.A.NI "(my) father" (*EA* 287:26; 288:13, 15, lit. "his father," see DUMU.MUNUS.A.NI-*ia* "my daughter," *EA* 3:7, Babylonia) is very learned; according to *CAD* A/1, 67, AD.DA is confined to lexical texts, except in É AD.DA (see É AD.DA.NI *BE* 14, 40:10, MB). In view of Ugaritic *'adn* (*a-da-nu, Ugar.* V No. 130:9') "father," which is perhaps also attested in biblical Hebrew (Joshua Blau-Jonas C. Greenfield, *BASOR* 200 [1970] 16, n. 23; Delbert R. Hillers, ibid., 18), one might consider *ad-da-a-ni* = *addānī* "my father." Against this interpretation are: (1) the syllabic writing *a-da-nu* favors *'ad*, not *'add*; (2) if, as the Jerusalem writing when taken as West Semitic would suggest, the word is *'ad(d)ān*, in the south one expects *'ad(d)ōn* (at Jerusalem, note *a-nu-ki, EA* 287:66, 69).

53 For the various uses of the "Glossenkeil" at Boghazköy, see B. Schwartz, *ArOr* 10 (1938) 65; on the main thesis of this article we are not competent to judge. C. Kühne and H. Otten, *Der Šaušgamuwa-Vertrag, StBoT* 16, 52, n. 1, also point to the "Glossenkeil als Interpunktionszeichen." Before commenting on P. Artzi's study of the Amarna glosses, *Bar-Ilan Annual* 1 (1963) 24ff., we await its completion.

54 Feminine plural {āte} is very common, as are the demonstrative pronoun (adjective) *šūt* and verbal suffix {šunu} (if indeed these are Assyrianisms and not survivals from OAkk or an early OB dialect). Other Assyrianisms like *abat šarri* "the word of the king" (*EA* 211:19-20; see also 173:15-16), *adi ūmi an-ni-e* (*PRU* VI 4:10), *išaṭṭurū* (*PRU* III 97:19), *ṣarpu* "silver" (*EA* 161:44), etc., occur here and there.

55 The apparent exception *an-ni-am* (*EA* 369:2) does not exist. Collation shows that the upper slanting horizontal of the alleged *ni* is not on the tablet; instead, there are clear traces which establish the reading *an-na*!*-am*, which also occurs in *EA* 45:13; 237:20.

56 See Mayer, *AOAT* Sonderreihe 2, 36. It is the absence of contraction that is noteworthy, not the possible allophones.

57 Despite our "minimalist" approach and the resolution of almost all orthographic ambiguities in favor of Babylonian, we make an exception here and do not read *la-ma-di*$_{12}$*-ka*, since not only is *di*$_{12}$ extremely rare, but the scribe's use of *de*$_4$ is otherwise quite consistent. A "hyper-Assyrianism" certainly belongs in this linguistic potpourri.

58 Elsewhere there are scattered Assyrianisms like *šēzibanni* (*EA* 318:8, 14; see also 62:30) or *lērub* (*EA* 149:19), but they are not only quite sporadic, frequently they are probably due, not to influence of Assyrian, but to ignorance of Babylonian (see after *lērub* in *EA* 149:19, *līmur* in the next line).

59 We take *le-lu-ub* simply as a mistake and doubt its relevance for the problem of EN-*ri* (see n. 52, above).

60 For Böhl, *LSS* V/2, 63, these two forms of the infinitive were simply errors.

61 Rather than assume with Albright (*ANET* 488, followed by *CAD* E 209b) two errors (present for preterite, singular for plural) and an omission (*ana muḫḫī*<*i̯a*>), we translate *tippaša epša lamna ana muḫḫi amēlūt māt kāši* "May you treat the crime as the responsibility of (lit. "against") the men of the land of Cush."

62 On the "hyper-Assyrianism" *la-ma-de*$_4$*-ka* in *EA* 287:59, see n. 57, above. Besides various forms of *idû*, the only other instance of *de*$_4$ is *ša-de*$_4$*-e* (*EA* 287:56), where /de/ rather than /di/ is obviously intended.

63 Whether Wilhelm, *AOAT* 9, 46, is justified in denying that comparable forms at Nuzi are to be explained as Assyrianisms since some of them also exhibit Babylonian features (see *te-le-qé-ú*, not *ta-la-qé-ú*, in *EA* 288:38; however, *ta-ša-mi-ú*, not *te-še-mi-ú*, in *EA* 286:50), we need not decide here. In view of all the other Assyrianisms in the Jerusalem letters, we think our explanation of the forms in question the most likely and see no real difficulty in taking *teleqqe'ū* as a hybrid of even three languages: Babylonian assimilation of the vowels, Assyrian lack of contraction, and Canaanite verbal prefix {t(a)} in 3 plural **taqtulū(na)*.

64 Contrary to *EA* II 1390, *EA* 286:57, 58 are not pertinent, for the subjects in question, LÚ.MEŠ.ERÍN *piṭati* and KUR.ḪI.A, respectively, are treated as singular (*lūṣi*, 54; *ḫalqat*, 60); this also calls into doubt *EA* 287:20. The only other Amarna parallels are in *EA* 1 (Egypt), 35 (Alašia), and possibly 125 (Byblos, but perhaps ŠE.IM.ḪI.A is to be taken as a collective).

65 For MA, see Mayer, *AOAT* 9, 97.

66 This peculiarity was first noted by Nakata, *ANES* 2 (1969) 22-23.

67 Occasional exceptions to the prevalence of *le'û* in the Amarna archive are, besides the two passages in the Jerusalem letters: *EA* 137:27 (Byblos), 241:18 (Syria? note also *abat* 10, 19–see n. 54), 326:15 (Ascalon).

68 See Labat, *L'akkadien de Boghaz-Köi,* 141; Dietrich and Loretz, Festschrift F. Altheim, I, 20. An instrumental meaning is also to be noted in *PRU* IV 36:35 (*ištu kakkīka* "par tes (propres) armes") and several passages of the Byblos letters (*ištu manni* "with what," *EA* 112:10-12; 123:31; 125:11-12. That this is the meaning is clear from: (1) the general context, which makes it obvious *from* whom or what Rib-Addi is to defend Byblos; (2) the parallel passage, *EA* 126:33, where *kī* "how" replaces *ištu manni*; (3) the parallel passage, *EA* 122:11ff., where after quoting the pharaoh's *uṣur* . . . , Rib-Addi immediately answers that in the past he had a garrison with which to defend himself, a situation quite different from his present one; (4) *EA* 125:14ff., where after *ištu manni* . . . , the days of former strength are again recalled; (5) the question, "Who (what) will protect me?" in *EA* 112:13 and 119:10, in the latter case following immediately upon the citation of the pharaoh's *uṣurme* . . . , just as *ištu manni* . . . does. In *EA* 112:11-12, *ištu nakrīi̯a û ištu* LÚ.MEŠ *ḫupšīi̯a* "with my enemies or with my *ḫ*" is ironical. On the background of these passages, see the important article of M. Liverani, *OA* 10 (1971) 262-63).

69 The basic language is still (Canaanitized-)Babylonian. Besides the Babylonian (or hybrid) forms already listed, note especially: *ii̯i̯anu* (not *laššu*), *inanna* (unknown in Assyrian), *šāšunu* (not *šunāšunu*? *šunātunu*?), probably {ūtu} (not {uttu}), lack of vowel harmony (*tarai̯i̯amu, tazai̯i̯aru, ušai̯i̯aru* [?]), *teleqqe* (not *talaqqe*), *u̯uššera* (not *u̯aššera*), etc.

70 For Amurru, see the very strongly Assyrianizing language of *PRU* IV 141ff.; for Alašia, *Ugar.* V no. 22; for Ugarit (i.e., found there, but provenience not certain), *PRU* IV 228f., 289; F. Thureau-Dangin, *Syria* 16 (1935) 118-93; for Boghazköy, *KBo* I 14, 20; *KUB* III 73, 75, 77-79. The provenience of the letter published by Thureau-Dangin poses a special problem. In general it is written in Assyrian (with *AHw* 382a, read line 7 *a-na i-ni* "why?" < *ana mīni*), but Thureau-Dangin's opinion that it was written at Assur does not seem to take into sufficient account the following: (1) KUR URU *ú-ga-ri-ta* (5, and see above on KUR URU GN); (2) *inanna anumma* (12, neither word attested in Assyrian); (3) after a temporal clause, *u* introducing main clause (24, "waw of apodosis"); (4) [*m*]*īnummê* (24, strictly peripheral; see *AHw* 656); (5) the lapse *du-ub-bu* (20) for *dubub*, and, probably, *šul-ma-ka* (10) for *šulamka*. Though we cannot rule out, especially in view of *EA* 16, the possibility of a scribe at Assur writing a mildly barbarized Assyrian, we must also allow that, as Assyrian political and commercial influence extended westward, (barbarized) Assyrian may have tended in some areas seriously to compete with, or even to replace, the older "Reichsakkadisch."

71 See A. Goetze, *Kizzuwatna and the Problem of Hittite Geography* (New Haven, 1940) 32.

72 Abdi-Ḫeba's correspondence is probably to be dated in the early years of Amenophis IV; see Edward Fay Campbell, Jr., *The Chronology of the Amarna Letters* (Baltimore, 1964) 104-5. In other words, Assuruballit had probably not yet begun even to reign.

73 Why *CAD* A/2 132 considers the Jerusalem occurrence "uncertain" is not clear. In context the meaning "here" makes perfect sense: Abdi-Ḫeba's emphasis ("and send a royal commissioner *here*") reflects his conviction that the crisis he faces is due to the absence of a commissioner in Jerusalem, where he really belongs rather than at Gaza (see lines 46ff.). Note the punctuation mark before *annikānu*.

74 *enūma ʿapiri* "like an ʿApiru" (*EA* 288:29), *enūma eleppi* "like a ship" (*EA* 288:33), *enūma āl ʿazzati* "like the city of Gaza" (*EA* 289:16-17), *enūma* <*mārī*> *Lab'ayi* "like <the sons> of Lab'ayu" (*EA* 289:21-22), as seen by Albright (see the translations in *ANET* 488). This meaning probably developed from the lexical overlap of *kīma* and *enūma* as conjunctions, with the former's prepositional meaning then extended to the latter.

75 These postscripts have been studied by A. L. Oppenheim, *AS* 16, 253-56. (To the examples of covering letters which he has pointed out at Mari, the Assyrian letter referred to in n. 70 should be added. On the identity of the addressee, the royal scribe El(i)-milku, see Nougayrol, *Ugar.* V 13, n. 2.) J. J. Finkelstein, *Eretz Israel* 9 (1969) 9, 34, has added the interesting observation that Abdi-Ḫeba's assertion of loyalty "I would die for you" (*mattī ana kāta*) is at the end of the letter, as in the postscript in *EA* 12. The imitation of MA and MB models, as argued by Finkelstein, would be another example of the scribe's learning.

76 For the evidence, besides Oppenheim's article, see Nougayrol, *Ugar.* V 67, and H. Otten, *MDOG* 87 (1955) 17.

77 On the modified sense in which this is true of the Assyrianisms, see above.

78 Missing, besides the typical confusion of stops (on the sibilants, see nn. 50-51, above), are characteristic lexical entries like *kīmê, mannummê, mīnummê*. The number of Canaanitisms is considerable, but a complete list, which would demand long discussion, is unnecessary. Suffice it to note: *a-nu-ki* "I" (*EA* 287:69), *zuruḫ* "arm" (*EA* 286:12; 287:27; 288:14, 34); *ṣaduq* "the right is" (*EA* 287:32), *ḫanpa ša iḫnupū* "what they have done is sacrilegious" (*EA* 288:7-8), **i̯aqtulu* as present-future (*EA* 286:6, 18, 20, 21, 24, 50; 288:61), **qatala* as perfect (*EA* 288:7, 41, 45), 3 plural **taqtulū(na)* (*EA* 288:38; see *JCS* 5, 33ff.), infinitive **qatāli* (*EA* 287:46; see *JCS* 6, 77), etc., etc.

79 Another crux is the title LÚ *ru-ḫi šarri* in *EA* 288. Unfortunately, its significance and its possible implications for the background of Abdi-Ḫeba still escape us; see H. Donner, *ZAW* 73 (1961) 269-77.

80 See *AHw* 235, 4)j); S. O. Simmons, *JCS* 13 (1959) 82; and the accession years of Sabum and Apil-Sin (*RLA* 2, 176, nos. 51 and 65).

PART III: SOCIOLOGY AND RELIGION

- 8 -

THE CONFLICT BETWEEN VALUE SYSTEMS AND SOCIAL CONTROL

George E. Mendenhall

The title of this paper is the main theme of the Bible, from the Exodus to the crucifixion of Jesus. It is also the main theme of contemporary daily newspapers, but contemporary theology seems largely unaware of the contrast, and seems determined to stamp it out. The wording of the title I have found to be interesting and attractive to university students and faculty alike, but since it is not traditional to biblical scholars or theologians it is almost certain to be rejected or misunderstood by both. What we are talking about is simply the conflict between Yahweh and Baal-worship. For the latter is simply what much, if not the dominant, theology of the present day takes for granted, namely, that religion consists of elevating a particular social control system to the position of an ultimate concern, and the only argument is over the question of which control system. Social scientists by and large seem to agree that "religion" is merely another competing control system, so weak that it can be safely ignored or dismissed as a primitive survival among the ignorant into a modern technological society.

If the theologians past and present agree with the social scientists as to the nature of religion, illustrated not only by the Inquisitions of the Middle Ages and Renaissance, the heresy trials of the nineteenth and twentieth centuries, and by the ambitious superstructures of academic organizations busily engaged in establishing a superpecking order among "departments of religion" across the country, it must be admitted that the present thesis has a very heavy burden of proof. It always has had, from Moses on, and is inseparable from the question increasingly asked among biblical scholars, as to what it is that really distinguishes the biblical faith from ancient paganism to which it so rapidly became assimilated during the ancient monarchy.

Though it may be freely admitted that most religious systems throughout history have been and remain social control systems, the main theme of the Rule of God that constitutes the contrast to ancient paganism still does not seem to be understood even by specialists. That contrast I have very briefly summarized in the contrast between covenant and law,[1] and the purpose of the present paper is to describe further the structural contrast in a larger social and historical context.

Since modern man seems to understand nothing but social control systems, not much space need be spent upon their description except to point out that they consist of far more, especially from the biblical point of view, than merely armies and police. In fact, the narrative of Jesus' temptation by Satan (Matt. 4:1-11) is based upon a long traditional recognition of the tripartite nature of such systems that is already adumbrated in Jer. 9: 23f.[2] As the latter passage clearly illustrates, the foundation of these means for social control is actually to be placed in the internal motivation of large numbers of persons. For

Jeremiah is warning against the sort of personality that finds a source of pride and satisfaction merely in wealth, prestige (always a consequence of technical specialization, especially political–the "wise man"), and power. At the same time, he affirms that the "*doing* of love, justice, and righteousness" is the product of a transcendent factor, not of a social control system. This biblical foundation of Luther's famous dualism of the Kingdom of the Sword versus the Kingdom of the Spirit has been vehemently attacked by theologians especially under the impact of the Nazi regime and its horrors.[3] Curiously enough, it is people in the fields of jurisprudence and economics--the two major modes of social control–who are in effect reaffirming most powerfully the biblical contrast, not only as a reality, but as a necessity if civilization and orderly social life are to survive at all. To this we shall return below. To summarize the biblical concept of social control systems, any action induced by such systems that is based upon individual motivations of economic gain, prestige (publicity), or ambition for power has nothing to do with the Kingdom of God. This is most powerfully stated in the Sermon on the Mount: "They have received their reward."

The description of the contrasting "value system" is a much more complex matter, and what theology should be all about, but is not, since it has rarely been able to transcend its own dependence upon ecclesiastical or academic social control systems.

The problem in ancient as well as modern times is that most of humanity cannot conceive of the existence of any legitimate and functional motivation for behavior other than money, publicity, and power. At the same time, power structures since the dawn of history have claimed legitimacy on the grounds that they produce "justice and welfare of the people." When they did not, as was usually the case, the solution was always sought in some competing power structure that turned out to be the mirror image of the one overturned. In the words of the old popular song, "Is that all there is, my friend?" The social sciences, theology, and ecclesiastical as well as political establishments seem to agree in saying "yes." So did the ancient religious and political establishments against which Moses and the mixed group that left Pharaonic Egypt asserted the higher authority of Yahweh, the states of Israel and Judah that repeatedly tried to silence the prophets, and the religious and political establishments in Palestine that agreed that Jesus was not for this world.

There is very little evidence indeed that modern political or religious or academic establishments have any more insight into the nature of the biblical Kingdom of God than their ancient counterparts ("Are you a leader in Israel and know not these things?" [John 3: 10]). There is even less evidence that modern dissident movements in the secular world have any faith in anything but the modern counterpart to the ancient "baal-worship," and this is true of all quasi-religious movements from the Israelis, Women's "Lip," the various minority movements covering the rainbow of skin color (which is usually all they have in common), and the various "political activist" movements of university students or clergy organizations. It is not surprising, then, that the Bible is relegated to the category of "ancient barbarian mythology," as one spokeswoman for a women's theology of the AAR recently put it, or to "the fairy tales of my race," as Moshe Dayan put it not long after the 1967 war.

It is characteristic that value-based movements are always regarded by social control systems as extremely dangerous competitors that must be wiped out by force. In 99 percent of the cases the social control system has analyzed the situation with considerable accuracy. It is the exceptional case that does not fit which remains unrecognized until it is too late–for the survival of the control system, not the value system.

The biblical history illustrates the continuity of a value-based community over a period of more than a millennium. During that period there was gradually worked out in the crucible of historical experience the structure of a value system, usually in opposition to social control systems, that has been completely confused by repeated attempts to identify the two. This attempt to identify the merely historical control system with a transcendent rule of God must always founder upon the shoals of the religious ethic, but the natural instinct of corporate self-preservation that is the first law of political science virtually demands the destruction of the religious ethic.

The structures of control systems and of the Kingdom of God are radical opposites, but they need not be long at war with each other. They simply belong to different categories, each with its own independent validity ("The powers that be are ordained of God"; "Render unto Caesar the things that are Caesar's, and unto God the things that are God's.") Indeed, the clear message of the Bible is that social systems can continue to exist only where a minimally tolerable value system has already become operative and still succeeds in functioning to some extent, but the social control system can never produce it, and often succeeds in destroying it.

Before describing the systemic contrast between values and social control, attempt must be made to describe what is meant by values in this context of biblical thought, for it seems to be foreign to both theology and social science. Actually the contrast becomes comprehensible only within the context of the biblical experience (i.e., history), as I hope to demonstrate, simply because any purely formal contrast is merely a contrast *between* social control systems, and all that is left is a *functional* contrast that can be observed or recognized (like atomic particles) only in action ("By their fruits you shall know them"). For the concept of values as used here is simply the translation of an old Anglo-Saxon word into its equivalent Latin-derived semantic equivalent: "worth(-ship)"=*valuta*.[4] A value system is that which motivates behavior of a person, and this of course is usually identified with the factors of power, prestige, and wealth that society uses always in an irrational way as means of social control. Arbitrarily, due to the inadequacies of the English language, and following the Sermon on the Mount as well as the prophets, I shall designate all action motivated by such factors as "interests" not values, and therefore secular ("That which is born of the flesh is flesh. . . .") over against that which is of intrinsic and transcendent value ("That which is born of the Spirit is Spirit"). The mainstream of biblical faith is, then, the affirmation of a real factor in human life and experience that is independent of, not produced by, but ultimately essential to the existence and satisfactory operation of any social control system. To deny this is simply to reaffirm the ancient pagan identification of the state with God, and at the same time to deny that there can be any legitimate *qualitative* concerns binding upon the all-powerful state, or upon any other social organization, for that matter. Such a proposition is patently absurd when couched in such terms, but it is a description of the dominant theory of foreign policy ever since the tired liberalism of the 1930s received its classical expression in the works of Walter Lippmann, who could not conceive of any concern other than "national self-interest."

The rejection of ethical controls over political power has always had and will always have catastrophic consequences, but that rejection is comprehensible within the framework of Lippmann's limited vision. Indeed, the present critical situation in the Near East is a classical illustration of the sacrifice of American national "self-interest" for the sake of an allegedly "moral" consideration. It is not, however, the structure of national interest, but the structure of moral values that is the issue, and here modern man is in the stage of primitive barbarism to such an extent that even specialists in the Bible often have not been able to comprehend the real issues. This is the central thesis of the present paper, for the whole history of mankind outside the biblical tradition is the record of the attempt to substitute social power structures for value systems, and always to identify the two. The result is simply a competition between power structures that must constantly lead to violence and war. The identification of power with Satan is highly unpopular in all social circles now as always, for the faith in something else has never been long characteristic of any large part of the human race, but it cannot be denied that it is that something else that has accounted for human survival up to the present.

The first of the three major structural contrasts between value and control systems is the contrast between private and public matters. A corollary to this is the contrast between the kinds of social relationships that are involved. It is surprising to find in contemporary literature an increasing awareness of this contrast, and very considerable confusion about it. At its clearest are those examples of politicians who use public office as a means of enhancing their private economic status. But in a society such as the contemporary United States where public organizations lose far more goods and money to their own employees than they do to professional criminals, it would seem probable that there are many millions of people who have no business throwing the first stone at politicians. The principle is the same: the idea that because the goods or money belong to an impersonal organization with large resources rather than to a person, there is no guilt incurred in taking what one wants. Both assume that a morality that they would not think of violating in dealings with friends and acquaintances does not apply in dealing with public corporations.

But this is only a minor illustration of a much more serious problem, and I can only attempt to describe it and suggest that others may succeed in bringing about more clarity in an issue that is shot through our corporate and private life. In the first place, what I define as a value is something that can be recognized and experienced only by a real human being, not those legal fictions that we call corporations. As Georges Bernanos put it decades ago in *Tradition of Freedom*, only a human being has a conscience. If corporations occasionally seem to act as though they have one, it is only because there is a real person in that corporation who does love and who is able to make his voice heard. It is most unfortunate that a lot of irresponsible balderdash about "corporate personality" and the "collective Spirit" or some such modern mythology has obscured the fact that corporations are mere legal fictions. What is true of real persons can be true only in a public, legal, sense of corporations, political, business, or even religious.[5] All a corporation can do is establish a "policy," and apply it as evenhandedly as possible to everyone. To do anything else simply invites chaos, disintegration of the organization and its functions, or even worse, arbitrary misuse of authority by giving its agents too much discretionary power.

It is for this reason that no corporation can be identified with the Rule of God--only persons. The conflict between such collectivities and value systems comes inevitably when the corporation recognizes *no* obligation binding upon it other than its own self-interest, and thus they must be carefully watched over by a superior law–the state. But who watches the watchmen? The state that recognizes no obligation other than self-interest is itself corrupt, and usually incompetent as well, for it is usually run by politicians who are incapable of looking beyond the next election, and therefore completely unconcerned for the long-range consequences of their own misuse of power. The same has long been and is characteristic of many religious organizations, and all incorporated ecclesiastical institutions are, from the value system of biblical faith and thought, mere public institutions for the perpetuation of ritual labors and the real estate thereto appertaining--the sort of thing that can be found in any primitive or ancient society. The real estate perpetuates the primitive concept of the "sacred and profane" that is such a favorite theme in contemporary comparative religion, but is poles apart from the normative mainstream of the biblical tradition.

Since the corporate control system as such cannot experience (or sometimes even recognize) love, justice, and compassion, its modes of control can be only the budget--appropriation of funds and therefore economic security of its employees so long as they are "loyal," i.e., submissive to the policies of their superiors in power--the opportunity for obtaining prestige by a combination of submissiveness and cautious initiative that obtains "recognition" and election to higher office, and for the chosen few, positions of real power where they can make decisions that can make or break those under their authority. This description seems to fit almost any social organization of any type of the present day, and ecclesiastical organizations seem to be unaware of the fact that it is incompatible with the Rule of God, and are not even concerned with the latter. ("It shall not be so among you.") Therefore, any attempt to identify a corporate organization with the Rule of God, or even the Community of God is a contradiction in terms, since the perpetuation of the organization rests upon appeals to motivations that are by definition temptations of Satan that strongly erode, if not drive out, those motivations that are in the Bible characteristics of human personality that are recognized as the "fruits of the Spirit." A church authority, like any other politician, is a prisoner of the prestige system that created his position, and as such he must represent the existing value system of the group he rules in its purest form -which is rarely very pure, since the group itself is ruled by motivations that have nothing to do with the Kingdom of God; otherwise the authority and prestige systems would not exist.

The corollary to this first contrast has already been introduced above. It is the contrast between a power structure and a community. A power structure needs no community to undergird it; in fact a community constitutes a very real danger to the power structure in many contexts, as we can illustrate by examples from the eighteenth century B.C. to the modern day. A power structure maintains control either by physical power of armies and police, or by economic controls over community or potential community leadership. Its members typically have little really in common except the power structure itself, and the common interests that it manipulates for self-perpetuation. Political entities have characteristically since the dawn of history been militarily controlled and territorially defined monopolies of force over populations that constituted a most diverse complex of communities that contrasted to each other in a multitude of ways: in social status, specialized function, residential proximity, "ethnic" origin, language, and even value-based communities. Ancient polytheism is nothing less, and probably much more, than the simple fact that this complex of parochial interests must be recognized by the all-powerful state in the hierarchy of the pantheon, in which the godlet of the king is of course always the top dog, ruling over the minor gods and their worshippers, from the powerful and ubiquitous god of the "scribes"--the royal bureaucracy--to the minor godlet of the female bartenders' union of ancient Sumer.

A community, on the other hand, is a complex of persons who have something in common other than a power structure, and a value system in which economic well-being is not in the control of a centralized power structure. Prestige likewise is not based upon superior ability in political dirty tricks, and power is regarded as demonic. The biblical community was originally based upon such a value system that is widely known to contemporary scholarship as the covenant, but which is also usually misunderstood as simply a "primitive" form of a power structure. To be sure, much of the biblical history, as well as its ancient distortions, records the fact that a control system pretended to be the historical realization of the Rule of God, through his anointed of course. But it is clear that the control system was constantly concerned to protect itself from outrageous proclamations that there might be a difference of opinion between God and the power-holder who claimed the divine right of kings, i.e., in modern terms the god-given right of "national sovereignty," which is, of course, constantly upheld by lavish use of Phantom jets, since God is no longer quite reliable enough to guarantee "national security," and has not been since the Nazi regime. Curiously enough, though the Nazi propagandists proclaimed that "if the German race did not exist, god would not exist," the downfall of the "German race" and its godlet has led to an unparalleled well-being for the German people.

Though it would be easily possible to argue also that a control system and a community differ greatly with respect to their goals or purposes that are appropriate to their nature, such discussion will be dispensed with here except for the observation that a community has no goal or objective except a qualitative one--the realization in the process of daily life of those values that make life Good, and in which its members find satisfaction. It is essentially a private structure, in biblical language an *'am* over against a *goy*. It follows, then, that the community is ruled by a structure radically different from that of a *goy*, or social control system. And this leads us to the second major structural contrast: the difference between covenant and law.

THE DIFFERENCE BETWEEN COVENANT AND LAW

Notwithstanding amateurish attempts on the part of various scholars to reduce covenants to mere primitive aspects of law, or even some mythical tribal wisdom, the structural and functional contrast between covenant and law is absolute. To be sure, they do coincide to some extent in the moral *content* of what they proscribe and prescribe, and this has misled innumerable theologians for millennia. It is the operational contrast between the two that opens up the New Testament to a much more adequate understanding, from the Sermon on the Mount to St. Paul's otherwise inexplicable polemic against the "law," which has been so often grotesquely misunderstood. For various reasons the contrast will be presented in parallel columns, and as succinctly as possible under a variety of headings, since this is not the proper forum in which to bring forth a monumental ten volume work that would easily be possible were the time and energy available.

I: Covenant	II: Law
1. Purpose	
Creates a community where none existed before, by establishing a common relationship to a common lord.	Presupposes a social order in which it serves as an instrument for maintaining an orderly freedom and security
2. Basis	
Gratitude: response to benefits already received=Grace.	Social fear: attempts to protect society from disruption and attack by threat of force.
3. Enactment	
By voluntary act in which each individual	By competent social authority. It is binding

willingly accepts the obligations presented.[6]	upon each individual by virtue of his status as a member of the social organization, usually by birth.
4. Validity	
Binding upon each person without regard to social context. It is universal as God himself and is, therefore, the real basis for the concept of the "omnipresence of God."	Entirely dependent upon social boundary lines. Completely irrelevant to one who has crossed the boundary of the social order.
5. Sanctions	
Not under control of social organization:[7] upredictable in specific cases, but connected with cause-and-effect concepts in human history. Both positive and negative sanctions included.	Enforced by social organization through its chosen authorities. Sanctions are largely negative though nonpolitical organizations use economic and prestige motivations to obtain conformity.
6. Norms	
Typically presented as verbal abstractions, the definition of which is an obligation of persons in concrete circumstances and the "fear of God"=Conscience.	Defined by social authority in advance usually with specific sanctions defined for specific violations. Arbitrary and formal in nature, since only forms of action can be witnessed to in a court of law.
7. Orientation	
Toward the future: makes individual behavior reliable and, therefore, a basis for both private and public security. Prediction of consequences extends to four generations in case of violation.	Toward the past: attempts to punish violations of the public order in order to make that public order more secure. It is oriented toward the future only in the sense that it gives warning in advance of the penalties that the society has power to impose upon the violator. Very short attention span (statute of limitations).
8. Social aspect	
Obligations individual, but consequences (blessings and curses) are of necessity social, since they are "acts of God"–drought, epidemic, defeat in war, etc. Powerfully reinforces individual responsibility to society, and social responsibility to refrain from protection of the guilty.	Obligations defined by society are binding upon all members, but sanctions are imposed only upon guilty individual, in adversary procedure and rite. Is a form of warfare pitting society against guilty person.
9. Evolution	
Forms basis for social custom especially in early stages. As social control takes over, may degenerate into mere ritual reinforcement of a social solidarity.	Presupposes a customary morality that it attempts to protect, but cannot create. Tends to become increasingly rigid in formal definition, and increasingly devoid of real ethical content.

10. Continuity

Since it is not produced by society, it cannot be guaranteed by society. Essentially private, individual, independent of social roles. Prophets, the Christ, Apostles. Destruction of a particular social control system, therefore, does not mean the end of the value system.	Cannot exist apart from social institutions–king, priest, political officers, legislative, executive, judicial. Ceases to exist when political structure falls.

The foregoing attempt to describe the contrast between the "parallel columns" is intended as a sort of theological shorthand to stimulate a new way of looking into innumerable problems that ancient and modern man share alike. At the same time, it can furnish a new approach to innumerable problems in biblical studies and the history of religions, and perhaps modern politics as well. For the scholarly mind that is sensitive to nothing but socially created "roles" certainly cannot cope with the problem of understanding the ancient prophets, or with the "life of Jesus," nor can such a modern theology cope with the problem of "identity crisis."

The problem as I see it and read it in the Bible is that most human beings throughout the course of recorded history have sought both physical (public) and emotional (private) well-being, and they simply cannot both be obtained from any social control system, in spite of political propaganda to the contrary. Public control systems have typically concentrated on protecting persons from physical violence from within and without (crime and war), and protecting persons from starvation (economic controls and welfare programs), but except for those of high-prestige political status, have never been able even to operate in the all-important area of personal self-evaluation except in transient periods (usually in wartime) when it has been possible to equate emotional well-being with self-sacrifice on behalf of the political power structure. This leads to the third and most crucial contrast.

VALUES VERSUS INTERESTS

No social organization can be equated with the Kingdom of God, and yet so long as human beings are capable of desiring, and responding to, those grand abstract terms that occur in most languages as "love, justice, and compassion" there will always be a conflict between value systems and social control systems. The problem arises when the latter pretend to be realizations of the former, when forms of behavior that are motivated by a social control system pretend to be expressions of the Rule of God. Professors Albright and Mann have not explored deeply enough the concept of "hypocrisy" in the New Testament, which is crucial to the present analysis. For in that concept, Jesus (it is impossible to conceive of any other source) did away with purely formal ideas of contrasts between the "sacred and the profane" that are so fashionable among modern professors of religion all over the country, if not the world. The idea that particular places or times are "sacred" over aginst "secular" counterparts seems to be common to most of recorded humanity, and the secularization of such sacred spots and times in favor of a proclamation of qualitative sacralization of *aspects* of human behavior seems to be that which brought about the crucifixion of Jesus, as well as that of his followers, which he could well have predicted, as the tradition maintains.

This contrast between *ritual* identification of the sacred and *qualitative* identification is crucial to the entire biblical tradition. Ritual identification is common to all religious traditions it would seem, and as any anthropologist knows, serves primarily to reinforce existing social solidarities. But though the Kingdom of God most certainly produces community, its function is to destroy artificial social boundaries, not create them. Therefore, hypocrisy is by definition a complex of behavior that claims to belong to the category of Column I–the sacred, value, orientation motivated by the love and rule of God, while as a matter of fact it belongs merely to a social control system, and the specific behavior ceases when the social reward system ceases–as when a person crosses the social boundary line. Though the biblical background of the concept is difficult to ascertain, I would suggest that it must be related to the semantic background of Hebrew *bagad*, "to deceive," and the Greek translation derived from the stage is entirely appropriate, for the actor is only a *persona* playing a role for social reward, not a real person.

The reality of the Rule of God is then the crucial issue, that seems effectively to be denied by much religious leadership, including theologians at present when they radically reject the contrast between the Kingdom of the Sword and the Kingdom of the Spirit. For the Kingdom of God is not a mere social lump of half-baked dough, it is the leaven–the qualitative functioning–of a transcendent factor that the Bible calls God, which is radically other than social control systems, which society benefits from, but which it can neither produce nor control. It can be recognized by individuals in themselves and others–the fruits of the Spirit–but it is and must be an act of faith, an affirmation of the reality of that transcendent factor in human life and experience that is just as historical as was Jesus of Nazareth, and with which that transcendent factor is identified, and with whom the believer identifies himself.

It is within some such frame of reference that the whole range of phenomena of early Christianity can be understood in its own context, from the teachings of Jesus to the proclamation of St. Paul, and the peculiar characteristics of the early church. In the first place, there is the rejection of social power as the ultimate realization of the Rule of God, which both Jewish and Roman power structures misunderstood. Included also is economic power used to induce ritually correct forms of behavior, which is so well illustrated by the actual function of ordination in many churches at present.[8] Next is the total rejection of law as a means either for control of behavior in the community, or as a description of a conformity that leads to "salvation." At the same time, law as a means of social control retains its validity–but it simply is not a means by which the Rule of God operates, for it of necessity can be relevant only to a particular social enclosure, and rigid definitions appropriate to a particular culture cannot be relevant to the multitude of "nations, kindreds, and tongues," over which the Rule of God is to be extended.

Finally, the reduction of the community of God to another mere competing social organization results in disintegration of the latter. For if the church has nothing to offer but another organization trying to preserve itself by social manipulation, economic pressures and inducements, and a little temporary glory (prestige) for selected individuals, plus the ritual reinforcement of a specious solidarity, then it has ceased to be the product of that transcendent power it claims to be. ("By their fruits you shall know them.")

Though the position described here has been rejected as "antinomian idealism" or some such term, such a judgment simply illustrates a naive blind faith in some kind of power structure and therefore comes close to the reestablishment of ancient Baal-worship. Though theologians may attack this description of a qualitative polarization, fortunately many in other fields are beginning to realize both the futility and the dangers to society of the idea that all kinds of personal and social problems can be solved by the unlimited use of social force and funds. For the vast majority of social problems arise out of the private sector of life. "Oppression and injustice" presuppose at least the existence of their opposites, but as specialists in the law have long pointed out in a multitude of ways, it is foolish, dangerous, and even silly to expect justice to result from the operations of the law. Quite the contrary, law must operate from the foundation of a sense of right and justice among the community it serves, but which it cannot create.

As Kenneth Boulding pointed out some years ago, the incredible elaboration of social organization in this country is a relatively very recent phenomenon. As withdrawal phenomena, scandals in power centers, and dehumanization of life progress to their logical conclusion, it would seem that the elaborate social organization we have built may be just as ephemeral as its ancient counterparts. The consequences could easily be just as catastrophic, and much more so as modern culture has far more destructive weapons at its disposal, and at the same time a far higher percentage of the total population is directly dependent upon social organization for its food supply. (One estimate is that in the United States only 4 percent of the total population produce food for the other 96 percent, and a goodly part of the rest of the world as well.) The practical deification of the social organization, ("God and country"=God *is* country) whether political or religious ("I suppose I do regard the . . . Church organization as God" said one professor of economics some years ago with regard to his own denomination, which happened to be protestant) has already foundered upon the reefs of political corruption, on the one hand, and the increasing withdrawal of persons from identification with institutionalized religion, on the other.

To sum up, the conflict between the two radically different structures is really a twofold one. The power structure induces conflict by its rejection of internal and external ethical controls over the behavior of its power-holders, and the age-old reaction is the development of a competing power structure that promptly feels obliged to reject ethical controls as well as a luxury that handicaps its chances for success. Thus Gresham's law operates in the realm of social ethic since the worse motivation drives out the better. The other side of the coin is the conflict that comes about when persons, acting as agents for a transcendent power and ethic, point out that the claims of power structures to be acting on behalf of that ultimate concern are sheer hypocrisy, for from their actions it is clear that they are sensitive only to the control mechanisms of power, glory, and money. Thus competing control systems always proclaim their concern for "justice," "liberty," and "human rights," which always turns out to be the obligation of someone else to give them more money, higher position in the pecking order, and power, while there is very little reason to believe that they have any concern for liberty, justice, and rights of those who are beyond the arbitrary social boundary line that creates the base of their claims to social control. Such social hypocrisy is dangerous because it effectively calls in question the reality of value systems and makes very difficult the affirmation that humanity is capable of a sense of justice and right that must take precedence over selfish interest. The permanent symbol of the necessity as well as the reality of that Rule of God is the crucifixion of Jesus–the equally permanent affirmation that "winning" in the jungle of social manipulation and social competitiveness cannot be the controlling motivation of those who hunger and thirst for righteousness and peace.

NOTES

[1] *TTG,* 200, n. 5.

[2] The wisdom, power, and wealth of Jeremiah correspond to the economic, prestige, and power motivations of the Temptation narrative. The virtual identity of wisdom with social prestige in ancient societies is very old, for it is an essential high prestige role in stratified political societies.

[3] There can hardly be a better illustration of a *non sequitur*. It was not only a portion of the German church that submitted to Hitler; a very considerable segment of American "liberals" admired him too, because he "worked economic miracles." It is the tired old "liberalism" that should be questioned, for it is seemingly incapable of imagining that there can be something more important than politics and economic manipulation. The critical situation in the Near East for the past couple decades is fundamentally due to this same "liberal" mentality that cannot see any historical factor other than the three temptations of Satan.

[4] According to the dictionary, "value, worth imply intrinsic excellence or desirability." Worship in the ancient world designated human response, usually in the form of symbolic action, to that intrinsic excellence.

[5] I have witnessed a number of occasions when ecclesiastical boards or synodical business meetings have acted upon the unquestioned assumption that the Christian religious ethic is irrelevant to the business at hand. It is for this reason that the old cliché about the "church being the conscience of the state" is pious twaddle. The church as an organization has not succeeded too well in being a conscience to itself, especially in its treatment of dissenters. Consider the religious establishment's contemptuous or even violent treatment of the prophets from Amos to Jesus.

[6] "Original sin" is therefore a recognition of the fact that no one is born into such a relationship to God, and no one is born with the value system that characterizes the covenant relationship.

[7] Such "acts of God" are given transcendent positive and negative value by tying them inseparably to the ethical system–the curses and blessings, and therefore powerfully reinforce qualitative controls over individual and corporate behavior. The modern situation is curiously illuminated by the fact that in law an "act of God" is simply an unforeseeable and uncontrollable event that relieves a defendant of legal responsibility. It was much easier in ancient peasant communities to recognize and find transcendent values in the processes that led to productivity, for factors such as climate and freedom from pests and epidemics most obviously were not under individual or social control. However, modern man is perhaps even more dependent upon such factors, for it is increasingly clear that the world-wide economy is not under anyone's control. Modern man is increasingly eroding away the value system that alone can make it operate for corporate well-being. See R. Heilbroner, *The Making of Economic Society* (Englewood Cliffs, N. J., 1962). "Where there is no vision, the people perish" is more than a figure of speech.

[8] The perhaps unconscious assumption that a person is a reliable preacher of the Gospel only if he receives his income from a unit of the church organization is illustrated by the virtually perfect correlation between ordination and economic dependence upon some

"jurisdictional unit" of the organization. Similarly my denomination has given up the attempt to define theologically what was meant by the "Call of God," and the "Call" has become simply a formal legal contract between the ordained person and a "jurisdictional unit."

- 9 -

DIVINE FREEDOM AND CULTIC MANIPULATION IN ISRAEL AND MESOPOTAMIA

J. J. M. Roberts

The reemergence of biblical theology in the years following World War I brought with it a renewed interest in the uniqueness of the biblical faith.[1] In terms of Old Testament studies, that meant an attempt to isolate the distinctively Israelite elements in Israel's religion from those elements which Israel held in common with her polytheistic neighbors.[2] G. E. Wright's *The Old Testament Against Its Environment* exemplifies well the mood and method of this theological approach to the Old Testament, and the title of his study would make an appropriate designation for this important aspect of the biblical theology movement.[3]

In spite of significant differences between Wright and other Old Testament theologians belonging to the movement, there seems to be a general consensus among them with regard to two fundamental contrasts between Israel and her neighbors: (1) Israel's religion was historically oriented and primarily concerned with bringing man's will into line with Yahweh's will, while the polytheistic religions were ahistorical, focusing on man's attempt to integrate himself into the rhythm of nature.[4] (2) The pagan ritual was an attempt to gain control over or manipulate the gods by sympathetic magic, while in Israel the cult by its emphasis on historical recitation, imaginative memory, and thanksgiving served to clarify God's will to man and to renew man's commitment to that will.[5] Thus, according to these scholars, the superficial similarities between Israel's religion and that of the surrounding nations obscures a far more profound discontinuity between the faith of Israel and that of the nations.

There is no doubt a significant element of truth in this comparative analysis--Israelite religion is undeniably different–and the analysis lent itself, as Childs notes, to a "hard-hitting, impressive new form of apologetic for Biblical religion."[6] The consequent popularizing, however, revealed certain weaknesses in the analysis that are not totally absent from the more sophisticated treatments, and it was inevitable that a reaction would set in. It came, along with a general decline in biblical theology,[7] in a two-pronged attack on the first thesis. Bertil Albrektson demonstrated that the pagan gods also act quite decisively in history,[8] and James Barr seriously questioned whether history was really as important a theological category to the ancient Israelites as the modern biblical theologians had made it.[9] Even if these critics have overstated their case, it seems relatively clear that the radical contrast between the polytheistic gods of nature and the Israelite god of history must be softened considerably.

As far as I am aware, the second thesis, which predicates a similarly radical distinction between the Israelite cult that preserves divine freedom and the pagan cult that seeks to manipulate the deity, has not received the same critical attention. Were the pagan gods, in fact, more susceptible to manipulation than Yahweh, and was the pagan cult a more blatant attempt to gain control over the deity than the Israelite cult? I think not.

To begin with, one must insist on a far more basic similarity in religious motivation between Israel and her neighbors than Wright's analysis would seem to allow. Despite whatever difference in historical emphasis there may have been between the Israelite and pagan cults, the rationale for serving the deity, especially on the individual level, was essentially the same in Israel as elsewhere. If one may generalize it, Satan's question about Job is very much to the point: "Does man fear God for nought?" The answer to this question in both Israel and Mesopotamia, to pick a specific area for comparison, was of course, "No!" Obedience to the deity, whether in ethical matters or in purely ritual concerns, paid. This is evident from the *Counsels of Wisdom* on the Mesopotamian side,[10] and one need only look at the covenant blessings to see how fundamental a role the incentive of profit or reward played in Israelite theology.[11]

Moreover, the rewards sought by the Mesopotamian and the Israelite differed very little, if at all. Both wanted long life, good health, numerous children (especially male children), material prosperity, deliverance from foreign enemies, peace and stability at home, and general well-being which would include what a modern would call mental health. Forgiveness of sins, for which both the Israelite and the Mesopotamian prayed, was related to these more concrete blessings, since it was only through the right relationship with the deity that these blessings flowed to man. If that relationship were broken through sin, the blessings would be lost.

In view of this basic identity in the ultimate goal of Mesopotamian and Israelite religiosity, the contrast Wright draws between the polytheist who saw the problem of life as an integration with the forces of nature and the Israelite who saw it as an adjustment to the will of God,[12] if it has any validity at all, is simply a contrast in the means used to attain the same end. When Wright speaks of an integration with nature in polytheism, he is, of course, referring to the origin of the polytheistic gods in the numinous awareness of the powers in nature, and the human need to bring oneself and these sometimes conflicting powers into a life-giving harmony. But, more than that, the polytheist accomplished this "integration with nature"–as the term "integration" itself suggests--by entering into the world of these powers, identifying himself with them, and through imitative action, forcing them to do what he wanted. As evidence for this fundamental role of sympathetic magic in polytheistic religion, Wright points especially to the underlying meaning of the major festivals of the pagan world.[13] Unfortunately, his argument is flawed here by a methodological inconsistency. When discussing the Israelite festivals, he emphasizes, not the original meanings of these celebrations, but the later Israelite historical reinterpretations, and in so doing he stresses the important point that even when rites and festivals are preserved in outwardly the same form, they do not always retain their earlier meanings.[14] Yet he completely overlooks this important insight when he discusses the pagan festivals. Of course, he did not have the benefit of Professor Jacobsen's paper on Mesopotamian religious drama,[15] but even in the *Intellectual Adventure of Ancient Man*, which Wright used extensively, there was already a clear intimation that Mesopotamian religion could not be understood as a static entity:[16]

> Though these functions of the human state have been integrated to some degree with the view of the universe as a state . . . the deeper significance, the inner sense of these festivals, lies outside of and is not truly founded in the view of the universe as a state. It should therefore not cause wonder that they cannot stand

out in true perspective in a presentation of that view; that they represent an older layer of 'speculative' thought.

According to the view of the world as a state, man is the slave of the great cosmic forces; he serves them and obeys them; and his only means of influencing them is by prayer and sacrifice, that is, by persuasion and gifts. According to the older view which created the festivals, man could himself become god, could enter into the identity of the great cosmic forces in the universe which surrounded him, and could thus sway it by action, not merely by supplication.

The point is, had Wright chosen as his object of comparison the later Mesopotamian view of the world rather than the more primitive, he would not have been able to paint such a sharp contrast between the pagan who could control the deity by sympathetic magic and the Israelite who could only adjust himself to Yahweh's will.

In the later Mesopotamian development, while the element of sympathetic magic never totally disappeared, the means by which one attempted to gain the desired blessings were modeled far more on the psychological devices one used with human superiors in line with the strong anthropomorphic and sociomorphic conception of the gods that had largely displaced their primary identification with natural powers. Note, for instance, the famous Old Babylonian letter which a certain suppliant addressed to his personal god:[17]

To the god my father speak: thus says Apiladad, your servant: Why have you neglected me so? Who is going to give you one who can take my place? Write to the god Marduk, who is fond of you, that he may break my bondage; then I shall see your face and kiss your feet! Consider also my family, grown-ups and little ones; have mercy on me for their sake, and let your help reach me!

With great sensitivity Jacobsen has captured the psychological pressures this sulking worshipper is applying to his personal god:[18]

His feelings are hurt because he thinks his god neglects him. He hints that such neglect is very unwise on the part of the god, for faithful worshippers are hard to get and difficult to replace. But if the god will only comply with his wishes, then he will be there right away and adore him. Finally, he works on the god's pity: the god must consider that there is not only himself but that he has a family and poor little children who also suffer with him.

One should also note, as Jacobsen does, that the man asks his god to write to Marduk for him.[19] Just as men call upon other men to intercede for them in the affairs of men, so the polytheist asks individual gods to use their influence on other gods in his behalf. In this case the personal god is called upon to use his connections with Marduk; in other cases a god like Marduk is asked to placate the personal deity who has deserted his ward in anger.

The ancient Mesopotamian also used various gifts, offerings, and promises of such to obtain the desired response from his divine overlords. One can hardly dismiss such practices as simply calculated bribery, but human nature being what it is, this approach to the deity always runs the risk of sinking to that level, and Mesopotamian literature offers some graphic examples of just such a corruption. In the Atra-ḫasīs epic, for instance, when Enlil decides to solve the noise problem by eliminating mankind through the plague, the people at Enki's counsel ignore their own gods and goddesses and shower all their gifts on Namtara, the god of plague. The maneuver has the intended effect of both pleasing and embarrassing Namtara, and he lifts the plague.[20] Subsequently the same ploy is used with success on Adad.[21]

But what normally strikes the Old Testament theologian as the most significant contrast between Israelite religion, which also had its sacrifices, free-will offerings, and vows, is the sometimes explicit statement that the Mesopotamian gods actually needed these gifts.[22] In the Atra-ḫasīs epic, for instance, after the flood has done away with the human slaves of the gods, there is no one left to provide them cult, and they sit weeping, their lips feverishly athirst, their stomachs cramped with hunger.[23] And everyone is familiar with the scene where the hero of the flood offers his sacrifice upon disembarking, whereupon the gods sniff the smell and gather like flies over the offering.[24] Or no less famous, the response of the slave when his master decides not to offer sacrifice:[25]

> Do not sacrifice, sir, do not sacrifice.
> You can teach your god to run after you like a dog.

Nevertheless, I think one should be more cautious than scholars sometimes are in citing such examples as evidence that the pagans could coerce or manipulate their gods while such would be unheard of in Israel. Do these passages in fact reflect normative Mesopotamian theology? Or could one with equal right quote Job 9:22-24 as the normative Israelite view on Yahweh's justice?

> It is all one; therefore I say, he destroys both the blameless and the wicked.
> When disaster brings sudden death, he mocks at the calamity of the innocent.
> The earth is given into the hand of the wicked; he covers the faces of its judges
> –if it is not he, who then is it?

But perhaps that is straining the argument.

It is true that the Israelites explicitly denied that Yahweh ate the sacrificial offerings,[26] and since there was no image of Yahweh, it was not easy to think of him as actually wearing the votive offerings of clothing, jewelry, and the like–in Mesopotamia these were directly connected with the care for the image.[27] But, apart from these rather crude anthropomorphisms which are to a certain degree tied to the presence of a physical image, all the Mesopotamian devices for influencing the god mentioned above are also present in the Old Testament in one form or another.

The highly stereotyped descriptions of physical and mental anguish characteristic of the individual psalms of lament clearly function to provoke Yahweh's compassion, and the use of vows and votive offerings in the Old Testament is too well known to need comment.

Because of Israel's monotheistic faith one would not expect a worshipper to call upon other gods to intercede with Yahweh, though intercessory spirits may be known in Late Israelite sources,[28] but to a large extent the same function is performed in Israel by men who stand in a particularly close relationship to Yahweh, such as Moses, Samuel, or one of the prophets.[29] Thus the use of influential mediators in approaching the deity with a request is a motif common to both Israel and Mesopotamia; the details are just altered to fit the differing theological systems.

Moreover, one should remember that physical needs are not the only needs an anthropomorphic god may have. If Yahweh could not be touched by the hunger and thirst that tormented the pagan deities deprived of their cult, his "spiritual" needs for praise and glory provided the Israelite with essentially the same bargaining point. Over and over again Yahweh is asked to do something for his "name's sake."[30] He must protect his name's honor:

> Remember your servants, Abraham, Isaac, and Jacob; do not regard the stubbornness of this people, or their wickedness, or their sin, lest the land from which you

brought us say, "Because Yahweh was not able to bring them into the land which he promised them, or because he hated them, he has brought them out to kill them in the wilderness." (Deut. 9:27-28; see Exod. 32:11-12)

Yahweh's need for praise and glory also finds expression in the Psalms where the psalmist, just as the Babylonian letter writer, sometimes reminds the deity that he is in danger of losing a valuable worshipper:

> Turn, O Yahweh, save my life; deliver me for the sake of your steadfast love. For in death no one remembers you; in sheol who praises you? (Ps. 6:5-6)

Or again:

> What profit is there in my blood, if I go down to the pit? Will the dust praise you? Will it declare your faithfulness? (Ps. 30:10; see 88:11-13)[31]

No doubt it is in this context that one should judge those passages in the Psalms where a request is concluded by such words as, "Then my tongue shall proclaim your righteousness, your praise all the day long."[32] As in the Babylonian *shu-ila* prayers, which characteristically end with a very similar vow,[33] the implication is that if the deity will give the man what he wants, the man will give the deity the praise he desires.

Moreover, strange as it may seem, the presence of such vows and other psychological pressure techniques in both Israelite and Mesopotamian prayers gives the lie, I think, to the widespread attempt on the part of Old Testament scholars to draw a sharp distinction between the manipulative quality of Mesopotamian and Israelite prayers. Arnold Gamper,[34] for instance, basing himself on R. G. Castellino's work,[35] refers to the prevailing Mesopotamian conception of the magical effect of prayer. "The thing prayed for," he says, "followed mechanically, as it were, out of the performance of the prescribed ritual."[36] If that were true, why bother making vows or indulging in the other psychological means of persuasion of which Akkadian prayers are full? At some point in the history of Mesopotamian religion the content of those prayers must have been taken seriously. After all, the appended ritual in many cases involves no more than a simple sacrificial offering, which in itself hardly implies a magical manipulation of the deity. Comparable ritual directions are lacking in the Old Testament Psalms, of course, but one should not make too much of this fact. One cannot safely argue on this basis--particularly for the preexilic period–that the Old Testament Psalms were recited independently of any ritual. In fact it seems clear that at least some of the Psalms were originally composed to accompany the sacrificial ritual–one thinks particularly of the correspondence between the *tôdāh*-prayer and the *tôdāh*-offering.[37]

Even Wright's argument from the Old Testament's prohibition against magic and divination is strangely inconclusive for his thesis. In the first place, only one page after saying, ". . . the pagan world of magic and divination is simply incompatible with the worship of Yahweh,"[38] he must temper this judgment by admitting that official Yahwism did contain some elements which "we would consider magical practices or things verging closely thereon."[39] Among the more important elements he puts in this category are the Israelite purification laws, the power of the spoken word in blessings and curses, the use of sacred lots for divining Yahweh's will, and the goat for Azazel in the Day of Atonement ritual.[40] He does not really explain why these exceptions do not invalidate his thesis, but his discussion of Azazel, his comments on the use of Urim and Thummin, and his treatment of Samuel the seer, who revealed secrets for a fee, suggest that these elements were simply feeble survivals from a pagan background which, for the most part, either died out early in Israelite history, or whose inner meaning was reinterpreted.[41]

Once again, however, the logic of historical development is just as applicable to Mesopotamia as it is to Israel. Even when one turns to those Mesopotamian incantations which strike us as the least prayer-like, and whose accompanying ritual seems most clearly to have originated in the realm of sympathetic magic, one must still reckon with the possibility that the original significance of the rite has been overlaid with a new interpretation. In some cases where such rituals are given a mythological interpretation, it is clear that the two do not really correspond, that the later interpretation has altered the purely magical significance of the original rite.[42] In other words one cannot simply assume from the character of the ritual that the Mesopotamian understood his incantation as a device for by-passing the divine will and achieving his desired ends by his own actions.

To illustrate this last point one need only compare 2 Kings 13:15-19:

> And Elisha said to him, "Take a bow and arrows"; so he took a bow and arrows. Then he said to the king, "Draw the bow"; so he drew the bow, and Elisha placed his hands upon the king's hands. Then he said, "Open the window eastward"; and he opened it. Elisha said, "Shoot!"; and he shot. He said, "Yahweh's arrow of victory, the arrow of victory over Aram! You will smite the Arameans in Aphek until you have annihilated them." Then he said, "Take the arrows"; and he took them. He said to the king of Israel, "Strike the ground"; and he struck the ground three times and stopped. Then the man of God became angry with him and said, "You should have struck five or six times, then you would have smitten Aram until you had annihilated them, but now you will only smite Aram three times."

This text with its precise ritual directions, its account of their execution, and its incantation-like recitation--"Yahweh's arrow of victory, the arrow of victory over Aram! You will smite the Arameans in Aphek until you have annihilated them"--shows striking similarities to Mesopotamian incantations. Nor is it unique. It does not differ radically from other accounts of prophetic symbolic acts.[43] On the surface it seems to portray a purely magical rite, yet few Old Testament scholars would be satisfied with an explanation of this passage which saw in it an attempt to by-pass Yahweh's will. Whether explicit or not, the magic is subservient to Yahweh's purposes. The prophet speaks and acts in the name of and as the agent of Yahweh, not according to his own will, hence, as Fohrer argues, this and other symbolic acts of the prophets have only a "broken" or "dialectical" relationship to magic.[44] I would agree, but precisely the same argument may be made for the Mesopotamian material. The Mesopotamian incantation expert, the *āšipu*, also derived his authority from the gods and spoke their words in their name.[45] The priest acted not on his own, but as the agent of the gods, as the legitimation theme found in many incantation texts makes clear.[46]

The empirical experience of the Mesopotamians, as we shall see, must have made it clear that even the most meticulous performance of incantations and rituals could not guarantee with mechanical certainty the desired end. Those rituals which end with a positive statement that the desired blessing will be achieved do not really alter this fact.[47] They simply state the expectations of the specialist, presumably based on prior experience, and no doubt, like the optimistic prognostications of modern physicians, these expectations were often disappointed.[48]

Moreover, Wright and other Old Testament theologians have basically misunderstood divination, at least as far as the normal Mesopotamian practice is concerned, when they describe it as a way of tricking or coercing the deity into revelation.[49] It may be that the origins of divination go back to a view of the world in which its very structure is thought to contain a clue to the future–a clue which one may discover by examining some microcosmic reflection of that world such as the entrails of a sacrificial lamb, but in the later period, as one text says, it is the god who writes the message of the future in the entrails.[50] The Old Babylonian prayer of the divination priest recently published by Goetze is enlightening in this regard.[51] Running like a thread through the whole text, or at least the part Goetze published, is the constantly recurring and only slightly varied refrain in which the priest appeals to the various gods: "In the ritual act I prepare, in the extispicy I perform put you truth!"[52] This repeated plea, not only for an answer, but for a true answer, should make it clear that the success of divination depended on the good will of the deity. Even the pagan deities could refuse to respond to man's appeal. The omens did not always turn out favorably, and often enough, they were totally unclear–the gods simply refused to answer.[53] To quote a Hittite example, Mursilis, as his plague prayers eloquently testify, had no easier time evoking a revelatory response from his gods than the tragic Saul did from Yahweh.[54]

In the final analysis, whatever the differences between Israelite religion and that of their pagan neighbors, and I do not mean to unduly minimize them, neither the pagan nor the Israelite could really control the divine world. In spite of all the means of persuasion available to humans, the inscrutable gods sometimes turned a deaf ear to their human subjects. Not even the most submissive and conscientious obedience to the divine will could guarantee the desired blessings–covenant or no covenant.[55] The good man sometimes suffered while the wicked man prospered, and as a result of this observation, drawn from the actual experience of life, some thinkers in Mesopotamia as well as Israel, moved toward a more profound view of the relationship between obedience and the divine blessings.[56] Man in the finiteness of his knowledge and power was simply unable to strip the deity of his freedom. This insight is most clearly stated in the wisdom literature of both cultures, but at least a rudimentary awareness of its truth can be detected even in the more strictly cultic texts of both Israel and Mesopotamia.

NOTES

[1] Brevard S. Childs gives a very good historical sketch of this movement, with a necessary distinction between the European development in the 1920s and the American Biblical Theology Movement of the 1940s and later (*Biblical Theology in Crisis* [Philadelphia: The Westminster Press, 1970] 1-31).

[2] Ibid., 47-50.

[3] G. E. Wright, *The Old Testament Against Its Environment,* Studies in Biblical Theology No. 2 (London: SCM Press LTD, 1950).

[4] Ibid., 22-23.

[5] Ibid., 101.

[6] Childs, *Biblical Theology in Crisis,* 49.

[7] Childs has vividly described this breakdown in the biblical theology movement (ibid., 51-87).

[8] Bertil Albrektson, *History and the Gods: An Essay on the Idea of Historical Events as Divine Manifestations in the Ancient Near East and in Israel* (Lund: CWK Gleerup, 1967).

[9] James Barr, *Old and New in Interpretation: A Study of the Two Testaments* (London: SCM Press LTD, 1966) 65-102.

[10] W. G. Lambert, *Babylonian Wisdom Literature* (Oxford: Clarendon Press, 1960) 101-3: 57-65; 105:135-47.

[11] Deut. 28:1-14.

[12] Wright, *The Old Testament Against Its Environment,* 23.

[13] Ibid., 93-95.

[14] Ibid. 98-101.

[15] See pp. 65-97 of this volume.

[16] Thorkild Jacobsen, "Mesopotamia," in *The Intellectual Adventure of Ancient Man,* ed. Henri and H. A. Frankfort (Chicago: University of Chicago Press, 1946) 200.

[17] *YOS,* 2, 141; *The Intellectual Adventure of Ancient Man,* ed. Frankfort and Frankfort, 205-6.

[18] Ibid., 205.

[19] Ibid.

[20] W. G. Lambert and A. R. Millard, *Atra-ḫasīs: The Babylonian Story of the Flood* (Oxford: Clarendon Press, 1969) 68:378-71:413.

[21] Ibid., 74:9-77:35.

[22] Wright, *The Old Testament Against Its Environment,* 103.

[23] Lambert and Millard, *Atra-ḫasīs,* 96-97:12-22.

[24]*Gilgamesh,* XI, 155-61.

[25]*BWL,* 148-49:60-61.

[26]Ps. 50:9-13.

[27]W. F. Leemans, *Ishtar of Lagaba and her Dress,* SLB I (Leiden: E. J. Brill, 1952); A. L. Oppenheim, "The Golden Garments of the Gods," *JNES* 8 (1949) 172-93.

[28]See Zech. 3:1; Dan. 12:1; and Job 9:33; 16:19; 19:25; 33:23 (Job may not be such a late source).

[29]Exod. 32:30-32; 1 Sam. 12:23; Gen. 20:7; Jer. 15:1.

[30]Pss. 31:3; 69:6-7; 109:21.

[31]This motif is given a new twist in Ben Sira 17:25-28, where it has become a motivation for man to repent. If he does not, he will miss the joys of taking part in worship. This new use of the motif is obviously secondary to the usage in the Psalms, however, so it is illegitimate to reinterpret these earlier passages in the light of this later use of the motif.

[32]Pss. 35:17-18, 28; 22:22; 61:9.

[33]Walter G. Kunstmann, *Die babylonische Gebetsbeschwörung,* LSS NF 2 (Leipzig: J. C. Hinrichsische Buchhandlung, 1932) 39-42.

[34]*Gott als Richter in Mesopotamien und im Alten Testament, zum Verständnis einer Gebetsbitte* (Innsbruck: Universitätsverlag Wagner, 1966) 7.

[35]*Le Lamentazioni individuali e gli Inni in Babilonia e in Israele* (Torino: Società Editrice Internazionale, 1940) XX, n. 4.

[36]Gamper, *Gott als Richter,* 7.

[37]Lev. 7:11; 22:29; Amos 4:5; 2 Chron. 29:31; 33:16; Pss. 50:14, 23; 56:13; 107:22; 116:17.

[38]Wright, *The Old Testament Against Its Environment,* 86-87.

[39]Ibid., 88.

[40]Ibid., 88-92.

[41]Ibid.

[42]W. G. Lambert, "Myth and Ritual as Conceived by the Babylonians," *JSS* 13 (1968) 110-11.

[43]G. Fohrer, "Prophetie und Magie," *ZAW* 78 (1966) 32.

[44]Ibid., 28, 34.

[45]Edith K. Ritter, "Magical-Expert (=*Āšipu*) and Physician (=*Asû*): Notes on Two Complementary Professions in Babylonian Medicine," *AS* 16 (Chicago: University of Chicago Press, 1965) 299-321, esp. 321.

[46]Adam Falkenstein, *Die Haupttypen der sumerischen Beschwörung,* LSS NF 11 (Leipzig: August Pries, 1931) 23-27, 70-74; see *BWL* 49:15, 25-28; 51:41-44.

[47] E. Ebeling, *Keilschrifttexte aus Assur religiösen Inhalts* I, Wissenschaftliche Veröffentlichung der Deutschen Orient-Gesellschaft 28 (Leipzig: J. C. Hinrichs, 1919) Nr. 43; E. Ebeling, "Assyrische Beschwörungen," *ZDMG* 69 (1915) 92-95.

[48] Note the references to unsuccessful treatment in Ritter, *AS* 16, 315-17, and see *BWL* 45:108:11.

[49] Wright, *The Old Testament Against Its Environment,* 87.

[50] O. R. Gurney and J. J. Finkelstein, *The Sultantepe Tablets* I, Occasional Publications of the British Institute of Archaeology at Ankara 3 (London, 1957) 60:15 and duplicates.

[51] A. Goetze, "An Old Babylonian Prayer of the Divination Priest," *JCS* 22 (1968) 25-29.

[52] Ibid., lines 11ff., 17-18, 31-33, 40-41, 48-49, 52-53, 56-57, 64-66.

[53] Note especially the use of this motif in the Kuthean legend about Narām-Sîn (*STT* 1, 30:72-92; O. R. Gurney, *Anatolian Studies* 5 [1955] 102-3:72-92).

[54] *ANET* 394-96.

[55] Whatever advantages covenant provided the Israelite over his pagan contemporary, it did not provide the individual with certainty of success. Josiah's fate makes that too painfully clear.

[56] See especially *Ludlul Bēl Nēmeqi* and the Babylonian *Theodicy* (*BWL* 21-91) for Mesopotamia, and Job for the Old Testament.

- 10 -

THE HISTORICAL DEVELOPMENT OF THE MESOPOTAMIAN PANTHEON: A STUDY IN SOPHISTICATED POLYTHEISM

W. G. Lambert

While the term "history of religions" is in vogue at the moment, the content of this phrase is not. The sociology of religion, its economic interrelations, and similar topics are now thought to be the proper meat for scholars, but history qua history is hardly respectable. To use the language of linguistics, synchronic rather than diachronic study is the fashion. Yet for ancient Mesopotamia the historical method is almost the only way open to study religion. In any one period there is an imbalance in our sources. Some aspects are well documented, others sparsely or not at all. The result is that while one could write studies in the religion of a particular period, a "history" of religion of the same period is not yet in view. Perhaps one should say "religions" in the plural, since certainly in the better-known historical periods more than one kind of religion existed. The city cults were the preserve of the official priesthood, of the ruler, and perhaps of the upper classes. Ordinary people might share in the spirit of the more important annual festivals, but the city temple was not a place of their devotions. For them the niche at home or the street corner shrine was the place of religion. While excavations may bring to light some remains of this popular kind of cult, probably we shall never know much about them. Their practitioners were illiterate, and scribes rarely deign to take notice of such low class things. Written documents, which most clearly illumine the surviving material structures and their equipment, almost exclusively concern the official city cults. These, then, shall be our concern.

In the beginning the separation of state and private religion may not have been the case. The small first shrine at Eridu, traditionally the oldest Sumerian city, a shrine a mere six feet square, obviously belonged to a small community. Even if the "lay" members of that group never actually entered this one-room shrine, it is very likely that their religious lives revolved around it. In a very small community everyone is involved in everything. As the cities grew in size during the Early Dynastic period, the separation of state and private cult was one inevitable result. For the beginnings we depend entirely on physical remains, and it appears that each community had its own temple, in which its particular god or goddess was worshipped. The principle of one deity per shrine is suggested both by the remains of the structures, and also by later evidence, for while in historical times honor could be done to a number of deities in one temple, it remained a temple--with very few exceptions--of a single deity. The presence of a spouse, children, and courtiers never obscured the identity of the owner of the temple, and the facilities for the worship of still other gods was not in principle different from the veneration of saints which takes place in many Christian churches. The names and characters of these city-owning gods and goddesses are not of course known for the earliest times, but in historical times there is so strong a conservatism in such matters that it may be suspected that they had not changed since prehistoric times. However, the matter is not so simple, and this can be seen from a study of Sumerian city deities so soon as their names and attributes are known, that is, from the middle of the third millennium B.C. The remarkable thing is that in a land of independent city states generally speaking each city has a different patron deity. There is almost no duplication. T. Jacobsen was apparently the first to draw attention to this, and to suggest the only likely explanation of it, that somehow in prehistoric times deliberate action had been taken to secure this end.

The basis for this case may be stated as follows. Sumerian deities as known in the historical periods are personifications of forces, aspects, or parts of nature as then conceived. The sun, the power in grain, love, and the cosmic water believed to exist beneath the earth were personified as Utu, Nisaba, Inanna, and Enki. It is understandable that primitive peoples should try to come to terms with the natural forces around them, on which they entirely depended, by worshipping them. However, no community depended on one deity alone. It was no use the god of the waters flooding your fields if the sun god did not in turn help by bringing on the crop by his heat and ripening it. In short, each community depended for its livelihood on most, if not all, of the deities of the country. The country, as just explained, was politically divided though culturally unified. This unity of culture appears in the state religions in that the deities of the various cities were related to each other in a generally accepted scheme like members of a clan, for which the Olympians offer the closest parallel. It is not a coincidence that most of the major deities of the Sumerians belong within three generations, which is precisely the state of affairs at any given time with a human clan. The most senior gods were provided with ancestries of more than six generations, but these forebears were not major members of the pantheon, and most of them are not even known to have been worshipped. The remarkable thing about this general acceptance of the organization of the gods in the various independent cities is that it implies a ranking in importance. The most senior were the most important and normally the most junior the least important. In a few cases it can be shown that in the earliest times different cities had somewhat different versions of the genealogy of the gods, but these were eventually ironed out so that by the second millennium these relationships were firmly established and generally known among the cities. A further significant fact is that the most important god in earlier times, Enlil, was patron of the city of Nippur, which so far as our knowledge goes, never had political importance. Thus if one aligns the various factors: (1) a dependence everywhere on most superhuman forces, (2) one city one deity, and (3) a country-wide pantheon in a politically divided land, one is forced to accept Jacobsens's conclusion. How this state of affairs came about can only be guessed at. If the Sumerians at some time entered the land as invaders they might have restructured the shrines and imposed a system while settling down and before they began to fight each other. But we do not know that they did arrive as invaders. Or one might suppose that in early times when the cities were still very small a conference took place in which these arrangements were worked out by mutual agreement.

The last paragraph was concerned with the patron deity of each city only. It must not be supposed that only one deity was known and worshipped in each place. In historical times we know that a variety of gods and goddesses were worshipped in each place. Often, however, they were well integrated in the worship of the city patron, in that he had the personnel of a king around him: divine family and divine courtiers. One may suspect that many of these were gods who had been at home in the place for centuries back, and when the principle of one patron deity one city was being worked up they received a lesser place in that arrangement. However, there are cases of two important gods being at home in one city, for example An and Inanna in Uruk. In some cases the explanation is that the city embraced two or more early villages, which grew together as they expanded and so brought their respective deities into the amalgam. Girsu and Lagaš within the city Lagaš are an example. However, this would certainly not explain all the minor, little-known gods acknowledged in Lagaš. While the order of the major city deities attests the imposition of order on the gods of the country, the multiplicity of little gods in each place equally attests a primeval chaos.

The matter can be illustrated further from cases of the same god in more than one city. The only major case is that of the sun god as patron of both Larsa and Sippar. However, Sippar belonged to the Semitic northwest fringe of Sumer, so the presence of Šamaš there as well as the presence of Utu in the good Sumerian Larsa can be explained in this way. Certainly in their case no one would have disputed that they were one god worshipped in two places. More significant are the instances of one deity present in two cities under different names. Perhaps the best known is Ninurta, son of Enlil, worshipped as an important but not the patron god of Nippur. The patron of Lagaš was Ningirsu, also son of Enlil. In historical times they were certainly conceived, at least in many cases, as two names for one deity. For example, a Sumerian hymn, *SLTN* no. 61, praises this god under the names of Ninurta, Pabilsag, and Ningirsu. This of course might be syncretism, so what of their origins? As a name Ningirsu means "Lord of Girsu," so it might only have meant "the form of Ninurta worshipped in Girsu." However, its having meaning does not imply that it is not an original name. Ningirsu could have been a completely separate deity in the beginning, who was later equated with Ninurta of Nippur because of similar characteristics. Ninurta means "Lord Earth," *-urta* being a form of *uraš* "earth." Here, then, the alternatives can only be stated. Either the two were always understood to be one, like Ištar of Nineveh and Ištar of Arbela from Assyria, or their equating results from taking an overall view of the pantheon and identifying similar gods. This process of assimilation is well known in the ancient polytheistic world, when foreign gods were regularly equated with the most similar home one. With the pair just named evidence is lacking to settle the question raised, though the lack of the name of Ninurta from Early Dynastic inscriptions from the rulers of Lagaš does perhaps support the idea that in the beginning Ningirsu was separate from Ninurta. Another case where the evidence is more helpful is that of Asalluhi and Marduk. Marduk was always city god of Babylon. Asalluḫi was to begin with god of a small town Kuar/Kumar near Eridu. It is possible that originally he was unrelated to Eridu and its god Enki, but if so then in very early times he was drawn into the pantheon of Eridu and became Enki's son. The meaning of the name Asalluḫi is unknown today, and the same seems to have been the case with the ancients, at least from the beginning of the second millenium B.C. By the time of Hammurabi, Asalluḫi was identified with Marduk. The question again is, was the identification primary or secondary? The name of Marduk means "Bull-calf of Utu," (a)mar.utu.(a)k, and the correct form is *Marūtuk*, of which the conventional Marduk is only a later alternative. Utu was of course the sun god. The assurance as to the meaning of the name comes from the writing, which is attested as far back as the second phase of the Early Dynastic period, and which remained standard until the end of cuneiform as a means of writing. What it attests is Marduk's sonship from the sun god. The view of his paternity as known from direct statements from the ancient world is that he was the son of Enki. None of these statements is as yet earlier than Hammurabi. This contradiction between the plain meaning of the name and his then current paternity was well grasped by the ancients, who tried to resolve it by a piece of Midrash. The genitive element in the name is the final -*k*, which is not written in the traditional orthography in accordance with its rules. However, we know it was pronounced from more than a score of phonetic writings of the name in Assyrian and Babylonian texts, and from transcriptions in other scripts. Thus Babylonian scholars solved their theological problem by deliberately ignoring the unwritten genitive and taking the name as an apposition: "the son, the sun god."[1] The rendering of "bull calf" by "son" is a correct interpretation of the implication, and the further problem raised, that Šamaš, not Marduk, was then the sun god, was overcome by making Šamaš sun god of the peoples (he shines on the earth), but Marduk the sun god of the gods, a higher calling. A similarly authentic ancient testimonial cannot be given for the reason for the change in paternity, but one can be suggested. Babylon was a very unimportant place until Hammurabi's time. In the Early Dynastic period there is perhaps one mention of it. In contrast Sippar holds an important place in Sumerian traditions, and was certainly more important than Babylon, though the two were not far apart. It is, then, quite possible that in Early Dynastic times Babylon was drawn into the theological orbit of Sippar, as was Kuar into the orbit of Eridu. The subordination of Babylon would naturally be expressed in its god's becoming son of the god of the major city. Such a status, however, was totally unsuitable for Hammurabi's reign. He made Babylon the capital of the country, and its god had to rise in accordance with this change. As we are told in the Prologue to the Laws, Anu and Enlil elevated Marduk to be one of the "great gods," not, as some modern writers have misconstrued it, to be head of the pantheon. Šamaš at this time was second-ranking, and not even at the head of that rank, since Sin, the moon god, was his father and so superior. Thus the son of a lower second-ranking god was low indeed. Enki, in contrast, was a god of the first rank and to be his son was obviously higher than being son of Utu, alias Šamaš. One may, then, at least ask if Marduk was not equated with Asalluḫi quite deliberately in the reign of Hammurabi in order to give him more prestige for his recent promotion. Due to lack of evidence before Hammurabi's reign, there is as yet no proof or disproof to quote, but confirmation of the fact that the two were originally separate gods can be found in the absence of use of the name Marduk in texts about the god of Kuar, unless in theologically speculative and syncretistic literature. An exception is in bilingual texts, where Asalluḫi is "translated" as Marduk. This is simply giving the more common name in a period long after the equation of the two deities was accepted.

It is important to appreciate that the kind of problem just dealt with arises solely from an overall view of the Sumero-Babylonian pantheon. Within the confines of the cult of a particular city many of these problems could be ignored. Hymns of praise to deities even say that there exists no other god than the one being addressed. This is not monotheism, but harmless hyperbole. Here then are the factors at play in the history of the Mesopotamian pantheon, a multitude of city cults, and thinkers who tried to reduce them to an ordered whole. The place where the thinkers' results are most directly stated is in the tradition of written lists. From the beginning of writing, lists of signs had been compiled, whether for reference for the professional scribe, or for text books for beginners. The idea took root and out of it arose a whole "list science," as Landsberger entirely correctly called it. While it included the practical aids for the scribal schools, it also attempted to embrace everything in the world into categories, and within the categories to present things in some rational kind of order. Though this tradition was not very productive in world history, it is of course the beginnings of the scientific method, and the classifications of a Linnaeus or Darwin are based on the same premise. The names of gods are one of the Mesopotamian categories, and god lists are known from the middle of the third millenium and onwards. As with lists generally, there are those of purely philological purpose, in this case to give the readings of the names of gods, and those which present the pantheon as an organized list of names. Only the latter are of concern here.

The Early Dynastic lists, from Fara and Abu Salabiḫ, can be seen to offer an organized list in that Enlil appears at the head. Unfortunately too many otherwise unknown deities appear in these lists for their full exploitation. The lists are simple strings of names with no explanations. By the end of the second millennium the Babylonian scholars had begun the compilation of lists with explanations. These are double-column in format and are based on the principle that x = y. This is the common format for Babylonian lexical texts, whether signs are being given their phonetic values, Sumerian words are being equated with Babylonian equivalents, or one rarer Babylonian word is being equated with a more common synonym. Thus most commonly the double-column god lists explain by putting rarer names of a god opposite the common name. Less commonly a phrase stating family relationship or dependency in some capacity is used instead, and such phrases can also occur by themselves to sum up a group of gods. The largest god list ever of this format is An = *Anum*,[2] as it is known after the first line. It dealt with some 2,000 names, most of which survive. However, that does not mean 2,000 gods, since some gods had many names. Even with the help provided in equations of names and explanatory phrases, much knowledge is needed to understand the full significance of this list. This list can be dated to about 1300-1100 B.C. It is certainly not Old Babylonian, and a single-column Old Babylonian list survives, *TCL* XV no. 10, which is clearly the basis from which the much longer and detailed An = *Anum* is derived. The existence of Middle Assyrian copies by the well-known scribe Kidin-Sîn proves that it had reached Assyria by about 1100. Many features confirm the dating to the latter part of the Cassite period. As to the intended purpose of An = *Anum*, detailed study suggests that it was in essence a simple list, intended only to codify the numerous traditional god names so far as possible in accordance with the existing religious status quo. The legacy of tradition was paticularly heavy, in that many little-known gods were handed down in lists, but may not have been worshipped any more. But tradition had to be respected, and while the compiler could of course simply reject, that was not his custom. The general organization of the work appears only in Tablets I-IV in the edition which is followed here. The remaining tablets are added on without the same systematic arrangement, and in some cases it is clear that whole groups of names have been taken over without change from existing sources. For the well-organized first tablets the arrangement is by family in order of seniority:

Anu
Enlil with Ninurta
Ninḫursag
Ea with Marduk
Sîn
Šamaš
Adad
Ištar

In each case the names of the main god are given first, then those of his (or her in the case of Ištar and Ninḫursag) spouse, then those of their children, which is why Ninurta and Marduk occur within the sections of Enlil and Ea, and finally the names of the various officers and courtiers are given. For us the present concern is to see what happens with the equated gods already considered. Ninurta does indeed occur in his Nippurian context, but Ningirsu does not appear at all in the first four tablets. He appears in Tablet V in a group of about a dozen names, which include of course Bau, his spouse. There is no statement of his sonship of Enlil. Since Lagaš was a place of no consequence at this time, perhaps indeed not even occupied, this evidence cannot be pressed. With Asalluḫi and Marduk things are clearer. The Old Babylonian forerunner gives separately Asalluḫi and Panunanki, his spouse, from Marduk and Zarpānîtum, his spouse, see lines 89-107. This separation does not necessarily mean the compiler regarded them as two distinct couples. It is possible that he was incorporating items from, e.g., liturgical texts from Kuar and Babylon, and did not integrate them. Indeed, there are many such crudities in his work. In contrast the compiler of An = *Anum* has carefully integrated the male and female names in two long lists. In this matter the compiler is simply adjusting his material to express more clearly the common understanding of his day. With so important a god as Marduk he had little choice, but with many minor gods he was free to follow his own judgment. Here it will be best to compare another list, An = *Anu ša amēli*.[3] This is set out in three subcolumns, though it is really based on a type of lexical text entry which says, e.g., "(Sumerian) du_8 = (Akkadian) *kamāru ša šurīpi*." Here the Sumerian root only equates the Akkadian verb when it refers to "ice," not in other nuances. In the same way, each individual name of a god is not simply to be equated with the god, but refers to some particular aspect of him. Thus An is the name of Anu where men are concerned. His other names refer to other aspects of his. An = *Anu ša amēli* is much shorter than An = *Anum*. It only has 152 names, and 19 gods are dealt with. There are some spouses, but no courtiers unless they were sufficiently important in the pantheon to stand on their own feet. The largest section is Ea's, and its length is explained in that quite a number of craftsmen gods are equated with him. These were minor gods, deifications of the various crafts, and one is not sure that they were ever the object of serious worship, and certainly not sure that they were patron gods of the various craftsmen. Most probably they result from cosmological thinking rather than from a basis in the cult, since in this civilization it was held that man was taught all the arts of civilization by the gods.

A few examples will illustrate the different treatments of these craftsmen gods in An = *Anum* as compared with An = *Anu ša amēli*. As already intimated, in the latter they are all given as "names" or aspects of Ea, who was a god of crafts generally. Two of them are Nunurra, god of the potter, and Ninagal, god of the smith. Nunurra similarly appears in An = *Anum* as a name of Ea (II 149), but Ninagal appears later, in the court of Ea as a separate deity described by the phrase "the smith's god." A third example is Guškinbanda, the goldsmith's god. In An = *Anum* he has no connection with Ea whatsoever, but appears among the dependents of Enlil as spouse of Ninimma, a very ancient goddess (I 291-301). Further examples could be cited, but they would not be different in essence. What emerges from this is that while major deities could be identified with similar ones, as in the case of Ninurta and Ningirsu, minor deities were rather absorbed into a major one. The distinction between major and minor here rests entirely in their position in the cult at the time. Gods which lacked a well-established place in a city cult were floating deities which could be taken over as going concerns or merged in something bigger, just as weak firms in Western society are subject to take-overs of various kinds. The reason for this in the ancient world doubtless lies in the concept of the name, which was not an identification tag simply as today, but expressed the very nature and being of its bearer. Thus for one god to use another's name was equivalent to the merging of the two. Since gods traditionally had more than one name, because epithets by frequent use often became such, it was not necessary to deny the existence of any god that had ever been conceived to exist. The name, and so the existence, was transferred to another owner. Still another kind of absorption can be quoted from An = *Anu ša amēli*. The last name of Anu given there is Uraš "earth." Elsewhere Uraš is very properly Anu's spouse: heaven and earth form a natural pair. So even a wife can be absorbed into her husband!

This cannibalism among the gods is manifested at its most curious extreme in two very different cases. The one is involved in the ancestors of Anu. Both he and Enlil, being senior among the pantheon of worshipped gods, had somewhat artificial ancestries supplied to explain their origins. Since the clan structure of the pantheon involved each deity having his or her spouse, Anu and Enlil were no exceptions, and their ancestries most often involved male and female pairs. This sounds adequate enough, but if this is taken to mean that each pair gave rise to the next by bisexual reproduction, as it would at first glance seem to, then one must accept the idea of brother and sister marriages, which were as taboo in ancient Mesopotamia as in most other parts and periods of the world. Once in ancient Mesopotamia the concept of incest in these primeval pairs is plainly accepted,[4] but generally it was avoided, and An = *Anum* and some smaller, related lists merge all the males in Anu's ancestry with him, and all the females with Antum, his spouse. This is evolution, not creation. Anu became himself by developing through a series of stages represented by his ancestors' names.

Before proceeding to the other remarkable case of the merging of deities it may be well to stress two points. The first is that this kind of doctrine is not confined to god lists, but can occur elsewhere. For example, a hymn in which the goddess Gula sings her own praise in alternative sections with that of her spouse, uses a variety of names for each.[5] Since some of the spouses have concerned us above, these alone will be given here: Ninurta, Ningirsu, Ninazu, Pabilsag, Zababa, Utulu, and Lugalbanda. Of these only Utulu is in all likelihood an original epithet of Ninurta, not resulting from the assimilation of another deity. Ningirsu was dealt with above. Ninazu was at home in Eshnunna, Pabilsag in Isin, Zababa in Kish, and Lugalbanda was an early king of Uruk, later deified. The purpose of this hymn is quite explicitly to bring out the various names and aspects of this divine pair. Second, it should be stressed that theology of this kind did not have to be uniform: different opinions could coexist. In the cases of Ninagal, Guškinbanda and Uraš quoted, An = *Anu ša amēli* has a different opinion from An = *Anum*, though these two works probably originated at about the same time. The Middle Assyrian copies of An = *Anum* also bear the text of An = *Anu ša amēli*. Since the latter work could hardly be Old Babylonian in origin, it too is most likely from the later part of the Cassite period, like An = *Anum*.

Two very different things were being achieved by this merging. One was the tidying up of an originally unwieldy pantheon. The number of gods by Late Babylonian times was certainly much less than in the classical statement of An = *Anum*. The other thing was not so impartial: some gods were being further glorified by swallowing up their rivals. The supreme example of this occurs in a small god list after the style of An = *Anu ša amēli* devoted to Marduk alone. It is of such importance to merit full citation:

Uraš (is)	Marduk of planting.
Lugalidda (is)	Marduk of the abyss.
Ninurta (is)	Marduk of the pickaxe.
Nergal (is)	Marduk of battle.
Zababa (is)	Marduk of warfare.
Enlil (is)	Marduk of lordship and consultations.

Nabû (is)	Marduk of accounting.
Sîn (is)	Marduk who lights up the night.
Šamaš (is)	Marduk of justice.
Adad (is)	Marduk of rain.
Tišpak (is)	Marduk of troops.
Great Anu (is)	Marduk of . . .
Šuqamuna (is)	Marduk of the container.
[(is)]	Marduk of everything.

CT 24 50, BM 47406, obverse

This document was brought to the front by Friedrich Delitzsch before World War I, in a general onslaught against the originality of Hebrew religion, an attempt to prove that monotheism was not original among the Hebrews, but the Babylonians. The atmosphere of controversy was quite unconducive to dispassionate consideration of the question, and the document has been hardly touched upon since. Seen now against the kind of thought just presented, it must be stated that this has indeed every claim to present Marduk as a monotheistic god. The deities being identified with him are major ones of the pantheon, and if one asks who is left, then only two qualifications have to be interposed. The first is that no goddesses are mentioned. Presumably the compiler of this list would not have denied the existence of Zarpānîtum, spouse of Marduk in his temple in Babylon, in which case one must qualify this monotheism by allowing for the existence of one god and his spouse. The other possible qualification is that demons are not dealt with in so much of this list as survives. (It is not complete; some lines are missing at the bottom.) Demons were gods in Babylonian terminology. If we suppose that the compiler would have granted that demons existed in addition to Marduk and his wife, one might still call this monotheism, since many Christian churches have strongly professed monotheism while believing in a supernatural personal devil. But granting these qualifications, the compiler wished us to see Marduk as the sole possessor of power in the universe: all other powers of nature were but aspects of him. This extreme doctrine has other attestation. The commentary on *Marduk's Address to the Demons* describes Šamaš as "Marduk of judgment" (*AfO* 17, 313 and 19, 115). And there are two hymns with similar import. *KAR* nos. 337 and 304 are parts of one tablet, a hymn to Marduk, and one side is divided into sections in each of which one of the major deities of the pantheon is explained as an aspect of Marduk. The other text, *KAR* 25 ii 3-24 duplicated in part by K 8978, explains the major gods as aspects of Marduk, beginning "Sîn is your divinity."

It would be wrong, however, to leave the matter there. As with the speculations about much lesser gods, this idea was only one opinion in the ancient world. A brief summary of the changes in the headship of the gods will suffice to show this. So soon as our sources inform us, that is about the middle of the third millennium, Enlil is head of the pantheon. By early in the second millennium Anu had joined him, and they two remained in control until Marduk displaced them both toward the end of the second millennium. He then ruled supreme for a time, but his erstwhile vizier and later son, Nabû, rose to be his equal, so that by the time of the Late Babylonian empire the two of them ruled much as Anu and Enlil had been joint rulers before. Even this status quo was not unchallenged. Nabonidus tried for a time to put Sîn in place of Marduk, but failed.

This paper has tried to show the way in which scholars of the Sumero-Babylonian tradition grappled with the problems they inherited in their polytheism. Seen now from so much later their efforts, while sometimes striving in the right direction, ultimately failed.

And one cannot truthfully say that the last was better than the first in this case. The earliest attempts to worship the powers around them in the universe were in some way closer to reality than the later speculations of theologians about the various "canonized" deities. As their civilization grew, their dependence on the whims of natural powers decreased, and then they began more and more to see their gods as themselves but writ large in the universe. While the attempts to tidy up a host of minor gods and overlapping among the bigger ones were commendable, this was not enough to adjust a sophisticated polytheism to the reality of nature. And the one attempt to see all power in the hands of one god, Marduk, though now vindicated in principle by a scientific understanding of the workings of the universe, did not win the support which it deserved.

NOTES

[1] See *Enūma Eliš* I 101-2 and VI 127-28; V *R* 43 rev. 54-56.

[2] There is no published edition of this list, but one is being prepared by the writer from the thesis of R. Litke, but based on fresh study of the original tablets and much new material.

[3] This list is also unpublished except for parts given in cuneiform in *CT* 24, 39-44.

[4] In the curious cosmology *CT* 46, 43.

[5] Published in *Or* N.S. 36, 105-32.

- 11 -

UNITY AND DIVERSITY IN THE OLDEST RELIGION OF ANCIENT EGYPT

Hans Goedicke

Herodotus credits the Egyptians of his time with being "religious to excess, beyond any other nation in the world."[1] While other older Greek writers share his admiration,[2] this attitude also finds opponents, who emphasize the alien nature of Egyptian religious manifestations.[3] Lucian's[4] biting remarks about the dog-faced god of the Egyptians and their worship of ibis, ape, goat, and other animals are well known. For the Fathers of the Church this was a natural line to take and most of them revelled in their condemnation of the ancient Egyptians as a model of unenlightened heathens.[5]

Modern Egyptology has long stood under the shadows of those traditions. Such an eminent Egyptologist as Erman[6] considered most of what is known about Egyptian religion "törichte Einfälle und Spekulationen einer übel angebrachten Gelehrsamkeit." Even Sir Alan Gardiner[7] in understating his views speaks of "the bewildering multiplicity displayed by the Egyptian Pantheon as elaborated by its priestly exponents." These and similar verdicts by Egyptologists are only too readily accepted and repeated by scholars outside the immediate field[8] and, consciously or not, taken as confirmation of Exod. 12:12.

Already Herodotus in speaking about the Egyptian religion was conscious of the immense difficulty in grasping the religious ideas of others, "for"–as he puts it–"I do not think that any nation knows much more about such things than any other."[9] The materialistic approach of the last century produced large catalogues of features, but they remained isolated and incomprehensive.[10] Even the phenomenological approach did not lead to an understanding; it did, however, open the way to the recognition of a multitude of patterns.[11] The complexity of man's psychic structure as elucidated by modern psychology and the pluralism of viewpoints emerging in the sciences can provide a new base on which to approach the religious expression and expressions of ancient Egypt.

Trail-blazing in this direction was Henri Frankfort's[12] recognition of the "multiplicity of questions" and the "multiplicity of answers" prevailing in Egyptian religious thinking. Even for us, who are in one form or another bound by a religious code of relatively narrow definition, there can still be considerable variety in emphasis on and interpretation of what could be posed as commonly held religious doctrine. The existence of a pluralistic situation applies to the same degree to ancient Egypt. Not bound by the bridles of codified and integrated denominational doctrines as provided by religious expression governed by scriptures acclaimed as holy and thus doctrinary, the potential for variation would seem endless. The diversity of the attested religious phenomena from ancient Egypt appears to confirm this. The widely held opinion that ancient Egypt had a "pantheon" resulting from the conglomeration of a host of local religious patterns has thus its seeming justification.

flowing in the bipolarity

However, to consider the religious expressions of ancient Egypt as revealing polytheism is possible only when approaching the complex question in antiquarian fashion, collecting phenomena while disregarding their specific nature, their significance, their social setting, and timing. With enough myopia, the leaves of grass in a small patch of lawn might seem innumerable.

The complexity of the "Egyptian religion" as a historic phenomenon loses much of its terror when we begin to differentiate among the vast number of individual features by establishing a kind of stratigraphy. When we follow C. G. Jung[13] in his definition of religion as "a particular attitude of the human mind consisting of a careful consideration and observation of certain dynamic factors, understood to be 'powers,' spirits, demons, gods, laws, ideas, ideals, or whatever name man has given to such factors as he has found in his world powerful, dangerous, or helpful enough to be taken into careful consideration," it transpires that its primary form is an individual confrontation between man and some kind of extrahuman power flowing in the bipolarity of attraction and repulsion.[14] As neither one bears up under any qualification, the resulting relationship is arbitrary and accidental. The recognition of "power" has its roots in human instincts. The reaction is either fear or desire to possess, or when putting it in dynamic terms, it inspires conquest or defense.[15] Being primarily individual without structuring qualification, the possibilities of interaction between a human and an outside power arbitrarily recognized are potentially unlimited. In the area of religion they represent the magic realm where man aims to control or rebuke arbitrary powers considered useful or dangerous. Although some elements of magic due to their recurrence are integrated in the "religious" code of social groups, by their very nature they remain individualistic.

The necessity for a community to find its internal structure and stability as well as its specific aims for perpetuation provides a specific base for the interaction of its members with any power or powers considered essential for the very existence of the social organism. Depending on the nature of the community's existence, a single or a multitude of sources may constitute its "religion." As most communities pursue their perpetuation as an economic unit by attaining sufficient sustenance for all their members, the relation with those forces in nature, which make man's survival possible, provide the framework for communal religious concerns. The interaction with those forces is neither accidental, nor are they arbitrary. Their impact on man's life is governed by time as experienced in the agricultural year,[16] except in those cases where a specific single source provides man's livelihood. The nature religion, as the main form of religious expression for the community, has its dominating feature in the observation of time as governing the relationship with extrahuman powers. Communities with specific religious concepts can be small or large; while they are a more or less closely knit unit, they are not universal. As a specific expression of religious ideas a number of community religions can exist side by side in a geographical area, as none contains the possibility of universality or exclusiveness. The city cultures of Mesopotamia and Greece are a large-scale demonstration of this phenomenon.[17]

While the community can provide a self-sufficient base for continuous existence, the aim to integrate larger spaces into conceptual units leads to conglomerations of communities. Their interrelation necessarily requires structuring on the basis of value schemes which are universally applicable. They cannot be emotionally founded, but have to be the results of intellectual reflection. The resulting religious expression simulates the intellectual structure of the integrated society and manifests itself in theological speculation and fomulation. While communities are physically and spacially limited, their conglomeration into a "society" extends into a superior magnitude which, ideally, encompasses the entire world of which the society is conscious.[18]

For us, whose approach to ancient Egypt is by nature an academic or intellectual one, only the third of the outlined religious attitudes can offer any prospect toward an understanding, because neither magic nor cult are intellectually penetrable. Both require participation, physically or emotionally, which, of course, falls outside the possible. Only in the realm of rationality is there any chance of meeting and understanding the ancient Egyptians. The recognition of the limitations existing for any penetrating venture into the religious life of another culture is in itself a beginning for delineating intellectual principles or structures.

Theological speculation in ancient Egypt often manifests itself in forms different from what is commonly associated with this term. Mostly it is not analytic or deductive, although treatments in this vein, like the Memphite Theology, are preserved.[19] The common is rather the expression in pictorial symbols or their composites. Often decried as "paralogical" or "protological"[20] it is, especially in the case of ancient Egypt, the result of a predominantly visual thinking process reflecting the close interaction of visual impression and expression, additionally fostered by the pictorial peculiarities of hieroglyphic writing which dominated the Egyptian thinking process.[21] If this, for us, alien form of expression is taken into consideration, the store of reflections or indications of Egyptian religious thought is substantial. Its unravelling is closely intertwined with the understanding of the Egyptian concept of "writing" and its predominantly conceptual attitude.[22]

There can be no doubt that ancient Egypt in its historic form was anteceded by a host of more or less individual communities with their own particular set of problems and their answers.[23] Some phenomena resulting from this level were integrated into religious concepts of historic times.[24] However, too little is known about local religious expressions or about the range of religious practices to pursue this question with any worthwhile prospects. Any problem concerning the intellectual life of ancient Egypt has its delineation in the onset of historic Egypt, i.e., that event which the Egyptians themselves clearly conceived as their starting point and which they called "The Uniting of the Two Lands," attributed to a legendary king Menes.[25] To draw the line there is fully justified, because it indicates the transformation of a conglomerate of communities into an integrated society with an internal structure and a uniform expression.[26] The latter finds its reflection in the socio-political as well as in the religious domain. Needless to say, the religious ideas reflecting ancient Egypt as an integrated, all-encompassing society did not flow from nowhere, but represent a crystallization on the matrix of earlier religious beliefs. What is new is the mold into which they are cast. While its concept is monolithic, the formulations found for it during the first millennium of Egyptian intellectual history are certainly not monotonous, and a distinct theological development can be traced.

Different from any migratory people the ancient Egyptians lived in a defined world. As experienced in the landscape of the Nile Valley, their world was limited to the four cardinal points.[27] Not only the horizontal expanse of their world was delineated, but also the vertical one. The sky for the Egyptians was not an infinite expanse, but rather a definite entity which represented the upward limitation of their world.[28] In other words, the "world" of the ancient Egyptians, i.e., the locale in which their lives and their experiences took place, was a clearly defined cube with definite borders on all sides. This world concept or "Weltbild" has found various renderings in the course of the ancient Egyptian culture. Although it becomes increasingly differentiated, its primary nature as defined space remains constant.[29]

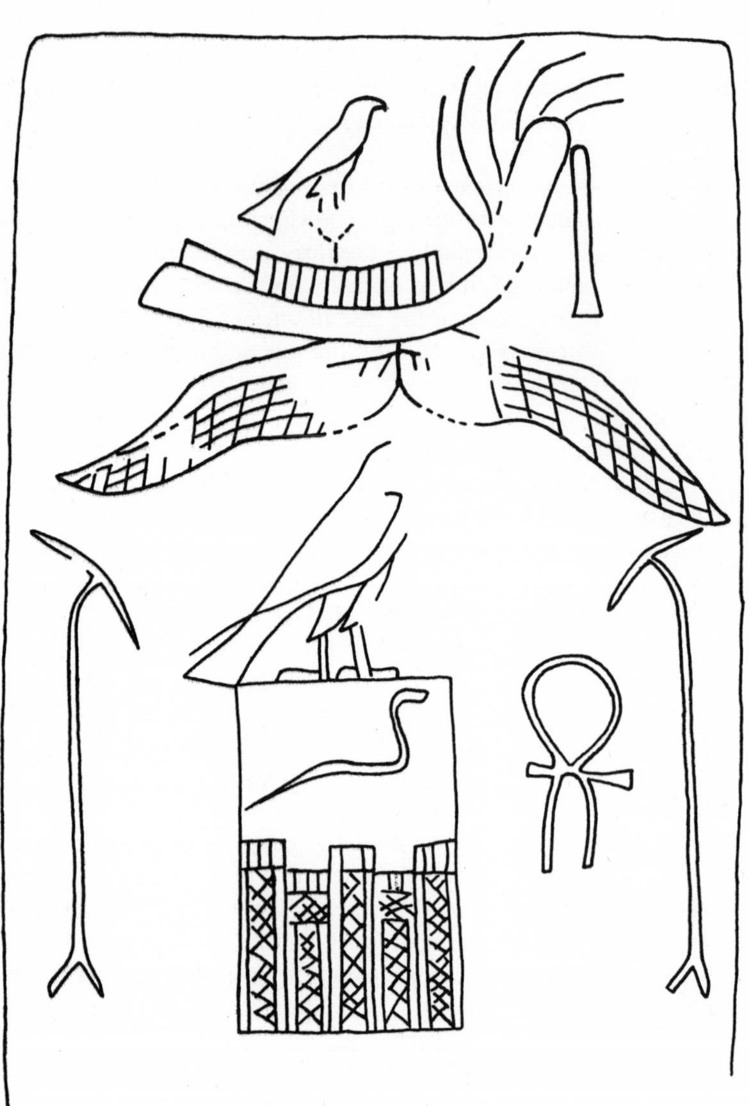

Figure 1

So far, our considerations have been mainly theoretical. We are in the fortunate situation of having pertinent pictorial evidence from very early times. It is a drawing carved on an ivory comb, which W. F. Petrie found at Abydos, and which was apparently part of the funerary equipment of the fourth king of the First Dynasty.[30] We have no idea of the background of the object nor of the reasons for putting the small design (it is only twelve centimeters) on it. There can be no doubt that we have in the design, not a naturalistic scene or impression, but a schematic drawing. It can thus justly be considered as the product of reflection and abstraction, for which elements were joined together which were part of the Egyptian writing system and served there to convey specific concepts. The picture can thus be analyzed like any conglomeration of hieroglyphs, which are used in this case as "sense" or "meaning indicators" rather than as phonetic reading signs.[31]

The entire design has two distinct tiers, separated by a pair of wings. The latter are supported by two particularly shaped scepters, originally a kind of shepherd crook, the hieroglyph *w3s*.[32] They, together with the wings above, form a defined area whose base line is not specifically marked. There is general agreement that the wings represent heaven;[33] however, they were repeatedly explained as the wings of an enormous heavenly god in falcon shape, whose span stretches between the horizons.[34] Tempting as it might seem, this explanation falls short in one point, which bars its attribution to the Egyptians. In all their symbolism, bewildering as it might seem at times, there always prevails an irreducible base of factual logic. Features drawn from different origins or beings can be joined together to phantasmic conglomerations, but partial features cannot be shown in total isolation. A pair of wings for an Egyptian cannot depict an animated being–and deities belong to them--as it has to have a body and a head. From his observation of nature, the Egyptian was thoroughly aware that no bird, small or large, can fly with wings alone. Thus the wings in the design cannot be taken as an indication or representation of an existential being like a deity, but they stand as a symbol conveying a specific meaning like any hieroglyphic sign. The Egyptian language has an old word *ʿnḏ* for "wing," while the more common later term is *šwt* or *šwty* "plumage."[35] To both exist homophons, i.e., words with the same consonantal structure.[36] For the first it is *ʿnḏt* "border" and without euphonic *n* the term *ʿḏ* "district"; for the second, it is *šwt* and *šwty* "side," in particular also the side of the body.[37] Either term is thus attested with a meaning "limit," "border," in addition to the ideographic application "wing." It is in the transfigurative sense that the pair of wings appears to be intended in the little design, indicating the upper limit or border of an area which is delineated at its horizontal expanse by the hieroglyphic sign for *w3s*. This stem has various applications, which can be reduced to a basic meaning "luck,"[38] i.e., an accidental event, which can be considered positive or negative, just as we distinguish between "good luck" and "bad luck." Integrating this meaning into our unraveling of the features of the early Dynastic design, it can be posed that for the ancient Egyptians the horizontal expanse or width of his world was set by two random points.

That space which we have established is the frame of existence for the ancient Egyptian. Within the defined and defining framework his mundane existence took place, so that it can be denoted as immanent sphere or immanence. In the design it is occupied by two elements, one the well-known hieroglyph for *ʿnḫ* "life" in an archaic shape,[39] the other the compound of signs used to indicate the "Horus-name."[40] The first denotes not only "life" as a physical process, but also the concept of an existential state. The "Horus-name" constitutes the most ritualistic designation of the Egyptian king as representative and executive of kingship as a metaphysically rooted institution.[41] The two indicators as sole contents of the defined space representing the immanent world constitute the dualism of principles which govern the immanence. They are complementary and juxtaposed at the same time as concept of life and as authority, exemplified in kingship. Its specific representative, i.e., the ruler for whom the design was carved, has the name *Ḏt-Ḥr*, i.e., "embodiment of Horus."[42] This name, like others of the First Dynasty, reflects clearly the Egyptian concept of kingship at that time, in which the king was seen as the physical manifestation of Horus.

Beyond the pair of wings, which we recognized as the upper delineation of the immanence, is a second area, but different from the one below it has no limitation in any direction. Being beyond the confines of the immanence we have to classify it as "transcendence." This undefined or unlimited realm beyond contains one element: a falcon perched in a vessel. It is generally agreed that this represents the god Horus traveling across the sky[43]—a picture which seems to have its later continuation in the image of Re', the sun, traversing heaven in his ship. Horus in the early representation has been identified as apotheosis of the prehistoric chieftain in his falcon "totemism."[44] As is recurrent in studies concerning religion, this is a circular argument, which sidesteps tackling the primary question of how to interpret "Horus." Since Horus is not akin to the generic Egyptian word for "falcon,"[45] i.e., the common theriomorphic representation of Horus, the origin of the designation has to be surmised as being an abstraction. *Ḥrw*, the Egyptian term behind the Greek ὧρος is a nominally used participle of a verb "to be distant,"[46] with the particular connotation of an upward direction. Thus the divine designation "Horus" is to be explained literally "the distant one," "the high one."[47] An identification of such nature has to be recognized as the product of abstract thinking rather than of mythic imagination. The clarification of the divine nomen also helps to understand the interconnection of the kings of the early First Dynasty with god. Horus is not an extension or projection of the prehistoric chieftain, but is rather the outcome of speculative reflection. It presupposes the existence of a fully developed world concept with a two-tier structure and the differentiation of immanence and transcendence.

The designation "Distant One" focuses exclusively on one quality of the divine and does not reflect any interaction between it and man, as is found with other divine names. The particular nature of the Horus concept conforms to the peculiarities of the cosmic structural design made for a king whose name means "embodiment of Horus," i.e., the physical immanent reflection of a distant power which was conceived as transcendental.

Theologically, this earliest formulation of the society-reflecting religion of ancient Egypt can be labeled "deism," i.e., the acceptance of an ultimate transcendental power which does not directly interfere in the affairs of the immanent world. However, these two spheres are not totally disjoined; they are intertwined in the authority resting in the institution of kingship as a reflection of the otherwise distant ultimate power.

Although still rudimentary, the structure elucidated by the design for King *Ḏt-Ḥr* constitutes the base from which all further theological speculation in ancient Egypt evolved. The differentiation of immanence and transcendence remains constant. The transcendental *ultima ratio*, always conceived as monistic, underwent other definitions, and the interaction between transcendence and immanence developed in increasing refinement.

The cosmological structure as transpiring in the design of the First Dynasty juxtaposes an ultimate transcendental power with the authority resting in kingship. The immediacy of this grouping dissolved by the end of the First Dynasty,[48] apparently in recognition of the irreconcilability of a transcendental ultimate single power and a defined immanence as its corollary. Intertwined is the necessity to conceive the *ultima ratio* as infinitely distant and, in order to qualify as Absolute, i.e., a kind of "Urgrund," as static, i.e., as resting in itself.[49] In consequence of the posing of a static Absolute in a transendence and its disconnection from the immanence with the social order of man, Egyptian theological speculation introduced a linking element at the beginning of the Second Dynasty.[50] It was conceived as prime dynamic reflection of the transcendental Absolute in the finite world of man and logically located at the borderline separating the two spheres. The concept of a supreme dynamic power is formulated in the image of Re' traveling along the heaven. Re' is without question a speculative formulation, as the designation is not the indigenous word for the sun as physical entity. Probably a development of Heliopolis, Re' makes its first appearance in the royal name *R'-nb(.i)* or *nb(.i)-R'* "Re' is my Lord" at the beginning of the Second Dynasty.[51]

In Egyptian etymology, the designation Re' is metathetically connected with the verb *i'r* "to ascend"; right or wrong from modern linguistic standards, it nevertheless indicates that for the Egyptians Re' was the ascendancy and manifestation of the transcendental Absolute above the delineation of the immanence. Iconographically, this is captured in the image of the winged sun disk. Although commonly interpreted as an expression of the lofty movement of the sun across the sky[53]–its flying–our earlier probing into the earliest Egyptian concept of cosmic structuring provides the correct answer. The wings of the sun disk have the same significance as those used in the design for King *Ḏt-Ḥr* to indicate the border between immanence and transcendence.[54]

The idea of Re' as dynamic manifestation of a necessarily static Absolute is also reflected in the formulation Re'-Atum, i.e., "the Re' of Atum." Often, though wrongly, declared a syncretism,[55] Re' in this formulation is dependent on Atum, another nomen defining the Absolute as "not-being One," i.e., transexistential, from the negative verb *tm* "not to be" attested since the Sixth Dynasty.[56]

As Re' was not absolute but a reflection, though a supreme one, Egyptian theological speculation had to find a solution for the interrelation of static Absolute and its supreme dynamic manifestation. It is significant that in the Second Dynasty when Re' first appears, the concept of *ma'at*, the specifically Egyptian idea of world order, is first attested.[57] It is this order by which Re' is defined in the universe as he is "lord of the ma'at and companion of the ma'at," as "Re' lives in/from ma'at every day."[58] The recognition of a universally valid concept of order and its formulation as ma'at to link the static Absolute and its dynamic manifestation is the theological achievement of the Second Dynasty. Although the original single ultimate power in the theology encompassing society had been divided into two aspects, a static and a dynamic one, its monistic character did not change in substance.

While the first step in refining the basic cosmological concept led to a clarification of the nature of the one ultimate source of all metaphysical force, all later theological developments concern the structuring of the immanence. There is not sufficient information available to discern any specific traces of an intellectual process during the Third Dynasty,[59] although its existence can be surmised in view of the impact it had as the formative period of the Old Kingdom, if not of ancient Egypt altogether. It is only in the Fourth Dynasty, and there in the reign of Radjedef, that the next step can be discerned with the appearance of Re' as integral part of the royal nomen.[60] With the formulation of the designation "son of Re'" (*z3-R'*) for the king, his position vis-à-vis the omnipotent divine ruler of the immanent world was defined. It is not, as has been voiced,[61] a decline of the king's metaphysical role, but is actually to be seen as a move to realign the position of the king as executor of authority in the world with the cosmic structure. As a consequence the mundane is brought into direct contact with the cosmic structure. Kingship as a metaphysical institution reflects the cosmological scheme in the immanence. It is important to note here that the monistic concept, i.e., the posing of a single source of all spiritual power, transcendental or mundane, continues as the basis of the theological thinking, although its flow is delineated by an increasing number of points: the (static) Absolute, Re' as its dynamic reflection, and the king as "Son-of-Re'."[62]

The increasing concern with the theological alignment of the immanent world becomes the theological question of the Fifth Dynasty. The details are still ambiguous, but nevertheless its main feature can be discerned. There appears to have been little interest in metaphysical problems during this period, judging from the information available.[63] The striking feature of the time is generally seen in the sun-cult and its promulgation in "sun-temples."[64] While the justification of this view is above doubt, the emphasis on Re' in the Fifth Dynasty is not isolated, but has its little-noted complementary in the religious interest in Hathor. The so-called "sun-sanctuaries" are at the same time places of worship for Hathor,[65] who occupies in them a role equal to Re'. In other words, the particular sanctuary conceived and construed in the Fifth Dynasty was dedicated to two deities, Re' and Hathor. Those two deities are not connected mythologically,[66] as in many later double or triple cults, but they have to be recognized as specific and independent theological concepts. We have already talked about Re'. Hathor, sometimes primitively explained as a "cow-goddess,"[67] has an elucidating name *Ḥwt-Ḥr*, which means "House of Horus" or "Domain of Horus," i.e., a mythological rendering of the realm in which the king as (immanent) Horus rules.[68] By her very name Hathor can thus be recognized as a theological formulation of the structured, ordered, and familiar world in which the Egyptians lived.[69] Hathor's worship side by side with Re' is thus to be understood as an expression that the world itself is manifestation of the ultimate divine and that it is permeated by order. It is an enormously positive attitude toward the world and life in it, making life an aspect of religion.

In the overall theological development, the Fifth Dynasty can be seen as a refinement of the concept reflected in the design for King *Ḏt-Ḥr* with its juxtaposition of kingship and life. Re' as dynamic power ruling the immanence corresponds to the former, Hathor to the latter. However, while the earlier formulation operates with "life" as an idea or principle, the Fifth Dynasty interpretation has a much stronger physical overtone. This is best demonstrated by that part of the "sun-temple" which is devoted to her. While the cult of Re' is centered in the stark obelisk,[70] the sockle supporting it has an inside chamber decorated with a chart of the multitude of phenomena in which "life" manifests itself during the course of a year.[71] It is a heroic attempt to see a structure in nature and to accept natural phenomena as religious expression.

The inconsistencies and shortcomings of intertwining cosmological ideas with the phenomena of nature were apparently realized by the ancient theologians within a relatively short time. The double cult of Re' and Hathor remains a restricted case. Fully implemented only in the sanctuary built by King Ny-woser-Re' at Abu Gurob,[72] the next reign, that of Djedkare'-Izezi does not see the construction of a "sun-temple" at all. Although it is still difficult to delineate its causes, the transition from the Fifth to the Sixth Dynasty is a period of major intellectual changes.[73] They have their most conspicuous demonstration in the emerging of Osiris and new eschatological concepts.[74] While in the spiritual order of the earlier Old Kingdom the service within the framework established by kingship as representation of the universal divine order was matched with the expectation of an existence beyond physical death in the company of the king served on earth,[75] the personal character of the expectations ceases with the Fifth Dynasty. It is followed by the introduction of Osiris as divine lord of the dead who grants life in the netherworld to anyone who has conducted his life ethically.[76] The life on earth takes on an expanded dimension. Its purpose does not find fulfillment exclusively in the service for the king, but is now placed under principles which concern all features of existence and also every person. Life accordingly holds a metaphysical potential, and existence on earth provides the framework for its attaining aspiration. Nature in its structure is conceived anew as a reflection of one ultimate godhead; however, different from the attempt in the Fifth Dynasty to see the natural phenomena as divine expression, the concept of the Sixth Dynasty is the result of abstraction.

Attested first in the reign of Pepi II[77] the theological system designed to intertwine immanence and transcendence is undoubtedly an achievement of the Heliopolitan priesthood. It conceives cosmology in a structure of nine, the Ennead.[78] The composition of the structure is in itself ingenious. *Psḏ*, the Egyptian word for "nine" is homophon to *psḏ* "to shine" "to appear."[79] Written as $\overset{|||}{\underset{|||}{|||}}$ it is optically conspicuous as plural of plurals, i.e., the total of forms.[80]

The Ennead, as structure of the universe, consists of eight pairs, each one composed of a male and a female element, and one single element from which everything emanated. This single or first principle is denoted as Atum. The designation is obviously a participle, either from the verb *tm* "to be complete" or from the negative verb *tm*. Atum can thus be rendered as "Complete One"[81] or as "not-being (i.e., transexistential) One."[82] In later accounts the cosmology, formulated in human experiences, is stated as a voluntary, self-indulged emission by the one all-lord.[83] The earliest account is less specific, but nevertheless makes it clear that the first pair of principles were an emission from Atum.[84] Denoted as Shu and Tefnut, they represent "light" (Shu) and "moisture."[85] The first as ordering force, and the second as procreative force, correspond to the pair of features in the immanent world as depicted in the design for king *Ḏt-Ḥr*. Shu and Tefnut are followed by the pair Geb and Nut, the first representing "earth," the second "heaven."[86] They are in turn followed by a generation of two pairs consisting of Osiris ("Benevolent nature") and Isis ("the throne")[87] on the one side, and Seth (the negative forces in nature) and Nephthys (Seth's complementary)[88] on the other. In their total they constitute the universe comprising transcendence and immanence. This formulation has two noteworthy features. It is a composition of metaphysical principles which stays aloft from defining the place of man in the universe and the existence of matter.

That even this encompassing theological system could not be maintained for long, once the pheonomenological world has been experienced as a reality, seems implicit in its purely metaphysical orientation. In the intellectual and political convulsions of the First Intermediate Period the ideal approach to the cosmos collapses.[89] When the sight clears again with the beginning of the Twelfth Dynasty,[90] the theologians of ancient Egypt have formulated a new approach to theology. The intertwining of transcendence and immanence was irretrievably lost, but the two spheres retain their balance. Although the phenomonological reality becomes fully accepted in theological thinking and with it the recognition of a number of powers active in it, the concept of the one and single godhead is continued, though less conspicuous than in the Old Kingdom. Sometimes referred to as Atum, the truly new theological formulation of the time is the name Amun, which denotes the godhead as "the hidden one."[91] He is no longer seen as directly influencing the affairs of the world, but as having retreated from it.[92] The immanent world is no more a mirror of metaphysical ideas, but is experienced as reality. Theologically, this leads to the posing of matter as a prime principle. Named Nun "the primeval water," it is conceived as "Urgrund" into which creation occurred.[93] As matter is seen as void of any independent dynamic force, the primacy of the godhead remains unrestricted.

Man is no longer in direct contact with the transcendental sphere. Between him and the ultimate godhead is the sphere of the gods, who are understood as reflections of the One.[94] This theological structure remains basically stable throughout Egyptian culture, although mostly in the background of a multitude of religious expressions.[95] Mainly concerned with immediate problems, they are directed to the gods who had the power to solve them. Only in rare occasions transpires the overriding deism of Egyptian theological thinking, as in *The Instruction of Ani* VII 15 "(The) god of this land is the sun which is on the horizon, and (only) his images are upon earth."[96]

NOTES

[1] *Histories* II 38.

[2] The sources are collected by Theodore Hopfner, *Fontes historiae religionis Aegyptiacae* (1922-25).

[3] Cf. also Georges Michaelides, "Vase en terre cuite portant une inscription philosophique Greque," *BIFAO* 49 (1950) 23ff.

[4] *Deorum Concilium* 10-11.

[5] See in particular, Friedrich Zimmerman, *Die ägyptische Religion nach der Darstellung der Kirchenschriftsteller,* Studien zur Geschichte und Kultur des Altertums, vol. 5, 5-6 (1912) 9ff.

[6] *Die Religion der Ägypter*[3] (1934).

[7] *Egypt of the Pharaohs* (1961) 216.

[8] In most general discussions about "religion," ancient Egypt is treated as a model of a "polytheistic" religion; e.g., William F. Albright, *From the Stone Age to Christianity*[2] (Anchor Books edition, 1957). For the need to distinguish levels among the religious phenomena see the excellent remarks by C. J. Bleeker, *Hathor and Thoth,* Studies in the History of Religion XXVI (1973) 10ff.

[9] *Histories* II 3.

[10] R. V. Lanzone, *Dizionario di Mitologia egizia* (1881-86); Heinrich Brugsch, *Religion und Mythologie der alten Ägypter* (1885-86); Sir Peter Le Page Renouf, *Lectures on the Origin and Growth of Religion* (1880); Sir Gaston Maspero, *La mythologie égyptienne* (1888-89); Alfred Wiedemann, *Religion of the Ancient Egyptians* (1897); Sir Ernest Budge, *The Gods of the Egyptians* (1904); et alia.

[11] James Henry Breasted, *Development of Religion and Thought in Ancient Egypt* (1912); Gerardus van der Leeuw, *Godsvoorstellingen in de oudaegyptische Pyramidentexten* (1916); Herman Kees, *Der Götterglaube im alten Ägypten* (1941); Eberhard Otto, *Die Religion der alten Ägypter,* Handbuch der Orientalistik I 8, 1 (1964); Jacques Vandier, *La religion égyptienne* (1944).

[12] *Ancient Egyptian Religion* (1948) 19ff.

[13] *Psychology and Religion* (1950) 5.

[14] The Halloween formula "trick or treat" uniquely demonstrates the bipolarity of the magical experience.

[15] Utilization and warding off are the applications of the magical attitude, which indeed, dominates technological thinking.

[16] It seems indicative that the Egyptian term for "time" (*tr*) is derived from the word for "agricultural season," while the word for "year" (*rnpt*) is a derivate of "to grow" (*rnp*).

[17] Egyptian religious phenomena likewise reflect this particular level, which manifests itself in a host of local cults. Especially Kurt Sethe, *Urgeschichte und älteste Religion der*

Ägypter, Abhandlungen für die Kunde des Morgenlandes, 18, 4 (1930) emphasized this stratum at the expense of the overall structure of Egyptian religion.

[18] See Mircea Eliade, *The Holy and the Profane* (New York) 19.

[19] This treatise, dating to the beginning of the Twelfth Dynasty (after 1990 B.C.), expounds on the role of Ptah as "creator" of the phenomenological world. The predominantly funerary or liturgical character of the preserved material results in part from the place of their ancient use and discovery, but cannot be used as the basis for any conclusions about the overall nature of Egyptian religious writing.

[20] First promulgated by Henri Frankfort, *The Intellectual Adventure of Ancient Man* (1949), chap. 1.

[21] The impact of their writing system on the thinking process of the Egyptians has never been sufficiently investigated. The peculiarities of intertwining semantics and pictorial meanings provided a strong stimulant resulting in a wide range of puns, which form the base for the so-called cryptographic writing; see Siegfried Schott, *Hieroglyphen, Untersuchungen zum Ursprung der Schrift* (Abh. Ak. Wiss. Mainz, 1950) 60ff.

[22] The affiliation of writing with the realm of ideas is, among others, demonstrated by its attribution to the god Thoth as its divine inventor. Egyptian, with the notable exception of Late Egyptian, is primarily a literary language ("Schriftsprache") and is not a direct reflection of the venacular.

[23] Their study is the main concern of Kurt Sethe, *Urgeschichte,* which overemphasizes parochial differences. His approach was widely followed despite its shortcomings.

[24] Not all religious formulations were coined in the historic period, not even those of the "high" religion. While many of the aboriginal "deities" remained restricted to the level of parochial significance, others, in particular Seth, were incorporated into the universal theological scheme.

[25] The Egyptian conceived it as a distinct beginning, especially in referring to it as "the first occasion" (*zp tpy*); see also Erik Hornung, *Geschichte als Fest* (Darmstadt, 1966).

[26] Despite the variety of contributors which made up ancient Egypt, the unity of idea and form emerging suddenly at the beginning of the historical period is striking.

[27] See in particular Heinrich Schäfer, *Weltgebäude der alten Ägypter* (1928).

[28] In the course of their history, the Egyptians came to conceive of more than one heaven. Nevertheless, the sky represented always a definite delineation; see also Hellmut Brunner, "Die Grenzen von Zeit und Raum bei den Ägyptern," *AfO* 17 (1954/55) 140ff.

[29] The concept of a "round" world, which might have influenced Ptolemy the Geographer, did also exist; see J. J. Clère, "Fragments d'une Nouvelle Représentation Égyptienne du monde," *MDIK* 16 (1958) 30ff.

[30] W. F. Petrie, *Tombs of the courtiers* (1921) pl. XII; see also Wilhelm von Bissing, *ZAS* 64 (1930) 112; R. Engelbach, "An Alleged Winged Sun-Disk of the First Dynasty," *ZAS* 65 (1931) 115f., Tf. VIII.

[31] See Schott, *Hieroglyphen,* 72ff.

[32] See Sir Alan Gardiner, *Egyptian Grammar*[3], Sign-List S 41.

[33] Schäfer, *Weltgebäude,* 92f., 113; see also Wilhelm von Bissing, *ZAS* 66 (1932) 69.

[34] Kees, *Der Götterglaube im Alten Ägypten,* 42f.; Siegfried Morenz, *Ägyptische Religion* (1960) 35; Rudolph Anthes, in *MAW,* 34f.; Wolfhart Westendorf, *Altägyptische Darstellungen des Sonnenlaufes auf der abschüssigen Himmelsbahn,* Münchner Ägyptologische Studien 10 (1966) 22f.

[35] Adolph Erman and Hermann Grapow, *Wörterbuch der ägyptischen Sprache,* IV 423. It is part of the common epithet of Horus as *s3b-šwt* "many colored of plumage."

[36] The principle of homophony is the principle base of the hieroglyphic writing system, by using a depictable object to indicate the designation of an identically sounding immaterial concept; see Schott, *Hieroglyphen,* 82ff.; Gardiner, *Egyptian Grammar*[3], 6ff.

[37] Erman and Grapow, *Wörterbuch,* IV 425f.; I 207, 12; 239, 6; see also Hans Goedicke, "Die Laufbahn des *Mṯn*," *MDIK* 21 (1966) 20ff.; Bernard Grdseloff, *ASAE* 42 (1943) 108f.

[38] The antonymic use of the term as "to decay" and "to have dominion" has been disregarded in the discussions of its meaning by Gustave Jequier, *Les frieses d'objects* (1921) 176; Sir Alan Gardiner, *JEA* 36 (1950) 12; idem, "Minuscula Lexica," in *Ägyptologische Studien,* ed. Otto Firchow (1955) 2; Erich Winter, "Ägyptische Tempelreliefs der Griechisch-Römischen Zeit," *AWAW* (1968) 84f.

[39] See Heinrich Schäfer, "Das sogenannte 'Blut der Isis' und das Zeichen 'Leben,'" *ZAS* 62 (1927) 108ff.

[40] See Hugo Müller, *Die formale Entwicklung der Titulatur der ägyptischen Könige,* Ägyptologische Forschungen 7 (1938) 13ff.; Gardiner, *Egyptian Grammar*[3], 72.

[41] Hans Goedicke, *Die Stellung des Königs im Alten Reich,* Ägyptologische Abhandlungen 2 (1960) 3ff.

[42] This rendering was proposed in a paper delivered at the Deutscher Orientalistentag 1961 in Göttingen; the traditional "Horus Snake" might invoke reminiscences of red Indian tribal chiefs, but makes little sense otherwise. Against Peter Kaplony's translation in *Orientalia Suecana* 7 (1958) 54ff., see Siegfried Morenz, "Die Heraufkunft des transzendenten Gottes in Ägypten," *SSAW* 109, 2 (1964) 11, n. 1.

[43] E.g., Westendorf, *Altägyptische Darstellungen,* 22f.; Anthes, in *MAW,* 20f.

[44] See Otto, *Religion,* 11; Kees, *Götterglaube,* 39ff.

[45] The common Egyptian word for "falcon" is *bik* and not *Ḥrw,* which is restricted to religious usage.

[46] Erman and Grapow, *Wörterbuch,* III 145f.

[47] Morenz, *Ägyptische Religion,* 23, 35; Erik Hornung, *Der Eine und die Vielen* (1971) 274.

[48] The names of the Second Dynasty kings indicate an entirely different concept of kingship in relation to the divine than those held during the First Dynasty. While the royal names of the latter express a specific relationship of the ruler to Horus in the form of a

manifestation, the royal names of the Second Dynasty do not relate the ruler to Horus as the divine lord. They suggest a separation of kingship from its religious base. The names have not been sufficiently studied to establish a clear pattern. Political tension, possibly culminating in a breakdown of the union of north and south, transpires from the available sources; see Gardiner, *Egypt of the Pharaohs,* 415ff.; Etienne Drioton and Jacques Vandier, *L'Egypte* (Clio; 1962) 142f.

49 The juxtaposition of static and dynamic Absolute is particularly emphasized in Gnostic cosmological formulations, like in the *Apocryphon of John* (Codex II 2, 26ff.) 4, 10-12 versus 4, 22ff. However, it recurs in Egyptian theological literature; e.g., the Leiden Amun Hymn; for a translation, see Wilson, in *ANET,* 368.

50 Although the circumstances are highly obscure, an affiliation with Heliopolis seems a viable thesis. It is indicative that the title of the Heliopolitan high priest is attested first in this time; see Mohamed I Moursi, *Die Hohenpriester des Sonnengottes von der Frühzeit Ägyptens bis zum Ende des Neuen Reiches,* Münchner Ägyptologische Studien 26 (1972) 12-14.

51 Henry G. Fischer, "An Egyptian Royal Stela of the Second Dynasty," *Artibus Asiae* 24 (1961) 45ff.; Hermann Ranke, *Die Ägyptischen Personennamen* I (1935) 186, 1.

52 Pyr. 452 b "ascend to it in this your name of Re'"; similar Pyr. 1449 a.

53 Schäfer, *Weltgebäude,* 116ff.; Kees, *Götterglaube,* 418f.; Westendorf, *Altägyptische Darstellungen,* 23; Sir Alan Gardiner, *JEA* 30 (1944) 46ff.

54 See p. 205, above.

55 Erman, *Die Religion der Ägypter*[3]. Correctly explained as "Erscheinungsform des Atum" by Winfried Barta, *Untersuchungen zum Götterkreis der Neunheit,* Münchner Ägyptologische Studien 28 (1973) 137.

56 For a survey of the different interpretations of the name, see Barta, *Neunheit,* 78ff.

57 The earliest datable occurrence is in the Second Dynasty royal name *Pr-n-m3't.* For ma'at, see the excellent discussion in Frankfort, *Ancient Egyptian Religion,* 49ff.; and Morenz, *Ägyptische Religion,* 120ff.

58 Jean Francois Champollion, *Monuments de l'Égypte et de la Nubie, Notices déscriptives* (1844) I 303, 1; *Book of the Dead,* chap. 153 B 1.

59 Various attempts have been made to assign major intellectual developments to the Third Dynasty; e.g., Wolfgang Helck, *Geschichte des Alten Ägypten,* Handbuch der Orientalistik 1, 1 (1968) 49f.; Joachim Spiegel, *Das Werden der altägyptischen Hochkultur* (1953) 168ff. However, the available information for this period is extremely limited and does not suffice to substantiate any thesis.

60 The only earlier royal nomen containing Re' as an element is Re'-neb. Radjedef's successors retain Re' in their name with the exception of Shepseskaf and Weserkaf.

61 Müller, *Die formale Entwicklung,* 68ff.; Gardiner, *Egyptian Grammar*[3], 74; Otto, *Religion,* 26; Kees, *Götterglaube,* 250ff.; Hans Wolfgang Müller, *ZAS* 91 (1964) 129ff.; Erik Hornung, *Der Eine,* 32; Morenz, *SSAW* 109, 2 (1964) 15f.

62 "Son" in this designation expresses a specific relationship, which has not necessarily physical connotations. It is used similarly in connection with kingship; see Goedicke, *Die Stellung des Königs,* 29.

63 It is only during the reign of Djedkare'-Izezi that a major change in religious outlook becomes discernible. The causes are obscure but might be related with an event alluded to in a cryptic fashion in Sinai inscription no. 13 as "the god caused that a treasure be found in the chamber of the (sun-temple) 'Residence of Re'' in the god's own writing."

64 See Kurt Sethe, *ZAS* 27 (1889) 111ff.; Werner Kaiser, "Zu den Sonnenheiligtümern der 5. Dynastie," *MDIK* 14 (1956) 104ff.

65 See Schafik Allam, *Beiträge zum Hathorkult,* Münchner Ägyptologische Studien 4 (1963) 7f. Of particular importance are the hitherto unpublished seal impressions from the sun-temple of Ny-woser-Re' with several joint mentions of Re' and Hathor.

66 Mythological connection is meant here in terms of "family relations," which are used to express primary associations. In the myth of the "Eye of the Sun" and of the "Heavenly Cow" Hathor becomes affiliated with Re' but without entering an intimate relationship.

67 Frankfort, *Ancient Egyptian Religion,* 11. Kees, *Götterglaube,* 11; Otto, *Religion,* 5f.; Allam, *Hathorkult,* 26f.

68 Morenz, *Ägyptische Religion,* 24; Hornung, *Der Eine,* 274. The designation is clearly the result of theological speculation, secondary by nature to the forming of the concept of Horus. Thus the attempts to explain Hathor by connecting her to "primitive" sources, either as "cow" or as "treee goddess" disregard the prime feature of the goddess as reflected in her name.

69 That Hathor is a mythological rendering of the Egyptian "world" explains the image of Hathor as "heavenly cow"; see Anthes, in *MAW,* 31. It finds its political expression in the appearance of cults of Hathor in foreign territories subjugated to the rule of the Egyptian king and of Horus. In this capacity, Hathor's cult in Sinai is a reflection of the Egyptian sovereignty and not a reinterpretation of an indigenous cult. The same applies to Hather of Byblos, who is attested only during those times when Byblos was a vassal of the Egyptian king.

70 See Ludwig Borchardt, *Das Re-Heiligtum des Königs Ne-woser-re* (1905); Herbert Ricke, *Das Sonnenheiligtum des Königs Userkaf,* Beiträge zur ägyptischen Bauforschung 7 (1965).

71 See William S. Smith, *Interconnections in the Ancient Near East* (1965) fig. 178; Elmar Edel and Steffen Wenig, *Die Jahreszeitreliefs aus dem Sonnenheiligtum des Königs Ne-user-re* (1974).

72 See note 65, above.

73 The changes include the political sphere, although their nature is not fully established. See Spiegel, *Das Werden,* 493ff.; Goedicke, *Die Stellung des Königs im Alten Reich,* 91.

74 J. Gwyn Griffiths, *The Origins of Osiris,* Münchner Ägyptologische Studien 9 (1966); Morenz, *Altägyptische Religion,* 136ff.; Herman Kees, *Totenglauben und Jenseitsvorstellungen* (1956) 132ff.

See S

[75] See Kees, *Totenglauben,* 108ff.; Morenz, *Altägyptische Religion,* 119f.

[76] Hermann Junker, *Pyramidenzeit* (1949) 55ff.

[77] Pyramid Spell 600; for a translation see John A. Wilson in *ANET,* 3; R. O. Faulkner, *The Ancient Egyptian Pyramid Texts* (1969) 246f.

[78] See especially Barta, *Neunheit*; see also J. Gwyn Griffiths, "Some Remarks on the Enneads of Gods," *Or* 28 (1959) 34ff.; Raymond Weill, *RdE* 6 (1951) 49ff.; Morenz, *Altägyptische Religion,* 172ff.

[79] Erman and Grapow, *Wörterbuch* I, 556f.; see also Rudolf Anthes, *JNES* 18 (1959) 194ff.

[80] See Hornung, *Der Eine,* 217.

[81] See n. 56, above.

[82] Atum can be taken as a formulation of the *theologia negativa*, using negative specifications to express the excess of qualities beyond anything existing. The *Apocryphon of John* (Codex II 3, 18-28) is an excellent example for this theological approach, but it is found repeatedly in Egyptian theological writings, e.g., The Leiden Hymn to Amun, Leiden Pap. I 350 IV 17ff. A translation can be found by Wilson, in *ANET,* 369, while a detailed discussion is offered by Jan Zandee, *De Hymnen aan Amon van Papyrus Leiden I 350* (Leiden, 1948) 82ff.

[83] See Papyrus Bremner-Rhind XXVI, 21ff. = R. O. Faulkner, *JEA* 23 (1937) 172f.; another translation is by Wilson, in *ANET,* 6. Some, e.g., Junker, *Pyramidenzeit,* 21, see in the account a primitive realism which is later spiritualized. As mythological expression is a concentration of human experience, it draws its formulation from it. It was thus consistent for the ancient Egyptians to use autoerotic acts for describing Atum's unassisted emanation.

[84] The two principles Shu and Tefnut, which emanated from Atum, are differently related to their source. While the former is described as "what Atum spat out" (perfective passive participle), the second is called "what Atum sputters" (imperfective passive participle), distinguishing between a completed and a continuous or recurrent act.

[85] See Barta, *Untersuchungen,* 85ff.

[86] Barta, *Untersuchungen,* 94ff. This pair seems to be a mythological rendering of "space" and "time" in the cosmology.

[87] Barta, *Untersuchungen,* 105ff. For Isis, see also Maria Münster, *Untersuchungen zur Göttin Isis vom Alten Reich bis zum Ende des Neuen Reiches,* Münchner Ägyptologische Studien 11 (1968).

[88] Nephthys' name, Egyptian *nbt-ḥwt* "mistress of the house" does not indicate any specific function, and she plays in Egyptian mythology a shadowy role.

[89] See John A. Wilson, *The Burden of Ancient Egypt* (1951) 104ff.; Kees, *Totenglauben,* 100ff.

[90] The Theban Eleventh Dynasty does not seem to have been a period of theological concern, but found its fulfillment in political action. The documentation of the preceding

Heracleopolitan Period is limited to funerary texts. According to them this period expanded and refined the theological concepts formulated in the late Old Kingdom without aspiring new cosmological formulations.

91 The interpretation of Amun's name as "the hidden One" is unrelated to the etymological origin of the god's name; for the latter see G. A. Wainwright, "The Origin of Amun," *JEA* 49 (1963) 21ff.

92 See in particular *The Instruction for King Merikare'*, 124, "God, who knows (men's) characters, has hidden himself"; a translation of the wisdom text can be found by Wilson, in *ANET*, 414ff. and by R. O. Faulkner, in *The Literature of Ancient Egypt*, ed. William K. Simpson (1972) 180ff.

93 Nun is mentioned once in the Pyramid Texts (Pyr 604 a), but without cosmological connotation. For an early reference to Nun, see Hermann Grapow, *Religiöse Urkunden* (Jena, 1913) 4ff.; a translation is also offered by Wilson, in *ANET*, 3f.

94 For the uniqueness of "God," see Hornung, *Der Eine*, 180f. Of particular clarity is the formulation in the Leiden Amun Hymn (IV 17) "One is Amun"; see Jan Zandee, *De Hymnen aan Amon van Papyrus Leiden I 350*, 82ff.

95 See Junker, *Pyramidenzeit*, 11ff.; Hornung, *Der Eine*, 247ff.; and Morenz, *Altägyptische Religion*, 144ff.

96 The juxtaposition of religious phenomena and "Urgrund" has also been claimed for ancient Greece; see Wilhelm F. Otto, *Die Götter Griechenlands* (1947) 169ff.

INDEX

A. AUTHORS

B. BIBLICAL PASSAGES

Gen. 13:8ff., 144 n. 32

Gen.

Library of Congress Cataloging in Publication Data
Main entry under title:

Unity and diversity.

(The Johns Hopkins Near Eastern studies)
Papers presented at a symposium held at Johns Hopkins University, Jan. 9-12, 1973.
Includes index.
1. Near East–History–To 622–Congresses. 2. Near East–Religion–Congresses. 3. Oriental literature–Near East–Congresses. I. Goedicke, Hans. II. Roberts, Jimmy Jack McBee. III. Series: Johns Hopkins University. Near Eastern studies.
DS62.2.U54 956 74-24376
ISBN 0-8018-1638-6